WORLD BANK CO...RY

YO-BTD-308

Uganda

Agriculture

The World Bank
Washington, D.C.

World Bank Country Studies are among the many reports originally prepared for internal use as part of the continuing analysis by the Bank of the economic and related conditions of its developing member countries and of its dialogues with the governments. Some of the reports are published in this series with the least possible delay for the use of governments and the academic, business and financial, and development communities. The typescript of this paper therefore has not been prepared in accordance with the procedures appropriate to formal printed texts, and the World Bank accepts no responsibility for errors.

The World Bank does not guarantee the accuracy of the data included in this publication and accepts no responsibility whatsoever for any consequence of their use. Any maps that accompany the text have been prepared solely for the convenience of readers; the designations and presentation of material in them do not imply the expression of any opinion whatsoever on the part of the World Bank, its affiliates, or its Board or member countries concerning the legal status of any country, territory, city, or area or of the authorities thereof or concerning the delimitation of its boundaries or its national affiliation.

The material in this publication is copyrighted. Requests for permission to reproduce portions of it should be sent to the Office of the Publisher at the address shown in the copyright notice above. The World Bank encourages dissemination of its work and will normally give permission promptly and, when the reproduction is for noncommercial purposes, without asking a fee. Permission to copy portions for classroom use is granted through the Copyright Clearance Center, 27 Congress Street, Salem, Massachusetts 01970, U.S.A.

The complete backlist of publications from the World Bank is shown in the annual *Index of Publications,* which contains an alphabetical title list (with full ordering information) and indexes of subjects, authors, and countries and regions. The latest edition is available free of charge from the Distribution Unit, Office of the Publisher, The World Bank, 1818 H Street, N.W., Washington, D.C. 20433, U.S.A., or from Publications, The World Bank, 66, avenue d'Iéna, 75116 Paris, France.

ISSN: 0253-2123

Library of Congress Cataloging-in-Publication Data

Uganda : agriculture.
      p.   cm. — (A World Bank country study, ISSN 0253-2123)
   ISBN 0-8213-2461-6
   1. Agriculture—Economic aspects—Uganda. 2. Agriculture and
state—Uganda.   I. International Bank for Reconstruction and
Development.   II. Series.
HD2127.U37   1993
338.1'096761—dc20

                                             93-1591
                                                CIP

PREFACE

This report is the result of a collaborative effort between the Government of Uganda and the World Bank. The Government team, organized under the Agricultural Policy Committee, was coordinated by Mr. Lawrence Eturu of the Agricultural Secretariat in the Bank of Uganda. The collaboration of staff in the various ministries involved in supporting development in the agriculture sector, led by the Ministry of Agriculture, Animal Industry and Fisheries and the Ministry of Finance and Economic Planning, is gratefully acknowledged.

This report draws on two major Government/Donor reviews of the agricultural sector undertaken in recent years. The first was the Agricultural Task Force of 1986/87, which produced working papers on all aspects of the agricultural economy. The second was the Working Groups exercise of 1989/90 which produced 10 papers on selected aspects of the agricultural sector, and underpinned the reforms supported under the Agricultural Sector Adjustment Credit (Cr 2190-UG) approved in December 1990. In addition, there have been sector specific studies used in the preparation of IDA operations in the Livestock and Forestry subsectors.

The report synthesizes the findings of previous studies and projects, and presents a vision of opportunities open to Government (and donors) for stimulating sustainable agricultural growth. The analysis uses a careful review of specific cases to make generalized policy recommendations. Firstly the stage is set for the analysis with a brief review of agricultural growth since independence, and a description of the macroeconomic framework (Section I). The report then sets the parameters for action, with a description of the natural resource base and characteristics of rural Uganda (Section II). The analysis of constraints, and hence opportunities for change and progress, is woven into the detailed review of institutions and subsectoral performance. Thus, Section III provides a review of those institutions: Governmental, cooperative, financial and private, which interact with the farming community and through which change can be promoted. Problem areas, and measure needed to overcome these problems are identified for each case. Similarly, in Section IV, the report goes through the review of each of the productive subsectors in agriculture. The section is labeled "Sources of Growth", because it looks into the problems affecting each productive sector, identifying constraints, and proposing measures to overcome these problems, and obtain growth. This section begins with an evaluation of export competitiveness and market potential. The limits to expansion and profitability are then established for each of the sub-sectors. The detailed review of the "micro" problems affecting each crop and animal product, then leads naturally to Section V, where the problems are categorized, general conclusions drawn, and priorities and sequencing established according to Government's development priorities, and the flexibility of the response from each sub-sector.

The sector strategy provided in Section V is the result of "sifting" the various measures available to Government to stimulate agricultural growth through a "sieve" of national priorities. The costs and benefits of the various various policies, rapidity of results, effects on the balance of payments, regional growth, rural poverty, the environment, are then used to formulate a short term, export oriented strategy based primarily on the revival of cotton production. The medium term strategy proposes a series of actions on a broad range of production and institutional issues. Effects on the environment, the consequences for the alleviation of rural poverty, and the potential increases in exports which could result from the strategy (Section VI), are then evaluated.

The short term strategy advocates continued efforts to regain market share in traditional exports: cotton, coffee and tea. While production margins are very thin, and international prices low, our analysis shows that Uganda due to its excellent natural conditions, is a low cost producer of these products, and can compete in international markets, even at depressed prices, if processing and marketing efficiency is restored. There is need for a rapid restructuring and liberalization of the cotton ginning and export marketing industry. In coffee, choice of export routes should be liberalized. In tea, Government should divest itself of parastatal factories and estates, and conclude the Custodian Board review process, which is keeping a significant number of the estates out of production. These changes would generate significant increases in foreign exchange, and have a broad based income generation effect in rural areas.

At the same time, short term measures should be taken to support the process of export diversification, which can grow very rapidly, as experience with sesame and fish exports in recent years indicates. Priority should be given to dry goods such as sesame, tobacco, hides and skins, spices and other products which do not rely too heavily on specialized packaging, critical transportation timing, expensive cooling infrastructure, and a commitment to constant, standardized quality deliveries.

In the medium term, the report argues that a series of measures are needed to support further diversification in agricultural exports. Development of high value specialized crop exports will increase returns and taxable profits, and stabilize export revenue. Government's role in developing these new activities should be indirect. Its focus should be on reducing unnecessary regulation, improving transport infrastructure and telecommunications, and smoothing the responsiveness of the land, labor and financial markets to profitable production opportunities. In addition, to raise rural incomes and ease the growth in food production, Government should take indirect measures to improve migration into underutilized areas of good agricultural potential. Careful management of this process will be needed to minimize environmental costs. Growth in yields is another key element of the agricultural strategy. Many traditional food and cash crops face disease and husbandry problems. Experimentation with new high value crops will require a high class, responsive research and extension service. Continued support for agricultural research and extension services is argued for, as is the need to provide improved monitoring and regulation of the use of natural resources-- grazing lands, forests and fish--as population pressures are exacerbated.

CONTENTS

The report was a joint Government of Uganda/World Bank effort. The main fact-finding mission was held in September/October 1991. The Government Task Force on the Agriculture Sector Review was headed by Mr. Lawrence Eturu, Director of the Agricultural Secretariat, Bank of Uganda, and included Dr. E.S.K. Mwanga Zake, Dr. N.S. Shetty, Mr. K.M. Agarwal, Mr. J.S. Johnson, Dr. W.O. Odwong, Mr. J. Katunze, Dr. C. Tizikara, Dr. I.O. Isyagi, Mr. P.N. Karuhanga, Mr. J. Kyamanywa, Mr. J. Rwampwanyi (Agricultural Secretariat), Mr. K.G.N. Kakama (Ministry of Finance), Mr. L. Msemakwelli, Mr. J.C. Oloa, (Uganda Cooperative Alliance), Mr. A. Okello-Oketta (Bank of Uganda), Mr. E.K. Busingye, Mr. J.R. Kahangirwe, Mr. G. Okech-Ochwo, Mr. J. Bwanika Ddungu, Mr. F.E. Mwesigye (Ministry of Commerce, Industry and Cooperatives), Mr. J.M. Nsimbi, Mr. G.M.R. Kakama, Mr. W.A. Ainebyona (Ministry of Finance and Economic Planning), Mr. J.N. Tibisaasa (Ministry of Lands, Housing and Urban Development), Mr. J. Omoding, Mr. R. Muyiyi, Mr. R. Semakula, Dr. J.R. Turyahikayo, Mr. L.P.K. Sebikejje, Eng. H.D. Kakeeto, Mr. S.E. Okwakol, Mr. L.K. Yiga, Mr. C.B. Bazirake, Dr. T.S. Kuryapawo (Ministry of Agriculture, Animal Industry and Fisheries), Dr. P. Ngategize (Uganda Coffee Development Authority). The Bank mission was led by Mr. J. Coates, and included Mr. V. Ashworth (food production), Mr. A.R. Bunker, (cooperatives), Mr. S. Caiger (non-traditional agricultural exports), Mr. J. Cameron (cotton), Mr. A. Finney (coffee), Mr. S. Harris (non-traditional agricultural exports), Mr. K. Loganathan (tea), Mr. T. Moy (tea), Mr. R. Noronha, (land tenure), Mr. A. Ordu (seeds and cotton), Mr. A. Sodhi (agricultural inputs), and Mr. M. Walshe (livestock). The followup Bank mission in January/February 1992 was led by Mr. J. Coates, and included Mr. S. Carr (general agriculture). The Green Cover review mission of December 1992 was led by Mr. J. Coates. The assistance of Ms. M. Gunawardane in the preparation of the report is gratefully acknowledged. There has been extensive discussion of this report with Government, and the main directions and conclusions reflect a consensus of opinion. Ultimately, however, the statements in the report are the responsibility of the Bank mission.

ABBREVIATIONS AND ACRONYMS

AEL	Agriculture Enterprises Limited
AfDB	African Development Bank
APC	Agriculture Policy Committee, Government of Uganda
AS	Ammonium Sulphate
ASAC	Agriculture Sector Adjustment Credit
ASN	Ammonium Sulphate Nitrate
BCGA	British Cotton Growers Association
BOU	Bank of Uganda
CAN	Calcium Ammonium Nitrate
CBPP	Contagious Bovine Pleuropneumonia
CDC	Commonwealth Development Corporation
CMB	Coffee Marketing Board
CMBL	Coffee Marketing Board Limited
CPI	Consumer Price Index
DANIDA	Danish International Development Agency
DFCU	Development Finance Company of Uganda
DRC	Domestic Resource Cost
EEC	European Economic Community
EPADU	Export Policy Analysis and Development Unit
EPC	Export Promotion Council
FAO	Food and Agricultural Organization
GTZ	German Agency for Technical Cooperation
IDA	International Development Association
IDRC	International Development Research Center
IFAD	International Fund for Agricultural Development
IFPRI	International Food Policy and Research Institute
IMF	International Monetary Fund
LTC	Land Tenure Center, University of Wisconsin
MAAIF	Ministry of Agriculture, Animal Industry & Forestry
MCIC	Ministry of Commerce, Industry and Cooperatives
MPED	Ministry of Planning and Economic Development
MISR	Makerere Institute of Social Research
NARO	National Agricultural Research Organization
NGO	non-governmental organization
NICU	National Inputs Coordination Unit
NTAE	Non Traditional Agricultural Exports
OECD	Organization of Economic Cooperation and Development
PTA	Preferential Trade Area
SDR	Special Drawing Right
TAMTECO	Toro and Mityana Tea Company
UCB	Uganda Commercial Bank
UCA	Uganda Coooperative Alliance
UCDA	Uganda Coffee Development Authority
UDC	Uganda Development Cooperation
UNDP	United National Development Program
UNEP	United National Environmental Program
USAID	United States Agency for International Development
UTGC	Uganda Tea Growers Corporation
WFP	World Food Program

EXECUTIVE SUMMARY

Sectoral Background

1.   Agriculture is the mainstay of the Ugandan economy. Eighty-nine percent of the population is rural. The sector accounts for 51 percent of GDP (1991) and over 90 percent of exports, and employs 80 percent of the employed household population. Agricultural output comes almost exclusively from about 2.5 million smallholders--80 percent of whom have less than 2 hectares each. Only tea and sugar are grown on large estates, which total 40,000 ha. The predominance of smallholder farming implies that the benefits from sectoral growth will be equitably distributed. Income per capita in 1990 was estimated at US$ 140 using the market exchange rate.

2.   Food crop production carries the agricultural sector in Uganda--totaling 71 percent of agricultural GDP, with livestock products another 17 percent (average 1989-91). Export crop production is only 5 percent of agricultural GDP, the fisheries subsector accounts for 4 percent, and forestry for 3 percent. Only one-third of food crop production is marketed, compared with two-thirds of livestock production, and all export crop output.

3.   Although the agricultural sector has grown rapidly in recent years--achieving a 4.9 percent average annual growth rate between 1986 and 1991--this should be seen in the context of the past twenty years. Economic development in Uganda since the early 1970s has been hostage to the effects of armed conflicts, the disintegration of public infrastructure and services, the collapse of Government regulation, and the uncertainties of high inflation and scarcities of foreign exchange. Agricultural output has only recently reached the levels achieved in the late 1970s. Indeed, if the average annual agricultural growth rate of 2.7 percent achieved between 1963 and 1978--a rate above the average for sub-Saharan Africa then--had been sustained through 1991, agricultural output would be about 26 percent higher than present levels. As it was, agricultural output has grown at only 0.9 percent per annum since 1968. Total GDP increased at 0.4 percent per annum in the same period. With population growing at 2.6 percent per annum, GDP per capita has declined markedly.

Lessons From This Review

4.   As a prelude to proposing a strategy to support growth in agriculture, this section summarizes the main conclusions of this report, and lists the market and production constraints that determine Uganda's alternatives in its drive to promote growth and alleviate poverty.

5.   Three main conclusions on the nature of past performance--and the possibilities for future expansion emerge from this report: agricultural expansion has resulted from the rapid increase in the production of food for a resurgent domestic market, the increase in food production has resulted from expansion in area cultivated, and the international markets for Uganda's traditional export crops have become much more competitive than in the early 1970s.

Growth in Food Production

6.   The engine of growth in the 1980s has been the re-establishment of peace and security, combined with release of the foreign exchange constraint, rehabilitation of key infrastructure, and the adoption of free-market policies--including the decontrol of food prices and trade. This has

resulted in an expansion in food production as production and marketing costs fell and the population tried to recapture consumption levels of the mid-1970s. Food production has been the lead sector in agriculture, both in 1980-83 and since the advent of the current Government in 1986. Trend growth in food production was 3.2 percent per annum for the decade, and 4.8 percent per annum since 1986. Since 1986, growth in agricultural demand has been led by the urban demand for food. The rapid rise in urban incomes--and demand--resulted in part from the refurbishment of industries, services and Government, which was undertaken with high levels of donor support.

7.	Food has become an attractive cash crop. For fifteen years--with the exception of the early 1980s and 1991 (Figure 40)--the relative returns on production of food versus cash crops has been above the levels of the early 1970s. Because access to land is almost universal, wages needed to hire labor away from own production have risen as well. The rise of labor costs has squeezed profit margins on estates. With lower returns to export-crop production, farmers' time devoted to export crops has declined, affecting yields and quality. The main cash earners for rural families are now food crops or dairy products sold in urban areas, rather than the export crops of the 1970s.

8.	One consequence of having food as the engine of agricultural growth is the dependence on the growth in domestic demand for continued impetus. Based on projected population and income increases (para 51) the domestic market is expected to increase at no more than 3 to 4 percent per year over the next decade. Much of the potential for growth through import substitution in the dairy, sugar, and tobacco subsectors has already been exploited. During 1991 and early 1992, the markets for "matoke" (bananas--the main foodcrop), milk, sugar, beef, and maize has been soft. And real food prices have been falling in the last half of the decade, except for a sharp increase in 1989. If current levels of growth in the domestic market are to continue, the focus will have to be on raising rural incomes through technological change and increases in labor productivity, diversifying of export markets, and raising urban incomes through increased import substitution and processing of local raw materials.

9.	Growth in agricultural output slowed considerably in 1990. From increases of 8.7 and 6.4 percent in 1988 and 1989, growth dropped to 2.9 and 2.5 percent in 1990 and 1991. The main cause of the slowdown was slow growth in food crop production, down to 2.5 in 1990 and 1.0 percent in 1991 from a high of 7.6 percent in 1989. Export crop GDP actually declined between 1986 and 1990 at -0.8 percent per annum, reflecting poor incentives for coffee production. A sharp recovery in 1991 brought the average rate of growth in traditional export crops since 1986 up to 3.6 percent per annum. In response to the incentives for diversification, fish products grew at 12 percent per year between 1986-91. The drop in growth in the food sector could have resulted from a several factors: completion of the reoccupation of the cultivated areas abandoned in the 1970s; the successful substitution for imported foods, such as sugar and milk; the saturation of the domestic market for food, given income levels; and the slow growth in incomes in nonfood sectors of the economy.

Table 1: Rural Population and Land Availability by District

Region and District	Rural Pop'n 1991 1/	Cultivable Land Area (Km²) 2/	Density 1991	Avge Area Cultivated per Person (ha) 3/	Area Required for 1991 Pop'n (Km²)	Percent Cultivable Land Used in 1991	Broad Soil Class
Central							
Mpigi	796	4,406	181	0.38	3,025	69%	I
Mukono	717	4,061	177	0.38	2,725	67%	II
Luwero	408	7,986	51	0.38	1,550	19%	II
Masaka	747	5,542	135	0.34	2,540	46%	II
Rakai	366	3,500	105	0.34	1,244	36%	III
Mubende	463	8,963	52	0.32	1,482	17%	II
Eastern							
Iganga	899	4,489	200	0.328	2,949	66%	III
Jinja	208	619	336	0.328	682	110%	II
Kamuli	473	3,694	128	0.328	1,551	42%	III
Kapchorwa	112	1,064	105	0.386	432	41%	II
Kumi	225	2,454	92	0.787	1,771	72%	III
Mbale	645	2,022	319	0.384	2,477	122%	II
Soroti	384	8,407	46	0.787	3,022	36%	II/III
Tororo 5/	842	3,887	217	0.387	3,259	84%	III
Northern							
Apac	454	4,962	91	0.542	2,461	50%	III
Arua	598	6,578	91	0.255	1,525	23%	III
Gulu	296	11,321	26	0.533	1,578	14%	IV
Kitgum	340	13,536	25	0.533	1,812	13%	IV
Kotido	181	10,352	17	N/A			III
Lira	471	6,950	68	0.542	2,553	37%	II
Moroto	158	7,540	21	N/A			IV
Moyo	168	4,313	39	0.255	428	10%	IV
Nebbi	292	2,689	109	0.255	745	28%	II
Western							
Bundibugyo	116	394	294	0.2	232	59%	III
Bushenyi	735	3,559	207	0.25	1,838	52%	II
Hoima 5/	395	6,633	60	0.316	1,248	19%	II/III
Kabale 5/	598	2,353	254	0.286	1,710	73%	II/III
Kabarole	741	7,607	97	0.25	1,853	24%	II/III
Kasese	343	1,478	232	0.2	686	46%	II
Masindi	275	5,369	51	0.316	869	16%	II
Mbarara	930	9,477	98	0.174	1,618	17%	III
Rukungiri	388	1,391	279	0.286	1,110	80%	II/III
Total	14,764	167,596	88		50,973	30%	

1/ National Census Figures.
2/ B. W. Langlands, "Soil Productivity and Land Availability Studies", Makerere 1974.
3/ Report on Uganda Census of Agriculture; Langlands, op cit.
4/ Langlands: I = Very good; II = Good; III = Moderate; IV = Poor.
5/ 1991 Census: Tororo + Pallisa, Hoima + Kibale, Kabale + Kisoro

Expansion of Area Cultivated

10.   Agricultural growth this decade has been due to an expansion in cultivated area, rather than an increase in yields. The area under cultivation--4.6 million ha--is still below the level of the late 1970s. Food crop cultivation, at 4.3 million ha, is at the levels of the early 1970s.Cash crop cultivation--at 0.3 million ha, due to the decline of cotton--is less than half the level of the 1960s. Agricultural land, while not limiting growth for the country as a whole, is a constraint in certain, high-potential, high-population regions in the Southwest and Northeast (table 1). There is a gradual inter-regional migration, from the most densely populated areas to less-populated regions of good potential. Reestablishing peace north of Lake Kyoga will make large underutilized areas available for cultivation. The area currently under cultivation, while utilizing the regions of highest potential, is still less than 30 percent of potentially cultivable areas.

Competition in International Markets

11.   There has been a sea change in the international prices of Uganda's traditional export crops: coffee, tea, and cotton face much lower prices in real terms now than in the early 1970's. Prospects for trend improvements are limited. Profits and rents from these crops, most of which were captured by Government, have been severely reduced to keep the country competitive in international markets. Successful international competition now requires continued increases in the efficiency of export production and processing, with little margin for taxation. Uganda, due to its excellent agricultural resources, is a low-cost producer in these three crops and with improved efficiency in the processing industries can expect to profitably sell all it can produce.

12.   The regional market for food, especially maize and beans, can be expected to increase. Uganda's landlocked status and reliable rainfall provide it with the opportunity to supply food cheaply to several of neighbors--one of whom, in any given year, can be expected to be undergoing a drought. Growth in this market depends however, on the annual food import requirements of a client country in a given poor agricultural year, and may not go beyond 300,000 to 400,000 tons of food per year.

Structural Adjustment in Agriculture and Constraints to Growth

Agriculture Rehabilitation Project

13.   Government's efforts to reform the production and marketing arrangements in agriculture since 1980 have received support from two IDA funded projects supporting sectoral adjustment: a) the Agriculture Rehabilitation Project (ARP) Cr 1328-UG of February 1983, and b) the Agriculture Sector Adjustment Credit, (ASAC), Cr 2190-UG of December 1990. Under the ARP the physical rehabilitation of export processing facilities in the cotton, coffee and tea sectors was successfully financed. No provision had been made for supporting operational reforms, however, and not all of the facilities have been used profitably. The ARP also financed a large share of agricultural imports between 1983 and 1992, when it closed. Perhaps the most important contribution was support for the newly established Interministerial Agricultural Policy Committee and its executive arm, the Agricultural Secretariat in the Bank of Uganda. Through this structure, Government kept in touch with production and incentives problems facing farms and processing industries and was able to implement ARP conditionality which required that farmgate prices for export crops be adjusted to maintain production incentives. While still administered by

Government, prices and margins for export crop purchase and processing were adjusted upwards during the early 1980s to maintain production and export incentives within a monopolistic, state controlled system. There was some response in the coffee, tea, cotton, and tobacco sectors, subsequently dampened by security problems in the mid 1980s, the collapse of international markets (Figure 6), and a decline in real farmgate prices.

Agriculture Sector Adjustment Credit

14.   ASAC was designed in 1990 to address the salient issues in adjustment of agriculture and their macroeconomic ramifications. ASAC's main focus was to control credit expansion for crop finance and improve export marketing efficiency and production incentives for coffee -- which in 1990 provided over 90 percent of export revenue. Its share has since declined, due to the growth in non-traditional exports, and the drop in coffee prices. In addition, funds were provided to improve policy making in the agricultural sector and strengthen agricultural research and extension capacity. The project has been successful and provides a model for how to proceed in the liberalization of other export crop marketing systems. Government has gone beyond the conditionality set forth in the operation in order to achieve the agreed objectives. Control of credit expansion to finance the purchase of the coffee crop, the largest single source of demand for funds in the financial system (Figure 9), has been achieved by shifting the responsibility for providing this credit to the commercial banks, thus removing the Bank of Uganda from its position as financier of last resort and improving Government's capacity to monitor developments in the subsector. Inflation declined from around 240 percent per annum in FY 1988 to around 30 percent in FY 1990 (Main Report, para 5.11). Coffee exports have been maintained in a time of declining world prices (Figure 29) by improving processing efficiency and farmgate production incentives. First, this was achieved through the promotion of competition. The monopoly control on exports held by CMB was dismantled. Participation by cooperative unions and private sector exporters was promoted. Government-imposed farmgate prices and marketing margins have been discontinued. The farmgate price of coffee, which had been declining in real terms since 1986, rose in May 1991 (Figure 10) when Government set the procurement price for the last time. Since then the market determined price for coffee at the farmgate has been market determined, and has fallen from its May 1991 level. CMB's regulatory functions were shifted to a separate Uganda Coffee Development Authority (Main Report paras 4.29-4.56). Second, Government has significantly reduced its tax on coffee exports. At present coffee export earnings are converted at the market rate of exchange, and the tax rate--having dropped to a flat 5 percent on export value in late 1991--is now zero. In addition to conditionality on coffee marketing and rural credit policy, ASAC is strengthening Government's policy formulation capacity for agriculture with technical assistance and training in the three main Ministries: MAAIF, MCIC and MPED. The Agricultural Secretariat, the locus for policy analysis in agriculture, continues to be assisted, although its role has shifted from administration of export prices and margins towards monitoring of product and inputs markets and prices, and providing analytical support for further adjustment and regulatory initiatives of Government. Agricultural research and extension are scheduled to receive long term support under two IDA funded projects, recently appraised, prepared with resources provided under ASAC. Also, ASAC provides support for the promulgation of a new Land Law which would extend freehold tenure. ASAC has addressed the first tier of constraints to agricultural growth. There is still an agenda for adjustment in agriculture, which is discussed below.

Constraints to Growth

15.   Growth in agriculture in Uganda has been hampered during the 1980s by a series of structural constraints related to: (i) Government control of food and export crop marketing and pricing which inhibited incentives to improve the quality and quantity of output in the farm and factory; (ii) inadequate transportation infrastructure and shortage of vehicles; (iii) shortages of foreign exchange, and high and unpredictable inflation; and (iv) physical insecurity. In addition, agricultural growth has been held back by a series of institutional factors which include: (v) ineffective Government research and extension services; and (vi) segmented, inefficient and discriminatory markets for capital, labor, and agricultural inputs. The effects of the above mentioned constraints on the development of each subsector are described, by institution and by crop, in Sections III and IV of the Main Report.

16.   Over the past six years, many of the structural constraints to growth in agriculture listed above have been removed. As the sectoral analysis undertaken in the Main Report indicates, since 1986 growth in the agricultural sector has been due, at different times, to: (i) the re-establishment of peace and security in the Center, South and West, which resulted mainly in increases in cultivated area under food; (ii) the decontrol of food marketing; (ii) improvements in transportation infrastructure between food producing areas and Kampala; (iv) rehabilitation of production and processing capacity for estate-based cash crops (tea, sugar); (v) decontrol of coffee processing and export marketing--which prevented serious declines in output, and (vi) the establishment of an open market in foreign exchange, which has provided an incentive for the development of non-traditional agricultural exports. The effects of the structural changes in the framework for agricultural growth undertaken over the past 6 years will continue to work themselves out during the 1990's. Increased competition in the coffee industry should result in improved processing and export marketing efficiency. Open markets in foreign exchange will result in investment export oriented industries. The rehabilitation of the tea sector will proceed slowly, helped by the resolution of Custodian Board cases.

17.   There is still an agenda for structural change in agriculture. Rapid increases in output in the cotton sector should result from changes in ownership and the introduction of more efficient management, improved access to credit, and increased competition amongst ginneries and export marketing agents. Adjustment in the cotton sector will be fairly complex and cumbersome however, given the dispersed location and ownership of ginneries, and the significant changes in ownership, management and finances involved. In tea, half of the gardens and many factories have yet to be rehabilitated. However, this is contingent on progress in the divestiture of Government-owned enterprises, the resolution of ownership claims for tea estates held by the Custodian Board, and the restructuring of factory ownership and management in the smallholder tea sector.

18.   The quickest gains from structural change have already been captured. The constraints to economic growth now facing the agricultural economy are not so easily dealt with. This point has already been made for food (para 9). Continued growth in agriculture will have to come from joint improvements in: (i) technology generation and dissemination; (ii) the responsiveness of the capital market, and the availability of long term finance; (iii) access and infrastructure to hitherto under-utilized areas; (iv) the re-establishment of peace and security North of Lake Kyoga; (v) the fluidity of the labor market; and (vi) tenure security, and the establishment of freehold tenure. The gradual release of constraints to growth in these areas will result from improvements in the

effectiveness of Government in the provision of essential public goods and establishing indirect regulatory mechanisms. All these efforts require a long term commitment to slow, steady change.

An Agriculture Sector Strategy

Development Objectives and Priorities

19.   In designing a development strategy for agriculture, priorities in the use of scarce financial and managerial resources should be set. The Government's objectives in stimulating growth in the agricultural sector are to meet the country's food requirements, generate foreign exchange, and improve living standards (Main Report, paras 5.13-5.14). Rapid growth in the food sector since 1986 has returned the country to food self sufficiency and brought about a broad based increase in rural incomes. The most fragile aspect of the recovery program in Uganda now is the lack of response in exports--which must grow in value in the next few years if economic growth is to be sustained. The capacity to finance imports has declined sharply due to the drop in coffee prices. Imports in 1990 were 3.5 times export revenue (Main Report, para 1.21). The availability of concessional donor funding to continue to bridge this gap is unlikely to be sustained at current levels,1/ and additional private sector finance is practically unavailable.

20.   The strategy to be followed must also acknowledge that the nature of agricultural growth will have to change over the next ten years. The lead will have to shift, from food production for the domestic market, to production of raw materials for processing and/or direct export. Over the past 6 years improvements in physical security in rural areas, reductions in economic uncertainty and inflation, increased availability of foreign exchange, and reductions in transport costs have driven the increases in agricultural GDP. The most responsive sector was food production, for the market and for own consumption, where marketing and pricing controls had been removed early on. Food production, excluding livestock, grew at 5.9 percent per annum between 1986 and 1990. Growth in export crop production languished due to continued Governmental interference, depressed world markets, and financial and managerial weaknesses in the marketing and processing industries.

21.   The scope for continued rapid growth in food production will be limited in future, due to its dependence on the size of the domestic market. Growth in domestic demand for food will be constrained to the increase in population, and increases in per capita income induced by expansion in urban based industries and services, and revitalized agricultural exports, the new lead subsector. If these factors produce a growth rate of 1.5 percent per annum in per capita income, then the demand for food is likely to be in the order of 3 to 4.5 percent per annum, in order to also cater for population growth (Main Report paras 4.13-4.16). Projections on this and other variables are developed in Section VI of the Main Report.

22.   In light of these imperatives, the report argues for a two pronged agricultural development strategy. In the short term, the agenda for adjustment and investment should continue to focus on increasing agricultural exports in traditional cash crops as rapidly as possible, while seeking diversification amongst the least investment-intensive non-traditional

---

1/   Mr. F.X. Colaço, Director, Eastern Africa Department, assessing the outcome of the Annual Meetings of September 1992 at Departmental Meeting of September 25, 1992.

agricultural exports. This will provide for a new source of growth in the sector, not limited to expansion of the internal market, and will address one of the key macroeconomic disequilibria and constraints to sustainable growth. In the medium term, deeper measures should be taken to diversify agricultural exports, improve technology generation and dissemination in the sector, and reduce transactions costs, entry barriers and market failures in the land, labor and capital markets as described below.

23.   The short term strategy advocates continued efforts to regain market share in traditional exports: cotton, coffee and tea. While production margins are very thin, and international prices low, our analysis shows that Uganda due to its excellent natural conditions, is a low cost producer of these products, and can compete in international markets, even at depressed prices, if processing and marketing efficiency is restored (Main Report, paras 4.18-4.21). There is need for a rapid restructuring and liberalization of the cotton ginning and export marketing industry. In coffee, choice of export routes should be liberalized. In tea, Government should divest itself of parastatal factories and estates, and conclude the Custodian Board review process, which is keeping a significant number of the estates out of production. These changes would generate significant increases in foreign exchange, and have a broad based income generation effect in rural areas.

24.   At the same time, short term measures should be taken to support the process of export diversification, which can grow very rapidly, as experience with sesame and fish exports in recent years indicates. Priority should be given to dry goods such as sesame, tobacco, hides and skins, spices and other products which do not rely too heavily on specialized packaging, critical transportation timing, expensive cooling infrastructure, and a commitment to constant, standardized quality deliveries. While the contribution to agriculture GDP from these crops is small (under 5 percent) their contribution to exports has been rising rapidly, and reached 20 percent in 1990, with the collapse in the price of coffee.

25.   In the medium term, the report argues that a series of measures are needed to support further diversification in agricultural exports. Development of high value specialized crop exports will increase returns and taxable profits, and stabilize export revenue. Government's role in developing these new activities should be indirect. Its focus should be on reducing unnecessary regulation, improving transport infrastructure and telecommunications, and smoothing the responsiveness of the land, labor and financial markets to profitable production opportunities. In addition, to raise rural incomes and ease the growth in food production, Government should take indirect measures to improve migration into underutilized areas of good agricultural potential. This will reduce the hunger for land in the densely populated districts of the Southwest and the Northeast, and permit labor augmenting technology to be used, increasing output per person. Careful management of this process will be needed to minimize environmental costs. Growth in yields is another key element of the agricultural strategy. Many traditional food and cash crops face disease and husbandry problems. Experimentation with new high value crops will require a high class, responsive research and extension service. Continued support for agricultural research and extension services is argued for, as is the need to provide improved monitoring and regulation of the use of natural resources --grazing lands, forests and fish -- as population pressures are exacerbated.

26.   The growth strategy advocated in this report should take place within bounds set by acceptable levels of environmental impact, self determination and equity. The approach utilized in promoting growth should lead to sustainable use of natural resources, enable local communities to participate and direct the development process, and provide the largest number of employment

opportunities possible to the rural poor. Uninhibited pursuit of a strategy to expand cultivated area could result in the mining of poor soils and the devastation of natural vegetation without providing a base for sustained increase in crop or livestock agriculture. Under the proposed strategy, policies which lead to increased internal migration should take into consideration the rights of the residents of the receiving areas, as well as the difficulties of adjustment faced by both incoming as well as resident families. Decisions on how production-processing-marketing relationships are structured, and the use of smallholder outgrower production schemes, can have broad beneficial effects. Prevention of concentration of land ownership through judicious management of titling and tenure of public lands will also benefit the rural poor. The effects of the proposed strategy on the alleviation of rural poverty, and the development of sustainable farming systems and participatory production relationships are noted below (paras 59 and 60), following the description of the growth strategy.

Short Term Strategy: An Export Action Plan

27.   **Coffee.** With coffee exports 80 to 100 percent of annual exports in the past fifteen years, it has been the clear initial target for improvements. As described in Main Report paras 4.29-4.56, and para 14 above, over the past two years there have been a series of radical reforms in the structure of the domestic coffee processing and export business--opening the industry to competition, reducing governmental control, and taxation. The policy reforms have gone as far as was necessary to set the stage for a competitive, aggressive attempt to win back some of the country's share of the world coffee market. No further basic changes in export policy in the coffee sector should be made for at least three years. While continuing evaluation of the effectiveness of current policies should continue, the industry should be allowed to adjust to the market-oriented framework established to date. With a no tax, and exports converted at the bureau exchange rate, there are strong incentives for exporters to raise quality and volume as much as possible. It will take time for the incentives to raise export output and quality--to filter back through the processing industry to the producers. There is, however, one area where action in the short term will significantly improve export incentives, and reduce uncertainty:

● Coffee exporters should be allowed to select the most competitive export channel and route (road or rail), and export inspections and customs procedures should be streamlined to reduce wasted time--and resulting cost increases.

28.   **Cotton.** The third largest export earner (after sesame seed) in 1990-91, cotton should be the focus of the Government's efforts to raise export earnings. The reasons are compelling.

● At market-based prices and reasonable levels of ginning efficiency--well above current levels--even low-input, low-output cotton production as practiced in Uganda is profitable;

● An important constraint to increased efficiency and growth in the sector is the lack of competition in ginning and export marketing. This can be solved with changes in policy, adjustments in laws and regulations, and assistance in rationalizing ginnery ownership, now held entirely by cooperative unions of which many are insolvent;

● The production response from farmers is expected to be rapid. In spite of the unsatisfactory system of cotton purchases and payment now in place--with routinely long delays--some 70,000 ha were planted in 1991. When payment is adequate and prompt, the incentives for increased production should be strong;

- The regions north of Lake Kyoga, where cotton has traditionally been grown, are not as severely affected by security problems as they were one or two years ago, and the situation is improving,

- Capital has already been invested in a partial refurbishing of nominal ginning capacity, which far exceeds current output;

- The three key ingredients to improving operations in the cotton sector--working capital finance, managerial and technical skills--can be provided by private entrepreneurs, without additional Governmental involvement, once it is clear that a stable policy based on freely convertible export earnings and a competitive ginning and export marketing environment is put in place.

29.   The steps necessary to revitalize the cotton sector include:

- The re-establishment of peace and security in production regions North of Lake Kyoga;

- The revocation of the Lint Marketing Board's monopoly on cotton exports, and other restrictive provisions of the LMB Act,

- The revocation of area monopsony power provided to cooperatives in the purchase of seed cotton, and other restrictive provisions of the Cotton Act,

- Provision of assistance to cooperative unions to enable them to solve financial and managerial constraints, and increase use of their ginning facilities. Sale, lease and/or management contracts with viable private sector entities are envisaged;

- The establishment of a cotton development authority, funded by a small cess--less than 1 percent--on cotton exports, to assure quality standards, to promote the industry at home and abroad, and to fund research and extension once industry profitability has been established.

30.   **Tea.** Whereas the estate sector has by and large been privatized, there remains the question of the tea estates and factories of the Government owned Agriculture Enterprises Ltd (AEL). These estates are inefficiently run at well under capacity. Privatization of their operations would permit these resources to be brought back into operation, with gains in employment and foreign exchange to the country.

- The Government should divest itself of AEL holdings in the tea sector as soon as private sector buyers with capacity to make full and profitable use of the assets have been identified.

31.   **Nontraditional Agricultural Exports.** The other area for immediate attention, and where the production response can be rapid, is in nontraditional agricultural exports. Growth can be rapid, as the evolution from 1989 through 1992 showed when NTAEs jumped from US$2.1 million to US$23.8 million in 1990 to US$ 42.6 million in 1991. The most important products

include sesame seed, beans, maize, other cereals, hides and skins, fish, and fruit and vegetables. This rapid growth must be supported. But markets for these products are small and volatile. The measures to foster this type of growth are indirect, and focus on the need to improve the reliability and efficiency of export channels, and facilitate access to term finance. Support from MAAIF and NARO on resolution of production problems for little known crops of high potential (spices, silk) is also needed. Priority measures would include:

- Review of the functions of the Export Policy Analysis and Development Unit, the Export Promotion Council and the Investment Authority, to harmonize their policy making, promotional and regulatory activities, and simplify the array of review and approval procedures faced by potential investors and entrepreneurs. These agencies should jointly develop a plan to address potential constraints to new investors in Uganda: improve export facilities, including regular air freight availability to Europe, reduce license and approval procedures, provide specialized communication services, and provide specialized export processing and storage infrastructure, targeted at key industries.

- Design of a mechanism to improve the availability of local and foreign funding to qualified investors. While the financial sector is under adjustment, the need for exports in the short term may justify the creation of a dedicated line of credit, or the establishment of an organization capable of providing venture capital finance and reducing the business risk to investors with likely new projects.

Medium-Term Agricultural Development Strategy

32.   The medium-term strategy outlines Government's role in inducing structural change and investment in agriculture until the turn of the century. The framework for the strategy cites the need for Government intervention in three main areas: (a) improving incentives for agricultural production and processing, (b) improving the efficiency of the land, labor, and capital markets, and (c) inducing technological change through improvements in agricultural research and extension, and strengthening management of natural resources. Recommendations, which are provided by crop or institution, synthesis the most important of the detailed recommendations contained in Section IV.

33.   **Incentive Framework.** Government administration of prices and processing and marketing margins in the agricultural sector has been almost completely discontinued. Only cotton, tobacco, cocoa and tea continue to have farmgate prices set by fiat. Government intervention in the sector will be justified to: (a) take direct or indirect measures to increase efficiency in processing, mainly through the promotion of competition, and (b) enter the market on the side of the producer in cases where processing industries exercise monopsony control on crop purchase prices. The cotton, tea and sugar subsectors are cases in point. The implementation of these measures is very dependant on accurately designed policies and programs which achieve desired objectives without diminishing production and investment incentives.

34.   The key entity in the formulation of Government policy in the sector is the Agriculture Policy Committee, which brings together the top civil servants in the Agriculture, Finance and Economic Planning, Commerce and related ministries, the Bank of Uganda and the Uganda Commercial Bank. Much effort has been made in recent years (under ARP, ASAC and various donor funded Technical Assistance projects) to develop Government's policy analysis and formulation capacity. The agriculture planning departments in the MAAIF, MCIC and MFEP

have all received support, as has the Agricultural Secretariat of the Bank of Uganda, the executive arm of the Agriculture Policy Committee. The system has worked well to date. Many of the major reforms liberalizing marketing, processing and exports have been successfully carried out under this structure. The system has now to be redesigned to play a role in the more indirect management appropriate in a market based economy. A Task Force constituted under the APC has addressed the question of planning and policy formulation for the agricultural sector. 2/ Points made in this report include the need to:

- Establish comprehensive and reliable sources of regular data on product and factor prices across the country;

- Strengthen policy analysis and strategic thinking in the Ministry of Agriculture, Animal Industry and Fisheries, to enable it to lead in the formulation of sectoral development policy;

- Consolidate the interministerial planning framework for annual budgeting and public investment program review in the agricultural sector, under the leadership of MFEP;

- Encourage producers and agro-industries to organize their own associations to represent their points of view before the policy makers. Such associations should be encouraged to "self regulate" their industry in their own interest;

- Maintain, for the present, the use of an Agricultural Policy Committee for the formulation of agricultural development policy, with the Agricultural Secretariat as an executive arm. This system is flexible and efficient and has proven well able to bring about consensus and produce results to date.

35.   In the coffee industry, competition is developing in export processing and marketing following the recent structural adjustment process (para 14). The recent Cabinet decisions freeing producer prices and processing and marketing margins to market forces, and allowing exporters to convert coffee export proceeds at the bureau exchange rate should fundamentally improve the incentive environment in the industry, assure fair competition between cooperatives and private-sector operators, and improve the responsiveness of the coffee industry to international conditions. In addition to the recommendations made for the short term plan, the report notes that:

- Coffee sector incentive policies, on pricing, taxation and licensing should be stabilized for at least three years, to allow the industry to adjust to the new rules. Monitoring of industry parameters should be constant, to permit a Government response to unpredictable destabilising events;

- Measures should be designed and enforced by UCDA to prevent collusion and maintain competition among coffee processors and exporters,

- Privatization of the Coffee Marketing Board Limited should be completed, with ownership shares gradually sold off to the private sector,

2/   Government of Uganda, APC, "Programme for Strengthening Agricultural Sector Planning (PASP)", Report of the Task Force on Agriculture Sector Planning, Kampala, January 1922.

- Alternative export sale procedures should be assessed--including an auction--to maximize medium-term export revenue, establish a fair basis for tax assessment, provide an open, fair pricing process, and encourage buyer commitment to the Ugandan product.

36. Measures to revitalize the processing side of the cotton industry have been spelled out in the short term plan. In the medium term, attention should be given to the production side. Cotton yields and acreage will respond to the efforts made to strengthen the inputs supply market, the rural financial market and to improve the responsiveness and relevance of Government's agricultural research and extension services. A resurgence of oxen based ploughing and cultivation will occur when the security situation in the Teso, Lango and Acholi areas improves sufficiently for farmers to hold animals without fear of rustlers. In addition, particular attention should be given to:

- Assistance in restocking with animals for draft powered land preparation and cultivation;

- Refinement and improvement of the cotton seed varieties by agroecological area. Previously adapted varieties have been mixed.

37. In the tea industry, to improve processing efficiency and increase output in estate and UTGC factories, the following measures are recommended, in addition to those noted under the short term plan:

- For the UTGC and its factories, reform should follow the plan outlined by the proposed EEC project, whereby factory management is separated from the extension and overhead-support functions of UTGC, and put in the hands of a professional management concern, and factories are eventually sold off to the farmers who use them;

- Retention accounts for foreign exchange earned from tea exports should be brought under strict supervision of the Bank of Uganda, and gradually phased out in favor of the open market in foreign exchange;

- UTGC's monopoly over procurement of green leaf should be removed. Factories should be encouraged to enter directly into contracts with outgrowers, which include leaf collection, input supply, and credit recovery. UTGC should play the role of "buyer of last resort" in order to maintain an equitable farmgate greenleaf price;

- Deliberations by the Custodian Board on ownership of private sector tea estates should be concluded, under the framework provided by the IDA-funded Structural Adjustment Credit, and incentives provided for the rapid rehabilitation of privately owned factories and gardens,

38. In the sugar industry, incentives for domestic production--with freely determined domestic market prices and competing privately owned producers--will be determined by trade policy. While the sugar industry is being rehabilitated--which may last another five years--competition from imports should be regulated through tariffs to permit the sugar producers to realize prices of

more than US$400 per ton needed to permit profitable factory operation and self-financing of the rehabilitation works.

39.   **Product- and Factor-Market Efficiency and Infrastructure.** Government influence on the functioning of markets supporting agricultural growth will, for the most part, be indirect. The key indirect instruments will be reforms in the financial market, a retreat from the inputs market, and investments in transportation and communication infrastructure, as discussed below. Direct intervention and change will need to be fostered amongst farmer cooperatives and in land markets.

40.   The major player in rural factor and product markets in Uganda over the past twenty years has been the <u>farmer cooperative network</u>. The existence of this network, its infrastructure, and the loyalty of its customers, means that rural cooperatives and their unions can continue to play an important role. Increased liberalization in rural trade and processing means, however, that these organizations will have to compete with other private sector entrants. Steps should be taken to assist cooperatives to emerge from their protected environment and take advantage of trade and processing opportunities. In this regard:

- Market protection for cooperatives should be reduced to force competition with private enterprises. At the same time, special social taxes and obligations imposed on cooperatives should be reviewed to avoid raising operating costs and placing cooperatives at a competitive disadvantage;

- Legislation governing the democratic operation of cooperatives should be used by Registrar to make the management cadres of primary societies and their unions more responsive to the majorities in the membership. At the same time, the Registrar's powers of direct intervention in the cooperative system should be diminished;

- Technical assistance in finance and management will be needed in the cooperative system to assist in the rationalization and divestiture of businesses, the negotiation of joint ventures with private entrepreneurs (especially in cotton), and the improvement of operating efficiency and profitability. Subsidies on this technical assistance may be needed in its initial phases to achieve the necessary restructuring of these entities;

41.   The market for <u>agricultural inputs</u> is distorted by Government participation, and by the difficulties of operating an import-based business in a rapidly changing macroeconomic environment. Steps should be taken to reduce market distortions and improve industry responsiveness by having:

- MAAIF withdraw from the physical distribution and sale of agricultural inputs. Donated fertilizer should be made available at commercial prices ex Kampala to the private trade for sale to farmers,

- Inputs--including donations of fertilizer--made available through donor funded agricultural projects should be sold by the Government through auctions, or in ways that will develop the private trade.

- MAAIF should to identify and promote the importing of products which, consistent with agronomic requirements of various soils and crops, can provide the required nutrients or active ingredients at minimum cost to the country and the farmer.

42.   The development of <u>rural financial markets</u> will have to follow on the measures being taken under the recently appraised Financial Sector Adjustment Credit (FSAC), proposed for IDA support. In addition to reestablishing confidence in the financial system and improving prudential capabilities of the Bank of Uganda, the following measures advocated under FSAC should improve the responsiveness of rural financial markets:

- Restructuring and recapitalizing the Cooperative Bank and the Uganda Commercial Bank--both of which have wide rural branch networks that can mobilize rural savings and supply finance to rural enterprises. Effective use of the branch network will depend on the development of a "branch orientation" in the commercial financial system which emphasizes the development of a lending relationship, and a deposit-taking relationship with customers. Branch managers should be encouraged (within the bounds of prudence) to identify and encourage local business development.

- Restructuring the development finance institutions. The supply of medium-term finance is crucial in the modernization of agroprocessing infrastructure.

- Maintenance of positive savings and lending rates leading toward a freely floating system.

- Continued testing of innovative approaches to market-based rural lending and saving. These pilot approaches should combine group-based savings and lending schemes with crop marketing and production finance, while targeting programs to needy areas, the rural poor, and rural women, in an attempt to use informal-finance methods to create sustainable village-level financial contracts and organizations. Such community-based pilot schemes should interact effectively with the "informal" financial network, make it more liquid, and link it more closely to commercial finance.

43.   The operation of <u>land markets</u> is a delicate area, confused by the existence of a reform decree passed in 1975, whose provisions have been only partly implemented. The approach proposed in this report is to:

- Focus tenure-related efforts on the mechanisms for the resolution of tenure-related disputes in the short term. The land market appears to work well in most areas, under traditional tenure systems.

- Regulate access to hitherto unoccupied--or underdeveloped--areas and public lands in ways which foster smallholder occupancy and ownership by persons committed to making the land produce. Speculative concentration of land holding in public lands and unoccupied areas should be avoided. Supportive treatment for smallholder immigrants, and extension of squatters rights where appropriate, should be provided.

- After sufficient national discussion to obtain broad agreement, new land legislation should be passed which would re-establish freehold tenure. Mailo 3/ tenants holdings would be separated from the mailo estate and vested in the Land Commission in freehold. The Commission may then grant this freehold to the mailo tenant. The rights of customary tenants on public lands would be restored, and tenants permitted to obtain freehold tenure. Freehold tenure will reduce the land-related barriers to migration by labor and small farmers which are inherent in many customary tenure systems.

- Once agreement on the new land legislation and regulation has been reached, the Land Offices through which the legislation will be implemented should be strengthened.

44. Whether there are obstacles to the functioning of the rural labor market is not clear. Cursory observation indicates that it functions fairly well and that labor responds predictably to employment opportunities around the country by migrating when the expected returns outweigh remuneration from local jobs and the costs of moving. The absence of migrant workers of Rwandan origin since the early 1980s has affected production relationships and wages for export crop production in estates and on smallholder farms. Migration of poorer farmers from the land-poor Southwest to the western and central areas continues. Migrants often work on existing farms while struggling to establish their own holdings--especially in the West. When the returns to food production improved in the latter half of the 1980s, the flow of migrant labor diminished. The flow of labor into urban areas has only gradually started again. Urban incomes are, on average, 69 percent higher than in rural Uganda, and rural areas have grown at 5.9 percent per annum, above the national average growth rate of 2.5 percent. Further work is needed to identify labor flows, the nature of the work contract, the influence of customary tenure arrangements in different regions, and ways Government can influence the efficiency of this market. The location of improvements in schools, hospitals, and rural feeder and access roads combined with improved access to land and tenure security under a freehold system can facilitate the flow of families from overpopulated areas into areas of labor shortage, where land is still available for smallholder use.

45. The role of Government in developing strategically placed rural infrastructure cannot be overemphasized. The efficiency of all the markets discussed above depends on the availability of reliable, low-cost transport and effective power and communications networks. Rural feeder and access roads play a vital role in determining whether and how a region is developed. The location and design of rural infrastructure can determine whether development of an area is environmentally benign. The availability of health and schooling facilities seriously affects population movements, and the human costs of migration and development. For this reason, this report recommends:

- Planning of rural infrastructure--roads, schools, and health care facilities--should be closely coordinated with agricultural development expectations, and environmental degradation considerations in regional and district-level development plans. Such plans, which could be developed with full community participation as part of the "decentralization to the districts" initiative, would smooth the flow of labor to areas of opportunity. The negotiation of these "zoning

---

3/   Mailo refers to freehold tenancies established in the Buganda region in the early 1900s.

plans" would crystalize the tradeoffs between environmental preservation and economic growth;

- Rural infrastructure development should be planned--and executed--with the full knowledge and cooperation of the communities affected. Such communities should be encouraged to participate in operation, maintenance, and rehabilitation of this infrastructure.

46.   **Research and Extension Services and Natural Resource Management.** Research is vital to the development strategy identified for the agricultural sector. Although expansion of cultivated areas is expected to continue in the medium-term, technological change will play an increasingly important role in agricultural growth. For resource-poor smallholder farmers faced with limited cropping alternatives, technological change, embodied in higher-yielding--or disease-resistant-seed or planting stock, a chemical, or a husbandry technique, can provide one of the few affordable means of raising incomes. Government is moving, with IDA assistance, toward the establishment of a centralizing National Agricultural Research Organization, which will set the research agenda and stabilize funding. Existing research institutes will belong to this organization.   Funding--and the agenda--for research will come from: (a) Government, for work on the broad array of food and livestock problems, where cost recovery is difficult; (b) export crop-related "cesses"--in coffee, tea, sugar, and cotton--to support crop-specific research programs; and (c) privately funded requests to resolve specific production problems. Measures would be taken under the IDA financed project to improve the incentives for collaboration with farmers and extension staff in finding research results which are relevant and profitable.

47.   Increased agricultural output and rural incomes are important Government objectives. The country cannot wait for the gradual dissemination of technological improvements through word of mouth and curiosity. To speed technological change, the Government should continue to operate an extension service dedicated to the dissemination of appropriate profit-enhancing, environmentally-appropriate technology.   Linking the widely dispersed, broadly diversified users of this service to its costs is difficult. For this, and equity reasons, the Government, with IDA assistance, will continue to fund a redesigned, streamlined, national extension service. The focus will be to provide intensive, high quality technical assistance through a "unified" service on all aspects of agricultural production. Management will be compatible with the "T & V" system. Extension staff will initially cover select portions of priority districts, extending coverage where economically justified, and as budgetary funding permits. Private operations--especially one such as tobacco production--with tightly linked input finance, production, and marketing, can be expected to finance their own, crop-specific extension agents.

48.   On natural resource management Governmental departments charged with controlling the use of forest and fish resources, and with management of wildlife, are notoriously weak and underfunded.   These organizations should be restructured and performance incentives provided so that the regulatory legislation and framework can begin to function. Natural resources and wildlife are under severe pressure due to population growth and fuelwood needs (forests), and due to incentives to export (fish).

49.   For the above-mentioned Government services to be effective in rural areas, personnel should have strong performance incentives, as well as the vehicles and equipment and supplies necessary for operation in difficult and taxing environments. For this reason:

- Funding for Government agricultural research, extension and natural resource management services should be given high priority within the National Budget. Annual budgetary allocations of locally generated resources in support of agriculture-related services, with emphasis on research and extension, be increased to at least 0.75 percent of GDP (about US$ 17 million in 1990);

- The NARO, the extension service and the natural resource management services should have terms of service remunerative enough to strongly motivate innovative and responsive performance;

- A portion of the funding by the NARO of its institutes be provided on a "results" basis, with continued funding contingent on the production of usable conclusions.

Prospects and Consequences of Agricultural Growth

Prospects for Growth in Agriculture

50.   Growth in the sector should raise incomes and consumer demand in the country. Most important is the effect that growth in agricultural exports could have on the economy. This section provides a brief treatment of growth prospects in the food sector, broadly defined to include livestock products, and the export sector. These two sectors contribute about ninety percent to agriculture GDP.

51.   **Food.** Growth in food output, will in large part determine sectoral growth. The fastest growing agricultural subsector in the past decade has in fact been food production. There are, however, limits to how rapidly production for the domestic market can grow. Using 0.95 as the income elasticity of demand for all food, a projected population growth rate of about 3.15 percent, a per capita income growth rate of 1.5 percent per annum (the trend since 1986), and assuming constant relative prices, the demand for food is estimated to grow at 4 to 5 percent. This is also the rate at which supply would have to grow, to keep relative prices constant. With no growth in per capita income, food production would still have to grow at 3.1 percent per annum, to keep up with the projected population increase. To put this in perspective, the annual increase in the value of food crop production between 1981 and 1990 has averaged 3.3 percent. Since 1986, growth in food crop production has been 5.9 percent per annum.

52.   Growth in the demand for food could see a shift out of root crops into livestock products, as incomes rise. The Rwanda study and the Uganda Household Budget Survey both support the hypothesis that the income elasticity of demand for livestock products is much higher than for food as a whole, well above 1 and perhaps as high as 2. As incomes improve, the demand for livestock products should increase significantly. Conversely, the demand for starchy foods is likely to decline. The income elasticity of demand for bananas, cassava, and other root crops, the basis of the Ugandan diet, is estimated to be well below 1.

53.   **Exports.** While the prices for traditional export crops are low, the markets are very elastic for Uganda: its market share in a given commodity is small, and it will be able to sell all it can profitably produce without influencing the price. An optimistic scenario for the largest export sectors is set forth in table 2 below, and shows how the value of exports could be more than doubled over the next five to seven years. It assumes that the action programs put forward in

this report are implemented and succeed. Base prices and exports are for 1990, and the projections are for seven years.

Table 2: Projection of Potential Export Performance Under Export Action Plan, through 1997			
	1990	1997	Annual Growth Rate
Volumes ('000 MT)			
Coffee Beans	142.40	195.00	4.6 %
Cotton Lint	3.80	45.00	42.3 %
Made Tea	4.80	16.00	18.8 %
Value (million US$)			Incremental Value (US$ M)
Coffee Beans	141.60	193.90	52.30
Cotton Lint	5.80	68.70	62.90
Made Tea	3.60	15.50	11.90
Non Traditional Agricultural Exports	20.00	100.00	80.00
TOTAL	171.00	378.10	207.10

54.   The **cotton** sector should grow rapidly, if the liberalization measures advocated above are successfully put in place, and substantial amounts of private sector capital and managerial expertise--both local and foreign--enter the industry. A major precondition for growth in this subsector is the continued reduction in security problems north of Lake Kyoga, in the traditional cotton growing areas. The projection is that, if the program is successful, cotton exports could go from 20,000 to 250,000 bales in five years. While this is well within ginning capacity and historical limits, it would be a huge undertaking. The implied growth rate is about 40 percent per annum over seven years. Were this successful, exports would increase by some US$60 million per year at current prices.

55.   The **coffee** sector, with the liberalization of processing and export marketing that has taken place, and improvements in the production and dissemination of the new planting stock, should rise to perhaps 4 to 5 percent per annum. A return to export levels of 3.2 million bags, a level that was reached in the early 1970's, would add another US$ 50 million to exports at current prices.

56.   In the **nontraditional agricultural exports**, a careful review of growth possibilities, given current production, shipping, and marketing constraints, indicates that total annual exports from this subsector could reach US$100 million in 7 years, an additional US$80 million over 1990 levels. Exports from this sector almost doubled to about US$ 43 million in 1991. Most of the growth would come initially from sesame seed, maize, hides and skins, and spices and essential oils. Floriculture, fruits, and vegetables would come later in the period.

57.   Longer term projections (through the year 2005) have been developed in the context of the World Bank Country Economic Memorandum 4/. These projections of economic results focus on what could be achieved, if all goes well. These projections thus represent a feasible target. A summary of the results of these projections is provided in Table 3 below:

Table 3: Projected Average Annual Compound Growth Rates for Agriculture GDP for the Period 1992-2005 (in percentages)			
Subsector	Actual Growth Rates		Projected Growth Rates
	1981-1991	1986-1991	1992-2005
Foodcrops (Domestic)	3.2	4.8	3.2
Livestock Products (Domestic)	1.3	4.6	4.6
Horticulture, Spices, High Value Non-traditional Crops for Export			11.2
Traditional Export Crops	2.3	3.6	3.1
Food (Domestic Crops plus Livestock)			3.5
Exports (Traditional plus Non-Traditional)			9.5
Agriculture GDP (Monetary and Non-Monetary)	2.9	4.9	5.0

58.   If these targets are met, it will mean that a series of profound and positive changes will have taken place in export agriculture in Uganda, enabling it to play its role of generating the foreign exchange needed to support continued development in agriculture and other sectors with higher returns to labor.

Environmental Impact of Agricultural Growth

59.   There has been a clear environmental cost to the years of civil disorder from which the country is emerging. Uganda's wildlife, forests, fish, grazing lands and other natural resources are in danger of being overused, polluted and driven to extinction. Soil erosion is a problem in high-population density, high rainfall areas. Natural resource management programs and policies have broken down during the period of civil unrest, and have yet to be re-established. The strengthening of the Government services related to regulating natural resource use, wildlife management and conservation, as mentioned above, will have to be accomplished quickly if the irretrievable loss of high forests and wildlife is to be avoided. Measures taken in this regard should incorporate the needs, interests and participation of the local residents. The encouragement of natural migration patterns into under-utilized areas will have to be undertaken following careful assessment of soil quality and sustainable agricultural potential to prevent settlement in regions unsuitable for stable development. These measures have been described above, and are contingent on the development of a strong management and regulatory capacity for natural resources within Government, as well as on the use of environmental, agricultural and social criteria in the planning of new roads, schools and hospitals. Within crop agriculture, environmental criteria will have to be used by the research and extension services to develop

4/   World Bank, "Country Economic Memorandum", Report No. 10715-UG, Green Cover version, Chapter 5.

solutions to pest and disease problems that are as benign as possible. The rapid development of cotton advocated in the report is based on the continued use of the traditional low-input, low-output methods. As productivity and input use rise, care should be taken by the extension service and Government to limit pesticides to those with minimal environmental consequences.

The Alleviation of Rural Poverty

60.   The strategy developed above is intended to cause agricultural GDP to grow as rapidly as possible in the next five to ten years, within the bounds imposed by climate, soils, markets, and the capacities of Uganda's institutions. Food production is widely dispersed, with all smallholder farmers producing food both for own consumption and the cash market. The structure of export crop production is also based on the use of large numbers of farmers, each of whom produces small quantities of the crop for a central processing center. The implication is that, once the processing industries have become competitive, growth in exports will carry with it strong backward linkages to the rural population. For this reason there is, in broad terms, **a close correlation between measures that produce agricultural growth, and those that will contribute to a reduction in rural poverty.** But, some aspects of the growth strategy are likely to have a greater effect on rural poverty--and gender differences--than others. For example:

- The rehabilitation of the **cotton industry** is likely to have a broad rural-poverty mitigation effect.

  o   Cotton was grown by thousands of smallholder farmers in the North and Northeast. These areas have been under severe security-related restrictions until recently, which significantly diminished economic activity. Although grown using low-input low-output--environmentally neutral--techniques, cotton provides cash and an excellent seed bed for the follow-on crop of millet;

  o   Cotton ginning is labor intensive, and can generate substantial wage employment;

  o   Cotton can be produced easily in certain areas in the West, contributing to the opening of new areas there;

- The enforcement of carefully designed minimum cane and greenleaf prices, guaranteeing farmers a share of the export parity price, can prevent factory owners from exploiting their strong monopsony positions in these industries. There may be a case for such a system in the cotton industry. This would depend on an assessment of the ability of farmers to sell to competing ginneries. There appears to be sufficient competition in the coffee industry not to warrant such interference.

- The use of **outgrower production** strategies for rainfed industrial crops such as tea and sugar, can include more families (as families) in the export industry, and in the cash generation possible from such an industry. A detailed assessment would be warranted in each case, however. While riskier for factories than for nucleus estates--in that supplies are not as secure or well regulated--such an approach could save an estate the costs of recruitment, supervision, and investments in living facilities.

- The inclusion of **inheritance rights for women** in the newly designed land legislation can permit women to continue to raise families and pursue their own lives upon the death of a spouse.

- The formalization of **squatter rights,** within well-defined circumstances taking into consideration ethnic differences and customary land rights--and the facilitating of smallholder occupancy of environmentally suitable public lands and unoccupied areas--can give smallholders from the poorer, crowded areas easier legal access to the underutilized regions in the West and North.

- The use of **rural women's groups** in the design of pilot rural savings and credit schemes can help incorporate women into the financial system, and provide finance for trade and food production, activities that rural women specialize in.

- The maintenance of an open, **unregulated market in liquid fresh milk** permits small one-and two-cow operations on the periphery of Kampala and near other urban areas to participate in a lucrative market.

- Support for **small rural processing and service enterprises**--sewing, brickmaking, metalwork, carpentry, and bicycle repair--provides additional rural employment in the production of articles and services that would otherwise be imported from the metropolis.

61.   If the projected rates of agricultural growth take place and the rural institutions and relationships noted above are developed, then the benefits of agricultural development will be sustainable, and will improve living standards for a broad spectrum of the rural population.

I. AGRICULTURE AND THE ECONOMY

1.1   Agriculture is the mainstay of the Ugandan economy. Eighty-nine percent of the population is rural. The sector accounts for 51 percent of GDP (1991) and over 90 percent of exports, and employs 80 percent of the employed household population. Agricultural output comes almost exclusively from about 2.5 million smallholders--80 percent of whom have less than 2 hectares each. Only tea and sugar are grown on large estates, which total 40,000 ha. The predominance of smallholder farming implies that the benefits from sectoral growth will be equitably distributed. Income per capita in 1990 was estimated at US$ 140 using the market exchange rate.

1.2   Food crop production carries the agricultural sector in Uganda--totaling 71 percent of agricultural GDP, with livestock products another 17 percent (average 1989-91). Export crop production is only 5 percent of agricultural GDP, the fisheries subsector accounts for 4 percent, and forestry for 3 percent (fig.1). Only one-third of food crop production is marketed, compared with two-thirds of livestock production, and all export crop output.

Sectoral Growth

1.3   The normal process of a structural transformation, from agriculture to other sectors, has not been smooth in Uganda. Agriculture's contribution to GDP declined from 48 percent in 1963 to 44 percent in 1968 (fig. 2). Then, in nine years, the agricultural share spiraled up to 73 percent of GDP, showing a virtual return to subsistence as the industry and service sectors broke down. Agriculture's share has declined unevenly since then. Since 1987, when agriculture's share of GDP was about 62 percent, the share has been declining gradually, in consonance with the normal process of industrialization, to reach 51 percent in 1991. About 56 percent of agricultural GDP--31 percent of GDP--consists of subsistence crops--for home consumption--that never enter the cash economy.

1.4   Although the agricultural sector has grown rapidly in recent years--achieving a 4.9 percent average annual growth rate between 1986 and 1991--this should be seen in the context of the past twenty years. Economic development in Uganda since the early 1970s has been hostage to the effects of armed conflicts, the disintegration of public infrastructure and services, the collapse of Government regulation, and the uncertainties of high inflation and scarcities of foreign exchange. The most serious internal conflicts occurred between 1979 and 1980--with recovery stretching to 1982--and between 1984 and 1986. These conflicts caused serious declines in agricultural output.

1.5   The rapid growth between 1980 and 1983, and between 1986 and 1991, is in effect a recovery from a very low base. Agricultural output has only recently gone above the levels achieved in the late 1970s (fig. 3). Indeed, if the average annual agricultural growth rate of 2.7 percent achieved between 1963 and 1978--a rate above the average for sub-Saharan Africa then--had been sustained through 1991, agricultural output would be about 26 percent higher than present levels. As it was, agricultural output has grown at only 0.9 percent per annum since 1968. Total GDP increased at 0.4 percent per annum in the same period. With population growing at 2.6 percent per annum, GDP per capita has declined rapidly.

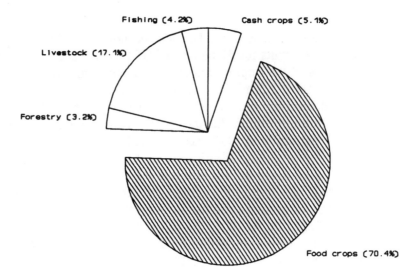

Figure 1   Shares in Agricultural GDP, Three-Year Average 1989-91

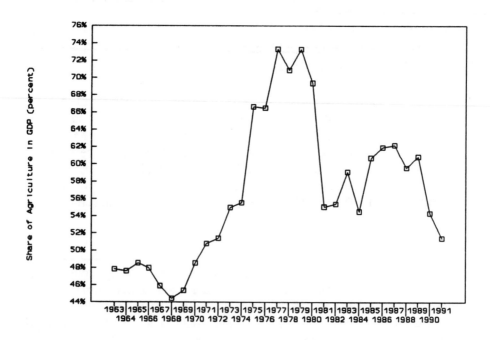

Figure 2   Share of Agriculture in GDP, 1963-91

1.6   Other lessons can be learned from the agricultural growth pattern between 1981 and 1990. The 2.9 percent annual growth in agricultural output achieved in 1981-91 was consistently led by higher growth in food crop production. Growth in the value of food production was 3.2 percent per annum for the decade (fig. 4). Export crop and livestock production grew more slowly, at between 1 and 2 percent per annum for the decade.

1.7   Between 1981 and 1991 there were two periods of recovery, and rapid growth--1981-83, and 1986-91. In the first period of recovery from the 1979-80 war--from 1981 to 1983--growth in agriculture was led by an 8.2 percent-per-year increase in the food sector, and a 20 percent-per-year increase in the export sector. The smallholders' response to the return of stability and to sharply increased price incentives was to cover basic food needs and rapidly increase export crop production.

1.8   The decline in output in the internal conflict of 1984-85 was less dramatic. Subsistence needs were not as dramatically affected. The second period of recovery starting in 1986 was led by growth in food crops and livestock products for the domestic market.   Food crop output led the sector with an average annual growth rate of 5.9 percent per annum through 1990. Slower growth in 1990 and 1991 brought the average annual rate of growth since 1986 to 4.8 percent (Fig. 4). 1/ Export crop GDP actually declined between 1986 and 1990 at -0.8 percent per annum. A sharp recovery in 1991 brought the average rate of growth in traditional export crops since 1986 up to 3.6 percent per annum. In response to the incentives for diversification, fish products grew at 12 percent per year between 1986-91.

1.9   In comparison with other countries in Africa, Uganda did well during the decade. Between 1980 and 1989, agricultural output for Sub-Saharan Africa grew at 2 percent per annum--below Uganda's 2.2 percent per annum, as it climbed back from the nadir of 1980. Growth in agriculture in Kenya (3.2 percent), Zimbabwe (2.9 percent) and Cote D'Ivoire (2.3 percent) was higher than in Uganda during this period. Agriculture in Ghana (0.9 percent) and Rwanda (-1.4 percent) grew more slowly.

1.10   Growth in agricultural output slowed considerably in 1990 and 1991. From annual increases of 8.7 and 6.4 percent in 1988 and 1989, growth dropped to 2.9 and 2.5 percent in 1990 and 1991. The main cause of the slowdown was slow growth in food crop production, down to 2.5 in 1990 and 1.0 percent in 1991 from a high of 7.6 percent in 1989. This could reflect the saturation of the domestic market, with much of the substitution for food imports completed, and slow growth in incomes from other subsectors.

1.11   The sources of growth in each subsector will be analyzed in this report. In food production, the substantial growth rate has resulted from area expansion, especially for bananas. For livestock, the main source of growth has been in the dairy industry. Perennial export crop production has been a function of increased yields (coffee, cocoa)--as husbandry levels improved with better production incentives--and of the rehabilitation of old stands, in the tea subsector. Annual export crops (tobacco, cotton) have expanded on the basis of increases in area cultivated.

1/   The crops included cassava, sweet potatoes, Irish potatoes, sorghum, finger millet, maize, beans, groundnuts, simsim (sesame), rice, and varieties of bananas suitable for cooking, brewing, and consumption as fruit.

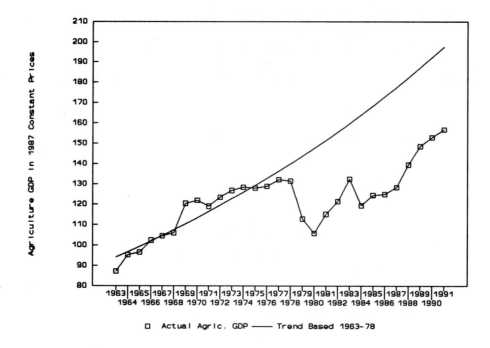

Figure 3   Agriculture GDP, 1963-91 in Constant 1987 Prices, and Forecast Growth in Agriculture GDP, Based on 1963-78 Trend.

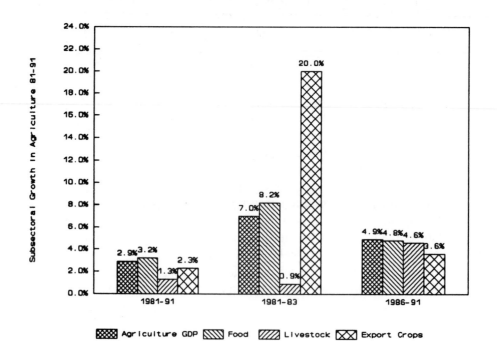

Figure 4   Annual Growth Rates in Agricultural GDP, 1981-91

1.12   This report is structured as follows. Section I provides background on the national economy and looks at trends in output. Section II reviews the natural resource base, and characterizes the rural population, farm ownership, and family living standards. Section III describes the services and institutions that support agricultural development. Section IV looks into constraints and opportunities in agriculture, reviewing export competitiveness and market prospects, before analyzing constraints and strategies for subsectoral growth. Section V considers the subsectoral strategies as part of an overall agricultural development. And Section VI suggests the implications of the strategy on public investment and on potential growth rates.

Agricultural Exports and Imports

1.13   Uganda has recovered from its expansion of agricultural imports necessitated by past disruptions. But continuing declines in revenues from coffee--the key export--are hurting the trade balance, when imports are needed to underpin economic growth.

Agricultural Exports

1.14   The health of Uganda's balance of payments in the 1980s depended almost exclusively on coffee exports. This was not always so. In 1970 coffee was only 50 percent of exports (fig. 5). Its share increased to more than 95 percent during the years of political instability and macroeconomic uncertainty. Only recently has coffee's share declined, due both to an increase in alternate exports, and a drop in the international price of coffee. Why this increased dependence on one crop? The answer lies in the production response to disruption and civil war. Coffee retained its importance as an export crop because of the low marginal costs of obtaining a crop, once the coffee trees are established. As a rainfed perennial, planted on family farms in the favorable Ugandan climate, the Robusta coffee tree--native to the northern shores of Lake Victoria--yields with minimal maintenance. Once the Robusta is well-established, low-level production can be maintained by family labor inputs for weeding, pruning, and harvesting. Hulling requirements are simple, cheap, and diversified. Export processing was centralized, until recently, in the Coffee Marketing Board. Since production is based on family labor and a simple manufacturing process, exports can be maintained for a few years even as production incentives decline. Continuously well-tended coffee trees are still productive after 60 years. But, the abandoning of weeding and pruning practices, as relative farmgate prices drop, weakens the coffee trees, which cannot regain their former vigor.

1.15   Although the tea tree is more robust, the tea industry is more fragile. A perennial crop, tea is grown on large estates and family farms. It requires constant attention. While marginal plucking and husbandry costs are all labor-based and low, tea has a more complex, centralized processing procedure than coffee. The effect of the political disorder and financial and economic uncertainty in the 1970s inhibited the functioning of the processing factories and export facilities, and forced the abandonment of plantations. Unlike coffee trees however, tea stands profit from a rest, and--if carefully rehabilitated--Uganda's tea gardens can yield as much as they did previously.

1.16   Cotton, the other important export in 1970, is an annual crop and hence has higher marginal costs of production. It competes directly with food and other annual cash crops in the annual planting decision. Reductions in returns on cotton can lead to a fairly rapid decline in production, as farmers switch into other crops. Cotton also requires a centralized capital-intensive ginning and marketing. Cotton's higher production costs, and its dependence on centralized capital-intensive ginning and marketing, have made it more vulnerable than coffee to political and economic uncertainty. Because cotton is an annual, however, the resurgence of production, in response to high relative prices and a revitalized ginning industry should be rapid.

1.17   Uganda's exports have been losing value rapidly. When export receipts are deflated by the index of prices of manufactured goods, 2/ then it becomes clear that exports have declined by - 5.4 percent per year from 1970 to 1990 (from relative economic prosperity, through the drop in coffee prices in the late 1980s). More recently, exports dropped by - 16.2 percent per annum from 1983 to 1990 (the beginning of the mid-1980s coffee boom through the 1989 dissolution of the ICO quotas).

1.18   Uganda's exports sold for just under $166.3 million 1990-91 (table 1).

Table 1:	Composition of Ugandan Exports by Volume (thousands of tons) and Value (millions of US$ FOB) for 1989-90 and 1990-91			
Commodity	**1989-90**		**1990-91**	
	(thousands of MT)	Value (millions of US$)	Volume (thousands of MT)	Value (millions of US$)
Coffee	165.2	180.432	115.8	118.638
Cotton	2.66	4.290	5.03	7.710
Tea	3.61	3.212	6.52	5.409
Tobacco	-	-	1.00	3.743
Maize	13.31	1.464	13.52	1.634
Beans	1.08	0.631	N/A *	2.664
Simsim	-	-	N/A	10.670
Other Pulses	-	-	N/A	0.582
Cereals	-	-	N/A	2.195
Fish products	-	-	N/A	1.981
Fruit & vegetables	-	-	N/A	0.682
Hides & skins	-	-	N/A	3.102
Timber	-	-	N/A	0.261
Minerals	-	-	N/A	4.872
Other	-	1.470	N/A	2.146
TOTAL		192.847		166.289

*   N/A - Not available

2/   MUV Index: unit value index in US dollar terms of manufactures exported from France, Germany, Japan, UK and USA weighted proportionately to the countries' exports to the developing countries, defined by the World Bank, International Economics Department, International Trade Division.

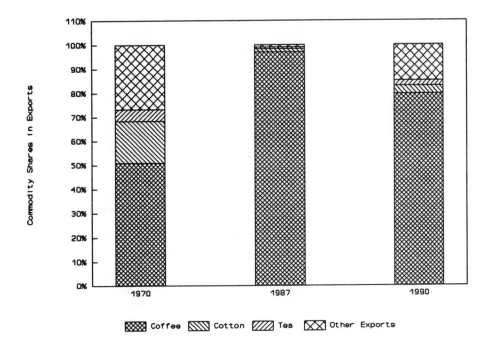

Figure 5   Shares of Agricultural Commodities in Total Exports

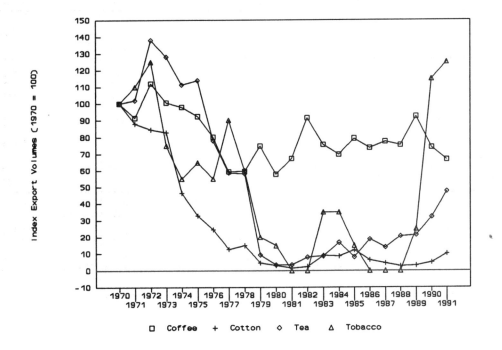

Figure 6   Indices of Export Volumes of Agricultural Commodities, 1970-91

1.19   The story of Uganda's agricultural exports can be seen in volume and price indices (fig. 6 and fig. 7). As of 1978 exports of crops other than coffee dropped way off, due mainly to the disruption of production and processing industries. Prices for two of Uganda's main export crops--coffee and cotton--maintained their real value from 1970 into the mid-1980s before a decline set in. Tea and tobacco prices declined sharply in real terms between 1970 and 1980. Prices for these key exports are well below the levels of the early 1970s, and they are unlikely to recover in the medium term. It can be seen however, that the performance of agricultural export volumes has not been a function of international prices. Whereas the international prices of cotton and coffee have followed roughly the same trajectory, their export performances differ radically. Cotton exports dropped dramatically through the 1970s, and have not risen above 10 percent of the 1970 level during the 1980s. Coffee exports on the other hand, while falling during the 1970s, recovered after the 1979 conflict, and--in the 1980s have remained at or above 50 percent of the 1970 peak volumes.

1.20   The drop in value of Uganda's coffee exports has been because of both the decline in world coffee prices, and to a decrease in the quality of its Robusta and Arabica exports. The production of washed Arabica--formerly about 10 percent of the crop--has stopped as processing costs have outweighed the returns in a tightly controlled market. Robusta exports in the highest grade also have declined as a share of coffee exports.

1.21   Because coffee is Uganda's main export, the drop in its real value has meant that the terms of trade--which stayed even throughout the 1980s--have declined dramatically. With the demand for manufactured imports and petroleum products increasing as the economy starts to grow, the deficit in the balance of trade has increased to unsustainable levels. In 1990 imports of US$618 million were about 3.5 times the value of exports of US$178 million.

Agricultural Imports

1.22   Domestic production can satisfy all Uganda's food and raw material needs. But, during the declines in production caused by two decades of economic and political disruption, urban food requirements--for milk, sugar, and wheat flour in particular--were met through imports. Imports of food and sugar totaled US$8.6 million in 1987, declined in 1988, totaling US$3.2 million in 1989 and US$1.4 million in 1990. Imports of milk powder were provided on a grant basis by donors, and these had dropped substantially in 1991 with the resurgence of the local dairy industry. Cereal imports of 16 thousand tons, and cereal aid of 17 thousand tons adds up to roughly the quantity of cereals received as food aid in 1974. By 1991 most of the imports or donations of sugar, cereals, and milk had been replaced with local production. Uganda's current food imports, at less than under 1 kg per capita, are well below the requirements of comparator sub-Saharan countries.

Macroeconomics and the Agricultural Sector

1.23   The predominant role of agriculture--and the importance of coffee to the cash economy--link agricultural performance closely to key macroeconomic variables. First, exports of coffee--and of other crops to a lesser degree--determine import capacity, a key factor in growth and modernization. Second, the coffee export tax was a major contributor to Government recurrent revenues in the mid 1980s, but its share of tax revenues has been declining rapidly, until the tax was removed in 1992. A third linkage is that agricultural finance--especially for the purchase, processing, and marketing of coffee (and other crops to a lesser degree)--is a large

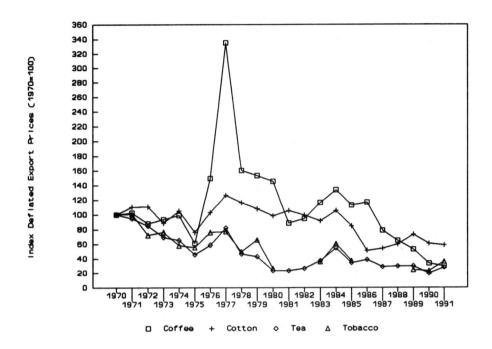

Figure 7   Indices of Real Export Prices for Agricultural Commodities, 1970-91

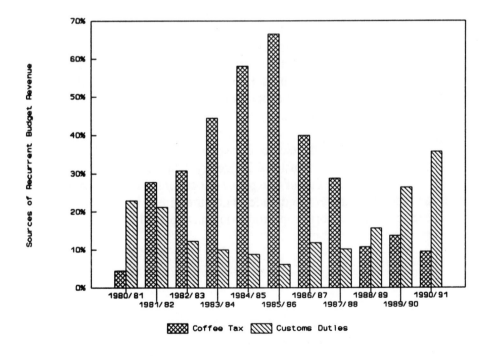

Figure 8   Coffee Export Taxes as Share of Recurrent Budget, 1980-81--1990-91

proportion of the total demand for credit, and determines the monetary aggregates. Fourth, in a less direct, but still crucial mechanism, efforts at budget containment and deficit reduction affect the availability of local funding for key agricultural services.

1.24   The decline in Uganda's terms of trade, and in the volume and value of its agricultural exports has been discussed above.

1.25   The decline in coffee revenues directly affected the recurrent budget (fig. 8). The windfall returns from the increases in the international price of coffee in the mid 1980s were siphoned off by Government--not into the Development Budget, but into the funding of recurrent expenditure. At the height of the international coffee boom in 1985-86, coffee tax receipts were more than 60 percent of recurrent budget revenues. It should be noted that the swings in coffee export tax revenue are counterbalanced in part by duties on imports. Imports are largely donor financed. This places in stark relief the country's dependence on donor funds, not only for imports but for budgetary support.

1.26   Other sources of revenue can affect agricultural incentives. An example is the annual sale of 20,000 to 30,000 tons of vegetable oil provided as a grant or long-term loan by the U.S. Such sales, while a useful source of Government revenue, lower the price of vegetable oil, a crop that Uganda produces and could export.

1.27   The financing of stocks of agricultural produce during export processing and marketing puts strains on the financial system. The main financing requirement is for the coffee crop. Crop finance has fluctuated between 16 and 57 percent of total credit outstanding during the decade (fig. 9). The peak for both the real value of crop finance and its share of total credit was reached in 1986. Then crop finance absorbed 92 percent of agricultural credit. Inflation in 1986 was 350 percent, the highest it has been during the decade. One step taken to contain inflation was to reduce credit creation by the banking system. To do this, and maintain the volume of coffee purchases, the Government-set minimum farmgate price for coffee was not changed in nominal terms during this inflationary period (1986-90) (fig. 10). The real price fell sharply, and has only recently started to climb back to previous levels. Production incentives in a key agricultural sector were sacrificed--in the short term--to contain inflation and monetary expansion.

1.28   Support for agricultural development has conflicted with macroeconomic objectives in one other area--the provision of local budgetary support for agricultural services. As will be shown in Section III, the real value of budgetary allocations for Government services that support agriculture has fallen throughout the decade--when the spread of disease in livestock and food crops and the need to expand export crop production have placed increasing pressure on the agricultural support system.

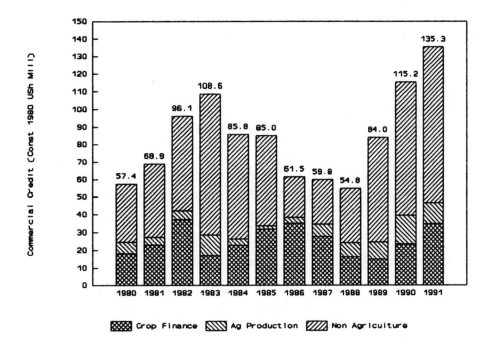

Figure 9 Credit for Crop Finance, Other Agriculture and Non-Agriculture (in constant 1980 Ush)

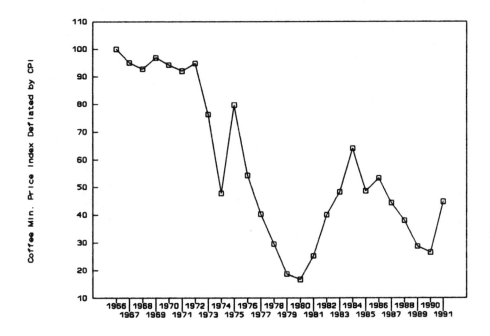

Figure 10 Real Farmgate Price for Robusta Coffee, 1966-91

II. THE RESOURCE BASE AND THE RURAL POPULATION

Natural Resources

2.1   Uganda's agricultural potential is good. 3/ The country is on the equator, and temperatures average about 21 degrees Centigrade, ranging from 15 to 30 degrees. More than two-thirds of the country is 1,000 to 2,500 meters high. Precipitation is fairly reliable, and varies from 750 mm per year in the Karamajong pastoral areas in the Northeast, to 1,500 mm per year in the high-rainfall areas on the shores of Lake Victoria, around the highlands of Mt. Elgon in the East, the Ruwenzori in the Southwest, Masindi in the West, and Gulu in the North (see map). South of the equator there are two rainy seasons, providing two growing seasons.

Soils

2.2   Soil type and topography are key determinants of land use.   The soils have been classified in seven groups:

- The Buganda surfaces (42,200 square kilometers) cover much of the region south of Lake Kyoga, including the districts north and northwest of Lake Victoria--and embrace five types of deep, sandy clay loams with medium-to-high productivity.

- The Tanganyika surfaces (78,200 km²) cover much of the area North of Lake Kyoga, West Nile, and parts of the southwest. They consist of sandy clay loam soils with low to medium productivity.

- The Karamoja surfaces (16,400 km²) in the Northeast comprise sandy clay loams and black clays of low productivity.

- Rift Valley soils (12,500 km²) in the West and North are sandy clay loams with alluvial parent rock of high productivity.

- Volcanic soils (5,000 km²) of high productivity are found on Mt. Elgon and in the extreme Southwest. In northern Karamoja these soils have low productivity.

- Alluvial soils (27,400 km²) found in central and northern Uganda--Lango and Acholi--as well as west of Lake Victoria, are sandy and of low productivity.

- Other soil types in the North (15,000 km²) are of low productivity.

3/   For a full description of Uganda's natural resources, see J.D. Jameson, "Agriculture in Uganda", Oxford University Press, 1970.

Farming Systems

2.3   Using soil, rainfall, and cropping characteristics, Parsons has defined five agricultural production systems. 4/ First are the high-rainfall areas around Lake Victoria, with bananas, Robusta coffee, and food crops grown in mixed farming systems. Fallowing is minimal.

2.4   **Teso systems** in Eastern Uganda are a second system, characterized by annual crops grown in two distinct rainy seasons. The rains are separated by a four-month dry period. Finger millet has given way to cassava as the main food crop, and cotton was the main cash crop. Prior to the disturbances of the mid-1980s, large numbers of cattle were kept, use of draft oxpower was widespread, and intercropping, rotations, and fallow periods were common to maintain fertility and reduce soil loss.

2.5   Third are the Northern Systems also descriptive of the Northwest--in which rainfall patterns restrict cultivation to one season. Rainfall declines from south to north. In the central northern zone, communal cultivation is customary. Annuals such as cotton, maize, and finger millet are common. Further south, groundnut and sweet potato are more common, with sunflower and tobacco the main cash crops.

2.6   Fourth, the **mountain systems** in the West and in the East feature bananas as the main food crop, with Arabica coffee and tea as cash crops. The higher altitudes permit cultivation of temperate fruits, vegetables, and Irish potatoes, as well as some of the traditional food crops.

2.7   Fifth, in the **pastoral systems** in the Northeast, rainfall totals less than 800 mm per year, and pastoral livestock production is combined with sorghum and millet cropping.

Land Use

2.8   A large proportion of the country's 241,000 km^2 could be cultivated. After lakes, swamps and forest reserves are excluded, more than 75 percent of the country--18 million hectares--is available for cultivation, pasture, or both (fig. 11). It is not clear what share of this is unsuitable for cultivation. Much further work is needed to determine where protective measures are justified to ensure that production systems are sustainable. Even the cursory studies undertaken to date, 5/ however, indicate that large areas of land are potentially productive and under-utilized. Of the 17 million ha classified as arable on a preliminary basis by Langlands, only 4 million to 5 million ha are under cultivation.

2.9   Comparing the 1974 Langlands data on cultivable area and census information, rural population density on cultivable land has increased from 53 people per km^2 in 1969 to 88 in 1991 (table 2). Eleven of the thirty-two districts analyzed had a rural population density exceeding twice the national average, in 1969 and 1991. The distribution of these densely occupied areas has not shifted. In eastern, southern and western Uganda, more than half of the districts have a rural population density of 180 persons per km^2 of cultivable land.

4/   D. Parsons, Agricultural Systems, in Jameson, op. cit., p. 127.

5/   B.W. Langlands, "Soil Productivity and Land Availability Studies", Makerere University, 1974

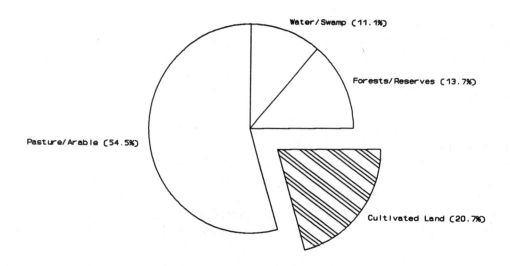

Figure 11   Land Use Estimates (by United Nations Environment Program)

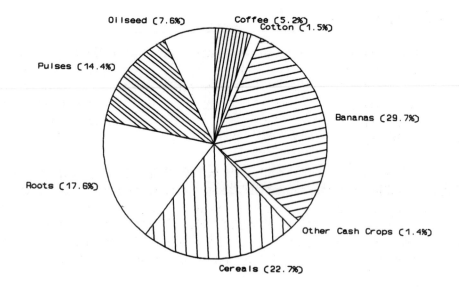

Figure 12   Distribution of Cultivated Area, 1990

2.10   A rough calculation of the share of cultivable land actually cultivated in each district--based on the cultivation capacity of the rural family--shows that only 30 percent of total cultivable area is being used.   Of the thirty districts reviewed, 6/ nineteen did not cultivate 50 percent or more of the available arable area. These calculations fit the gross calculations of availability of uncultivated agricultural land, based on national crop data. Although admittedly rough, these assessments do indicate that many districts appear to have substantial land of moderate-to-good potential available for crop-based production.

2.11   With the return of security and stability, and the migration of small farmers from the densely populated Southwest and Northwest into underutilized zones in the West, the cultivated area will continue to be expanded, as it has in the past (para 2.15). The Government should adopt a more active--although indirect--role in this process, in order to prevent conflicts with inhabitants of areas of immigration, and to encourage land use patterns which are sustainable in the long run.   Additional study on agricultural potential is recommended, albeit on a large scale, to map out sustainable farming systems for those areas which are underutilized in order to indirectly influence the migratory flow to go into the less ecologically fragile regions.   Criteria for identification of areas appropriate for agricultural expansion should include (a) agricultural potential, (b) intensity of use by current residents and claimants, (c) access to markets, (d) environmental fragility and risk of degradation,; (e) conservation criteria (to protect moist tropical forests and wildlife preserves), and (f) the existence of debilitating disease affecting people or livestock, such as trypanosomiasis. Government interventions to channel the migration flow should be indirect, and should include placing physical and social infrastructure--feeder roads, schools, hospitals--to encourage migration in the desired direction. Government can also facilitate the flow by providing supportive legislation on squatters' rights, tenant rights, and public land use and by defusing ethnic tensions between prior residents and new entrants with enhanced benefits-- from rapid agricultural growth--for the entire community. .

Currently Cultivated Area

2.12   An estimated 4.6 million ha were under cultivation in 1990,   but the data are weak. The proportion of cultivated area double cropped, or intercropped, is not known. The Agriculture Census of 1966 showed none of the crops grown completely in purestand.7/ Only 60 percent of bananas was then in purestand, 50 percent of cassava, sorghum and finger millet, 40 percent of Robusta, and 75 percent of cotton. For this reason it is likely that the global estimates of area cultivated are significantly higher that the actual area utilized.

2.13   Of the total area under cultivation in 1990, (fig. 12) 36 percent is under perennial crops. Of the 1.7 million ha under perennials, about 1.4 million ha are under bananas, and 0.25 million ha is under coffee. Sugar is grown in about 20,000 ha and tea--the other significant perennial crop--covers about 20,000 ha. Except for about 70,000 ha of cotton and 4,000 ha of tobacco, annual crops are all food crops. Of the 2.9 million ha in annual food crops, 1 million ha are in cereals, 0.8 million in rootcrops, 0.7 million in pulses, and 0.4 million in oilseeds.

6/   Two districts did not have information on area cultivated by family

7/   Report of the Uganda Census of Agriculture, Vol. 3, 1966, in Jameson, p.cit.

Table 2: Population and Land Availability by District

Region and District	Rural Pop'n 1991	Cultivable Land Area (Km²) 2/	Density 1991	Avge Area Cultivated per Person (ha) 3/	Area Required for 1991 Pop'n (Km²)	Percent Cultivable Land Used in 1991	Broad Soil Class
Central							
Mpigi	796	4,406	181	0.38	3,025	69%	I
Mukono	717	4,061	177	0.38	2,725	67%	II
Luwero	408	7,986	51	0.38	1,550	19%	II
Masaka	747	5,542	135	0.34	2,540	46%	II
Rakai	366	3,500	105	0.34	1,244	36%	III
Mubende	463	8,963	52	0.32	1,482	17%	II
Eastern							
Iganga	899	4,489	200	0.328	2,949	66%	III
Jinja	208	619	336	0.328	682	110%	II
Kamuli	473	3,694	128	0.328	1,551	42%	III
Kapchorwa	112	1,064	105	0.386	432	41%	II
Kumi	225	2,454	92	0.787	1,771	72%	III
Mbale	645	2,022	319	0.384	2,477	122%	II
Soroti	384	8,407	46	0.787	3,022	36%	II/III
Tororo 5/	842	3,887	217	0.387	3,259	84%	III
Northern							
Apac	454	4,962	91	0.542	2,461	50%	III
Arua	598	6,578	91	0.255	1,525	23%	III
Gulu	296	11,321	26	0.533	1,578	14%	IV
Kitgum	340	13,536	25	0.533	1,812	13%	IV
Kotido	181	10,352	17	N/A			III
Lira	471	6,950	68	0.542	2,553	37%	II
Moroto	158	7,540	21	N/A			IV
Moyo	168	4,313	39	0.255	428	10%	IV
Nebbi	292	2,689	109	0.255	745	28%	II
Western							
Bundibugyo	116	394	294	0.2	232	59%	III
Bushenyi	735	3,559	207	0.25	1,838	52%	II
Hoima 5/	395	6,633	60	0.316	1,248	19%	II/III
Kabale 5/	598	2,353	254	0.286	1,710	73%	II/III
Kabarole	741	7,607	97	0.25	1,853	24%	II/III
Kasese	343	1,478	232	0.2	686	46%	II
Masindi	275	5,369	51	0.316	869	16%	II
Mbarara	930	9,477	98	0.174	1,618	17%	III
Rukungiri	388	1,391	279	0.286	1,110	80%	II/III
Total	14,764	167,596	88		50,973	30%	

1/ National Census Figures.
2/ B. W. Langlands, "Soil Productivity and Land Availability Studies", Makerere 1974.
3/ Report on Uganda Census of Agriculture; Langlands, op cit.
4/ Langlands: I = Very good; II = Good; III = Moderate; IV = Poor.
5/ 1991 Census: Tororo + Pallisa, Hoima + Kibale, Kabale + Kisoro

Trends in Cultivated Area

2.14   Allowing for the weaknesses in the data, the countrywide series since 1970 lead to several observations. First, there was a sharp drop in the area under cultivation in 1979 and 1980 from which the country has still not recuperated. Total area cropped fell from an all-time peak of 5.5 million ha in 1978 to 3.6 million ha in 1980 (fig. 13). This may be due, in part, to statistical problems associated with the deterioration of Government statistics collection during the Amin regime. The sharp drop also may reflect a one-time adjustment for the gradual decline in area cultivated from 1970 (0.5 ha per capita) to 1980 (0.3 ha per capita). Since 1980 the data gathering effort appears to have been more consistent.

2.15   Second, the area under food crops expanded from 1970 to 1978, and dropped sharply during the war years of 1979 and 1980. In spite of rapid growth during the 1980s, areas under cultivation for food have still not reached the levels of 1976-78 (fig. 14).

2.16   Third, in spite of the rapid growth in agricultural output during the 1980s, less food is produced per capita, now than in the early 1970s (fig. 15).

2.17   Fourth, despite internal dislocations and economic uncertainty--or perhaps because of them--the area under bananas has increased continuously since 1970 to 1.4 million ha in 1990 (fig. 16) at a trend-growth rate of 1.8 percent per year.

2.18   Area production and yield characteristics of food and the other major crops are discussed in depth in Section IV.

Land Use and the Environment

2.19   Demographic pressures are exacerbating the stress on Uganda's environment. Nowhere is this more apparent than in the loss of tropical high forest, which has declined from 1.2 million ha in 1958 to 0.7 million ha in 1987. 8/ Efforts to protect Uganda's forests will have to deal with upwards of 50,000 people who have encroached on forest reserves--largely since 1970--and with indiscriminate logging associated with industrial expansion. Pressure on forests also comes from the growing demand for charcoal and building poles resulting from growth in population--estimated at 3.1 percent per annum--9/ and incomes.

2.20   Successful management of environmental issues in Uganda will require the updating of old legislation and the establishment of new policies on wildlife and forest conservation, the minimization of degradation, and the sustainability of agricultural and industrial development. Environmental evaluation and monitoring methods for major public and private investments will have to be put in place to ensure that the objectives of such legislation are met.

8/   UNEP, Natural Resources and Environment in Uganda, Strategic Resources Planning in Uganda.

9/   Shaw, Paul, Demographic Prospects and Consequences of Population Growth, contribution to the Uganda - Social Sector Strategy, White Cover, April 9, 1992.

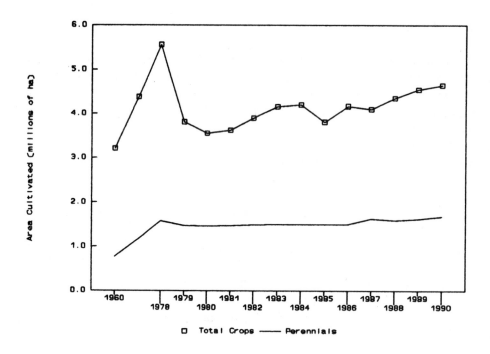

Figure 13   Changes in Total Cultivated Area, 1960-90

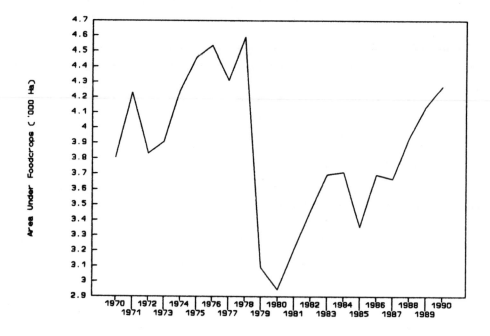

Figure 14   Changes in Area Under Foodcrops, 1970-90

Institutions capable of following through on such policies will have to be created, and the participation of local communities in conservation efforts obtained if such policies are to succeed. 10/

2.21   A recent study 11/ shows that nine of the thirty four districts (those around the northern perimeter of Lake Victoria) have between 60 and 79 percent of their total area cleared for agriculture. It is in these areas that soil erosion and over-exploitation of forests is greatest. A comparison of land use between 1973 and 1986 shows that net clearing of land for farming or livestock rearing was barely 1 percent of the 24 districts studied (table 3). Only nine districts accounted for 90 percent of the changes. This surprisingly small net change, in a period of severe disorder and absence of natural resource management, is the result of having the widespread clearing in certain regions compensated for by the regrowth of natural cover in other regions. There were substantial declines in natural vegetation cover in the Northern Region (around 345,000 ha) and large increases in the Western and West Nile Regions (280,000 ha).

Table 3: Land Use Changes Between 1973 and 1986			
Region	# Districts	Area in Farming or Livestock (km²)	Area in Natural Vegetation (km²)
West Nile	3	- 576	+ 897
Northern	4	+ 3,446	- 3,626
Northwest	4	+ 66	- 76
West	4	-2,651	+ 1,966
Mount Elgon	2	+ 410	- 699
Southern	5	+ 809	- 984
Karamoja	2	- 22	- 36
TOTAL	24	+ 1,482	- 256

2.22   Population density does not explain the differences in land clearing in the thirteen years 1973 to 1986. The environmental study mentioned previously notes that with one exception for thirteen years the districts with highest population density had practically no change in the area cleared for cultivation. The sparsely populated areas, on the other hand, suffered extensive clearing. Again, the districts with the highest population growth rates--more than 4 percent per year--actually had a reduction in their agricultural area, and an increase in forests. The reverse happened in districts with population growth rates of below 2 percent per year. The road network has also had no effect on land use in the thirteen years under review--which is consistent with the decline in agricultural markets. The analysis concludes that the key factors determining land use have been the location of the wars and civil disorders, the breakdown of governmental control, and the abandonment of economic policies that used to support cash crop production.

10/   Grant Slade, and Keith Weitz, 10/Uganda - Environmental Issues and Options, draft, February 19, 1991.

11/   N.V. Jaganathan, H. Mori, and H.M. Hassan, World Bank, "Applications of Geographical Information Systems in Economic Analysis: A Case Study of Uganda", April 1990, Environment Working Paper No. 27.

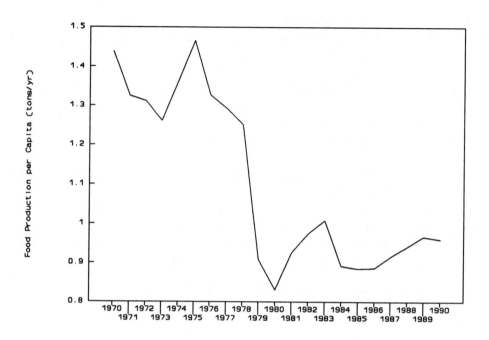

Figure 15   Food Production Per Capita (tons/year), 1970-90

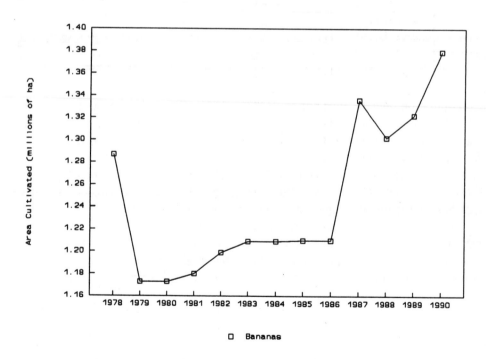

Figure 16   Area Under Bananas, 1970-90

2.23   Uganda's wildlife, forests, fish, grazing lands, and other natural resources are in danger of being overused, and driven to extinction. Soil erosion is a problem in high-population-density, high-rainfall areas. Natural resource management programs and policies have broken down during the civil disorder and have yet to be reestablished. Sustainable management practices should be established by the Government in key areas such as wildlife and forest management to prevent complete loss. The private sector has little incentive to protect these public resources. Private ownership may solve some of the sustainability problems, but would enable a privileged few to capture the returns from the use of these resources.

2.24   The establishment of a Ministry concerned with Environmental Protection in 1986 indicates that the environmental issues are of national importance. This ministry is weak, however, with its role poorly defined. Environmental activities are horizontal, by nature, and cut across the concerns of sector ministries. The ministry concerned with environmental action should monitor the effects of the development programs of the sector ministries, and guide sector policy along lines that will be environmentally benign. The charge of the Ministry of Water, Energy, Minerals and Environmental Protection at present is to develop a national environmental policy, and put in place the mechanisms to regulate and enforce its provisions. The United Nations Environment Program has done a detailed survey of environmental problems in Uganda. This is being sharpened and transformed into an operational plan under a donor-supported National Environmental Action Plan. The recommendations were scheduled for public review and discussion in mid-1992.

Forests

2.25   Forest reserves cover some 7 percent of the country, with 700,000 ha in tropical high forests, 632,000 ha in savannah forests, and 24,300 in plantation forests. The tropical high forests are found in western Uganda, around Lake Victoria, and on Mt. Elgon in the East. They include rare plants and animals--some in danger of extinction--and unique ecological systems. Until the early 1970s the Forest Department strictly regulated logging, charcoal burning, and revenue collection. In the mid-1970s as resources available to the Forest Department declined, the system of high-tropical-forest management broke down, and sawmill management deteriorated. As a result, indiscriminate logging practices degraded the forest environment and damaged wildlife habitats. Timber resources also have been depleted. Reserve boundaries have not been respected; both reserves and savannah forests have been subjected to uncontrolled and damaging harvests. Management of the softwood plantations--first planted in the late 1940s, and now totaling 13,400 ha. also deteriorated in the early 1970s, reducing quality and yield of the standing stock. These trees reached maturity after 1971, but the plantations have never been exploited commercially. Their sustainable yield of 90,000 cubic meters of sawn timber per year represents about two-thirds of Uganda's demand for timber in the year 2000. Careful use of these softwood stands could relieve pressure on the ecologically fragile natural hardwood forests.

2.26   The Government--with the assistance of EEC, DANIDA IDA and UNDP--has been working to regain control over the exploitation of the country's forests. The donor-funded Forestry Project (IDA Cr 1824-UG) has as its objective the development of forestry management plans to determine how the country can better manage this resource. This includes reducing indiscriminate logging in natural forest areas. The project would seek to improve boundary demarcation and maintenance in high forests and savannah reserves. Areas of natural forest would be reforested and activities of charcoal burners would be controlled. The proportion of natural forest area to be set aside as nature reserves would be increased from 5 to 20 percent. A "protected forest" category would be applied to another 30 percent of the natural forest area, under which only limited logging would be permitted.

2.27   The eventual levels of logging in Uganda's forests will depend on the resource-management plans adopted. To develop these plans, the Government, with project assistance, is undertaking forest inventories, testing detailed small-scale forest management plans, redesigning forest harvesting licenses so as to conform with sound forest management practices for increasing control and protection, and improving revenue collection from logging operations. It is intended that this development activity will be sustainable in the long term while also meeting societal objectives for conservation and biodiversity.

2.28   Work in this subsector is severely hampered by lack of government funding, and by the weakness of the Forestry Department. A strong governmental commitment to fund and support the activities of the Forest Department is needed to make the regulation of forest use effective.

Land Tenure

2.29   Land tenure systems differ across Uganda. Tenure practices are a mix of traditional practice, colonial regulations, and post-colonial legislation.

Current Status

2.30   Before the Land Reform Decree of 1975 there were four main types of land tenure in Uganda: customary tenure, freeholds (ordinary and adjudicated), Mailo tenure (owners and tenants) and leaseholds. 12/

2.31   Customary tenure is the most widely used system, and prevails outside the precolonial kingdoms of Ankole, Buganda, and Toro.   Conditions vary by ethnic group and location. Customary tenure did not recognize individual ownership of land, but did recognize the rights of individuals to possess and use land--subject to the superintendency of family, clan, and community. The individual landholder had the right to use his/her holding as he/she thought best; rent or lend land temporarily; pledge the crops, but not the land; sell the land, subject to family approval; dispose of land according to customary laws of inheritance; protect the homestead and cultivation from grazing or other predations; and dispose of trees.

2.32   The family or clan had the right to settle disputes, approve all land transactions, prohibit the sale of land to undesirables, and purchase land offered for sale in its jurisdiction. The wider community had the right to graze animals within its jurisdiction, as long as homesteads and crops were preserved. The community also retained the right of access to water, salt licks, and other key resources.

2.33   Freehold rights were provided under the British Government Agreements with the Buganda Kingdom (1900), the Ankole Kingdom (1901), and the Toro Kingdom (1900). Few freehold titles were actually given out by the Colonial Government, outside of Buganda. Just

---

12/   Makerere Institute of Social Research and Land Tenure Center, University of Wisconsin, Land Tenure and Agricultural Development in Uganda, January 1989, pp. 4-23.

before independence, three small schemes in Ankole, Bugisu and Kigezi provided "adjudicated" freehold title to smallholders.

2.34   Within Buganda, a system of--mailo--tenure was established, whereby members of the nobility received freehold rights to estates (determined in square miles). Large areas of Central Uganda were alienated on this basis. Customary users of these lands had their tenure translated into tenancy--kibanja rights on mailo land. Controversy over this shift in customary tenancy rights, resulted in the Busulu and Envujjo Law of 1927, which limited the ability of mailo owners to evict kibanja tenants or increase their rents. Much subdivision of mailo holdings has occurred since 1900. Mailo land titles have become easily transferable, smoothing the development of a market in land, and its use as security in credit transactions.

2.35   Leaseholds are provided by private owners, or by the Government under the Public Lands Act of 1969. These have been used by influential farmers to obtain access to large tracts of land in under-utilized areas.

2.36   In 1975 the Government of Idi Amin promulgated a Land Reform Decree. The decree was revolutionary in that it nationalized all land and introduced a uniform system of tenure; converted both mailo and other freeholders into lessees; and reduced the status of tenants to tenants at sufferance who could be evicted without notice (customary tenants on public lands) or with six months' notice (on mailo lands).

2.37   The goals of the decree were to facilitate the use of land for social and economic development and to introduce land use planning, including land use zoning. Development conditions were to be imposed--and leases terminated--if the conditions were not met.

2.38   It is difficult to objectively determine the impact of the Decree. It has been on the statute books for more than sixteen years and, despite widespread criticism, its validity has never been tested in a court of law. On the face of it, the Decree appears to have decreased security for tenants--especially kibanja. It appears to have been a mixed blessing for lessees (former freeholders) who, though their terms of holding were curtailed--to leases of ninety nine years for individuals, and 199 years for "legal persons" such as churches or corporations--were now entitled to evict tenants and regain possession of lands. To suggest that the legislation was "ignored because it was not enforced," as some have, is not quite accurate--except, perhaps, for the zoning provisions. On the other hand there is evidence that customary tenants were evicted and that pastoral routes and grazing lands were taken over by "developers." The opportunity to treat land "not developed substantially" in accordance with development conditions or land not occupied under customary tenure as "unused" land could also encourage land invasions -- as did happen in a few cases. Even for a mailo owner or lessee, the ability to evict a tenant would depend largely on the potential social reaction to such evictions.

A Strategy for Change

2.39   Under the aegis of the Government's Agriculture Policy Committee, studies and workshops have been held on this topic. A consensus among the students of this problem has developed, and been translated into a draft for proposed legislation. This proposal was approved by the Agriculture Policy Committee, and has been forwarded to the Ministry of Lands, Housing and Urban Development for review, prior to submission to the Cabinet.

2.40   The proposal for reform is based on the adoption of a land tenure system which provides for freehold tenure as a national system. Thus, the proposed legislation would, first, restore freeholds, and second, separate mailo tenancies from the mailo estate and vest them in the Land Commission in freehold which the Commission may then grant to the mailo tenant. A third position would restore the rights of customary tenants on public lands and permit them to obtain freehold tenure--exception in urban areas where freehold would be vested in the urban authority and landholders would be entitled only to obtain leaseholds.

2.41   The main assumptions underlying the proposed new legislation are familiar, but worth repeating, that (a) a freehold title is necessary to encourage investments in and sound management of land; (b) the possession of a freehold title facilitates the use of land as collateral for credit--which, by implication, can be directed to long-term capital investments; (c) freeholding enhances the title-holder's desire to engage in long-term investments; (d) a land market can be created--or restored--where none exists; (e) Uganda needs a uniform land tenure system rather than the current myriad systems; and (f) a freehold system with registration of titles would permit Government to capture some of the rents to which it is entitled, and to introduce a land tax to spur further development.

2.42   It should be noted however, that freehold tenure and a registered title are necessary, but not sufficient, elements in promoting security of tenure and agricultural development. Also necessary are political stability, economic incentives, and the development of markets and infrastructure. Despite the 1975 decree, land transactions have increased in the last three years. As an indication of activity, some 5,720 leases a year were authorized, of which 48 percent were new titles. There was an average of 5,500 dealings in mailo land a year in the Kampala office, and 14,000 dealings a year in the last three years in the Masaka office of which an estimated 50 percent were new transfers. There were an estimated 5,000 applications a year to the Uganda Land Commission for consents to transfers.

2.43   The preceding analysis supports the adoption of a uniform national policy for the introduction of freehold tenure and the repeal of the decree. But, registration and titling of the entire country would be prohibitively expensive. For efficiency reasons, it is necessary to adopt criteria for implementing a titling program. Traditional systems of tenure do provide as much security of tenure as freehold, providing Government monitors land transactions in areas where these systems exist. Titling should be considered where the traditional system appears to be under threat. In the meantime work should be begun to legally recognize traditional systems, to develop a record of rights of use and occupation, and to prevent incursions into the traditional system. The focus of governmental intervention should be to improve the efficacy of the mechanisms for resolving disputes--within the framework of the traditional tenure system--while the policy of freehold titling is gradually implemented under the new law, with priority given to issues of conflict.

2.44   Titles are not enough to spur agricultural development. A titling program should only be undertaken if linked with the development of a national land use policy that recognizes the suitability of different land use systems and is fostered through the directed provision of infrastructure, and economic and fiscal incentives. Above all, farmers have to perceive continuity of policy to invest in their farms.

2.45   Compensation due mailo owners--for the vesting of kibanja tenant land in the Land Commission, and its eventual conversion into freehold--is probably the most sensitive aspect of the proposed legislation. Once the principle has been adopted, the mechanism for compensation should be dealt with separately in the regulation of the new law. By treating this difficult issue separately, the review and approval of the new law can be allowed to proceed. It is recommended that agreement first be left to the parties--with the intervention and assistance of private commercial organizations encouraged. Government should only intervene as a last resort.

2.46   Fragmentation of holdings in the densely populated rural areas of the Southwest and the Northeast was considered. It is felt that administrative measures to contain this fragmentation (which would entail modification of inheritance law, and official and customary tenure law) have not been successful in other parts of Africa. The experience in Kenya of trying to force consolidation of plots and prevent fragmentation in high density areas has not been successful. The process of fragmentation is likely to continue until economic non-viability of plot size forces sale and consolidation. If allowed to operate freely, normal transactions in the land market will produce consolidation of holdings once untenably minute sizes are reached.

2.47   Implementing a freehold tenure system requires ordering existing records in the Land Offices, reconstructing the records where they are no longer available, and rehabilitating Lands Offices. The gradual decentralization of registration services to the district level would be undertaken as a second phase, once the system had been brought up to date, and new procedures compatible with the new land law put in place. Improving these services will be justified once the new law is approved, given the need for an efficient, fair and open registration system to realize the benefits of the "freehold" system noted above.

The Rural Population

Consumption and Expenditure

2.48   The share of Uganda's population living in cities is one of the lowest in Africa. Among its neighbors, only Rwanda has a level of urbanization below Uganda's 11 percent. The urban ratio for all of sub-Saharan Africa is 28 percent. While the rural-urban migration that normally accompanies development is occurring in Uganda, the rate of growth of the urban population, at 5 percent per annum, is still not high by African standards. The rural population is growing at 2.15 percent per annum, 13/ below the average rural population growth rate for sub-Saharan Africa, and below the level estimated for Uganda prior to the recent census.

2.49   The National Household Budget Survey (1989-90) reveals the following characteristics of rural dwellers:

- There are an estimated 2.5 million rural households. The average rural household has 5.59 persons, compared with 4.50 in urban areas. Males exceed females by 2 percent in rural Uganda (table 4),

- Average rural expenditure per capita, per year, is valued at about US$10, compared with US$218 per capita in urban areas, and US$116 for Uganda as a whole (table 5). 14/ Consumption levels cannot easily be

---

13/   Based on the intercensus period 1980-91.

14/   At the parallel exchange rate, which reflects the marginal cost of foreign exchange in the economy.

compared, however, food prices at farmgate are likely to be significantly below urban prices,

- In rural areas, 71 percent of total expenditure goes for food, (including beverages and tobacco), compared with 51 percent in urban areas (table 5);

Table 4: Estimated Number of Households, Household Population, Gender Ratio, and Household Size, 1989-90			
	Urban	Rural	Total
Number of Households	377,529	2,509,887	2,887,416
Houhsehold Population Total	1,699,191	14,027,544	15,726,735
Household Population Male	800,738	7,077,102	7,877,840
Household Population Female	898,453	6,950,442	7,848,895
Male/Female Ratio	0.89	1.02	1.00
Household Size	4.50	5.59	5.45
Source: National Household Budget Survey, 1989-90			

- The distribution of spending in rural areas is considerably more skewed than in urban areas. About 54 percent of rural households live on less than US$ 526 per annum, compared with 26 percent of urban dwellings for the same income level (table 6), 15/

- The rural diet is higher in starch, and lower in protein than its urban counterpart. About one-third of the rural diet is matoke, potatoes, and other tubers compared with less than one-quarter of urban food consumption. Lower farmgate prices exacerbate this difference. Some 21 percent of rural household food expenditure goes into meats, milk, and eggs, compared with 28 percent of the urban household expenditure, 16/

- Expenditure on meat, eggs, milk, and sugar increases dramatically in absolute terms--and in shares of food expenditure and total expenditure-- indicating that markets for these products should improve as incomes increase (assuming that the increased spending is due to volume and not price differences),

- More than 97 percent of rural households had no running water or electricity.

15/ On a per capita basis, the rural distribution is even lower, because family sizes are larger.

16/ Again, the rural areas are worse off than these figures indicate, because larger family sizes means lower per capita consumption.

Table 5: Rural-Urban Breakdown of Monthly Household Budget (1988-89 Ush)						
	Urban		Rural		Total	
DESCRIPTION	Monthly Expenditure	Share Total Expend	Monthly Expenditure	Share Total Exp.	Monthly Expenditure	Share Total Exp.
MATOKE, POTATOES & OTHER TUBERS	6,274	12%	6,819	22%	6,750	20%
BREAD AND CEREALS	4,824	9%	3,299	10%	3,498	10%
MEAT AND POULTRY	3,048	6%	1,920	6%	2,066	6%
FISH	1,776	3%	1,037	3%	1,133	3%
MILK AND EGGS	2,733	5%	1,163	4%	1,370	4%
OILS AND FATS	977	2%	367	1%	445	1%
FRUITS AND VEGETABLES	2,871	5%	2,216	7%	2,301	7%
BEANS, LENTILS, NUTS, ETC.	1,735	3%	2,001	6%	1,967	6%
SUGAR, COFFEE AND TEA	2,625	5%	852	3%	1,083	3%
OTHER FOODS	391	1%	343	1%	349	1%
SUBTOTAL FOOD	27,254	51%	20,017	63%	20,962	61%
SUBTOTAL BEVERAGES	3,294	6%	2,048	6%	2,210	6%
SUBTOTAL TOBACCO	507	1%	331	1%	354	1%
SUBTOTAL RESTAURANTS	1,023	2%	162	1%	274	1%
TOTAL - FOOD, BEVERAGES & TOBACCO	32,078	60%	22,558	71%	23,800	69%
CLOTHING AND FOOTWEAR	3,500	7%	1,815	6%	2,036	6%
RENT, FUEL AND POWER	5,748	11%	1,515	5%	2,069	6%
EQUIPMENT & GOODS	6,333	12%	2,959	9%	3,399	10%
TRANSP & COMMUNICATION	1,770	3%	849	3%	969	3%
HEALTH & MEDICAL CARE	933	2%	599	2%	643	2%
EDUCATION	1,809	3%	629	2%	770	2%
RECR, CULT & OTHER	1,175	2%	721	2%	782	2%
MONTHLY EXP.	53,346	100%	31,645	100%	34,468	100%
ANNUAL EXP.	640,152		379,740		413,616	
ANNUAL EXP/CAPITA	142,256		67,932		75,893	
ANNUAL EXP. (US$) **	979		581		632	
ANNUAL EXP/CAP (US$)	218		104		116	
Average Persons Per Family	4.50		5.59		5.45	

Source: MPED, Uganda National Household Budget Survey 1989-90. ** US$ 1.00 = Ush 654 in FY 1988-89

2.50   The survey does not cover sources of income. This information would provide guidance on ways to target income-increasing opportunities. It must be noted, however, that rural dwellers are poor, and resources for investment in agriculture are limited. An agricultural development strategy cannot depend on the mobilization of large quantities of cash for inputs or labor, unless financing is provided. Even finance is not an immediate solution--as the capacity to borrow, and repay, will be limited.

Table 6: Frequency and Distribution of Households by Monthly Household Expenditure Class						
Annual Household Expenditure Class	URBAN		RURAL		TOTAL	
US$ per family (US$ 1 = Ush 654)	Number of Households	Percent	Number of Households	Percent	Number of Households	Percent
0 to 459	98,617	26.1%	1,363,311	54.3%	1,461,928	50.6%
459 to 917	130,302	34.5%	745,433	29.7%	875,735	30.3%
917 to 1,376	79,076	20.9%	232,745	9.3%	311,821	10.8%
above 1,376	69,534	18.4%	168,398	6.7%	237,932	8.2%
	377,529	100.0%	2,509,887	100.0%	2,887,416	100.0%
Average Family Size	4.5		5.6		5.45	

Farm Characteristics

2.51   Estimates of the amount of land cultivated by a family vary. The National Household Budget Survey (1989-90) indicates an average of 1.35 ha of farmland per household, with an additional 1.03 ha of other land available (table 7). There is above-average farmland available per family, in the West and North. Data on the distribution of landholdings by size, indicate that of those households which possessed land, 62 percent controlled plots of less than 1 ha, and 23 percent controlled plots of between 1-2 ha (table 8). About 2.1 million rural households--85 percent of the total--possess plots of less than 2 ha.

Table 7: Average Land and Livestock Possessed per Household by Region						
Item	Units	Central	Eastern	Western	Northern	UGANDA
Farmland	Ha	1.36	0.98	1.72	1.10	1.35
Other Land	Ha	0.84	1.18	0.96	1.59	1.03
Total Land	Ha	2.20	2.15	2.68	2.69	2.38
Cattle	Number	0.97	1.36	2.11	0.67	1.37
Pigs	Number	0.35	0.18	0.46	0.4	0.35
Goats and sheep	Number	0.92	1.51	2.03	2.43	1.54
Poultry	Number	3.58	6.75	3.50	5.73	4.50
Source: National Household Budget Survey 1989-90						

Table 8: Distribution of Rural Households by Farm Size									
Area of Farm Owned	CENTRAL		EASTERN		WESTERN		NORTHERN		UGANDA	
Hectares	Number House-holds	Per-cent Land	Number House-holds	Per-cent Land	Number House-holds	Per-cent Land	Number House-holds	Per-cent Land	Number House-holds	Per-cent Land
Urban	245,574		56,178		50,317		25,460		377,529	
Nil (urban)	263,062		99,209		83,900		5,725		451,896	
0 - 1	492,873	61.4	383,599	67.0	436,401	55.8	200,809	72.2	1,513,682	62.2
1 - 2	173,971	21.7	128,610	22.5	195,091	24.9	59,296	21.3	556,968	22.9
2 - 4	99,171	12.4	45,952	8.0	94,743	12.1	13,314	4.8	253,180	10.4
4 - 6	15,901	2.0	6,583	1.1	31,234	4.0	2,364	0.9	56,082	2.3
6 - 8	6,921	0.9	2,638	0.5	7,478	1.0	94	0.0	17,131	0.7
8 - 10	2,237	0.3	3,521	0.6	1,849	0.2	323	0.1	7,930	0.3
10 and above	11,121	1.4	1,875	0.3	15,812	2.0	1,739	0.6	30,547	1.3
TOTAL	1,065,25		671,987		866,508		283,664		2,887,416	
TOTAL w/Land	802,195	100	572,778	100	782,608	100	277,939	100	2,435,520	100

Source: Uganda National Household Budget Survey (1989-90). The survey covered all districts of Uganda except Kumi and Soroti in the Eastern Region, and Gulu, Kitgum, Kotido, Lira and Moroto in the Northern Region.

2.52   What do Ugandans do with their land?   How much is cultivated? Are cultivation levels near their limits? There is little systematic evidence available on farming systems. A survey undertaken by Makerere University and the University of Wisconsin Land Tenure center in Masaka and Luwero in 1988 analyzed cultivation levels and land use by type of tenure. The conclusion reached 17/ was that "there seems to be no difference in the proportion of land that is unused across the various tenure types. That is, mailo owners do not seem to have more unused land on average, than mailo tenants or customary tenants." The survey also indicates that "labor shortage was the major reason given for not using all of the land." Soil infertility--or fallowing requirements--were the next most frequent reason for less-than-full use. Cultivated area per farm shows a substantial increase in the share of each holding cultivated in Masaka (Center), Busoga (East) and Kigezi (Southwest) (table 9). 18/

17/   MISR and LTC, op. cit. 0. 116 (see p. 21).

18/   USAID/Uganda, Agricultural Census, 1962-63, and "The Uganda Profile,", 1984.

Table 9: Share of Holding Cultivated		
	1962-63	1984
Masaka	53.9	61
Busoga	33.1	63
Kigezi	75.4	92

2.53　　　　The Agricultural Sector Survey of 1986-87 permits a rough characterization of districts--and hence regions--by principal farming activities. Almost 70 percent of the farms in Uganda are primarily crop production oriented (fig. 17). In the Western Region the share of pure crop farming goes up to almost 90 percent, and declines in the Eastern Region to some 55 percent. The rest of the farms are mixed. Only in the Central Region does the share of farms oriented exclusively toward livestock rise to 5 percent.

Rural Labor Markets

2.54　　　　Surveys of production constraints, such as the survey of 1988 by the MISR/LTC identify the availability of labor as the key factor in smallholder expansion. In the plantation crops of tea and sugar, labor costs are cited as a make-or-break factor in farm profitability. The responsiveness of the rural labor market affects plantation profitability and size. According to the national Household Budget Survey 80 percent of employed persons listed agriculture as their main occupation. [19]

Smallholders

2.55　　　　Agricultural production in Uganda comes primarily from family farms, with the family--children included--providing most of the labor. The main difficulty in managing the labor input in family farms arises at the times of peak demand: weeding and harvesting. The strategy used to meet additional labor requirements has differed by region. Historically, [20] Buganda farmers took in permanent laborers, many of them immigrants from Rwanda or Zaire, who worked year-round on coffee and cotton. In the North and East, labor-sharing arrangements were more common. Labor was hired to meet peak requirements. In some of the northern areas there was a tradition of communal participation in opening up new land for individuals. More than half of the landholders, especially in central Uganda, paid for labor in cash.

---

[19]　　　MPED, Uganda National Household Budget Survey, 1989-90, Table 2.30

[20]　　　J.H. Cleave, and E.H. Jones, in Jameson, op. cit., p. 114.

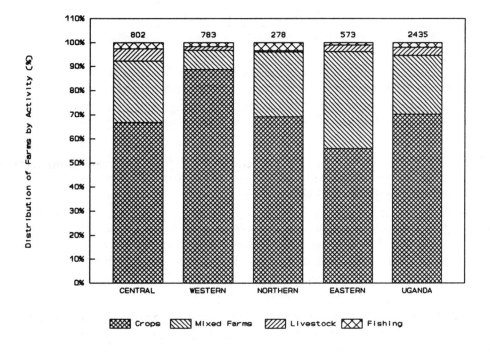

Figure 17 Distribution of Farms by Primary Activity

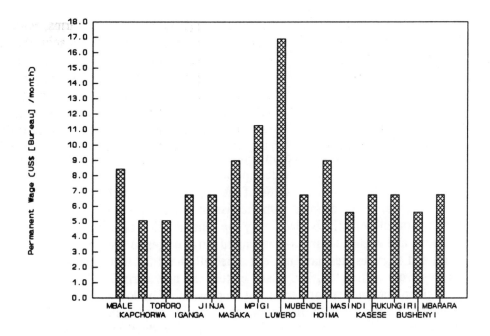

Figure 18 Monthly Rural Wage Rates

2.56   As noted in a recent review of Uganda's rural labor markets 21/

> "Labor market transactions at peak periods are common for most farm-households. In 1989 approximately 30 percent of total labor inputs on major cash and food crops were provided by hired labor. Escalating labor costs propelled by rising food and consumer goods prices are now placing considerable financial constraints on smallscale employers. Between 1989 and 1991 hired labor input on [smallholder] tea fell from 41 percent to 29 percent of total labor input and on Robusta coffee from 33 percent to 26 percent. The hired labor input on most food crops remained broadly the same."

2.57   The available data reveal significant differences in the casual, and permanent labor wage rates, across districts. Luwero had the highest permanent wage at Uganda shillings Ush15,000 per month in May 1991, equivalent to US$17 per month at the bureau exchange rate (fig. 18). The average permanent wage in the country was about Ush6,900 a month. The higher rates in Luwero may reflect a need for permanent labor to work the bananas and coffee--in a market where the immigrants are scarce, locals have fled the region, and others are reluctant to relocate.

2.58   Daily wages fluctuated between Ush350 and Ush700 in November 1991, equivalent to US$0.33 to US$0.65 at the parallel rate (fig. 19).   The average rural wage rate was Ush540 per day in November 1991, which, at US$0.50, is exactly equal to the dollar-equivalent wage in May 1991. These wages are below the average returns per person-day calculated for a wide range of food crops (fig. 27)--but above the returns per person-day on Robusta coffee. Daily wages were highest in Mbale, Tororo, and Iganga, densely populated regions in the East, and also in Masaka, in the Center, where production opportunities are best and daily returns high. Kabarole, in the West, a center for the tea industry, registered the lowest daily wage. The Evans study notes that Kapchorwa, Tororo--and possibly Iganga, among other districts--have been facing labor deficits, in terms of labor/land ratios. 22/ The daily wage differentials noted above also reflect the needs of the regional growing seasons, which differ in timing across the country.

The Estate and Nonfarm Market

2.59   Estates have traditionally relied on contract and permanent labor, often immigrants from Rwanda or Zaire. Political and economic disruptions in Uganda and neighboring countries in recent years, and sharp devaluations in the value of the Ugandan shilling have reduced the flow of immigrant labor to Uganda. This, coupled with the rise in food prices and the availability of alternate employment opportunities--which accompany the rehabilitation of infrastructure and the reestablishment of the tea and sugar industries--has caused rural wages to rise in real terms. Low productivity in the tea and sugar estates have made it especially hard for them to obtain sufficient labor, at the wages they were willing to offer. Cane cutters can now earn Ush 12,000 a month, which is within the regional parameters for permanent employees. The low green leaf price severely limits the ability of outgrowers to hire labor, and restricts garden size to the 1 ha to 1.5 ha that a family can handle. Tea factories are limited by the low productivity of their processing

---

21/   Alison Evans Rural Labour Market Assessment - Uganda, Preliminary Observations and Conclusions, Agricultural Secretariat, Bank of Uganda, April 21, 1992, p.1.

22/   Evans, op. cit., p.2.

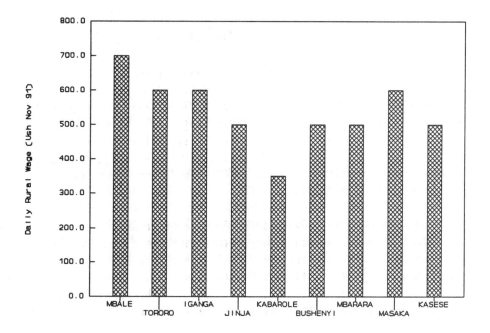

Figure 19   Daily Rural Wage Rates

operations, and their high debt-service obligations, from providing more than an absolute minimum to wage laborers. Consequently, estates have great difficulty in paying market wages, and hence, not surprisingly, in finding adequate supplies of contract workers.

Labor Migration

2.60   Cursory observation indicates that labor flows respond predictably to regional employment opportunities around the country. There is an element of unpredictability to the movements however, since the laborers are also smallholder farmers in their own right, who will react quickly to any change in the relative profitability of their own employment. The change in the returns from food production can produce an especially rapid reaction in labor availability, due both to the change in the returns from alternate employment, as well as to the increase in the cost of the minimum food basket. The absence of migrant workers from Rwanda since the early 1980s has affected production relationships and wages for export crop production--mainly in the tea and sugar estates and to a certain extent on smallholder farms. Migration of poorer farmers from the "land-poor" Southwest (Kibaale, Rukungiri) into the western (Hoima, Kibale, Kabarole) and central areas (Mukono, Luwero) continues. While migrants may start off as agricultural laborers, they will often end up establishing their own holdings (especially in the western areas).

2.61   The market for labor among smallholder farmers--while active--appears to be small, fragmented, and constrained by limited mobility and imperfect information. Relationships are localized and personalized transactions are preferred. Since smallholders enter the local market for casual daily labor at more or less the same time during the crop year--to meet peak land preparation, weeding, or harvest requirements--they become price takers. Smallholders with more cash at this crucial time can pay the scarcity wages and obtain timely assistance. This has consequences on yields and profits. The ability to obtain timely credit, not necessarily in large amounts, to finance hired labor during peak demand will be a key determinant of yield, cultivated area, and farm income.

2.62   The flow of labor into urban areas has only gradually started again. Urban incomes are, on average, 69 percent higher than those in rural Uganda in money terms, and urban areas have grown at 5.9 percent per year, above the national average growth rate of 2.5 percent.

2.63   Although more work is needed to identify barriers to inter district labor movement, the nature of the work contract, and ways the Government can influence market efficiency, the following recommendations can help to improve the responsiveness of the market, and reduce labor-related constraints to increased production. First, improved transport facilities--especially improved trunk and feeder roads--would improve labor mobility, permitting an elastic response to the strong seasonal demand from smallholders. More availability of bicycles, especially for women, also can improve responsiveness.

2.64   Second, the reestablishment of peace and security should loosen the market, making people more likely to move into ethnic areas different from their own. Third, increased availability of cash for smallholders--through improved payment systems, informal credit, and more work opportunities--would permit the employment of more labor and release a peak-demand bottleneck.

2.65   Fourth, labor-related constraints to expansion in smallholder agriculture can be softened, and returns to labor increased, with the increased use of labor-saving techniques. Equipment should focus both on farm-related tasks--using ox-drawn mechanization (ploughs, weeders, carts), for example--and on domestic chores (fetching water, grinding cereals, cooking), which could release male and female labor. Fifth, in addition to the measures already mentioned, constraints to female participation in the labor market, and the returns to traditionally female tasks should be identified. Interventions---using the extension service, or NGOs--should respond to regional female priorities.

2.66   Sixth, the gradual improvement in the processing efficiency of the tea sector--and hence the possibilities for raising the greenleaf price--should improve the sector's competitiveness in the labor market. Recommendations on Government intervention in establishing a floor price for greenleaf are discussed in Section IV on the tea industry. The private sector should be induced to produce innovative labor contracts, and bonus and incentive payments. Additional investment in housing, schooling, and other benefits should also improve supply.

Rural Women

2.67   A recent Bank report on the status of women in Uganda places rural women, appropriately, at the "center of agriculture." 23/ In a primarily food-based agricultural economy, women provide 68 percent of the labor for food crop cultivation, and 53 percent of the

---

23/   Eva Jarawan, "Women in Development: Current Issues and Agenda for Further Research," AF2PH Working Paper, June 28, 1991, p.20.

labor needed for cash crop cultivation. 24/ Some 94 percent of employed women gave their main occupation as agriculture, compared with 82 percent for men. Womens' responsibilities to the rural household do not end with crop cultivation, however. The National Household Budget Survey notes that the primary activity of 72 percent of economically active rural females-- excluding students or those unable to work involves attending to household duties. 25/ This compares to 20 percent for economically active males, whose primary activity (60 percent) is as "own account worker."

2.68   As the Jarawan report points out however, womens' contribution to the productive process is not matched by their control over the use of the resources generated.   Women decided on the use of the funds generated from the sale of crops in relatively few cases: 39 percent of the time for food crops (one-third of this jointly with men) and 17 percent of the cases for cash crops (a little less than half the time in conjunction with men).   In addition, as noted in the Jarawan report,

> "property acquired during marriage belongs to the husband. In the event of the husband's death, the woman is not the automatic heir ... According to the formal legal system, a wife or wives get 15 percent of the husband's estate while the children get 75 percent (in equal shares). The dependant relatives get 9 percent [of the estate,] and the customary heir 1 percent." 26/

2.69   Women may face lower returns and greater difficulties than men in competing in the rural labor market. As noted by Evans:

> "Female labor supply for wage work is restricted by the multiple demands of domestic food production and processing, household maintenance, childcare, health care and cash-earning, to meet daily and lumpy expenditures such as school fees and medical expenses. Inadequate crop and personal transport facilities limit women's mobility and further restrict their labor time. The loss of assistance from school age children in simple farm and household tasks ... has had a significant impact on female labor time. Restricted bargaining power and contractual inferiority in the labor market largely stems from these constraints on women's ability to allocate time and resources optimally. The greater inelasticity of female labor supply may pose a limit to the response of both family and hired labor to changed incentives. Although as already indicated distress selling of female labor during a period of food deficit and around the time that school fees are due is very common." 27/

24/   AFCODE Survey, 1989, in Jarawan, op. cit., p. ...

25/   MPED, Statistics Department, Report on the Uganda National Household Budget Survey 1989-90, Entebbe, February 1991, Table 2.20.

26/   Jarawan, op cit. p.9

27/   Evans, Alison, op.cit. para 18

2.70   Women are also at a disadvantage in education with respect to men: 43 percent of rural women are functionally illiterate, compared with 28 percent of rural men; and 51 percent had finished primary education, compared with 60 percent of men.

2.71   For these reasons, as the aforementioned report indicates, there is a need to consider gender in designing programs to transfer technology and improve production opportunities and incentives in rural areas.   If this is not done, the production effects of production programs will be lost, and the gender-based inequities exacerbated.   Of key importance in supporting rural development on this issue is redressing the gender inequities in the inheritance legislation and practices. Also, Government should make particular efforts to reach women in services that support smallholders, such as attempts to transfer improved cultivation techniques or foster savings generation and marketing initiatives. As mentioned in the previous section, the introduction of labor-saving devices and infrastructure into the rural household should have a effect on the welfare of rural women.

Regional Differences and Migration

2.72   As argued previously, there are still large areas of underutilized, medium-to-high potential farmland in Uganda (table 2). Only one-third of areas potentially open for cultivation or pasture are used for crop production.   But, the availability of land to farmers differs sharply by district. The density of the rural population by district varies from 20 to 60 inhabitants per square km in Masindi, Hoima, Mubende, and Luwero--all fairly high potential-areas-- to 250 to 300 in Kabale, Mbale, Iganga, Tororo, all of them districts with high agricultural potential (fig. 20). Why do farmers not move into the underutilized areas of good production potential?

2.73   The answers to this are complex, varied, and not clearly understood. With a population projected to increase at 3.1 percent per annum, there is a strong imperative for fuller use of areas of good agricultural potential. 28/ Because Uganda's population is largely rural, the number of farming families is increasing steadily. The new entrants will continue to look for opportunities to open their own farms rather than intensifying production on parental farms. This has been the means by which an increasing farm population has been fed in the past, and the absence of an overall land constraint would indicate that the same strategy will be used for the remainder of the decade. Given this underlying pressure, "security" appears to be a key determinant of interregional migration, and of expansion in cultivated areas. As argued in the review of the environmental effects of agriculture (para 2.15), area cultivated increased in those districts where the "security" situation improved. Population density in the Southwest and Northeast may have increased more rapidly than population growth during the years of "the troubles," as former migrants returned to their ethnic areas.   With the current improvement in "security" across the country (excepting portions of the North), a resurgence in the natural outmigration from the densely populated Southwest and Northeast, and a return to the "foreign" districts where homesteads were established can be expected. Spot observations by the mission confirm this hypothesis in western Uganda.

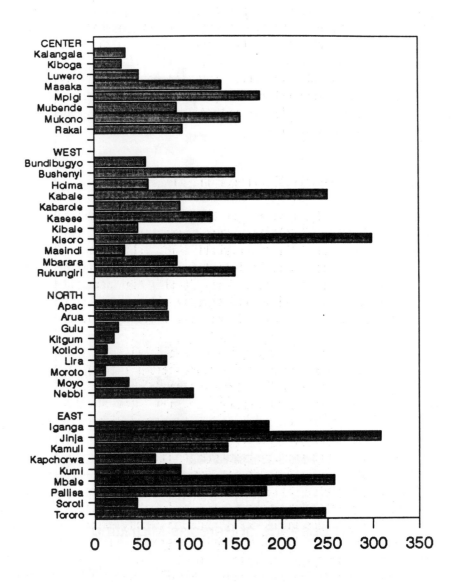

Figure 20   Rural Population Density 1991 (hab/km2)

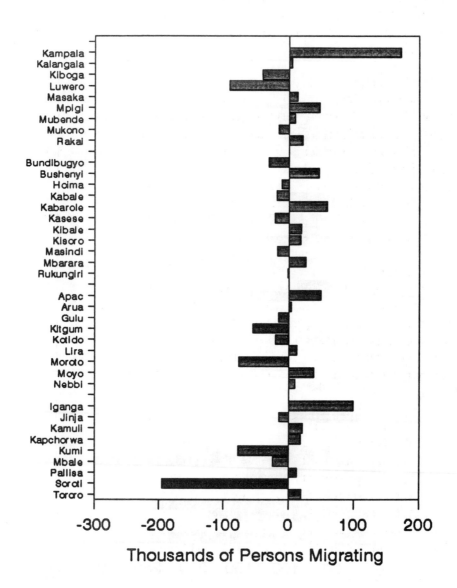

Figure 21 Net Migration 1980-1991, After Allowing for Population Growth

2.74   A rough attempt has been made to measure migration across districts by comparing the actual intercensal growth rate of population in each district with the national intercensal growth rate of 2.5 percent per annum (fig 21). Districts with a growth rate higher than the national average, show up with an inflow of migrants, and vice versa. The hypothesis is that three forces are inducing population movement: the normal rural-urban shift in search of better living standards, the exodus from areas where security risks are untenable and the quest for new land for cultivation.

2.75   The large move into Kampala during the intercensal period can be hypothesized to be mainly part of the rural-urban drift, with some components of security-driven migration. The exodus from Soroti, Kumi, and Mbale into Iganga, Tororo, and Pallisa can be hypothesized to be due to the decline in the security situation. The shift out of Luwero and Kiboga into Mpigi, Rakai, Masaka, and Kampala also can be thought of as due to security problems in these areas in the early and mid 1980s. Similarly, the exodus from Moroto, Kotido, Kitgum, and Gulu into Apac, Lira, Moyo, and Nebbi is believed to be a reaction to security problems. The small shift out of Kabale may be due to disruptions caused by the conflict in Rwanda.

2.76   The South and West have not seen serious security problems over the decade, except in the mid 1980s. Movement here is hypothesized to be a response to land pressure. The exodus from Kabale, Bundibugyo, and Kasese--where cultivable land per capita is very low, partly because of the presence of the Ruwenzori range into Kabarole, Kibale, Kisoro, and Bushenyi appears to be for such a reason. A mission visit to this area confirms the presence of large numbers of people from the Kigezi region in the western districts mentioned above. Detailed information on the distribution of people by ethnic origin, from the 1991 census, should permit a confirmation of these trends. Much additional work is needed, however, to establish how and why these movements occur, and to determine what role Government might play in channeling them.

2.77   It is a basic conclusion of this report that Government should be much more concerned with these "natural" flows of people and resources than it is at present. Interregional migration is a vital "engine" of growth. It is the mechanism that has been used in the past--and will continue to be used--to expand cultivated area. This type of expansion in output provides the greatest returns to labor, if the migration costs are not too high. There is substantial land with good potential for sustainable rainfed agriculture. Government should be guiding this migration-- indirectly--to ensure that expansion takes place in appropriate areas, that ethnic and environmental effects are minimized, and that the physical and social hardships of the migrants are reduced.

2.78   This report recommends that Government develop a policy on interregional migration to, first, establish those areas where immigration is most desirable. This would depend on assessments of agricultural potential, environmental consequences, and ethnic differences.

2.79   Second, the policy should investigate conditions in the areas of severe land pressure, evaluate measures being taken to improve productivity there, estimate potential numbers of migrants, and formulate indirect incentive measures to guide migratory flows to the desirable areas. The spatial location of economic and social infrastructure--feeder roads, schools, and hospitals--is believed to be a key determinant in population flows. Third, Government should clarify tenure rights of new occupants, with regard to those of traditional owners. New law should take the consequences of this type of movement into consideration.

2.80   Fourth, the policy should design Government's role in assisting recently established communities. Provision of production assistance, using the extension and research network, will be of key import. Consolidation of schools and health services, and road maintenance will have to be financed. The enhanced participation of newly formed communities in the operation of these services could be sought. Fifth, Government should implement mechanisms to monitor the levels, directions, and consequences of these migrations to permit adjustments in policy and response to any problems.

2.81   The formulation of such a policy will require substantial commitment to investigating the conditions in target areas, and to investing the infrastructure and services needed to carry out the policy.

Social Indicators and Food Security

2.82   There are marked differences in social indicators by region. 29/ Household expenditure was lowest in northern and eastern Uganda (table 10). The share of the population in the lowest income category was highest in these two regions. These data could reflect the fact that in 1988-89, when the Household Budget Survey was conducted, these two regions experienced severe civil unrest. The explanations for these regional differences are hypothetical, and will require further detailed analysis to strengthen the conclusions. The ratio of children suffering from "stunting," where height-for-age ratios were significantly below the norm, is highest in the Southwest. This may be associated with diet (see below). The Eastern Region, one of the most densely populated, also appeared to have the lowest living standards, with very low household expenditure, an above-average share of people in the lowest income category, and above-average child mortality.

Table 10: Regional Social Indicators					
Region (HBS)	Average Household Expenditure (Ush 1989-90)	Percent in Low Expenditure Category	Region (DHS)	Under 5 Mortality (Per 1000)	Stunting
Kampala	59,944	19.9%	Kampala	174	22%
Central	36,477	51.1%	Central	187	35%
Western	35,813	44.2%	West	179	47%
			Southwest	172	54%
Eastern	23,695	61.3%	East	207	45%
Northern	22,087	68.2%	West Nile	211	45%
UGANDA	34,468	50.6%	UGANDA	180	45%

2.83   Food security--access to food--appears to be a problem in certain areas of rural Uganda, based on a quick review of the available survey data. A rough calculation of the calorie equivalent of the food available per capita in 1991--about 960 kg per year--indicates that there are about 3,420 calories available per person (table 11). This level of consumption is adequate. But,

---

World Bank, <u>Uganda - Social Sector Study</u>, op. cit., p.6,7.

the World Bank Atlas 1991 shows per-capita calorie availability in 1988 at 2,013--which is significantly less than adequate. Whatever the actual value, two points should be made: the average food basket is low in protein, and (ii) and there are likely to be food security problems in at least some areas in rural Uganda. These points are discussed below, and will be elaborated on in the forthcoming Country Economic Memorandum, to be produced by the World Bank.

Table 11: Caloric Equivalent of Average Amount of Available Food Per Capita				
Food Item	Share	Kg of Food	Calories/Kg	Total Calories
Bananas	50%	480.0	670	321,600
Cassava	22%	211.2	1090	230,208
Sweet Potato	13%	124.8	970	121,056
Cowpea/Pulse	3%	28.8	3420	98,496
Oilseeds	2%	19.2	5740	110,208
Cereals	10%	96.0	3500	336,000
Total Food	100%	960.0		1,217,568
Calories per day				3,420

Source: Agricultural Compendium, Elsevier, p. 576/77

2.84   On the first point 85 percent of the average gross volume of food is provided by bananas, cassava, sweet potato, and other low-protein foods (table 11). The implication is that the diet may be protein deficient, while providing adequate calories. The lack of adequate protein would explain the high incidence of stunting--especially in the Southwest, where the diet of banana, potato, and sweet potato is especially prevalent. The consumption of millet and other cereals is higher in the North and Northeast. The availability of sufficient calories explains why the health data on weight for height (wasting), an indicator of acute malnutrition, were not so far from the norms.

2.85   On the second point, rural incomes average only US$104 per annum (at the bureau exchange rate), with 54 percent of households spending less than US$94 dollars per year, on food consumption (table 10). While these are very low absolute numbers, the farmgate price of home-grown food, on which this expenditure estimate was based, may be sufficiently low to permit an adequate consumption level. Substantial disparities exist in average incomes across regions, (table 10) with expenditure in the North and East at or below two-thirds of the national average. These data imply very low annual consumption levels, and may indicate the existence of rural areas where food security is a problem. Further investigation of select rural areas for evidence of food insecurity is warranted to identify those who suffer from it and design measures to address the problem.

2.86   In order to reduce the negative effects of seasonal food shortages on local prices and consumption it is important that the Government, international agencies, and NGO's be given sufficient time to react to threats of food shortfalls. The Early Warning System currently in place is weak and its ability to collect and analyze national production information as the crop season progresses should be strengthened to increase its ability to accurately predict harvests and improve its credibility with policymakers.

III. AGRICULTURAL SERVICES

3.1   Following the collapse of economic activity in the late 1970s, Government stepped in during the early 1980s to provide basic support to the farming sector, which the private sector was unwilling or unable to respond to. In addition to extension and research, the Government became involved in the importation and sale of agricultural chemicals and implements, and the provision of agricultural credit. The Government's continued presence in these markets in the early 1990s has inhibited the re-emergence of the private sector.

3.2   During the 1980s, services to the agricultural sector were provided by a series of ministries, each specialized in an aspect of rural production or organization. Agriculture, animal industry and fisheries, and cooperatives and marketing were supported from three ministries. A fourth ministry dealt with land tenure regulations, and a fifth ministry addressed environmental questions. This fragmentation hampered the execution of a coherent development program for agriculture.

3.3   The services performed by public sector institutions have declined considerably in quality since the 1970's. With the deterioration in economic performance, and the decline in the real value of the budget, salaries and funding for operation and maintenance have been allowed to go down. The politically unpalatable measure of reducing staff has been put off, with the result that salaries are now so low that outside employment is necessary to make ends meet. 30/ Government employment has become a parttime occupation for most staff, with the result that Government services are patchy, at best.

3.4   Much attention has been devoted recently to this problem. In its recent review of the effectiveness of public expenditure, the World Bank has recommended a program of devolving to the private sector those commercial functions assumed by Government during the periods of crisis, and the provision of other services that are potentially profitable. 31/ To improve the effectiveness of those regulatory and public good services which must remain with Government, personal emoluments have to be raised, personnel trained, and institutions and operating systems rationalized. The capacity to expand Government expenditure beyond the current 16 percent of GDP is severely limited. For this reason, sharp reductions in public service personnel are recommended. This question is eloquently described in the discussion of the revenue-wages-productivity nexus in a recent Bank report. 32/

Government Services for Agriculture

The Public Service

3.5   Government has an important role to play in supporting the development and dissemination of profitable technological advances, and in regulating production and commercial activities in the agricultural sector.

30/   Christine Obbo, "Women, Children and the Living Wage," in Holger Bernt Hansen and Michael Twaddle (eds) Changing Uganda, Eastern African Studies, James Currey Ltd., 1991, p.98.

31/   World Bank, Public Choices for Private Initiatives, 9203-UG, February 12, 1991.

32/   This question is eloquently described in a discussion of the revenue-wages-productivity nexus in a recent Bank report, Uganda - Managing Public Expenditure, 10512 UG, March 31, 1992, p. 27.

3.6　　　　Measures have been put in place to improve the effectiveness of the public service in agriculture. Funding for state-owned farms and ranches has been cut. Funding for the state-owned tractor service agency has also been reduced, and the agency is slated for sale. A study by the Public Service Review and Reorganization Commission of September 1990 has recommended a "minimum living wage." With support from the Bank's Structural Adjustment Credit (Cr 2314-UG), the Ministry of Public Service is undertaking a functional review of the structure and staffing requirements of four key ministries, one of which is the newly merged Ministry of Agriculture Animal Industry and Fisheries (MAAIF).

3.7　　　　The MAAIF was formed in June of 1991 from the two key ministries involved in promoting agricultural development. The MAAIF now provides extension services in every district and coordinates research covering crop and animal production. In March 1992, further ministerial restructuring took place. The Ministry of Commerce, Industry and Cooperatives now regulates the marketing of cash crops--and the development of cooperatives, commerce, and industry. In addition, the newly formed Ministry of Finance and Economic Planning collaborates with the two ministries just mentioned in the design and implementation of agricultural development policy through the Agriculture Policy Committee and the Agricultural Secretariat of the Bank of Uganda. Environmental and forestry questions covered by the Ministry of Water, Energy, Minerals and Environmental Protection. Land tenure issues are dealt with by the Ministry of Lands, Housing and Urban Development.

Funding

3.8　　　　Agriculture-related Government services received about US$ 18 million (at the official exchange rate) from local sources--4 percent of budgetary expenditure in 1990-91, excluding grants. That amounted to 0.5 percent of GDP in 1990. If donor contributions are included, agriculture-related services' share of GDP goes up to 1 percent. 33/ Comparator countries undergoing adjustment--(Ghana, Malawi, and Kenya)--averaged 2.4 percent of GDP on similar expenditures. Uganda's allocation of central government expenditure on agriculture, at US$ 3.4 per capita in 1982-87, was well below the US$ 21 per-capita average for ten other sub Saharan countries. 34/ Whether this amount is appropriate depends on the role Government is expected to perform in agriculture. The intention, at present, is to staff an extension service, with a presence in every district, to provide production assistance. It is also the intention--after the establishment of a National Agricultural Research Organization--to fund research from general budgetary resources, taxes on specific export crops, and private contracts for investigation of specific problems. All research on crops and livestock is Government funded. For these kinds of expectations, funding levels are grossly inadequate. Salaries and allowances for staff are well below the levels needed to provide a minimum living wage, and funds for operations are well below those needed to support constant daily activity.

3.9　　　　A recent study on extension systems in East Africa notes that expenditures on agricultural extension in the region averaged 1.2 percent of agricultural GDP in 1980. 35/

33/　　　See World Bank, Public Choices for Private Initiatives, 9203-UG, p. 35. and unpublished tables.

34/　　　Botswana, Mauritius, Swaziland, Egypt, Kenya, Malawi, Togo, Ethiopia, Madagascar, and Zimbabwe, from World Bank, Nigeria - Strategy for Agricultural Growth", 7988-UNI, p. 79.

35/　　　Lisa A. Schwartz, and Jacob Kampen, Agricultural Extension in East Africa, World Bank Technical Paper 164, p. 12.

Expenditure on research was another 0.81 percent of agriculture GDP. Uganda in 1990 was spending 0.9 percent of agricultural GDP on all agricultural services combined, which puts it below regional levels.

3.10   The extent to which a country should tap the resources available in agriculture to support the development of other sectors depends on where the country is in agricultural transformation. Timmer identifies four phases that characterize agriculture's contribution to economic growth. 36/ During the first phase, which he calls "Getting Agriculture Moving," resources flow out of agricultural decline. Agriculture is the dominant activity in the economy. The Government invests its resources--raised from taxes on agriculture--in infrastructure, research, and extension services, and ensures that incentives encourage farmers to adopt innovations and new technologies as they come available. The evolution into the second phase, characterized as "Agriculture as a Contributor to Growth," starts,

> "when agricultural productivity per worker rises. This increased productivity creates a surplus, which in the second phase can be tapped directly, through taxation and factor flows, or indirectly, through Government intervention into the rural-urban terms of trade." 37/

3.11   Uganda, which may have been evolving into the second phase in the early 1970's, has slipped in its developmental status, and can still be characterized as a "first-phase" agricultural economy, in Timmer's terminology. Productivity per agricultural worker, evaluated by observing agricultural GDP per rural inhabitant, dropped in the mid 1980's. It has been growing since 1986, and by 1990 had returned to the level attained in 1983. The emphasis in Uganda should be on investing in agriculture and supporting sectors, to raise labor productivity, and permit the generation of resources needed to support growth in the rest of the economy.

3.12   Over the past decade, Governmental expenditure in support of agricultural production has varied considerably in real terms, (fig. 22). 38/ But, from 1980 to 1990, both the level of resources, and the share of Recurrent and Development budgetary expenditure on agriculture have declined. Expenditure for agriculture since 1987-88 has remained at about 40 percent of 1984-85 and 1985-86 levels. Recurrent expenditure on agriculture is now half of what it was in 1984-85 (in real terms) and developmental expenditure has been at about 20 percent of 1985-86 levels since 1989-90. Agriculture's share in the total budget has also declined from 12 percent in 1980-81 to about 4 percent in 1990-91 (fig. 23).

36/   C. Peter Timmer, "The Agricultural Transformation," in Handbook of Development Economics, Vol. I, edited by H. Chenery and T.N. Srinivasan, Elsevier, 1988, p. 279.

37/   Timmer, op.cit., p. 280.

38/   Donor contributions to the development budget, which are substantial, have not been included for lack of reliable, consistent information.

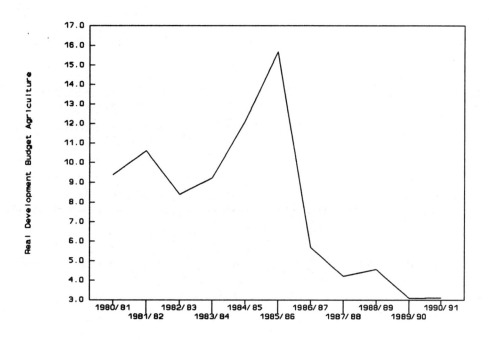

Figure 22   Real Budgetary Expenditure on Agriculture Related Services

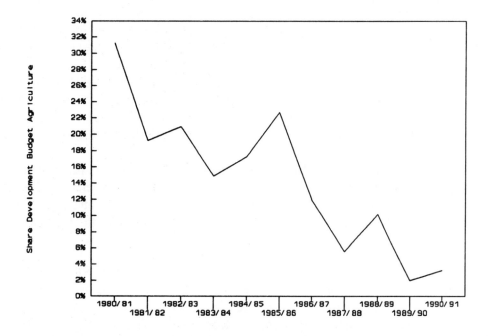

Figure 23   Share of Budgetary Resources to Agriculture Related Services

Agricultural Extension

3.13   In spite of these declines in relative and absolute allocations of resources, the three--now two--key ministries, have maintained the same level of field and headquarters staff throughout the decade. In all, there have been some 5,560 agents with "field" responsibility, all of them at least diploma or certificate holders. They are supported by a hierarchy of specialists and administrators extending through the county, district, and regional levels to Entebbe. Trials and training are provided mainly by the 16 District Farm Institutes, some of which have been rehabilitated. The distribution of field staff in 1990 was: in MAAIF, some 1,785 Assistant Agricultural Officers and Agricultural Assistants, 1400 Field Assistants, 450 Animal Husbandry Officers and Assistant Animal Husbandry Officers, 450 Assistant Fisheries Development Officers and Fisheries Assistants, and 228 Veterinary Officers; in the Ministry of Commerce Industry and Cooperatives, 850 Assistant Cooperative Officers and Cooperative Assistants; and in the Ministry Water, Energy, Minerals and Environment Protection, 400 Foresters and Forest Rangers.

3.14   Funding allocations in 1990, at the official exchange rate, total US$ 350 per field staff per person per year. This includes all locally financed Government expenditure for the ministries listed above, and covers all overhead charges for the agents. The allocation is too low. If all these funds were paid directly to field staff--which they are not--they would amount to just US$29 per month. In order to better evaluate future budgets, it is recommended that "norms" of expenditure, per field agent, be worked out, so that funding at the norm provides sufficient resources for a successful program.

3.15   Funding is not the only problem faced by the governmental agencies charged with supporting farmers in agricultural development. The bureaucracies are unresponsive to field-level needs and priorities. Links with the research network are hard to develop, given its centralization around Kampala. As noted forcefully by the Government's Manpower Development Task Force in 1987, at that time there was almost no coordination among the ministries, either at Headquarters or in the field. This made unified planning for the agricultural sector almost impossible. The results were fragmented overlapping services, and no integration between crop and animal production or between production and marketing. Coordinated services are vital for the farmer. Their absence in Uganda has contributed to agricultural stagnation. The ministerial reorganization of June 1991 represents a first step towards redressing these weaknesses.

3.16   **Project Implementation Experience.** Regional or crop-based projects have been funded over the past ten years in partial attempts to redress some of these problems. The Agricultural Development Project (Cr 1539-UG) in the North and Northeast, and the Southwest Region Agriculture Rehabilitation Project (Cr 1869-UG), both cofinanced by the International Fund for Agricultural Development and IDA, attempt to rehabilitate agricultural extension and adaptive research services, as well as rural infrastructure, on a regional basis. In addition, the EEC for five years has been funding a Farming Systems Support Program (FSSP), to increase the quality and volume of coffee production in select portions of central Uganda. These projects have had limited success in improving the quality of agricultural services. Implementation has lagged considerably behind schedule. Administrative support from Entebbe has been weak. Government funding allocations have been erratic and low, eroding staff commitment and credibility with farmers. The quality of expatriate technical assistance staff has been mixed, with some teams providing mediocre services.

3.17   The lessons to be learned from IDA-funded investment projects in the late 1960s and early 1970s are not new. 39/ The combination of a profitable technical package, a crop or livestock product with a good market, an effective and committed executing agency, and a stable and supportive economic environment will lead to success. Each element is necessary, but not sufficient for success. Weakness in any one of these areas will lead to failure. Unlike current commitments, these projects were small, and total costs lay between US$4 and $8 million. The projects were also focused in their objectives, with each project addressing one crop: tea, livestock, or tobacco.

3.18   **Future Prospects.** In improving the quality of services offered by the Agricultural ministry, the country will have to decide what the level of subsidized agricultural services it can afford. With a ceiling on the real resources available to the Government from the economy in the short-run--at 16 percent of GDP budgetary expenditures are well beyond revenue collections--and severe competition among ministries for these resources, it is unlikely that the sector can expect its real allocations to grow rapidly. Thus, services will have to be improved with resources similar to those available at present. In designing the new institutional goals, norms for the levels of funding adequate to run an effective agricultural support service will have to be utilized. Once more realistic goals have been agreed to, the MAAIF will have to be downsized to a level compatible with the resources available from the National Treasury.

3.19   Then will follow the long task of institutional development, as the organization is tuned to reach its objectives as effectively as possible. Some of the institutional development principles will be to (a) establish clear lines of authority and feasible spans of control, (b) reward the efficient use of resources in achieving institutional goals, (c) have managers and staff be accountable for services provided, (d) maintain a strong linkage between research and extension, (e) pay adequate salaries and adopt a merit based reward system, and (f) make sufficient operating funds available on a timely basis. The Ministry of Public Service is conducting a "functional rationalization" study of the Ministry of Agriculture, Animal Industry and Fisheries. A revised set of institutional goals, an adjusted institutional structure, and targets for reductions in force were due to be completed by mid-1992. The recently approved National Agricultural Extension Project (Cr 2424-UG) will work within the revised structure to improve the effectiveness of operations.

3.20   Not all extension services require funding from the national budget. The British American Tobacco Company has established a very effective extension service in the North and West of Uganda, funded entirely from operations in the tobacco industry, for assisting tobacco farmers producing for the company. The system works well, and fulfills the conditions needed for a successful extension service. It is based on a good cash crop with a proven market and well-researched production techniques. Extension agents are knowledgeable in their field, and recommendations can be acted on. Inputs and finance, provided by the company, are timely and appropriate, reducing the risks associated with cash crop production. This system cannot be replicated easily, however, dependent as it is on a cash crop with a centralized marketing and processing institution. The central institution is able to cover the costs of services such as extension and credit, diminishing the problem of having "users" of extension services in other, more widely traded crops pay for the service.

39/   The Tea Growers Corporation Project (Cr 109-UG) of 1967, the Livestock Development Project (Cr 130-UG) of 1968, and the Smallholder Tobacco Project (Cr 212-UG) of 1970.

Crop Research

3.21   Uganda has a long tradition of crop research, and contained well-established research institutes at Kawanda (coffee, banana, sugarcane, tea, cocoa, soils analysis), Namulonge (cotton, root crops, beans and maize), Serere (sorghum, millet, cassava, oilseeds, semi-arid production systems), and Entebbe (animal health). Food crop research has received little attention. Even without the civil disturbances and the intermittent wars between 1976 and 1986, it would have been necessary to redirect research efforts in Uganda. The complete disruption and destruction of the country's agricultural research capability has provided an opportunity to reconstruct this capacity in a manner best suited to serve the country's present needs.

3.22   The current research network comprises seven research institutes, eleven stations, four regional veterinary laboratories, and sixty-five varietal testing centers. The strategy for the rehabilitation of the research network will be to centralize the structure of research management in order to better guarantee funding, permanence, stability, and good working conditions to the research system. This National Agricultural Research Organization would secure Government or official donor funding; provide a forum for arriving at a consensus on research priorities, resource allocation, and coordination; ensure the existence of a work climate and facilities conducive to agricultural research in participating organizations; and ensure that two-way linkages to extension are in place. The national organization would also provide support on publications and human resource development to participating centers; provide for coordination of donors involved in agricultural research; and monitor and evaluate progress by affiliated research centers in achieving agreed-upon research program goals. A National Agricultural Research Organization Act incorporating these measures has recently been passed, providing legal sanction for the restructuring of the agricultural research system.

3.23   The basic research centers would have to participate in the national network and follow the priorities--and receive funding--from the national system. However, centers would be free to develop programs with additional funding from external organizations interested in particular crops or problems.

3.24   A minimum number of research stations would be maintained in each of the four agroecological zones, to study each zone's key agricultural problems. This would permit the extension system to respond to the production problems of the region. The proposal is to reduce the number of centers to six, and the number of variety testing centers to thirty-four. The more developed research institutes, located in the high potential zones around Lake Victoria, would continue to conduct basic research, and would house the one-of-a-kind facilities such as a soils laboratory. A mandate for an improved level of assistance to agriculture exists. A response to this mandate has been designed under the national Agricultural Research and Training Project, recently approved by IDA.

Animal Disease Control

3.25   Veterinary services and disease control programs deteriorated substantially during the upheavals of the 1970s and 1980s. Looting and epidemic disease during the 1980s led to an estimated 30 percent reduction in livestock numbers. Preventable diseases such as rinderpest and Contagious Bovine Pleuropneumonia (CBPP) are spreading. The reinvasion of tsetse in the West and South is increasing the incidence of trypanosomiasis, a danger to animals and humans. The existence of these diseases inhibits the development of ox-drawn mechanization and the use of exotic, high yielding milk cows in the dairy industry. To counter this, the Government's disease-control program should be strengthened, veterinary services developed, and the flow of drugs and inputs to the sector increased.

3.26   The new policies stress privatization and cost recovery. This includes full participation of the private sector in the supply and distribution of veterinary drugs and medicines. At present the PARC project supported by the EEC and the World Bank Livestock Services Project (Cr 2176-UG) has included financing for the establishment of private veterinary practices. In addition GTZ are providing valuable assistance to upgrade veterinary diagnostic facilities at Entebbe and demonstrate and undertake epidemiological studies to define disease incidence in selected areas of the country. The clinical service which is supposed to be provided by the public veterinary service is extremely inefficient and has a minimal effect on animal health. Although transport, inadequate allowances, and a gross shortage of drugs and medicines contribute to this situation, the main problem is staff remuneration.

3.27   A private veterinary practice, while clearly viable in the high productivity dairy areas, will not be profitable in all parts of Uganda. This report suggests that Government consider two models for the privatization of clinical services: (a) the use of nomadic animal health assistants, and (b) the contracting of veterinarians part time for Government work.

3.28   The first model proposed for consideration by MAAIF in formulating its assistance strategy involves the employment of mobile animal health assistants in arid pastoral or agropastoralist areas. These mobile animal health assistants are selected representatives of pastoral or agropastoral traditional groups who receive a short practical training course of two or three weeks from the veterinary service. They are trained to provide a basic animal health service by veterinary service staff but must make their own arrangements with the group regarding fees or payment. The assistants are supplied with basic drugs and medicines through the veterinary service or the private sector. They charge livestock producers the full cost of drugs and medicines and in addition they sometimes charge a markup of about 30 percent to cover their own remuneration. Methods of reimbursement vary, however, from place to place. A common feature is the establishment of a revolving fund by pastoral associations or other groups to ensure that funds are available to purchase replacement stocks as necessary. The Government should support the formation of such pastoral associations or rural cooperative groups, to permit the spread of disease-control services. The support of the veterinary service is essential as it must run an active program of epidemiological studies and cost-benefit analyses to define the diseases and treatments the mobile health assistants will recommend and provide training. Experience to-date in many African countries shows this to be a very attractive, cost-effective approach to providing veterinary services, especially in arid areas. It is recommended that this approach be tested on a pilot basis in predominantly pastoral livestock areas.

3.29   The second model involves contract work. Veterinarians or animal health assistants would be employed part-time under a contract for essential public sector tasks--compulsory vaccinations, sampling dips, meat inspection, quarantine and certification. Using this approach, for example, a veterinarian could receive some of his income from the Government under contract and earn the remainder in private practice. This model would give rise to considerable cost savings for Government, and increase the productivity of veterinary staff. The practice of contracting veterinary work is common in many countries. Veterinarians or veterinary assistants can also be employed by dairy cooperatives or other producer groups part-time or full-time.

3.30   If these concepts--of community-based and part-time contract service--were adopted, the veterinary service could be restructured and downsized considerably along the lines recommended in a recent consultant report reviewing expenditure and personnel planning for livestock services. The restructured full-time veterinary department should then be reoriented to concentrate on its main task of disease surveillance and monitoring--and to further develop an active approach to epidemiology, as is being done at present with German assistance. A key aspect of a new epidemiologically oriented veterinary service will be the cost-benefit analysis of the treatments currently recommended, especially for tick-borne diseases and trypanosomiasis. There is little evidence at present to justify expensive tick control measures in all indigenous cattle or blanket tsetse eradication.

3.31   **Tsetse.** The control of tsetse has now moved to the use of baits or pour-on products. Since the tsetse infrastructure and organization was set up to undertake block control there is now a strong case for a complete rethinking of tsetse control as well as the organizational structure to deal with it. It appears that control measures would not be justified for indigenous cattle on strictly animal-health grounds except possibly in isolated locations. Carefully conducted cost-benefit studies are badly needed to clarify the situation from district to district. The community will need to be much more involved, as will the veterinary and medical services and possibly agriculture extension. IDA is supporting work in this field through the Livestock Services Project mentioned previously.

3.32   **Artificial Insemination.** The maximum of 12,590 inseminations was recorded in 1970. They declined to 2,000 in 1982, and rose to 5,691 in 1991. Assuming two inseminations per conception accounts for about 2,800 calves--or 1,400 heifer calves. Its current impact on the livestock industry is minimal.

3.33   A decision has been reached to privatize the service. In designing the future service, attention must be given to testing, selection, and approval of sires for use in A.I; overall reproductive performance of the national herd, but, especially that portion serviced by A.I; and the need for an initial subsidy to boost the efforts for breed improvement.

3.34   **Livestock Research.** Veterinary research should emphasize the control of ticks, tick-borne diseases, tsetse, and trypanosomiasis. In addition epidemiology studies and cost-benefit analyses should be emphasized to quantify the disease challenge in different areas and formulate cost-effective prevention and control measures. Animal production research should center on grassland technology and animal nutrition. Attention should also be given to identifying and selecting animals with good genetic resistance to trypanosomiasis and tick-borne diseases. Attention should also be given to carrying out research on the establishment of an effective A.I. service--including the use of fresh semen--and a major program to improve fertility and reproductive performance. Pig and poultry research should also be emphasized (breeding, feeding, husbandry, disease control and management) to develop farming systems adapted to Ugandan conditions. The research should focus on adaptive rather than basic research, and economic aspects and cost-benefit analysis should receive special attention.

3.35   Four field stations will be the main locations for animal production research: Nakyesasa Livestock Husbandry Experimental Station, 600 ha, some 27 km Northeast of Kampala (dairy, poultry, pigs); Mbarara Field Station Ruhengere 1,300 ha, some 25 km north of Mbarara (dairy, beef, small ruminants, poultry, pigs); Aswa Field Station in Gulu District (beef, small ruminants); and the Animal Health Research Center in Entebbe, which will continue to provide limited laboratory facilities for production research until new facilities are established at the

Livestock Husbandry Experimental Station at Nakyesasa. Entebbe is and will continue to be the main center for veterinary research and veterinary diagnostic work.

Farmer Cooperatives

3.36   Cooperatives have a comparative advantage in some activities and can play a useful role in promoting efficient and equitable development of Ugandan agriculture if they can become more efficient businesses. Uganda has 5,300 cooperatives; 7 national unions, 37 district unions, and 5,256 primary societies. Primary societies, in most villages, are small businesses with a few employees--many with stores and warehouses. Two- thirds are called produce marketers, but in reality are multipurpose--selling inputs to and receiving produce from farmers. District unions are usually prominent businesses in their communities. They are multipurpose cooperatives with many primary societies as members. The Uganda Cooperative Alliance is a key apex organization.

Comparative Advantages

3.37   A major asset of cooperatives in Uganda today is the established distribution and collection network throughout the country. For almost any region there is a district union with experience in business. Further, most villages have a cooperative and people with experience trading with farmers, who know farmers in their trade area. This is a tremendous resource. To establish an effective regional and local distribution system is expensive. Farmer cooperatives organize where spacial monopolies exist, often in commodities such as cereals, oilseeds, cotton, and milk. Cooperatives often also handle feeds and farm inputs because of their established distribution and collection network. Primary societies in Uganda play an important role in assembling production of cash crops prior to transport to the processing centers. This takes place for crops such as coffee and cotton. In tobacco, primary societies act as intermediaries between growers and the British American Tobacco company, in a successful "model".

3.38   There are normally fundamental differences between cooperative and noncooperative businesses in the assignment of voting rights and distribution of earnings. In a noncooperative, or investor-owned business, both rights to vote for members of the board of directors and distribution of earnings are according to percentage investment in the company. The company is controlled by and operates for the benefit of investors. On the other hand, a cooperative assigns voting rights on the basis of one member, one vote. This is done to safeguard the interests of the individual, whatever his or her wealth and business with the cooperative. Distribution of earnings--net surplus in the case of Uganda--to its users is on the basis of the business conducted through the cooperative. A member, for example, with 8 percent of the business is entitled to 8 percent of earnings. The company is controlled by and operates for the benefit of member-users.

3.39   Cooperatives and investor-owned companies are equivalent in that capital of each is supplied by private individuals. Governments sometimes prescribe rules for use of cooperative assets, although they avoid making similar rules for investor-owned companies. While these rules can limit the competitiveness of cooperatives, they are needed in a country such as Uganda, with an incipient level of farmer involvement in the market economy. A certain level of Government supervision is needed to reduce the possibility of self-interested manipulation of a primary cooperative and associated unions by unscrupulous management. As owner-members become more aware of their rights, and of how the commercial enterprise system works, Government's supervisory role can be reduced to one of ensuring that membership's democratically expressed desires are indeed respected.

3.40   Because of the companies' differences in assigning voting rights and allocation of earnings, most countries have separate laws for cooperatives and investor-owned companies. An essential component of a cooperative law is protection from being declared monopolies. The cooperative law often includes other cooperative principles such as limited returns to capital, democratic control, self-help and self-reliance, limitations on nonmember business, operations at cost, and others.

The Cooperative Societies Statute

3.41   The Cooperative Societies Statue of 1991 maintains the office of the Cooperative Registrar in the Ministry of Commerce, Industry and Cooperatives, with the responsibility of regulating cooperatives. Duties include registration of cooperatives, approval of bylaws, approval of wages, approval of bonuses, audit or approval of auditing companies, supervision of elections, conflict resolution, opinions on the next year's financial plan, implementation of regulations prepared by the minister, and others. Other duties support cooperatives, such as providing model bylaws, helping small cooperatives with bookkeeping and accounts, some training and technical assistance, and conflict resolution upon request. District cooperative officers are a valuable resource for many primary societies.

3.42   In general, the new cooperative law still views cooperatives as needing protection, to be provided by the Government or an apex agency. Small primary societies may not be bothered by the restrictiveness of existing legislation, but unions and larger entities may increasingly elect to organize as noncooperative companies. Cooperatives are subject to higher taxes than noncooperative competitors.

3.43   Some general observations on the law are, first, that cooperatives are "private" companies owned by users. The requirement that cooperatives pay into reserve funds for education and other purposes imposes costs which other private companies do not bear. If membership accepts these contributions as part of their investment in the community's social insurance and welfare system, they should be aware that these additional operating charges affect competitiveness, and dividend payouts. The services provided by the cooperative system, such as by the Uganda Cooperative Alliance, the Uganda Central Cooperative Union, and other apex organizations should be provide on a fee-paying basis, much as UNEX provides its services to unions.

3.44   Second, cooperatives that are not financially viable should be allowed to go out of business. In rural areas where they provide key social as well as economic functions, time-bound efforts to return faltering enterprises to profitability can have have broad social benefits. However, following best efforts to assist such enterprises, they should be allowed to compete in the marketplace and if necessary go out of business in favour of more effective competitors. Third, cooperatives should be allowed to operate according to wise business management principles, free of political pressure except as provide by law and required of all companies.

3.45   Fourth, the Cooperatives Act governing the establishment and operation of cooperatives, and its regulation and enforcement by Government, should be adjusted to make the management cadres of primary societies and their unions more responsive to their membership.

3.46 Two provisions usually in cooperative laws of other countries are not in the Uganda law. The first is a provision allowing cooperatives to allocate net savings to users after year-end close of business but before tax reports are due. Usually the allocation is "paid" in stock certificates, allowing the cooperative to retain capital needed to operate its business. The second is an exemption from corporate income tax of net savings allocated to members.

Restructuring Primary Societies

3.47 The cooperative system faces the prospect of considerable change. Economic liberalization and increased competition in the processing and marketing of export crops are encroaching on monopolistic privileges enjoyed by the cooperative system, such as the processing of cotton, and the sale of inputs to the cotton sector. The enhancement of private sector participation likely will challenge the position of cooperatives, and their unions, in all sectors. To confront these challenges, cooperatives will need to improve their management and solvency. In attaining these objectives it is essential that cooperative management become more responsive to membership desires. Membership should be encouraged-under Government tutelage, as provided by law--to change management on the basis of democratic vote, consolidate their businesses, and restructure their finances. This change should be initiated at the grass root, primary society level. Under the new Cooperative Society Statute the Registrar and specialized Non-Governmental Organizations can play a key role in ensuring that a democratically elected leadership is indeed put in place, that the wishes of the membership are followed in defining a society's business strategy, and that commercial operations are carried out on a responsible and profitable manner. Following the renewal at the primary level, the Registrar should review the activities and role of the district unions.

Union Restructuring

3.48 District unions own and manage the largest assets in the cooperative distribution and collection system. Profitability in all but a few is affected by weak management, overinvestment, expansion into unrelated enterprises and debt. Most of the unions could be profitable ventures and provide efficient services to their members if they were able to compete with or utilize private sector entrants. A key principle in enhancing the effectiveness of a union is improving management responsiveness to the democratically expressed desires of the membership. This mechanism of internal control should be facilitated by the Government and the Cooperative Statute. Support of this principle will have to be strong enough to counter the entrenched interests of management.

3.49 Major changes in the structure of a union, such as staff reduction, selling assets, closing gins, and so on, would create concern in political circles, probably exceeding the ability of boards and management to resist. Change will probably have to be precipitated by an outside event, such as competition by a private company competitor, or foreclosure by a creditor.

3.50 The cooperative system functions under the overhang of debt incurred during the last decade in order to finance the rehabilitation of ginneries and other productive assets. Hullery and ginnery rehabilitation loans through the Cooperative Bank are now coming due. Foreclosure by a creditor does not appear at present to be a powerful enough threat to motivate self-restructuring within the cooperative unions however. There is only a minor effort at present to collect on the Cooperative Bank loans. More forceful collection measures would bankrupt many cooperatives, and require severe restructuring measures. Loans through Uganda Commercial Bank (UCB) were mostly completed in the late 1980s and, because of a five-year grace period, repayments have not yet begun. These UCB loans, together with other debts to the Lint Marketing Board, are resulting in interest charges which are accruing faster than current earnings are expected to grow, and could indeed induce change in management and structure of unions and primary societies if the lenders exercise their rights to require repayment.

3.51   Policy reforms in the coffee and cotton industries will encourage private sector companies to enter these markets and provide the entrenched cooperatives with competition. This will induce change in management and asset structure to make them more competitive, or succumb to competition. Assistance to the cooperative structure, if desired, should be undertaken while maintaining the same competitive conditions--a level playing field--for cooperatives and private sector enterprises.

3.52   Once the need for change or restructuring is accepted by the membership various support mechanisms can be put in place. The World Bank is funding an Enterprise Development Project (Cr 2315-UG) which provides technical assistance and a line of credit to support the process of industrial restructuring and rehabilitation. The cooperative system can make use of this facility. Also, UCA is able and willing to assist unions to restructure operations, and funding for such activities is available from projects funded by USAID and the Swedish International Development Agency (SIDA).

The Rural Financial System

Current Status

3.53   Uganda's once-well-developed formal financial system has deteriorated. Broad money holdings (savings and time deposits and cash) as a ratio of GDP, a generally accepted indicator of the level of development of a financial system, was 6.7 percent in 1988-89. 40/ This was the lowest ratio in Africa, after Zaire. 41/ Kenya, with a reasonably well-developed financial system had a financial depth ratio of about 38 percent in 1989. The level of financial intermediation in Uganda has been declining since the mid-1970s. In 1970 the above ratio was about 20 percent, and in 1974 about 30 percent, before the decline set in. The decline in the financial system has been due to two main factors: (a) the destruction in the value of loan portfolios, caused by the widespread economic and social disruption which took place between 1971 and 1986, and (b) the decimation of the capital of financial institutions, and of depositors' assets in these institutions, by the highly inflationary environment of the mid-and late 1980s-- when governmentally controlled lending rates, and deposit rates were highly negative in real terms. Faced with these events, foreign financial institutions retrenched into urban areas, and focused on trade-related and fee-generating financial services. Government-owned banks remained with the less and less profitable rural branch network (UCB has 190 branches, the Cooperative Bank 24 branches) and the poorly performing rural loan portfolio. Given the level of disintermediation, deposit mobilization shrank dramatically. Government-owned banks were left technically insolvent by the end of the 1980s decade. Term financing also devolved to the Government-run development finance institutions: the Uganda Development Bank, the East African Development Bank, the Development Finance Group in UCB, and the Development

---

40/   World Bank, Uganda, Financial Sector Review, 9099-UG, May 7, 1991, Vol. 2, p. 143.

41/   World Bank, World Development Report 1991, Oxford University Press, p. 228.

Finance Company of Uganda (DFCU). The development bank portfolio was also in poor shape, as a consequence of the poor performance of the industrial and agro-industrial sectors, leaving the development institutions also in a very weak financial position.

3.54   The rural financial system, the poor relation within the overall financial system, deteriorated as well. Deposits in rural branches declined. Lending from own resources also declined as business risk soared, and the returns to financial investments became negative. Because of inflation, resources moved rapidly from lenders to borrowers--via inflation-- particularly in the mid-1980s (fig. 24). Two kinds of credit are provided to agriculture: crop finance for the purchase of the major export crops (coffee, tea, and cotton) and production finance for on-farm investments in improved technology or working capital. Finance for agriculture as a share of monetary agricultural GDP is at about the same levels in 1989 and 1990 (4 to 8 percent) as it was in the mid-1960s (around 6 percent). With the decline in total lending however, agricultural credit has become a much larger share of total credit than it was prior to the disruptions of the 1970s and 1980s. In the mid 1960s agricultural credit was between 15 and 20 percent of total commercial bank credit outstanding. At the end of the 1980s the share of total credit going to agriculture varied between 30 and 60 percent. Of this, between 60 and 80 percent is marketing credit, provided to the cooperative unions, the Coffee Marketing Board Limited, and the Lint Marketing Board for the purchase of raw materials (fig. 9).

3.55   The only credit available in rural areas, outside of the crop finance, were occasional lines of credit funded by foreign donors. Two of these lines of credit are of particular interest: the Rural Farmers Credit Scheme, as an object lesson in directed small-farmer credit; and credit for reconstruction of rural agro-industries run by cooperative unions because lines of credit overhang the agroprocessing industries and constrain the financial viability of the unions.

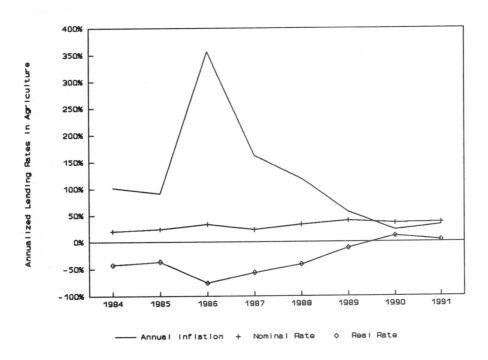

Figure 24   Annualized Lending Rates in Agriculture

3.56   The Rural Farmers Credit Scheme, administered by the UCB and financed from an African Development Bank loan, UCB's own resources, and grants from EEC and DANIDA was initiated in 1987.   It provided a line of credit to be disbursed directly to smallholder farmers in support of investment and working capital requirements for crop, livestock, or fishing activities. Some 23,000 loans were disbursed, valued at Ush2.9 billion. The fixed lending rate of 40 percent per annum resulted in a real rate of interest of about minus 18 percent per annum. Recovery rates were poor, about 65 percent. Program operating costs are estimated to be about 20 percent of loan value, so UCB was losing about 40 percent of portfolio value per annum on the operation, without taking into consideration bad-debt losses. Many of the investment goods were procured by UCB, and disbursed in kind to the farmers. Farmers both profited and lost from this scheme. Those that received funds at fixed nominal interest rates, received grants whose size increased with inflation. Due to the losses incurred by the financial institution, however, such lending has been sharply curtailed, and it is at present practically impossible to obtain direct finance for rural investment in smallholder farms. In this sense, farmers lost.

3.57   The other credit lines of interest were aimed at rehabilitating coffee hulleries, cotton ginneries, and tea factories affected by the depredations of the 1970s and early 1980s. Many of the loans were taken by cooperative unions. Repayment of these loans is now coming due, and some of the cooperative unions are facing cash flow problems because of this. The lines of credit were handled by the Development Finance Group of UCB, and the Cooperative Bank. Funds were provided by various donors, including IDA's Agricultural Rehabilitation Project (Cr 1328-UG through the UCB) and the African Development Bank (through the Cooperative Bank). Funding was provided to both private sector agroprocessors and cooperative unions. The cooperative unions, which have a monopoly on cotton ginning, absorbed all of the funds destined for the cotton sector. Cooperatives also took some of the loans provided for rehabilitation of coffee processing. IDA funds were onlent at the prevalent lending rate for the agricultural sector, with ten-year repayment periods and three years' grace. The lending rate was negative in real terms all through the 1980s, and has only now become positive. African Development Bank funds were onlent at a fixed nominal rate of 10.7 percent per annum, with principal carried also in nominal terms.   The recipients of loans in both programs have profited from the effects of the negative lending rates. However, those with loans from the Cooperative Bank have had practically all of their obligation canceled by inflation. About Ush2.4 billion are still held in loans to cooperative unions from the Cooperative Bank and the UCB.

3.58   The institutions involved in quasi-formal finance include savings and credit societies and nongovernmental organizations. While their overall impact is small, their experience in attempting different approaches to rural lending can be instructive in designing measures to extend the frontiers of the financial system. The essence of the NGO programs is the use of groups (often women's groups) to foster financial savings; reduce transaction costs associated with savings, lending, and supervision, and increase repayment incentives through joint liability and penalty arrangements. Such programs have high administrative costs--typically the administration and training cost is equal to the amount loaned--which limit their coverage and applicability.

3.59   Informal financial networks exist, but little formal study of them has been undertaken. These networks are understood to have three main forms: merchant and trader lending, group-based rotating savings and credit associations, and farmer-to-farmer loans. Merchant credit often operates in kind, with the trader or supplier financing the producer--or vice versa--and is the type of arrangement most easily linked into the formal financial system. Rotating savings and credit associations--believed to be very broadly used--are organized by groups of 25 to 50 members with some particular affinity (same village, same employer, same business). Every period funds are deposited with the group and every period these savings are allocated to one member of the group--by lot. Hybrids of these groups are also organized, with savings pooled for use on a group-determined project. Farmer-to-farmer lending supports productive investments, as well as consumption amongst the farmers in a given community. This practice, which existed during the mid-1960s, has been described in detail by D. Hunt.42/ It is not clear whether it continues in the early 1990s. In addition to the above-mentioned sources of informal finance, the Hunt study notes the presence of moneylenders in the Buganda area in the mid-1960s. Moneylenders, the other common source of informal finance in rural areas in other countries, did not appear to be present in the Lango area during this period.

A Proposal for Reform

3.60   The World Bank is working closely with the Government to address the problems underlying the financial system. Five major problems with the financial system were identified in a recent Bank study. 43/ These problems--and measures currently in place to address them-- are summarized below:

-     **Lack of confidence in the financial system** due to the uncertainties regarding the real economy, the foreign exchange regime, negative interest rates and inflation. This problem is gradually being resolved. Insecurity problems have been reduced to certain pockets in the North and Northeast. The foreign exchange regime has stabilized with the liberalization of the market. Inflation has been reduced to 30 to 40 percent per annum. Interest rates have been raised to positive real levels, with a concomitant increase in deposits. Rates are still administratively determined however.

-     **Lack of control of credit expansion by the Bank of Uganda** continues to be a problem, but is now associated mainly with the financing of the budget deficit. The expansion associated with the provision of crop finance for the purchase of the coffee crop is now provided by the commercial system, under arrangements agreed to under the Agricultural Sector Adjustment Credit (Cr 2190-UG).

-     **Internal and external constraints facing the Bank of Uganda** due to uncertainties in its mandate and institutional weaknesses. The Bank of Uganda is gradually being strengthened and many of the problems will be addressed in the context of the Financial Sector Adjustment Operation under preparation for IDA financing. The Bank of Uganda has had, and will continue to have, an important role in leading the financial system to increase domestic resource mobilization, to support export-finance, and to improve capacity to deal with rural credit issues. The Bank of Uganda will also play a key role in defining Government policy towards rural financial market development.

42/   D. Hunt, Credit for Agricultural Development: A Case Study of Uganda, East African Publishing House, Nairobi, 1975, p.248.

43/   World Bank, Uganda - Financial Sector Review, op. cit., Vol. I.

• **The high risk of financial instability arising out of solvency problems** at the two largest banks, the UCB and the Cooperative Bank. An increase in deposit rates has improved the position of the UCB recently, which when coupled with a process of portfolio review and an eventual capital injection will permit this bank to regain profitability. The Cooperative Bank receives assistance from the Swedish Cooperative Association, and is gradually being reformed. Its portfolio and management systems are in worse shape than those of UCB, however, and rehabilitation of the Cooperative Bank will require considerable institutional development efforts, along with capital injections. The restructuring of these two Government banks will be tackled under the Financial Sector Adjustment Operation.

• **The unsustainability of development-finance institutions** has still to be addressed. The low recovery rates and negative interest rates have had disastrous consequences on the banks' liquidity and solvency, and they have become little more than agencies for extending funds provided by donors. Term finance will be needed to sustain recent economic growth, once the excess capacity of existing capital investments has been utilized.

3.61   In addressing the question of rural financial market development, should anything more be done, over and above those steps noted above to improve the efficiency of the overall financial system?

3.62   One approach is put forward in a recent review of rural finance in Uganda. 44/ It advocates a "savings based" approach, utilizing the existing commercial financial system. The provision of financial savings services, through deposits of varying maturity and return, is by far the cheapest and simplest service a financial institution can provide. Commercial banks-- Government or private--should be encouraged to extend their networks into the rural areas, (clearly the more prosperous areas will receive priority) to capture rural savings through financial instruments. Once a bank-customer relationship is established, and a savings record built up, both sides are more willing to enter into a customer borrowing operation. Rural branches then should be encouraged to develop their own group of customers. This approach has been used successfully in Japan, the Republic of Korea, Taiwan-China, and--more recently--in the Dominican Republic and by the Bank Rakyat in Indonesia. 45/ Short-term loans are made at relatively high real interest rates--of perhaps 3 percent per month. Special incentives are provided for branch employees, based on loan recovery, deposit mobilization, and branch profitability. Minimalist lending procedures can reduce bank costs and improve recovery rates. Under this approach, individual loans are kept small, information requirements are limited, and disbursement is quick. In this way the bank can provide some of the characteristics of the informal sector lender. The loan is made on the basis of the relationship between the lender and borrower. Potential borrowers have to have a savings record. Loan repayment is required at frequent intervals. Loan rollovers and increases are contingent on prompt repayment, real rates of interest are kept high to ensure bank cost recovery, and staff are adequately remunerated. Loans can be

---

44/   Dale Adams, "Rural Finance in Uganda: Questions and New Options," attachment to Back to Office Report of August 8, 1991, from Ms. F. Aynur Sumer on the Preparation Mission for the Financial Sector Adjustment Operation.

45/   Jacob Yaron, Successful Rural Finance Institutions, AGRAP, World Bank, August 1991.

made through groups, but a bank should avoid the high costs associated with group formation and administration.

3.63   The process mentioned above improves intermediation, and may increase the availability of funds at the regional and village level. Funding available from a financial institution is provided to traders, cooperatives, and other intermediaries, as well as to producers of wealth. In this way farmers and other local entrepreneurs are reached, without a need for the bank to interact with each type of borrower. The very close financial, ownership, and labor-related relationships in the farming or village economy mean that providing financing to some key players in the local economy enhances liquidity and investment capacity in a much broader range of businesses.

3.64   The above-mentioned process takes time, as confidence and information is built up between banks and customers. Key preconditions for the successful evolution of a self-financed rural financial market include financially viable investment opportunities of low or moderate risk at the local and national levels--so that banks will be interested in intermediating between a rural deposit base, and high-return investments in other locations; positive real deposit and investment rates; and the exclusion of targeted, cheap, indifferently administered lines of credit. Such instruments diminish the system's ability to generate and sustain its own financing requirements.

3.65   In addition, a successful rural financial market requires the development of a "branch orientation" in the commercial financial system--banks, cooperatives, or other institutions--which emphasizes the development of a lending relationship, as well as a deposit-taking relationship with customers. Branch managers should be encouraged--within the bounds of prudence--to identify and encourage local business development. This development need not necessarily be smallholder-based. Business opportunities for larger-scale agricultural development should be reviewed and funded as well, within the ability of the bank to respond.

3.66   The other precondition is continued testing of innovative approaches to market-based rural lending and saving. These pilot approaches should combine group-based savings and lending schemes with crop marketing and production finance--while targeting programs to needy areas, the rural poor, and rural women--to use the methods of the "informal" finance network to create sustainable village-level financial contracts and organizations. Such community-based pilot schemes can interact more effectively with the informal network, make it more liquid, and link it more closely to commercial finance.

3.67   The development of an institution specialized in agricultural credit is not felt to be advisable now for four reasons--assuming that UCB and the Coop Bank continue to operate in rural areas. First, the strongest constraint to the development of competent rural financial institutions now in Uganda is the availability of skilled personnel. The rehabilitation of the Coop Bank, and the revitalization of UCB's rural operations will make impossible demands on the available staff even without the presence of an additional competitor.

3.68   Second, the development of such specialized organization would undercut the efforts of the more general approach advocated here. Third, an institution devoted exclusively to lending for agriculture would be exposed to all the production risks inherent in agriculture, the riskiest sector in the economy: production depends on unpredictable weather events, and prices fluctuate wildly, dropping sharply at harvest. More diversified organizations can sustain the risk of lending better than one specializing in the highest-risk enterprises.

3.69   Fourth, potential competition in the formal rural financial market exists already with Coop Bank and UCB. The contribution to coverage and intermediation efficiency of a new institution--unless it is extremely innovative and effective--would be marginal.

3.70   It is also true that the experience in Uganda and elsewhere in Africa with Government-owned, donor-funded, specialized term-lending financial institutions has not been satisfactory. In Uganda, the Uganda Development Bank and DFCU are facing recovery rates of 20 to 30 percent, and depend completely for survival on continued donor and Government support. Such organizations, in practically every case, end up providing funds on terms that are cheaper than those available on the financial market. Rather than addressing the capacity of the market to provide the new instruments, the specialized institutions--through the targeted and rationed lines of credit--channel available funds to targeted users, often chosen for reasons other than financial viability. These institutions do not remain financially viable, reducing their developmental impact to a one-time operation for the initial recipients of Governmental funds.

The Supply of Agricultural Inputs

3.71   As the agricultural economy becomes more sophisticated, additional reliance will be placed on purchased inputs.

Chemical Inputs, Implements and Machinery: Current Status

3.72   The agricultural market for fertilizers and plant protection chemicals is small, fragmented, and somewhat distorted. It is small in that the country's consumption of 2,000 to 2,500 tons of inorganic fertilizer nutrients is very low--for an estimated crop area of about 4 million hectares. The input market is fragmented--limited quantities of selected inputs are available in Kampala or at some district headquarters, but there is no price competition among regions. In fact, prices vary widely at different locations, sometimes by as much as 400 percent. The market is distorted because of the subsidized sale of some inputs by MAAIF and the pricing policies of donor-funded agricultural projects.

3.73   The private sector considers that the financial risks involved in importing, stocking, and selling agricultural inputs are too great to attract them into full-scale business. The risks relate to (a) the seasonal nature of demand for fertilizers and pesticides; (b) the long lead time required to import the goods (three to six months) after opening letters of credit, with the capital borrowed at high rates of interest (around 45 percent); and (c) continual heavy depreciation of the Ugandan shilling (in July, 1990 $1 was equal to 440 shillings; in June 1991 it was 700 shillings; and, in April 1992, 1,200 shillings). To break even and profit, a trader must be able to sell the inputs at prices nearly double the CIF cost to cover the interest costs and depreciation in the value of the shilling. As a consequence, barring some desperately needed agrochemicals and livestock drugs, which have an assured market despite high prices, most of the imports by the trade are against tenders floated by IDA or donor-funded projects or by MAAIF. The well-intentioned subsidized sale of imported inputs by MAAIF further undermines the confidence of traders in their ability to import and sell inputs at commercial prices. Fertilizer, probably brought in under a donor-funded project, can now be purchased commercially at Ush 120-200/kg depending on where in the country it is being sold. The landed price of urea in Kampala with no subsidies is on the order of Ush300-350/kg. At farmgate, the price is likely to be in the neighborhood of Ush 400/kg.

3.74 While the use of chemical inputs in agriculture is expected to continue to grow, the market is not expected to be commensurate with planted area, for example. Fertilizer use is predicted to continue to be used on high-value export--or import-substitute--crops, such as sugar, tea and tobacco. Growth in these exports will stimulate demand. It is not forseen, however, that much fertilizer will be used on subsistence crops, with the exception of hybrid maize. Fertilizer costs in Uganda are too high--if priced at market values--to justify use on crops other than those with the highest yield-response such as tea and hybrid maize. The dairy industry will generate demand for acaricides and medicines; continued growth in the use of these chemicals will depend on the viability of the dairy industry.

Chemical Inputs, Implements and Machinery: a Strategy for Reform

3.75 A strategy for developing a commercial input supply service is outlined below. To support this strategy, the Government should assist in the dissemination of precise information on imports, availability, and prices in different parts of the country, and share this information with all concerned. In addition, the Government should move to reduce market distortions caused by the distribution of inputs at below market prices, and foster a periodic dialogue with major consumers and suppliers of fertilizers, pesticides, and animal husbandry chemicals. The following action plan is recommended.

3.76 First, MAAIF should withdraw from the physical distribution and sale of agricultural inputs. Donated fertilizer should be made available at commercial prices ex Kampala to the private trade for sale to farmers. This withdrawal should be phased, to take into consideration the need to educate the trade on handling of highly toxic products, to ensure availability of strategic low volume high value products, and to assist with adjustment in industries built on the use of subsidized inputs. Eventually, however, Government should play only a regulatory role in the trade.

3.77 Second, as an interim measure, inputs provided from donor funds through agricultural projects, such as the IDA-funded Agriculture Development Project and the Southwest Agriculture Rehabilitation Project, should be sold by the Government in ways that will not distort the market and force out the private trade. Periodic regional auctions of available inputs to local traders would keep prices at market levels, put the goods into the regional market, and encourage the development of regional distribution networks.

3.78 Third, MAAIF should identify and promote the importing of those products which--consistent with agronomic requirements of various soils and crops--can provide the required nutrients at minimum cost to the country and the farmer. For instance--depending on the fertilizer product chosen for import--one kg of nitrogen can cost CIF Kampala US$0.60 in the form of urea, US$0.80 as ASN, US$0.90 as Ammonium Sulphate, or about US$1.00 as Calcium Ammonium Nitrate.

3.79 Fourth, to overcome the existing spatial discontinuities and high variability in retail prices from one location to another, the Government--through the NICU--should expand its program to disseminate input price and availability information. This will benefit consumers-- farmers--in the little-served, high-cost regions. The local business newspapers could be persuaded to carry weekly prices and volumes of key inputs by region. NICU could publish a newsletter with prices, volumes and trends, that would be available, at a fee, to the public.

3.80   Fifth, the Government should consider setting up a "procurement library", possibly run by NICU.   This library would provide information on different brands and world wide sources of supply for local dealers.   Users would pay a fee.   The information would be constantly maintained.

3.81   In the medium term, the Government strategy should be to continue to promote a liberalized market in agricultural inputs, by facilitating the availability of foreign exchange, eliminating subsidies on input use, barring Government agencies from competing unfairly in the inputs market, regulating the trade to prevent the use of environmentally damaging chemicals, and providing guidance on the most appropriate and cost-effective chemical inputs.   The Government also should explore the possibility of the viability of some domestic fertilizer production as well as domestic formulation of pesticides from imported active ingredients by the private sector.   In pursuing this strategy, training and trials are recommended.

3.82   Government should ensure MAAIF extension staff are trained in effective use of chemical inputs, marketing, environmental impact, and user safety, which will be passed on to farmers.   Training in these should also be provided to input supply dealers.   A program of trials should test the physical and financial viability of the use of agrochemicals--including fertilizers, herbicides, pesticides, acaricides, and antibiotics--as part of the nationwide agricultural research program.   And the Government should assess the feasibility of producing--or mixing--agrochemicals locally, including possibly phosphate fertilizer using Uganda's deposits.

Draft Power Use and Potential

3.83   Expansion in area cultivated has played a major role as a source of agricultural growth during the 1980s.   In certain areas of the country with underutilized areas of good potential agricultural land, expansion in area cultivated will continue to be a vital source of growth.   The increased use of draft power, both for cultivation and transport, and the improvements in draft power efficiency will play a major role in supporting this expansion.

3.84   Until the early 1970s the use of oxen for basic land preparation grew rapidly in parts of the Eastern Region where the demands of an annual cash crop (cotton), the availability of suitable cattle, the nature of the soil, vegetation and land conformation combined to make this an attractive and profitable practice.   Ox ploughing spread more slowly into the more heavily wooded areas of Lango and Acholi where the vegetation was less suited to mechanical cultivation. Ox ploughing was never adopted in those areas in which perennial crops dominated the farming system, where the natural vegetation was a dense grass sward or where tse-tse fly presented a challenge to cattle.

3.85   Ox power in Uganda to date has meant ox ploughing, unlike other parts of Africa in which weeding, transport and thrashing of grain can involve large numbers of working animals.   Even where primary cultivation was done entirely by oxen (Teso and parts of Lira) there was an insignificant use of weeders (maximum 250 ha in mid 1960s) or of ox carts.

3.86   In the early 1960s government policy deliberately focussed on tractors rather than oxen as the primary source of mechanical power.   The disturbances of recent years have not encouraged a resurgence of activity in this field.   The MAAIF does not have a separate department dealing with this topic at the national level, although there is a regional officer at the research station at Serere, and a small research unit on Agricultural Mechanisation at Bukalasa Agricultural College.   From the available information it would appear that:

- ox ploughing in its traditional heartland has declined dramatically because of the loss of animals from cattle raiding and the fear that introducing fresh stock will precipitate further raids;

- there has been an increase in ox plough use in Tororo district, where cattle loss has been less serious and where ox ploughs were supplied by donor funded projects;

- there has been an increase in ox ploughing in Apach and Karamoja;

- there has been no spread of ox cultivation in the banana/coffee zone, the hilly southwest nor the main tse-tse belt of Bunyoro; and

- there has been no significant uptake of the use of oxen for transport in any area.

3.87   In the absence of any concrete data it is not possible to undertake an analysis of the attractiveness of ox power in various parts of the country.   The areas most deserving of immediate attention for promoting ox cultivation are:

- those bordering on the districts of Teso and Lango (which used oxen intensively in the past) in which animals are still readily available and where there are individuals familiar with working oxen;

- the drier areas of Buganda (e.g. Mawogola, Gomba and Nakasongola) where zebu cattle are available and where annual cropping is widespread; and

- those parts of Bunyoro and West Nile which are relatively free of the tse-tse, have been cleared of forest and are limited by labour shortages from increasing the area under cultivation.

3.88   Ox drawn transport should be feasible in all those areas detailed above, as well as:

- areas where draught animals are available and bulky crops (e.g. bananas) are a major source of cash. This would include Buganda and parts of Ankole as well as the maize growing areas of Northern Bunyoro.

3.89   Factors which induce the use of ox power for agriculture and related activities should be the topic of further study to guide the production of appropriate implements and prior to the initiation of widespread promotional efforts. It appears at present that the main factors which will determine adoption are:

- the availability of suitable working animals. There is little experience of working Ankole long horn cattle and their suitability for ploughing as opposed to carting needs further investigation;

- the familiarity of the local populace with cattle and the social acceptability of being seen working oxen;

- the nature of the natural vegetation. This involves tree density, grass density and the growth habit of the dominant weeds; and

- the comparative costs of hand labour and ox-power, and bicycle and motor transport and ox carts.

3.90   In a number of countries oxen are more widely used for transport than for cultivation. The high level of motor vehicle ownership in Uganda in the past (the highest in Africa at Independence) has provided rural people with access to hired transport for their produce. There are now indications that the availability of motorised transport has not kept pace with population growth. Further investigations should be made into the comparative costs and acceptability of ox drawn carts and hired pick-ups. Ox carts are currently available (from donor funded projects) at a subsidized price of about US$ 130. This compares with $ 800 currently payed by farmers in Malawi. Despite the heavy subsidy there has been little interest in these ox carts. The reasons for this need to be thoroughly understood. Bicycles have also become a major means of transport in rural areas and an analysis of relative costs, speed and comparative acceptability of bicycles and ox carts should precede widespread campaigns to popularise ox drawn transport.

Rural Infrastructure

3.91   An important determinant of growth in agriculture is the cost of transport to market and the ease of access to price and volume information for both produce and inputs. Both are public goods in nature and reasonable areas for Government investment.

3.92   The road network consists of some 7,500 km of trunk roads and some 21,200 km of feeder roads. Rural feeder roads are themselves divided into four subcategories according to traffic levels and surface quality. In the course of the country's economic rehabilitation program, the paved trunk network has been substantially renewed, with very positive effects on rural development. Work continues on the main gravel roads. Rural feeder roads, however, remain in a state of disrepair, with an estimated 25 percent impassable in the rainy season. An estimated 46 percent of the entire network requires full rehabilitation, 33 percent requires only spot improvements to guarantee all weather access, and 21 percent requires culvert and drainage repairs. 46/   About 10 percent of the total network would require improvement every year on a continuing maintenance basis. If continued support to agricultural growth is to be provided, the next phase of infrastructure rehabilitation should pay serious attention to the rehabilitation of rural feeder roads.

3.93   Maintenance of these roads is the responsibility of the Works Departments of the District Administrations. These departments are chronically short of funds, equipment and trained personnel. Dependent in part on local revenue raising capacity, many districts will find it extremely difficult to finance the necessary civil works program. Benefits from these expenditure programs, and hence increases in the tax base, will only materialize in five to ten years time. While the increase in the revenue base can eventually be used for a district-based road

---

46/   Government of Uganda, Ministry of Local Government, "Strategy for Rural Feeder Roads Rehabilitation and Maintenance", March 1992, page 32

maintenance program, there is a strong argument for matching finance from the central government to kickstart this key aspect of rural development.

3.94   A strategy has been formulated to respond to these concerns. 47/ The approach put forward is to have the Ministry of Local Government (MOLG) undertake the first time rehabilitation works, and bring rural road conditions up to par, prior to handing them over to the districts for maintenance. The MOLG would also strengthen the rural road maintenance capability of District Level Works Departments so that eventually they can be entrusted with full responsibility for this task. The cost of a five year rural roads program, which would accomplish the bulk of the required rehabilitation and institutional strengthening, is estimated at US$ 171 million. While many donors have committed funding for this program a gap still remains.

3.95   In addition to the rural road network, interactions between producers and traders would be facilitated by measures which increase access to information on price and availability of products, improve competition at point of sale, and reduce transactions costs. Such measures are public goods, with limited possibilities for cost recovery. They are also tasks best undertaken by District Governments. As with the rural roads program, funding for the initial design and construction phase would have to come from the central budget, probably through MOLG, with maintenance and fee collection then becoming the responsibility of District Governments. The phased development of market infrastructure and information services at the district and county level should be included in the Public Investment Program, and become part of the Development Budget.

47/   Ibid.

IV. SOURCES OF GROWTH

Market Prospects for Uganda's Produce

Traditional International Markets and Prospects

4.1   Uganda competes with the rest of sub-Saharan Africa in its traditional export markets. It is very reliant on coffee, with tea, cotton, tobacco and cocoa also potentially important. These five commodities represented 21 percent of all sub-Saharan exports between 1984 and 1986, and 71 percent of agricultural exports. These five commodities account for 90 to 98 percent of Uganda's total exports. A recent World Bank study of the prospects for agricultural exports from sub-Saharan Africa provides a broad perspective on the market situation, and arrives at conclusions for sub-Saharan Africa that are equally valid for Uganda. 48/

4.2   Whereas world trade in food and agricultural raw materials increased at rates of 2.5 and 0.07 percent, per annum respectively, in real terms between 1970 and 1985, African exports of food declined at minus 2.5 percent per annum, and exports of agricultural raw materials declined at minus 4.0 percent during this period. As a result, Africa's share of food exports declined by 50 percent. Africa's market share in food and raw materials exports was absorbed by the rapidly growing agricultural exports of Southeast Asia.

4.3   The major reason for the decline in Africa's share of world markets in agricultural commodities is a failure to react competitively to meet growing world demand. Four factors explain Africa's performance: real exchange-rate movements, producer pricing policies, technological developments, and declining marginal export revenue.

4.4   Uganda's real effective exchange rate--which, if it increases, reflects an overvaluation of the official exchange rate--followed the trend for sub-Saharan Africa. The real effective exchange rate increased by more than 330 percent between 1977 and 1980 reflecting extreme overvaluation, before declining during the 1980s.

4.5   Real producer price levels have been allowed to decline in many African countries, whereas they increased in competing countries in Asia and Latin America. This occurred in Uganda as well (see below). Technological improvements have increased yields in coffee and cotton in competing countries. Uganda's coffee and cotton yields have remained static for twenty five years.

4.6   For some countries, whose exports are a sizable proportion of world trade in a commodity--such as Cote d'Ivoire with 30 percent of the world cocoa market, or Kenya with 15 percent of the black tea market--an increase in exports can reduce the unit price. Given the low price elasticities of demand for these commodities, the increase in export volumes will result in a less-than-proportional increase in revenues. While it may still be worthwhile to expand exports, careful consideration has to be given to production is still profitable at the reduced price.

4.7   Uganda does not face such a situation. Its contribution to world trade in Robusta coffee, the market where Uganda's share is largest, is about 15 percent. There is a fair degree of

---

48/   Takamasa Akiyama, and Don Larson, <u>Recent Trends and Prospects for Commodity Exports in Sub Saharan Africa</u>, PPR Working Paper WPS 348, December 1989.

substitution, however, in the medium term between the Robusta and the much-larger Arabica market. Uganda is estimated to have an effective share of about 7 percent of the world coffee market, a share well below levels that can cause a "marginal-revenue" effect. The country could double its coffee exports to perhaps 5 million bags, without significantly effecting medium-term international prices for Robusta coffee (see below).

4.8   The international market for primary commodities has softened recently due to the decline in demand--and an increase in primary commodity exports--from the former U.S.S.R., and the effect of recession on the countries of the Organization for Economic Co-operation and Development (OECD). In recent years, the price index for agricultural commodities has declined gradually--9 percent in the two years 1989 to 1991. This trend is expected to continue until the mid-1990s, when the OECD countries are expected to climb out of the recession.

Regional Markets

4.9   Uganda has a lopsided relationship with regional markets. Imports from neighboring countries since 1970--apart from the US$50 to $70 million a year of fuel brought in through Kenya--have averaged between 20 and 25 percent of total imports (fig. 25). Exports to the region, when the East African Community arrangements were still in place, were on the order of 15 percent of exports. Uganda's regional merchandise trade in the late 1960s and early 1970s was balanced. Uganda's main trading partner in the region is Kenya. Since the early 1970s. however, regional imports have remained at about the same level of total imports, but the exports have dwindled to less than 10 percent of the total. An increase in this market should be sought in the context of negotiations on the East African Preferential Trade Area.

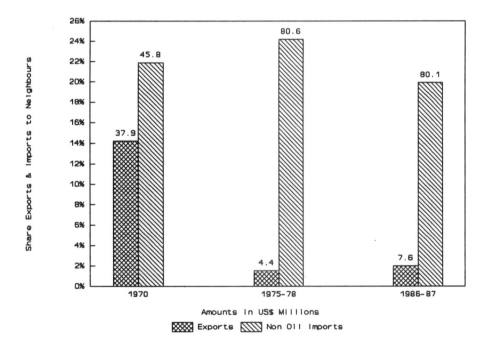

Figure 25   Shares of Exports and Non Oil Imports Exchanged With Neighbouring Countries

4.10   **Potential for Export Growth.** The regional market in food provides a reasonably attractive location for Uganda's produce, especially food. Uganda's climate is consistently good for agricultural production and varies little.   Neighboring countries, due to more variable climates, higher population density, or political instability, are likely to have food shortages which Uganda is well-placed to respond to. This market is limited, however, by the limited foreign exchange of these trading partners, the rapid response required to cover food shortfalls--usually less than a growing season--and the short-lived market opportunities, which can disappear with a good harvest in the importing country.

4.11   **Strategic Regional Export Reserve.** Because each of Uganda's neighbors could suffer a drought and food shortage in a given year--and because a rapid response would be needed--there may be a rationale for Uganda to hold a strategic regional food reserve against such an eventuality. The reserve would have to be profitable over the medium term. Much detailed analysis on such points as the likelihood of crop failure in neighboring countries, storage capabilities for different foods, and costs of operations and finance would be required to evaluate whether such a venture would make money. Perhaps funding to test a pilot export reserve could be obtained from relief-oriented donor agencies such as the World Food Program. In addition, cooperation could be sought from donor relief agencies, so that funding for relief supplies, which is normally used for procurement from OECD countries, could be channeled into purchases from local food producers--Uganda).   MAAIF has developed preliminary plans to food storage infrastructure at the border, to facilitate border trade in these commodities.

4.12   The potential stability and growth of maize and bean exports is tied to exports to the East African Protected Trade Area countries. In the medium term, a wider range of spices and essential oils could be developed to supply the needs of these countries than is currently met by imports. Kenya and Tanzania are looking at the development of a range of spices, spice seeds, and essential oils to supply local needs and replace imports, but Uganda with its range of climates and its land availability could become a highly competitive supplier to both countries and to other countries of the region. Consumption of these products could grow substantially. There is a substantial soap-making capacity in the region, and a hence a market for a number of essential oils widely used in scenting soaps and allied products.

Domestic Markets

4.13   The domestic food market buys most of Uganda's agricultural produce. More than 90 percent of agricultural output is consumed domestically. National accounts estimates indicate that about 57 percent of agricultural GDP in 1990 was produced and consumed on the farm, and did not enter the monetary economy. This is food--crops, livestock or fish--except for a small portion of forestry products. In addition, about 38 percent of agricultural production, sold in the monetized economy, is food for urban areas. Export crop production is only 4 percent of the value of total agricultural output, and monetized forest products about 1 percent.

4.14   Preliminary estimates have been made for the growth in demand for food. The income elasticity of demand for food, in a poor country such as Uganda, can be expected to be between 0.95 and 1.05. 49/ Household expenditure data from the 1988-89 survey would lead

---

49/   Harold Alderman, <u>The Effect of Food Price and Income Changes to the Acquisition of Food by Low Income Households</u>, IFPRI, Washington, D.C., May 1986, p. 38.

to the lower estimate. A recent study in Rwanda estimated this elasticity at 0.96. 50/
Assuming the income elasticity of demand for all food is 0.95, a projected population growth rate
of about 3.15 percent, 51/ a per capita annual income growth rate of 1.5 percent (the trend
since 1986), and constant relative prices, the demand for food is expected to grow at 4 to 5
percent per annum. This is also the rate at which supply would have to grow, to keep relative
prices constant. With no growth in per capita income, food crop volume would still have to grow
at 3.1 percent per annum, to keep up with the increases in demand due to population increase.
To put this in perspective, the annual increase in food crop production between 1981 and 1990
has averaged 3.3 percent. Since 1986, growth in food crop production has been 5.9 percent per
annum. The Rwanda study and the Uganda Household Budget Survey support the hypothesis that
the income elasticity of demand for livestock products is much higher, well above 1 and perhaps
as high as 3. As incomes improve, the demand for livestock products likely will increase
significantly. Conversely, the income elasticity of demand for bananas, cassava, and other root
crops--the basis of the Ugandan diet--is likely to be in the 0.5 range. Growth in income should
see a shift in types of food demanded.

4.15   The above estimates are rough, and will have to be refined to compare rural with
urban areas in further investigations. They do imply, however, that there will be continued
demand for agricultural output at growth rates which, while below the 5 to 6 percent rates
achieved since 1986, are still above long-term average growth rates for the country. Moreover,
if the food supply does not grow at this rate, on average, severe shortages, price increases, and
reductions in nutritional levels will result.

4.16   Domestic demand for agricultural output also includes raw materials required by
domestic industries producing for local consumption. The local demand for tobacco is about half
of total output, and can affect the quantities available for export. The domestic demand for cotton
by local textile mills could potentially be significant. The textile industry has been operating at
15 to 20 percent of installed capacity and consuming about 10,000 bales of lint cotton per year.
52/ Growth in the domestic textile industry could make a large claim on domestic cotton
output, now running on the order of 40,000 to 50,000 bales of lint per year. If lint production
were to recover, however, to its prior level of 450,000 bales per annum, then the share of total
output required by the local cotton industry would fall slightly to less than 20 percent.

Diversification and Expansion of Exports

4.17   This section specifies programs recommended to enable each main export crop to
overcome domestic production constraints and increase domestic profitability, international
competitiveness, and export volume. Following a brief review of the theoretical competitiveness
of Uganda's exports and a quick survey of potential supply response from Uganda's agricultural
sector, the coffee, cotton and tea subsectors are reviewed in detail. Current production

---

50/   Joachim von Braun, Hartwig de Haen, and Juergen Blanken, Commercialization of Agriculture under
             Population Pressure: Effects on Production, Consumption, and Nutrition in Rwanda, IFPRI, Research Report
             85, 1991, p.66.

51/   Shaw, op. cit., table 2.

52/   MPED, Background to the Budget 1991/92, June 1991, table 60.

constraints and the market for each crop are analyzed in order to provide justification for the measures proposed to induce growth with equity.

Comparative Advantage and Competitiveness

4.18   A recent study identifies crops that have the greatest potential profitability under a liberalized export regime. 53/ Using Domestic Resource Cost analysis, 54/ the study develops an index of theoretical comparative advantage and profitability for different crops. Using this type of analysis, at current economic values, all of Uganda's traditional export crops have a DRC ratio of less than one, and are hence theoretically competitive (fig. 26). Using this gauge, Robusta is less competitive than Arabica coffee, and tea is more competitive than cotton. Also, under this economic analysis, maize, groundnuts, soybeans, and rice cannot compete effectively in the international market, although there may be regional market opportunities. Products such as hides and skins, cardamom, cashew nuts, sesame, and other nontraditional exports appear to have export potential, at economic values.

4.19   Family labor costs--the largest production input--are evaluated, in the economic analysis, in terms of their opportunity cost which is staple food production. These "shadow" wages are 20 to 30 percent above the going--financial--wage at the time of the analysis (January 1990). Production and processing efficiencies are those which existed at the time of the analysis. Since yields and processing efficiencies were comparatively low, especially for tea and cotton, there is substantial room for improving competitiveness through better processing efficiency.

4.20   The financial analysis was less optimistic--until the recent decision to apply the bureau rate of exchange to coffee exports. At current financial prices (and the bureau exchange rate) robusta coffee, the least competitive of the traditional exports, becomes competitive, and local factors of production receive their "market-value" returns. The conclusions on other products do not vary from the economic analysis.

4.21   The conclusions of this analysis are twofold: the traditional export crops continue to be competitive in the international market, at nondistorted prices and exchange rates, and other agricultural products could be even more competitive than the traditional crops.

Supply Response for Agriculture

4.22   Growth rates for the agricultural sector in sub-Saharan Africa are low, and have averaged 2 percent per annum over 1980-89. 55/ The output response to changes in the real aggregate producer price for agricultural products is not high in Africa. A survey by the

53/   Bank of Uganda, Agricultural Secretariat, "Comparative Advantage and Competitiveness of Uganda's Agricultural Exports," Kampala, January 1990.

54/   Domestic resource cost analysis compares the net returns to domestic factors of production valued in foreign exchange--(after the cost of imports has been deducted--to their domestic "scarcity value." The DRC ratio is the scarcity value of domestic factors of production divided by the foreign returns to these factors--both in domestic prices. The ratio's size depends on the exchange rate used. The analysis discussed above was done used "economic" prices and exchange rates, with distortions removed, to establish a benchmark. The lower the DRC ratio, the more competitive a country's exports. A DRC ratio of one or less means that--at the official exchange rate--the product can compete effectively on the world market.

55/   World Bank, World Development Report 1990, table 2, page 181.

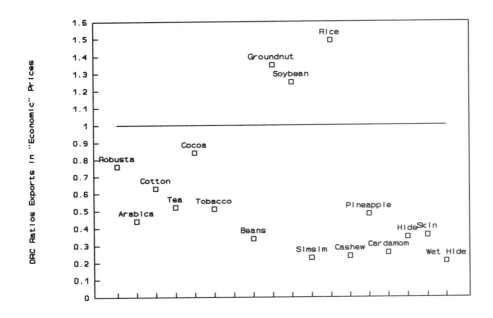

Figure 26   Domestic Resource Cost Ratios, Selected Commodities, 1990

International Monetary Fund showed that, on average in more than nine countries between 1963 and 1981, a rise of 10 percent in the real farmgate price index elicited an increase of 1.2 percent in output. 56/ The figure for Uganda was even lower, with a 10 percent increase in the farmgate price index producing a 0.5 percent increase in output. This estimate includes years of disruption and civil war, so the response is likely to be higher at present.

4.23   The response from individual crops to changes in relative output prices is much higher than for the sector, as farmers can switch into the more profitable commodities. The results of the above-mentioned study show that among traditional African export crops, coffee has the highest elasticity of supply to price changes. Data for smallholders in Kenya indicate a short-term (first-year) elasticity of 0.64, and a long-term elasticity--two or more years--of about 1.5. Thus, over two years, a 10 percent increase in the producer price of coffee will increase output by 15 percent. A price elasticity of supply of more than one implies that it could be possible to increase tax revenue from coffee exports, by reducing taxation levels. But price changes are only a first step in eliciting a supply response from the agricultural sector, and the level of the eventual response depends on the efficiency with which all the ancillary productive inputs and services are provided.

4.24   Estimates of the response in the Ugandan cotton sector to price changes show it to be significantly less elastic than coffee. A study in 1969 estimated the cotton supply elasticity (both

---

56/   Marian E. Bond, <u>Agricultural Responses to Prices in Sub-Saharan African Countries</u>, IMF Staff Papers, Vol. 30, Dec. 1983, 703-26.

short and long-term) at 0.25 in 1922-38 for Uganda. The estimates were the lowest of all the cotton-producing countries in Africa. The response in the Buganda area was much higher than the country average, at around 0.70, both short and long-term, for the same period.

Crop Returns

4.25   Every six months, the Agricultural Secretariat in the Bank of Uganda surveys farmgate production costs, input quantities, and output prices, and evaluates gross margins and smallholder production incentives for Uganda's main crops (fig. 27). Domestic prices are converted to dollars at the bureau rate of Ush 1,070 to the dollar, to facilitate international comparisons.

4.26   The Secretariat's most recent findings are that the financial returns to robusta production, per labor day--or any other measure--are low, well below matoke (banana). At US$0.32 per day, returns to coffee production do not even pay the market daily wage, which was Ush545 (US$0.51) at the time. The returns to greenleaf tea production are not much better than for coffee, and are well below returns to food production.

4.27   In addition, cotton looks attractive, when weighed against maize, beans, and cassava, which are its main competitors. Millet, a complementary crop, also has good returns. Rice, tobacco, groundnuts, and soybeans look good on paper, but a series of infrastructural and husbandry problems restrict their cultivation to relatively small areas.

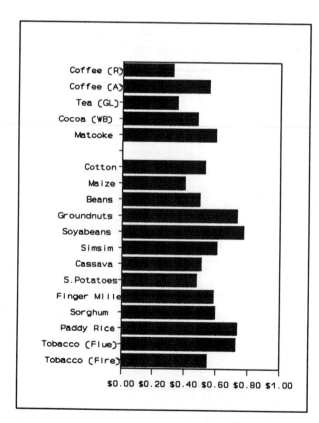

Figure 27   Returns per Labor Day, 1991 (in US$)

4.28   The returns to food crop production fall on or around the going wage of US$ 0.51 per day. The weighted average return--with weights allocated according to shares of total food area--would be very close to the wage. This indicates a certain coherence between the food market, the labor market, and the returns from alternatives to food production (which most of the laborers have).

Coffee

4.29   The coffee industry is based entirely on smallholder production. Robusta accounts for 94 percent of output and Arabica 6 percent. Robusta is traditionally dry processed. The small Arabica output is classified as secondary African mild, due to its poor quality and limited availability. Precise statistics on area cultivated are not available. The area under production appears to have been effectively reduced, mainly by the stumping of the coffee trees and intercropping with more lucrative banana and annual food crops. A realistic estimate for the total area currently under coffee is 272,000 hectares, with robusta at 250,000 ha and Arabica at 22,000. Yields have been low and quality declining for robusta and Arabica over the past fifteen years. Output reached a peak of 213,000 tons in 1972 (195,000 tons robusta and 18,000 tons Arabica), fell sharply in the late 1970s and early 1980s and has still not regained its former high levels (fig. 28).

4.30   **Production Constraints.** The soil, rainfall, and climate are very favorable for robusta. Actual robusta yields do not exceed 600 kg/ha clean coffee, which are 75 to 80 percent of yield levels that should be expected with low input techniques. Arabica yields have remained

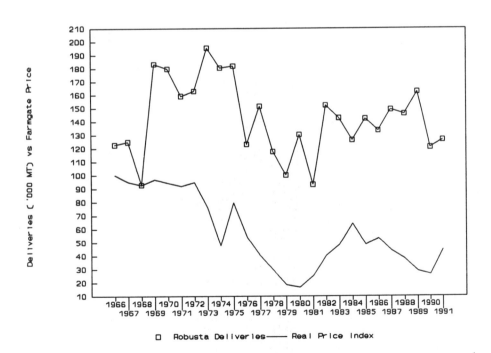

Figure 28   Robusta Deliveries and the Real Farmgate Price Index, 1966-91

at around 450 kg/ha clean coffee, 60 to 75 percent of reasonable yields under smallholder conditions. Some of the reasons for these returns include aging robusta trees, a lack of new robusta planting material, competition from other crops, poor field practices, declining robusta quality, and fungus diseases in Arabica.

4.31   The old Nganda varieties, accounting for about 40 percent of planted coffee are estimated to be 50 to 60 years old while the erecta types planted in the 1950s and 1960s are estimated to be 30 to 35 years old. Under good standards of management the 30-35 year old coffee would still be in healthy bearing condition. But trees that have been subjected to poor pruning, lack regular clean weeding, and are subject to couch grass invasion have aged prematurely.

4.32   Most robusta now in production originated from seed propagation and is hence extremely heterogeneous in yield potential. Six high-yielding clones have been available since the mid 1970s but the output from the twenty eight existing nurseries has been small. Up to 1990--before the start of MAAIF's Farming Systems Support Project, supported by the European Economic Community--the small amount of replacement and infilling was mainly from seed. At the same time, due to low returns from coffee, farmers have devoted more effort to bananas, beans, and vegetable crops which--on most farms--are intercropped with the coffee. Hence although weeding of the interplanted crop has helped to keep the coffee clean weeded, the annual pruning and de-suckering is poorly done. Cycle conversion is too long (more than five years). No fertilizing is done, except by progressive farmers, some of whom use coffee husk.

4.33   Three factors are responsible for the decline in robusta quality: decreasing bean size from aging trees, aggravated--in some cases-- by poor husbandry; the harvesting of much of the crop while underripe, which requires less labor; and the poor standards of drying. At present most farmers dry the kiboko (dried Robusta cherry) on the bare ground where it is subject to rewetting, mould, and rot. This, along with insect damage, leads to the formation of "black beans."

4.34   All existing varieties of Arabica, particularly SL varieties --70 percent of total planting--are susceptible to leaf rust (at lower altitudes) and Coffee Berry Disease (at higher altitudes) leading to severe annual crop loss. Virtually no sprays for leaf rust are done.

4.35   **Production Incentives.** Coffee has played such a large role in Uganda's economic development, that its industry has been under tight governmental control since the colonial era. The passage of the Coffee Marketing Act in 1969 established the Coffee Marketing Board with monopoly control over coffee exports. The declines in export value and volume noted previously have led the Government to liberalize the industry. The Government has recently taken bold steps to increase the financial incentives for coffee exports (see below). The first and most difficult stage in restructuring the coffee processing industry and coffee pricing and taxation policy--initiated in 1990 with assistance from the IDA--funded Agricultural Sector Adjustment Operation (Cr 2019-UG)--has now practically been completed. A proposal for a second stage of liberalization and stimulation of production will be put forward below.

4.36   Farmgate prices for kiboko and Arabica parchment (washed Arabica) have been established by Government since the colonial period. The farmgate price of coffee has been dropping in real terms--as measured by the Low Income Consumer Price Index, the most appropriate indicator of consumption expenditure for rural Uganda--since 1972, the start of the

Amin years. The price reached its lowest point in 1980 with the fall of Amin. Under the structural adjustment efforts of the early 1980s the farmgate price for coffee gradually rose to 64 percent of its 1970 value in 1984. Deliveries to the Coffee Marketing Board responded. Since that year, however, the real farmgate price of coffee has been allowed to decline, until a policy reversal in 1991. Real farmgate coffee prices are now 45 percent of 1970 levels. Given the weakness in international markets, it will be difficult for real farmgate coffee prices to regain their former value in the medium term.

4.37   Contrary to the trend in farmgate prices, international prices were at or above real 1970 prices in eleven of the eleven years to 1986. Uganda's export volume bear little relationship to the international price of coffee (fig. 29). Exports declined during the late 1970s while the price remained high in real terms. Substantial income-earning opportunities were lost by having the domestic market disconnected from international incentives. Since 1986, international prices have declined every year, and in 1991 were at 32 percent of the 1970 price in real terms, (fig. 29). Farmgate prices were set in nominal terms in domestic currency by Government. Coffee prices were observed by the cooperative unions, who acted as buyers and hullers for the Coffee Marketing Board. The price was supposed to permit smallholders to cover their costs of production, but ended up being arbitrarily adjusted, or not, as short-term macroeconomic circumstances dictated. The nonadjustment of the nominal farmgate price, in an environment of 150 to 300 percent annual inflation, starting in 1986, resulted in a serious loss of real value. The farmer's share of the export price--at the official rate of between 30 and 50 percent is low by world standards (fig. 30).

4.38   The coffee industry is now riding a razor's edge of profitability. Gone are the days when large rents were available between production and processing costs and export receipts. A crop budget analysis in September 1991 indicates that at clean coffee yields of 400 kg/ha or more, the producer price for robusta established in July 1991 of Ush210/Kg of kiboko roughly equaled the marginal costs of production--which are about half the average costs of production. A price any lower than this would seriously hurt production. Prices higher than this are needed to provide incentives for investment in renewing the stock of coffee trees.

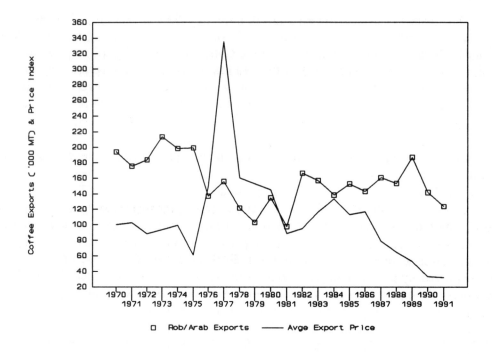

Figure 29 Coffee Exports in Thousands of Tons, and Real Index of Export Prices, 1970-91

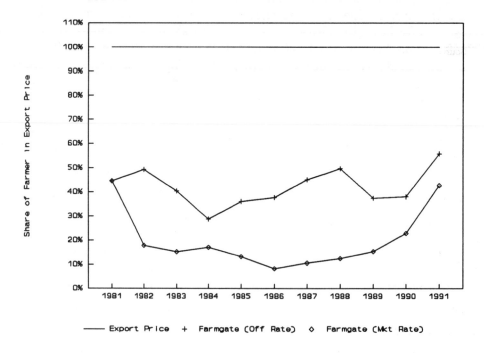

Figure 30 Farmgate Robusta Coffee Price as Proportion of International Price, at Official and Market Exchange Rates, 1981-90

4.39 The effects of the sector restructuring program, and the structural adjustment program on the coffee industry can be seen in 1991. Farmers' shares of the international price have increased rapidly--to almost 60 percent at the official rate--due to the upward adjustment of the farmgate price, and the reduction in the difference between the market and official exchange rates.

4.40 The final step in the liberalization process was taken in March 1992, when coffee exporters were allowed to convert their earnings at the market rate of exchange, and the determination of the farmgate price of coffee was left to the market, with Government continuing to provide an indicative minimum price.

4.41 **The Processing Industry.** Hulling and primary processing are done by cooperative unions and private sector processors prior to delivery to the Coffee Marketing Board Limited (CMBL). The share of the cooperative unions in this activity has declined in recent years, from 58 percent in 1983-84 to 23 percent in 1989-90. In addition to farmgate prices, prior to 1991, the Government also established processing and marketing margins in the coffee industry. These margins were set at or above average processing costs, and had grown to comfortable levels by 1990 (table 12).

Table 12: Coffee Processing Costs for, Milling and Bagging and Transport (1990 Prices)	
Details	US$/Ton
Kenya (milling, grading, bagging - Arabica)	41
Costa Rica (milling, grading, bagging - Arabica)	66
Uganda (transport, hulling, bagging - robusta)	126

Source: Agricultural Secretariat, CMB, MCIC.

4.42 As a result there has been over investment in hulling capacity. The figures for the 1988-89 crop year indicate that there are now more than 300 hullery factories and nearly 600 huller machines. On the assumption that annual capacity per huller working one shift for 200 days is 800 tons of rough hulled coffee, the country has a primary processing capacity of about 450,000 tons, and hulleries are working at about 35 percent capacity (table 13).

Table 13 : Hullery Output and Capacity Utilization - 1988-89			
Zone	Factories	Hullers	Capacity Utilization
Central Zone	244	463	35%
Western Zone	49	70	34%
Eastern Zone	14	45	44%
National Total	307	578	35%

Source: APC Report No 2, Coffee Marketing and Organization, August 1990.

4.43 Uganda can significantly increase its competitiveness by improving the efficiency of its processing industry, and lowering transport and marketing related costs. Comparisons with

Costa Rica and Kenya indicate Uganda has significantly higher costs for all aspects of processing and marketing. Processing and marketing charges for the higher-valued Arabica in Costa Rica total US$300 per ton and, in Kenya, US$176 per ton. Processing and marketing costs, for Uganda's robusta total US$448 per ton, of which only US$77 represents transport costs to the coast. Uganda has been receiving only US$800 to US$900 per ton for robusta which declined to US$ 700 per ton in February 1992. This leaves little room for the producer. The elimination of Government-set processing margins and the abrogation of the CMB's monopoly on exports in July 1991 has opened the way for increased competition amongst processors and exporters of coffee. A shakedown in the coffee processing industry is under way, and it appears that the cooperative societies and unions are suffering in the competition.

4.44   **Competition Among Exporters.** In 1990, in measures which IDA supported under the Agricultural Sector Adjustment Operation (Cr 2190 UG), the Government agreed to permit competition with the CMB in the coffee export market. The four largest cooperative unions then entered the trade. Government agreed in addition to separate CMB's regulatory functions from its trading activities. In 1991, the Coffee Act was repealed and the CMB was constituted as a private company, Coffee Marketing Board Limited, wholly owned by Government at present, but with the intention to broaden ownership soon. A Coffee Development Authority (UCDA) was established in 1991 to regulate the coffee trade and promote sector development of the sector. Eight private sector firms were licensed to compete with CMBL and six cooperative unions in the export trade.

4.45   **The Export Tax.** The last link in the chain of governmental control was the export tax. Until 1991, with all the margins fixed by Government, the difference between the export receipts and the Government-set price of exports in local currency remained with the Government. The marginal tax rate was 100 percent. Under the system installed with the budget speech of July 2, 1991, coffee exports paid tax only if the realized price exceeded a threshold, set initially at US$ 1.05/kg for both Arabica and robusta. Above the threshold, robusta exports paid 5 percent of the total price, and Arabica exports, 20 percent. The preestablished margins for coffee processors and exporters were ended, "allowing the processor and the exporter [to] compete for the margin between the minimum producer price and the export realization." 57/

4.46   The revised system, while it represented a substantial improvement over the previous method, had three serious flaws. First, export earnings from coffee continued to be converted to shillings at the official exchange rate, 15 to 20 percent below the market rate. This implicit tax seriously affected industry profitability (see table 14). Second, the "reference price" for Arabica should have been well above the reference price for robusta.

57/   Budget Speech of July 2, 1991, by the Minister of Finance.

Table 14: Effect of Exchange Rate on Coffee Industry Profitability		
	Auction Rate	**Bureau Rate**
Bureau Exchange Rate (Ush/US $)	990	1,250
International Coffee Price (US $/Kg)	0.75	0.75
Export Realization (Ush/Kg)	727	937
Farmgate Price Coffee (clean) (Ush/Kg)	389	389
Est. Processing/Marketing Costs (Ush/Kg)	385	457
Expected Profit Margins (Ush/Kg)	63	80
Actual Intermediary Margin (Ush/Kg)	(47)	91
Share of Expected Profit		114 %

4.47   A flat tax--of, say, 5 or 20 percent--on the full realized price, when this realized price is above a reference price, causes a drop in net returns to the exporter at the reference price. This undermines any incentive to raise realized prices when the export price is in the neighborhood of this reference price.

4.48   This situation was corrected in March 1992, when the Government(a) allowed coffee export earnings to be converted at the bureau rate, and (b) converted all taxes to a 5 percent tax on the full realized price. In June 1992 the Government removed the 5 percent tax on coffee exports with effect from the beginning of July 1992. This new framework should provide sufficient production and export incentives to the industry. After a year of adjustments, the Government is expected to stabilize coffe export policy, and allow participants in the industry to see how quickly they can increase exports.

4.49   **Weak Institutional Support.** Governmental services provide only minimal support to coffee producers and processors. Some of the problem areas include (a) lack of agrononomic research, inefficient nursery management, and inadequate extension services. Apart from the production of the six robusta clones, little or no original research has been done since the 1970s in breeding, crop husbandry, smallholder production economics (input packages), or postharvest activities. A particular constraint is the lack of disease-resistant hybrids or cultivars of Arabica.

4.50   With assistance from the FSSP the MAAIF nurseries have been rehabilitated and are again producing planting material. But output is less than 20 percent of the demand for plants from farmers and about 6 percent of the nurseries' maximum capacity. In addition, extension services from the MAIIF for coffee are severely understaffed, underfinanced for their work, and often lack adequate crop-specific know-how.

4.51   **Incentives for Quality Control.** Robusta quality has also declined. The raw bean size which for most buyers is a determining factor has seen a noticeable decline, as will be noted from table 15 below. The share of coffee in the large-screen "18" and "15" sizes has diminished.

Table 15: Robusta Quality Grades		
	1986-87	1990-91
Screen 18	12.2 %	7.1 %
Screen 15	64.2 %	60.2 %
Screen 12	17.9 %	27.8 %
B.H.P.	5.2 %	4.9 %

Source: CMB, UCDA

4.52   Although there are significant price differentials in the international market for different qualities of robusta or Arabica, these incentives are not translated to the internal market. This has led to the disappearance of wet processing for robusta and has discouraged processors from maximizing quality by careful hand-sorting of defective beans. Currently only the UNEX organization (10 percent of exports) appears to carefully hand-sort beans before exporting. CMBL has recently taken steps to improve the quality of wet coffee receipts by establishing a scale of price penalties on coffee delivered with a moisture content in the range of 13.1 to 20 percent, which is higher than acceptable, and a new differential price scale, with penalties based on the percentage of defective beans.

4.53   The increases in the penalties appear to have had some effect since--according to statistics for 1990-91-- about 72 percent of deliveries now fall into the highest two quality grades. However much remains to be done, since about 80 to 90 percent of wet coffee deliveries to CMBL have a moisture content of 13 to 14 percent. The level of penalties in this range are very low, and at 2 percent of value, do not make it worthwhile for the processor to dry the coffee.

4.54   The current premium for coffee with no black beans does not provide sufficient incentives for cleanliness, however, improving a given grade to the next-higher one involved 0.5 days of hand labor as well as the 3-kg weight loss. The differential in the rough hulled grades-- 10.10, 10.15, 10.20, 10.25--are such that a primary processor loses money by hand-picking three of the four main grades to improve the rough-hulled quality (table 16). Currently this is as follows:

Table 16: Costs of Upgrading Robusta	
Hand-Sorting to Upgrade Quality (by grade)	Loss/Gain to Processor (Ush/ton)
10.15 to 10.10	(23,737) loss
10.20 to 10.15	(6,316) loss
10.25 to 10.20	(10,158) loss
10.30 to 10.25	8,895 gain

4.55   There is no price and grading structure for kibooko purchases at the farm level. Farmers can do a considerable amount to improve bean quality, from husbandry and variety selection, to harvesting and drying. But farmgate incentives for improving quality are nil. Hence, kibooko is purchased at a moisture content above 12.5 percent, and a considerable number of outturn ratios--the proportion of green coffee bean from the red cherry-- are below 54 percent, indicating a high percentage of immature beans.

4.56   It should be noted that, with the liberalization of the coffee market, these pricing penalties by the export processor may be market determined, as export buyers bid on lots according to quality.

4.57   **Market Prospects**. Uganda's share of the world robusta market has declined in recent years. Uganda's current share of 15 percent--down from 18 percent in 1970-75--totals between 2.0 and 2.5 million bags (120,000 to 150,000 tons). Uganda's share of the Arabica market is much smaller, and has declined sharply, from 0.7 percent to 0.3 percent of world exports. The world trade in Arabica, about 75 percent of the world coffee export market, has grown at 1.6 percent per annum over the past eighteen years. The world robusta market has grown at less than half this rate, or 0.7 percent per annum, due to a shift in consumer tastes. Trade in the world coffee market is regulated under a series of International Coffee Agreements, using quotas and trigger-price mechanisms. Since 1989 quotas and control mechanisms have been suspended, even though the current International Coffee Agreement has been extended.

4.58   World coffee prices have been in decline since 1986 (fig. 29). The prospects for reaching a new International Coffee Agreement within the next year or two are not good. The record Brazilian 1991-92 harvest of 30 million bags, of which 7 million are robusta, and Colombia's record harvest of 16 million bags contributed to a further serious decline in international coffee prices in early 1992. The price of robusta dropped to US$0.70 per kg. Prices are now so low that border prices--at market exchange rates, with no export taxes--**are below the cost of production and processing** in many countries. An international coffee-market "shakedown" is underway. The higher-cost producers--and processors--will be forced out, as prices drop to the minimal levels that justify production. In two or three years, supplies and stocks likely will have been reduced sufficiently to bring the price up. The large Brazilian and Colombian harvests are delaying market recovery for longer than analysts had expected.

4.59   **Strategy for Coffee Development**. Uganda is well placed to survive the market shakedown, because of its comparative advantage in its production. Uganda also has few short-term alternatives for the generation of export earnings. The areas where Uganda can improve its competitive position have been identified in this report. Processing and marketing costs are high, due to years of protection and overinvestment. Crop yields are lower than they need be, due to neglect caused by a decline in the onfarm profitability of coffee compared with food crops. Yields can be increased without large expenditures through husbandry improvements, if the incentives for the use of additional labor are favorable and secure. In the robusta industry an upgrading of varieties used would further raise yields and bean quality.

4.60   The continued liberalization and revitalization of the coffee sector would require a second phase of marketing and processing liberalization measures. These measures should address incentives for improved quality, improved productivity at the farm level, and increased processing and export efficiency.

4.61   Export tax charges should include a review of the one percent "cess" (a tax) on coffee exports to support UCDA research and marketing efforts to ensure that it does not create a further disincentive to export. The effects of recent pricing and tax changes on competition and supply response should be closely monitored. And the pros and cons of an auction compared with a tender system should be evaluated, with identification of the preconditions that determine when a given system is preferred.

4.62   Processing and export licensing measures should enable more to compete in the export business. Coffee exporters should be allowed to select the most competitive export channel and route. And export inspections and customs procedures should be streamlined to reduce wasted time and the resulting cost increases.

4.63   Pricing measures should establish two grades for farmgate kibooko coffee based on an outturn ratio of good beans of 54 percent. The price differentials between the rough hulled grades of robusta--10.10, 10.15, 10.20, 10.25--should be increased to 8 to 10 percent from the present 2 percent, to encourage hand sorting. The re-development of fully washed Arabica in central pulperies should be carefully reviewed and tested on a pilot basis. The eventual objective would be to achieve 20 percent of Arabica production as fully washed--about 5,000 tons annually. And the re-development of washed robusta should also be carefully evaluated--both for indications of potential demand and price, and for assessment of investment and operation requirements. A small pilot pulpery should be established to test the idea prior to massive investments. The aim would be to wet-process 10 percent of robusta production.

4.64   Nursery management should be improved and financial autonomy provided to the operation. Productivity of existing nurseries can technically be greatly increased for example by splitting cuttings down the middle, and/or by reducing the time the seedling is in the nursery. Farmers should pay a price commensurate with seedling costs. Returns from sales should remain with the nurseries. Rewards for nursery profitability should be provided to the staff. Consideration should be given to leasing each nursery to licensed cooperatives or private operators, who would operate them on commercial lines. A test case of one or two nurseries should be tried prior to complete privatization. MAAIF should continue to supervise seedling quality and provide extension assistance to buyers.

4.65   Support services should include efforts by UCDA, in collaboration with the National Agricultural Research Organization to define and license the importation of new hybrids and hybrid cultivars of Arabica--seed, cuttings, or both--suitable for a replanting program and for use in adaptive research. Interesting varieties would include Catimor hybrid from Kenya, Zimbabwe, Colombia, or Papua New Guinea, or a Ruiru 1.1 hybrid cultivar from Kenya. Strong coffee research services should be reestablished under the National Agricultural Research Organization, funded in part by UCDA from a "cess" on coffee exports. Initial emphasis should be on adaptive research on imported planting material for Arabica, and development of recommended inputs packages for cultivation of Arabica and robusta.

Cotton

4.66   Cotton was introduced into Uganda in 1902 by the colonial Government.

> "The circumstances ... show exceptionally clearly the links between industrial interests in Britain, the colonial Government, the missions and the local population: the BCGA [British Cotton Growers Association] supplied cottonseed which was distributed through the Uganda Company [the outlet for the commercial activities of the industrial missions] to Ganda chiefs who were

then ordered by the Government to make sure it was planted by the peasants..." 58/

The ginning and marketing of cotton in Uganda was open to free competition until 1907, when hand gins were prohibited, and the licensing of ginneries begun. Ginning and marketing of cotton were progressively restricted by Government, through the establishment of the Cotton Control Board in 1921, culminating in the 1929 Cotton Commission. The restrictive recommendations of this commission led to the Cotton Zone Ordinance of 1933, which carved the country into fourteen zones, and allocated an area to each ginnery where it became the monopoly buyer. A minimum pricing scheme was set up by the Government, in agreement with the ginners, and

> "the competition between gins for the cotton crop and the movement of prices according to supply and demand was finally ended. "Commerce" and "agriculture" were thus legally separated, the cotton industry was to be regulated as far as possible by Government dictate, but profits remained in private hands. This system of controlled marketing and prices to growers has lasted to the present day." 59/

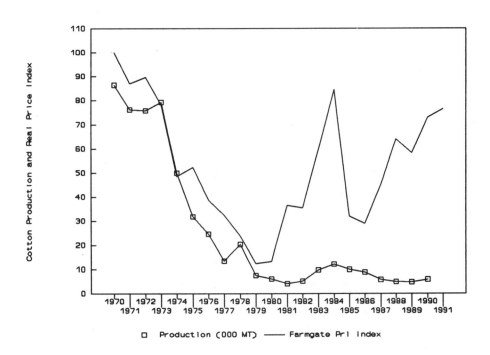

Figure 31   Lint Cotton Production in Thousands of Tons, and the Real Index of Farmgate Prices, 1970-91

58/   R.M.A. van Zwanenberg, with Anne King, <u>An Economic History of Kenya and Uganda 1800 - 1970</u>, Humanities Press, New Jersey, 1975, p.60.

59/   van Zwanenberg, op. cit. p. 210.

- 84 -

4.67   Production grew rapidly until the mid-1930s, when coffee began to compete in the cash crop market. Cotton output and area continued to grow at a slower rate until around 1970, when the area under cultivation peaked at some 900,000 ha, and production reached 470,000bales--86,900 tons--of lint. From this point on the industry has declined steadily (fig. 31). Output in 1990 was about 31,900 bales (5,900 tons) of lint, and the area under cultivation was estimated at 70,000 ha.

4.68   **Current Status.** Ugandan cotton is a rainfed annual crop of medium staple, grown using low input-low output methods. The use of fertilizers and pesticides is small. It is grown at less than 1,500 m, and requires a rainfall regime of over 800 mm/annum. It competes mainly with annual food crops. At the peak of production in 1970, it was grown mainly north, east and southeast of Lake Kyoga, and in the Kasese area in the West. Yields from 1924 through 1968 varied between 200 and 450 Kg/ha of seed cotton 60/, which is low by world standards. Yields for 1980-90 continue this trend. Field surveys indicate, however, that yield levels vary significantly by farmer. A survey in 1989 61/ found mean yields of 1,100 Kg/ha of seed cotton in the West (Kazinga Channel); 750 Kg/ha in the East, and 650 Kg/ha in the North.

4.69   Two varieties have been in use since the mid 1960s. The BPA variety, bred for cultivation in the West (Kasese to Masindi), is also suited to the areas south and east of Lake Kyoga. The SATU variety was adapted for use North of Lake Kyoga (Acholi, Lango, and Teso). Production of the SATU variety has declined and seed supplies are reportedly inadequate to supply even the traditional areas.

4.70   The ginning and marketing of cotton are currently regulated under the Cotton Act, revised in 1964, and the Lint Marketing Board Act of 1959, amended in 1976. The Lint Marketing Board now has the right to purchase all cotton for export. Ginneries are free to sell lint to the two domestic mills. Traders in cotton lint and seed had to be licensed by the LMB. Profits from cotton trading by the LMB were transferred to a "Cotton Price Assistance Fund." The Cotton Act provided for the zoning of cotton production, the setting of fixed seed and cotton lint prices, restrictions on the importation or trade in cotton, and the licensing and siting of ginneries. This Act was used to allocate "areas of influence" to each ginnery, prevent the use of hand ginneries, and confine ginning activities to the unions, who now own and operate all ginning capacity in the country. In late 1991, the Government declared its intention to liberalize the ginning and marketing of cotton.

4.71   The theoretical ginning capacity in Uganda far exceeds demand. There exist some 35 ginneries with some 700 stands, and a theoretical capacity of 280,000 bales per season. This is what remains from the peak capacity of 50 ginneries and 500,000 bales per season. Even this estimate is theoretical. Actual operational capacity is well below this. In spite of rehabilitation programs in the 1980s, many ginneries are still in poor condition, and actual operating capacity is some 60,000 bales per season. The rehabilitation programs of the mid-1980s were financed by lines of credit provided to the cooperative unions by the UCB and the Cooperative Bank (para 3.57). Recently, the Government has been working through the LMB to provide finance, technical assistance, and spare parts to key ginneries, in an attempt to increase production further.

60/   Stephen Carr, The Impact of Government Intervention on Smallholder Development in North and East Uganda, Wye College, University of London, May 1982, p. 23.

61/   Agriculture Policy Committee, Government of Uganda, Agroeconomic Study of Cotton Production, February 1990, annex 1, p 16.

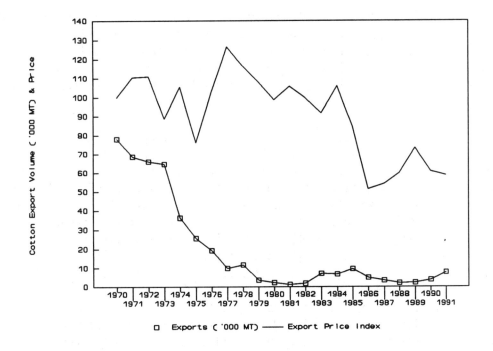

Figure 32   Lint Cotton Exports in Thousands of Tons, and Real Index of Export
Prices, 1970-91

These efforts have been moderately successful. Farmgate prices have been raised. The
production response has been strong, but is not matched by operating capacity of the
monopsonistic unions, which have been unable to purchase and gin the available cotton due to
financial and managerial problems.

4.72   **Key Constraints.** The cotton industry in Uganda collapsed when international prices
were high. Exports dropped from 65,000 tons of lint in 1973 to 10,000 tons in 1977 (fig. 32).
This dramatic decline was due in part to the dislocation in the ginning and export industries,
caused by the expulsion of the Asians in late 1972, who owned and ran many of the ginneries,
and in part to the decline in real prices paid for seed cotton.

4.73   Price Factors. The decline in production after 1973 closely follows the decline in
real farmgate prices (deflated by the Low Income Consumer Price Index) (fig. 31). The ratio of
the seed cotton price to that of "next best" cultivation alternatives, such as millet, maize, or
cowpea, shows a similar trend. During the early 1980s, the Government raised real cotton prices
substantially, in an effort to restore output levels. There was an output response--although slight
when compared to the changes in the real farmgate price. The lack of significant response in the
production of lint, can be attributed to "nonprice" factors (see below).

4.74   As was the case with coffee, farmgate prices for cotton provide the farmer with a
relatively low share of the international price, especially when valued at the market rate of
exchange. As of 1990, the Government allowed the earnings from cotton exports to be valued at
the market exchange rate, raising industry earnings. In 1991 the farmer received about 55

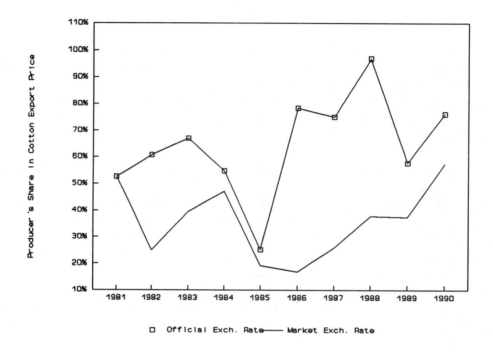

Figure 33   Farmgate Price of Cotton as Proportion of Export Price, 1981-90

percent of the world price for lint, which while not out of line for Africa, is below international levels (fig. 33).

4.75   The elasticity of supply with regard to the price of seed cotton can be quite high. Response elasticities of over 2.0 have been estimated for Kenya and Nigeria. 62/ In Uganda however, the supply response elasticities which have been estimated are much lower at 0.2-0.7, suggesting that other, nonprice factors inhibit rapid increases in output in the country.

4.76   A key non-price factor is vertical integration--which is more important in the cotton industry than in coffee. This is because a market only exists for the cotton lint and maybe for seed, the final products of the cotton ginning process. Picked seed cotton (as with greenleaf tea or sugarcane) cannot be transported too far before transport costs become prohibitive. Ginneries are thus located near producers. Should any links in the chain fail, the intermediate product has little value, and the production effort to that point is wasted. Lack of competition among ginneries and exporters is believed to be the main source of the institutional problems facing the cotton industry. Both ginning and exporting have monopsony buyers--unions and the LMB--working with captive clients on a predetermined margin.

62/   Uma Lele, Nicholas van de Walle, and Mathurin Gbetigouo, "Cotton in Africa. An Analysis of Differences in Performance", MADIA Discussion Paper 7, World Bank, 1989, p.33.

4.77   Some reasons for the failure to respond to price incentives include late farmer payments, problems with input availability and costs, ginnery malfunctions, and the classification system. Late farmer payments for seed cotton deliveries to primary societies reduce the effective price received. These result from the difficulty of obtaining crop finance at the union level, because of outstanding bad debt to the LMB or the commercial system, and administrative inefficiency at the union or primary society where the payments are made.

4.78   Any attempt to raise cotton yields above the 400 kg/ha level will depend on the use of insecticides. (Fertilizer use has not been proved profitable). 63/ An important and profitable input is the use of ox-drawn ploughs, 64/ which have been used extensively in the North and Northeast 65/. The timing of the first two weedings coincides with the harvest of early planted crops, which means that labor must be hired. All of these measures to raise yields require financing, yet direct access to formal finance is very hard for the farmer. Finance and the inputs are most efficiently provided by the marketing entity--the cooperative society. The financial insolvency of the cooperative societies, however, has severely restricted the provision of production finance. Even were finance available from informal sources, the market in agricultural inputs, dominated by MAAIF and the Uganda Central Cooperative Union, is haphazard and poorly developed.

4.79   In addition the quality of another input seed has deteriorated. Seed is cleaned and distributed free of charge by the ginneries. This service has been poorly run. Due to low yields and insecurity in the North, the SATU variety has practically disappeared. It has also been mixed with BPA. The mixture has led to poor genetic purity and low germination rates.

4.80   And ginnery malfunctions are a serious problem, with a lack of spares and qualified mechanics contributing to long delays in the ginning of cotton stocks. This reduces cotton quality and increases production costs. The Cotton classification systems used are based on "hand-pulling" methods, which are inadequate for the world market. More comprehensive and accurate methods would allow Uganda to charge a premium--where warranted--for its product, while generating confidence in its quality.

4.81   **Market Prospects.** Given current slim margins efficiency at all levels of the industry will have to be promoted to keep Uganda competitive in the international market. Uganda will be trying to revitalize its cotton industry at a difficult time in the cycle of world cotton prices. International cotton prices are lower in real terms than in the early 1970s, due to the resurgence of cotton production in China in the mid 1980s. As with coffee, real prices are unlikely to return to their former pre-1984 levels. The deep trough in international cotton prices in 1986 caused a rapid resurgence in demand, and substitution of natural for synthetic fibers in North America and Europe. The subsequent rise in prices peaked at about US$ 1.85 per Kg (Cotton Outlook A index CIF Europe) in early 1991. Since then prices have fallen to about US$ 1.24 per Kg (February 1992) due to the record world crop in 1991. Prices are projected to remain low in 1992 and 1993, and to return to 1991 levels--in real terms--by 1995. The long-term forecasts for the cotton market do not predict any seachanges from current low real prices. The effect of the potential entry of the republics of the Commonwealth of Independent States into

63/   APC, Government of Uganda, "Agroeconomic Study of Cotton Production" op. cit. Annex 5, p.20

64/   APC, op. cit., p. 19-20.

65/   Carr, op. cit.

- 88 -

the world cotton market is mitigated by the decline in productivity of their cotton-producing areas, and the increased demand for food in these republics, which competes directly with cotton acreage. The price is projected to return to the relatively high real levels achieved in 1989 by the year 2000, and decline thereafter.

4.82   Domestic demand comes from two textile firms: Nytil and Ugil, currently operating at about 14 percent of capacity. They produced some 8,150 square meters of cloth in 1990, down from 11,750 the previous year. Domestic purchases of lint in 1990 totaled some 1,300 bales by Ugil, and roughly 20,000 bales by Nytil. Demand from local mills could be a useful market, up to the limits of the domestic market for cloth. Once the limits of the domestic market have been reached, the regional market for clothing could also be tapped by Uganda, if quality improves sufficiently to compete successfully with Kenyan products.

4.83   **Future Development Strategy.** The country is at a crossroads on cotton development strategy. The nonprice factors are severely restricting sector response. Production levels continue to be low, in spite of increased "minimum" prices from 1986 to 1991. The existing institutional structure has to be changed. Two approaches can be taken in restructuring the industry: the centralized francophone West African model, or the decentralized anglophone East Africa and Nigerian model. 66/

4.84   One approach would be further centralized control of the industry, recognizing the interlinked nature of production, processing, and export. Such an approach, similar to the system evolved by British American Tobacco,(BAT Uganda) in the production and processing of tobacco, or by the *Compagnie Francaise pour le Developpement des Fibres Textiles* (CFDT) and associated cotton processing and marketing parastatals in West Africa, would strengthen the role of a central marketing organization. This organization, in the West African model, would own and manage all ginning and export marketing facilities. It would engage in research to improve on farm productivity and cotton quality. It would provide production finance for inputs to farmers, recovered against delivery of the crop. Credit for production and marketing finance would be negotiated by the centralized company for the whole industry. In this system, research results could be passed efficiently on to the farmer, using company credit and personnel. Repayment would be guaranteed by the company's monopsony marketing position. Large quantities of technical assistance (an annual average of 162 staff in 13 French-speaking African countries over 1985-87) are used in running CFDT and associated national cotton companies. Use of this approach in West Africa has resulted in average, national, rainfed seed cotton yields of more than one ton per ha in Burkina Faso, Burundi, Cameroon, Cote d'Ivoire, Madagascar, Mali, Senegal, and Togo. 67/ Cotton exports grew by 740 percent between 1960 and 1985 for the French-speaking African countries.

4.85   The centralized approach described above, while showing positive results on yield levels and export growth, has deficiencies. It is heavily dependant on technical assistance from CFDT. The centralized approach stifles private sector initiative and flexibility. The monopolistic countrywide parastatals can be fairly inflexible, and the size and diversity of interests can mask profitability of the cotton sector. This can result in substantial losses when international market

66/   Lele and others, op. cit., p.33.

67/   Lele, op. cit., p.14.

conditions change, as occurred in Cameroon in 1986-88. 68/ The general criticism of the CFDT system is based on "(a) CFDT's high financial costs associated with monopoly operations and unnecessarily advanced technology in cotton processing; (b) an alleged bias against foodcrops, and (c) the high environmental costs". 69/

4.86   The other approach--advocated in this report--is to decentralize cotton production, processing, and export marketing, with each layer of the industry competing for raw material and exports. Pricing, down to the farmgate, would be determined by market forces. Ginneries would compete for seed cotton. Export companies would compete for lint. Research by Government institutions would continue, possibly with industry funding. A central regulatory agency would set quality standards and collect statistics. The proposed structure existed when cotton production was successfully started in Uganda early in the century. A similar model has been followed, with a fair degree of success, for the Ugandan coffee industry. This approach would benefit from the incentives provided by competition and profit-seeking at every stage of the process. It diversifies against the risk of collapse or default of a centralized organization. It makes the industry responsive to international market conditions. By keeping units small the system links cost elements directly to profits, leading to efficiency in investment decisions. Such a system accepts that cotton production, will be on an extensive, low-input, low-output basis.

4.87   The proposed strategy was put forward by the Agriculture Policy Committee. 70/ A small regulatory authority body would be established, a Uganda Lint Authority, in place of the current LMB, to set quality standards, maintain production and export statistics, facilitate the estimation of credit requirements, and administer a small cess on exports to fund cotton research. In addition, initial impetus should be given for the establishment of a private, nonprofit, apex representative organization, formed by representatives from the marketing, processing, and production aspects of the industry, and capable of representing industry views to the Government and public. On the production side, extension advice would be provided to all entrants by MAAIF. Ginneries could finance inputs and labor for favored clients. Decentralized input supply and credit mechanisms would be developed domestically to serve all sectors including cotton.

4.88   An important aspect of the development strategy in the industry will be to focus on "lead ginneries," in an effort to solve their financial, managerial, and technical problems and return output to full capacity. Key ginneries in four important producing areas should be targeted: North Busoga; Bukedi, Apac; Lira, West Nile; and Kasese. The cotton regulatory agency, or the UCA, or another temporary parastatal body should take the lead in this effort, marshaling Government, donor, and private resources to get the industry started again. In the context of a competitive industry, interested banks and export trading concerns would help the unions to resolve their bottlenecks. Self-financing credit and technical assistance agreements could be crafted, for example, between a union, a foreign trading concern, and a bank to enable operations to begin and expand.

68/   Lele, op.cit., p. 30.

69/   Lele, op. cit., p. 24.

70/   Government of Uganda, Cotton Subsector Development Strategy, Kampala, August 1991.

4.89   The structure of a liberalized industry can be easily described, but a transition from the current monopolistic structures would have to be carefully managed. The following phased approach is envisaged:

- The <u>legal framework</u> would have to be changed to support a competitive, decentralized approach. Having the National Resistance Council revoke the Cotton Act and the Lint Marketing Board Act would permit public debate on the industry's future. A new law sanctioning the establishment of a regulatory body would be needed.

- An industry <u>regulatory</u> body would be needed, especially during the initial phase of the introduction of competition. New cotton grades would have to be established, and enforced. Guidance would be needed in coordinating foreign intervention in ginning and exports. <u>Research</u> priorities would have to be communicated to the research system. A small cess--variable within prescribed limits, depending on industry needs could be imposed to finance research on cotton varieties and husbandry.

- Following the enabling legislation, the regulatory agency, possibly a Uganda Lint Authority, should seek <u>private sector participation</u> in ginning and export operations and registering approved companies. In the initial stages, when production volumes would be low, interested foreign trading organizations should be encouraged to put together a "package" with interested cooperative unions and local banks, combining ginnery use-- lease, management contracts, or sale--and crop finance. UNEX, an apex union already active in coffee exports, is well-positioned to establish an export trade in cotton.

- The <u>LMB</u> should be restructured and privatized, with shares sold eventually to private investors. It should be encouraged to compete in an open market with private entrants. The board should be permitted to restructure its holdings, and divest itself of productive assets, such as stores and vehicles as needed to restore profitability.

- The cotton industry should bring a few key ginneries, and their catchment areas, back into production and export. The unions in these key ginneries, should be assisted by the regulatory agency, by the Uganda Cooperative Alliance, or another management agency to resolve financial, managerial, and technical difficulties--by entering into lease, purchase, financing, or other agreements with other unions or private parties. Successful rehabilitation of a few key ginneries would boost industry redevelopment. Nine efficient ginneries could likely handle the whole crop.

- The <u>chemical inputs</u> market would be opened to the private sector. It is expected that ginneries will enter into agreements with suppliers and farmers to supply inputs against deliveries of seed cotton. Insecticides are expected to be the main input sold. Foreign exchange for these imports is available from the bureaus or donor-funded importation schemes.

- Reintroduction of the ox-drawn plough will only occur once civil peace and security is reestablished in these areas. Formal finance through the banking system, for the purchase of oxen and ploughs may be necessary if such funds are not available informally.

- Extension advice would continue to be available from the MAAIF extension service, backed by the research establishments at Namulonge and Serere. IDA-funded projects in support of the Government extension and research networks are expected to revitalize these services.

- In addition to the need for purified, reissued seed cultivars, and improved germination rates, and increased ginning outturn is needed--the proportion of lint in seed cotton--for varieties suitable to the North, Northeast, and West--and the MAAIF-led research establishment could focus on that. West African rainfed cotton has significantly higher ginning outturn rates than cotton in Uganda--40 percent in Cameroon compared with 33 percent for Uganda. 71/

4.90   The cotton industry likely can respond rapidly, once the support infrastructure is operating and finance is available. A precondition for the reestablishment of a vigorous cotton industry is the achievement of peace, and the establishment of the rule of law in the northern and northeastern cotton growing zones. The redevelopment of the cotton subsector, as with other aspects of the agricultural economy, depends on the improvement of the feeder and minor road network, the deepening of the rural financial system, the reduction of inflation, and the maintenance of an undistorted market for imports and exports of produce. The international cotton market is much more competitive than in the heyday of the Ugandan cotton industry. To be successful, participants will have to pare production costs and processing margins to a minimum.

71/   Lele, Uma op.cit. p. 10

Tea

4.91   Made tea represented between 5 and 6 percent of exports in the early 1970s, third in importance behind coffee and cotton. In 1972--the peak year--some 23,000 tons of black tea were produced, and 21,000 tons exported, 6.7 percent of total exports. Tea exports dropped a catastrophically in 1979 to 1,500 tons, when the war with Tanzania forced closure of the factories, all of which are in the Southwest or West (fig. 34). Production has never recovered from this shock. Under the adjustment policies engaged in the early 1980s, production recovered slightly, climbing to some 5,800 tons in 1985, before continued security problems caused a decline in 1986. Since then, policy reforms such as removal of the Uganda Tea Authority monopoly on exports, valuation of export proceeds at the market exchange rate, liberalization of export marketing, and permission for foreign exchange retention accounts have stimulated production. Output is back up to 9,300 tons of made tea, almost half of early-1970 levels. The domestic market currently absorbs about 2.6 million kg, and the remainder is exported.

4.92   **Current Status**. Tea is grown on good soils at altitudes of over 1,200 meters, and rainfall of more than 1,200 mm/year. These conditions can be found in the western districts of Bushenyi, Rukungiri, Kabarole, Hoima, and Masindi, and on the northern shores of Lake Victoria. Uganda has the potential to be a low-cost, competitive producer of tea. The crop has been well-established--free of pests and diseases and requiring minimal cultivation, mainly weed control and fertilizing. The cut, tear and curl (CTC) method of manufacture used in Uganda is relatively uncomplicated, and hence lower-cost than orthodox manufacture. And the two enforced rests--in 1975 and in 1985--have done the tea bushes no harm, and may have helped them. Since 1987 some rehabilitation of tea fields and factories has taken place with about half the total planted area back in production (table 17)

Table 17 : Status of Tea Industry in 1990					
Estates	Planted Area (Ha)	Area in Production (Ha)	Made Tea Production (Metric Tons)	Operating Factories (Number)	Capacity Utilization (Percent)
Joint Ventures					
TAMTECO	2,326	2,000	2,066	3	44 %
Uganda Tea Company	900	753	1,372	2	76 %
Parastatals					
Agricultural Enterprises Ltd (AEL)	3,086	1,150	720	5	12 %
Uganda Tea Growers Co. (UTGC)	9,440	4,400	1,847	5	20 %
Privately Owned					
Private Estates	6,250	950	622	9	5 %
TOTAL	22,000	9,253	6,627	24	19 %

4.93   There are two company estates: the Toro and Mityana Tea Company (TAMTECO) with some 2,300 ha of land planted in tea and managed by Mitchell Cotts Group, and the Uganda Tea Company, with nearly 1,000 ha of planted tea managed by the Mehta Group.

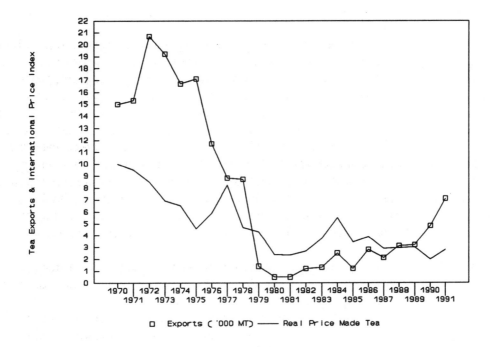

Figure 34   Made Tea Exports in Thousands of Tons, and Real Index of Export
Prices, 1970-91

4.94   Of TAMTECO's 2,300 ha under tea, approximately 2,000 ha have been rehabilitated and
brought into plucking on their three properties: Toro Kahuna, Kiamara, and Mityana. Present
yields are on average 1,200 kg made tea per ha. Feasible estate yields are estimated at 2,500 kg
per ha. TAMTECO has had financial problems repaying earlier loans. Because of a lack of
finance and factory capacity it has seemed advisable not to maximize crop intakes--and
consequently fertilizer has only been applied in small measure. This has meant low crop intakes,
low yields, and therefore high production costs. Until the financial problem is solved, the
profitability of these properties cannot be achieved.

4.95   Of the 900 ha that the Uganda Tea company has under tea, 790 have been rehabilitated
and are in production on their two properties Luwala and Kasaku. Very satisfactory work has
been done in rehabilitating the tea. Yields are expected to be in the order of 2,400 kg per ha, the
highest achieved so far since rehabilitation started. The problem of labor shortage has been
successfully overcome, in this and other estates, by giving blocks to families for maintenance and
plucking after they have been rehabilitated by estate labor. Chemicals and fertilizers are supplied
by the estate and the families are paid on the basis of greenleaf plucked.

4.96   Like TAMTECO, the company owes considerable sums on loans for the development of
factories and field rehabilitation. One consequence of this debt burden is that the factory capacity
has not been rehabilitated sufficiently to cope with present harvests. Until additional machinery is
installed, present policy is to make as much tea as possible even if the quality is poor.

4.97   There are six <u>Government estates</u>, each owned by a separate company managed by Agricultural Enterprises Ltd. (AEL), a wholly owned subsidiary of the Uganda Development Corporation. The total area originally planted in tea was 3,085 ha, of which 1,172 ha--or 38 percent--have been rehabilitated. The rehabilitation work has not been of a high standard. Due to the difficulty of recruiting hired labor, about half of each estate has been parceled out to farm families in one-to-two ha blocks, for rehabilitation, maintenance, and harvest. Yield is less than 1,100 kgs per ha. There seems no reason, with good husbandry, why 2,000 kgs per ha should not be achieved again.

4.98   A complete reorganization of the managerial structure is needed--as well as enough working capital--to restore efficiency to this group. Considering the lack of working capital, shortage of labor, and general disorganization, it is creditable that over 1,100 ha have been rehabilitated and are now in production, even if work standards are not of a high order. This enterprise needs to be privatized if it is to become a viable commercial enterprise again.

4.99   Each of the six estates has a factory, although Bugambe factory is not yet functioning. Mwenge, Kiko, and Ankole factories were rehabilitated under the World Bank Emergency Tea Rehabilitation Project while Muzizi and Salama factories still need further attention. Around US$3.3 million has been loaned from the East African Development Bank and Barclays Bank for factory development and over Ush376 million was borrowed for field development. At current levels of efficiency and output there seems little prospect of making enough profit to service these debts.

4.100   There are said to be thirty 30 <u>privately-owned estates</u>. They average about 160 ha and have about 6,250 ha in planted tea. Made tea production in 1990 was nearly 700,000 kg, of which 63 percent was from two factories, Maco and Mutesa. Less than one-quarter of the total tea hectarage owned by private estates has been rehabilitated. This is because final ownership of those estates, now owned by Asians and held by the Custodian Board, has not yet been determined. Out of the thirty estates, nineteen have factories, but only nine factories, as far as can be ascertained, are in production--and none at full capacity. All the factories will need rehabilitation to different degrees.

4.101   The <u>Uganda Tea Growers Corporation</u> (UTGC) buys greenleaf tea from some 3,800 smallholders and small estates. Smallholder farmers manage 0.5 to 1.5 ha of tea, and small estates may manage up to 200 ha of tea. These farms have some 9,440 ha of tea, with about 5,750 ha in production. Ownership is concentrated in the hands of the small estates. In the six districts with smallholder and small estate tea (Kabarole, Bushenyi, Rukungiri, Hoima, Mityana/Mubende and Mukono) 270 farmers--or 7 percent of the total--own 48 percent of the total hectarage (2,745 ha).

4.102   All outgrowers and private estates without factories rely on UTGC to collect and arrange processing for their green-leaf, except in Masaka and Mukono districts where there is no collection service yet. UTGC has a monopoly on the collection of greenleaf and, in a district where it is not managing a factory, delivers the leaf to a UTGC factory. Lorries and tractortrailers are dispatched daily from depots to collect leaf from some 400 collecting centers. The practice is to charge the outgrowers Ush2 per kg for collection. The factory to which the leaf is delivered pays Ush3 per kg so that UTGC recovers USh5 per kg. But, the cost of collecting and delivering leaf far exceeds this reimbursement.

4.103 Eight factories come under UTGC management. The following five are in production:

Table 18: UTGC Factories Currently in Production		
	Present Maximum Capacity (kg green-leaf per annum)	Proposed Extended Capacity (kg green-leaf per annum)
Igara	3,190,500	4,190,500
Mabale	4,761,900	5,238,100
Mpanga	2,714,300	4,047,600
Kayorza	3,000,000	4,333,300
Kisaru	1,428,600	2,047,600
	15,095,300	19,857,100

4.104 The first four factories were rehabilitated under the World Bank Emergency Tea Rehabilitation Project, along with AEL factories at Mwenge, Kiko, and Ankole. Construction of UTGC factories at Buhweyu, Kyenjojo, and Mityana was aborted for security reasons. The reinitiation of construction is under negotiation with the African Development Bank, and completion is expected in 1994. When all eight factories are running, total greenleaf capacity will be 34,107,100 kg which is in line with present UTGC/EEC projection of a crop of 33,578,680 kg from outgrowers by the late 1990s.

4.105 Is tea production profitable? Will it be profitable in the future? The tea sector has been able to retain its foreign exchange earnings, and exchange them at the bureau rate, since 1987. One of the main problems affecting the sector is low factory utilization, which drives up unit costs. Also, world market prices for tea are well below levels of the early 1970s in real terms. While current prices enable established factories and estates to operate profitably, financing the cost of factory and field rehabilitation reduces the margins in the tea industry to low levels. The illustrative calculations below (table 19) are based on an efficient factory, operating at 1,200,000 kg per annum.

Table 19: Production Costs for Made Tea (assuming an efficient factory of 1,200 MT output/year, and Ush950	
Greenleaf (Ush85/kg) and 21.5 % output 1/	395
Leaf Collection	43
Leaf Processing	310
Marketing Costs	152
TOTAL COST (FOB Mombasa)	900
Average Sale Price (Mombasa) All Grades	1,200
Profit to Factory	300
Profit to Outgrower (after payment of labor)	10

1/ With fertilizer at market prices, allowing a profit margin to the outgrower.
Source: UTGC estimates

4.106 Preliminary financial and economic analysis based on current yield levels indicates that the sector--is profitable--at current yields, using projected prices for tea at the market exchange rate, assuming efficient processing and marketing costs. Cost of production, processing, and marketing, of which only 42 percent is foreign, is about 75 percent of the export price. The domestic resource cost ratio works out to 0.72 for outgrowers and 0.55 for estates. The theoretical payback period for rehabilitation of a standard factory and its nucleus estate and outgrower fields financed by equity and long-term loans is satisfactory, assuming efficient operation of the enterprise. The financial problems faced by the various enterprises have been due, in part, to the need for two rehabilitation efforts--before and after 1985. There also have been difficulties in operating enterprises far from Kampala, in an economy which has only recently stabilized. With improved infrastructure, stabilized labor markets, more efficient export corridors, coupled with the privatization of Government-owned enterprises, and improvement in factory management, enterprises in this sector should gradually return to profitability.

4.107   The European Economic Community has been assisting the Government with the rehabilitation of outgrower-based tea production. During the course of phase I, the project has succeeded in increasing tea production, expanding the capacity of the five operating factories, strengthening UTGC, supporting an extension service, and providing inputs--mainly fertilizer, at subsidized prices--for outgrowers. A second phase of EEC assistance is under negotiation. The second phase approach would be consistent with the development strategy for the sector (para 4.101).

4.108   There remains constraints to sector development involving labor, finance, transport, and parastatal management. The apparent shortage of labor--the main constraint at present--is seriously affecting the plucking of the greenleaf. In the smallholder sector, at most 0.5 ha of tea can be managed by one person. If family members assist, it is possible to manage up to 1.5 ha. More than that means hiring labor. All estates hire labor. Prior to the industry decline in the 1970s, immigrant labor from Rwanda and Zaire worked the plantations. With the decline in the Ugandan tea industry, the decline in the value of the Uganda shilling, and the development of tea in Rwanda and Zaire, this source of labor disappeared. Now, wages paid for labor in the tea industry have to compete with the returns available from own-farm production (dairy, bananas) or wages from public works. Wages in the tea industry--from estates and smallholders--are well below daily wages in the regional market.

4.109   Wages for labor hired on smallholder farms are a function of the price the factory pays for greenleaf. This price is set by the Government, to prevent factories from exercising monopsony power over the outgrowers. The price is enforced by the UTGC, a parastatal, with a monopoly over procurement of greenleaf from outgrowers. In spite of these good intentions, producer prices have been allowed to decline to low levels--affecting production (fig. 35). The adjustment of the greenleaf price to Ush60/kg in mid-1991 permits smallholders to cover costs, as long as the price of fertilizer is subsidized. At this price, however, incentives for rehabilitation of tea gardens are still very low.

4.110   A review of this question by the Agricultural Secretariat concluded there is no shortage of labor for hire in rural Uganda. 72/ At a competitive wage, and with adequate inducements on estates--such as housing and schooling--sufficient labor will be forthcoming, according to the review. This study also shows that the costs of running a mechanical plucker--which produces lower-quality leaf, and requires foreign exchange--was about Ush100/kg greenleaf, well above smallholder production costs. A planned release of the UTGC monopoly should permit factories and outgrowers to reach an accommodation on greenleaf prices that are attractive to both parties, in keeping with the minimum price set by the Uganda Tea Board.

72/   Agricultural Secretariat, Bank of Uganda, Tea Subsector - Labor Constraints, July 1991.

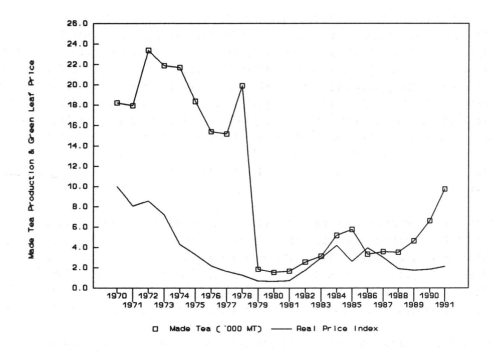

Figure 35   Made Tea Production in Thousands of Tons, and Real Index of Green
Leaf (Farmgate) Prices, 1970-90

4.111   A major problem in the sector is the lack of working <u>capital</u>. Government enterprises--both
AEL and the UTGC--are saddled with debt-servicing costs on donor-financed rehabilitation programs.
Government is not willing or able to inject more capital, and these enterprises have difficulty
borrowing from banks because of the enterprises' debt load. Government has decided that these
enterprises will eventually be restructured and sold to private shareholders. Joint venture operations,
although operating profitably, are unable to raise the working capital needed to harvest the greenleaf
needed to bring factory operations up to capacity. These operations never fully recovered from the
setback caused by the decline in security in 1984-86. TAMTECO is having to abandon sections of its
estate that have already been rehabilitated. The Government has offered to sell its 51 percent holding
in TAMTECO to the private sector partner for fresh injection of funds. The Commonwealth
Development Corporation is also examining the possibility of providing additional equity.

4.112   The development of feeder roads in the tea growing areas has not kept pace with the recent
rehabilitation of the subsector. Under the Transport Sector Review IDA is examinining the most
efficient transport methods (e.g. road as compared with rail) along the Kasese-Kampala-Mombasa
corridor, the main outlet for the tea industry.

4.113   For parastatal enterprises, <u>ineffective management</u> seems to be the major constraint. Both
UTGC and AEL are highly centralized in Kampala. Field units do not have informationon production
levels, costs, or product prices needed to make sound managerial decisions. Also, uncertainty over the
ownership of factories managed by UTGC and the lack of separate and complete accounting records
for each processing and production unit contribute to the managerial inefficiency.   Under the EEC-
funded project, however, impressive gains have been made on the extension and input supply system.

4.114 **Market Prospects.** Uganda is a price taker in the world market. With total world trade of about 1 million tons of made tea in 1991, Uganda's maximum exports of 20,000 tons do not affect the market. Price prospects are not good. Prices are not expected to improve very much from the historic low obtained in 1988. The main reason is that producing countries have continued to increase production, in spite of the low international prices, by maintaining domestic incentives through currency devaluation, and by increasing yields. In recent months, demand has softened with the withdrawal of the former U.S.S.R. the buyers' market. Prices--in 1985 terms--are expected to fluctuate between 135 c/kg and 150 c/kg through the turn of the century, after which they should rise, as the possibilities for continued yield increases in producing countries diminish.

4.115 **A Strategy for Growth.** The strategy for the development of the tea sector is based on the premise that the export of tea is profitable for Uganda. The main task at present--prior to the rehabilitation of more tea gardens--is to improve efficiency at the factories, and reduce processing margins. At the same time the interests of the outgrowers, are at a bargaining disadvantage with respect to factories, should be taken into consideration in the eventual agreement on the price of greenleaf.

4.116 To address these questions, the following strategy is proposed. First a regulatory body to be known as the Uganda Tea Board should be established for the industry and staffed with a majority of industry representatives. This board would be responsible for setting quality standards, setting the greenleaf price, monitoring the trade, and funding research and development from a small assessment to be agreed upon with the industry. Second, once tea production and exports are back up to the 15,000 to 20,000 ton level, a threshold-based marginal export tax with a marginal tax rate below 50 percent--similar to that proposed for coffee--should be formulated for the tea sector to permit the country to partake in the windfall gains from swings in the international tea market. Retention accounts for foreign exchange earned from tea exports should be placed under strict supervision of the Bank of Uganda, and eventually phased out, in favour of the free market in foreign exchange.

4.117 The Government also should divest itself of parastatal estates and factories--AEL and UTGC-- and consider divestiture of its majority share in the joint-venture operations. To implement divestiture a minimum producer price for greenleaf should be established, based on export receipts, rather than the farmer's cost of production. This will give the farmers a share in the gains (and losses) provided by swings in the international price. The Uganda Tea Board would set a minimum green leaf price based on average ex-factory sales receipts, less the cost of processing, and a reasonable greenleaf-to-made tea output ratio. The price levels should be subject to biannual review.

4.118 At the same time, UTGC's monopoly over procurement of greenleaf should be ended, and factories encouraged to enter directly into contracts with outgrowers which include leaf collection, input supply, and credit recovery. Deliberations by the Custodian Board on ownership of private sector tea estates should be concluded--under the framework provided by the IDA--funded Structural Adjustment Credit--and incentives provided for the rehabilitation of factories and gardens.

4.119 The Government and EEC have been formulating policy for the smallholder tea sector and UTGC prior to proceeding with a second phase of the Smallholder Tea Rehabilitation Project. The two elements of this policy with which this report agrees, are, first, that potentially profitable UTGC factories should eventually be privatized, starting with Mabale, Mpanga, Igara, and Kayonza. At first, ownership should be vested in a local holding firm--DFCU for example--for eventual sale to the outgrowers. In the restructuring of factory ownership, long-term liabilities would be reduced and rehabilitation would be financed by a capital injection through the holding company (funded by EEC). The Government and UTGC would relinquish ownership claims.

4.120   Second, UTGC should be restructured into two operating entities--a management agency, charged with providing management services (for a fee) to operate the factories, and a development agency, charged with supporting smallholder development with extension, research, and other services funded by the Government but separate from the Tea Board.

4.121   The Government has indicated its intention to divest itself of its holdings in AEL. This report supports that position. At issue is the selection of a divestiture procedure that will provide adequate incentives for investor interest, while providing the Government with a reasonable return. Based on the recent study by the CDC, three categories of management and ownership for AEL are listed, in increasing order of risk to an investor:

- A new company be formed to lease and manage assets of AEL. With management lease for a fixed period, with option to purchase on expiry. Working capital would be injected by shareholder of the new company. Lease payments could be performance related. Finance for rehabilitation could be provided from the IDA-funded Enterprises Development Project (Cr 2315-UG).

- Immediate privatization, with the Government retaining a minority share. Assets would be the Government share. The majority would finance rehabilitation and working capital, supplemented by loans from financing agencies and IDA under the Enterprises Development Project.

- Immediate privatization, with complete Government divestiture. The shareholders of the new company would purchase assets from Uganda Development Corporation, the current holding company. Proceeds of the sale would be credited to a Divesture Fund to pay existing AEL creditors a proportion of their outstanding loans. This arrangement would also qualify for financing under the Enterprises Development Project.

4.122   The Government should select an option and initiate negotiations with prospective investors. Discussions should be based on a detailed divestiture study, including an assessment of factories, infrastructure, vehicles, estates, and smallholder outgrowers. This study would also focus on ways of enhancing the attractiveness of this package to investors. The possibility of attracting smaller investors by breaking AEL into individual estates and their complementary factories, within the framework outlined above, should be considered.

Nontraditional Agricultural Exports

4.123   **Current Status.** Uganda exports a number of nontraditional crops and commodities: simsim (sesame seed), hides and skins, Wet-Blue hides, maize, beans, and some horticultural crops. In 1990-91 nontraditional agricultural exports totaled a record US$18.8 million, 11 percent of total exports. Standard measures of comparative advantage such as the domestic resource cost ratio, show Uganda to be a competitive producer of the above-mentioned crops. Import substitution, as valid as export expansion and diversification in its impact on balance of trade and the national economy, has also been actively pursued through the increased production of sugar and dairy products.

4.124   While Ugandan climate, soils, topography, and rainfall are conducive to the production of a wide range of crops, the choice of high-value products for export development is restricted by a producer's ability to deliver to the buyer promptly, in the correct season, in good condition, and at a competitive cost. Ugandan agriculture is rainfed and smallholder based. Farm incomes--and thus capacity to invest in new technology--are very low. Applied research and extension systems are weak and improved inputs are expensive and difficult to buy. Agricultural credit is also scarce. These conditions are not conducive to the development of high-value output agriculture, except on a small scale.

4.125   The costs, speed, and efficiency of export delivery channels are key factors in determining comparative advantage. Transport costs are a large part of the final price of specialty produce in Europe, especially if shipped by air. Fruit and horticultural products are standardized, and permit little differentiation. Competition takes place on transport cost, and the ability to ship into the window in the European market created by the absence of supply from domestic, or traditional suppliers.

4.126   Practically all Ugandan exports go overland to Mombasa or Dar es Salaam. Most of the agricultural long-haul traffic in Uganda is by road. Freight charges from Kampala to Mombasa vary from US$35 to US$70 per ton, with the competitive rate at about US$60 per ton. Delivery times from Kampala to Mombasa by lorry range from three to seven days, depending on delays at the border or vehicle breakdown.

4.127   Rail freight charges are US$57 per ton from Kampala to Mombasa and US$65 per ton to Dar es Salaam. Average delivery times are ten days to Mombasa and twelve days to Dar es Salaam, though express trips reduce times to seven and ten days respectively. When the Port Bell facilities are finished, transit times for Kenya and Tanzania should be further reduced. Three trips per week are made to Kisumu (for onward transit to Mombasa) and one to two trips per week to Mwanza (for Dar es Salaam).

4.128   Overland transport--by rail as well as road--is complicated by border delays. There is a general lack of container capacity on the rail route and refrigerated containers on the overland route must be carried by Kenyan registered vehicles. Trunk roads are in good condition but feeder roads are poor.

4.129   Air freight space is limited by the lack of scheduled direct flights to Europe and by the capacity of the aircraft used. Chartered air freight capacity remains limited because of the lack of southbound cargo. Competition for northbound air freight space from Kenyan and other neighboring country exporters also affects availability. Cargo handling facilities at the airport remain a constraint, although the Civil Aviation Authority has recently announced the completion of repairs to cold storage facilities at Entebbe. Lack of sufficient cold storage space to date also inhibits the bulking of sufficient cargo (35-40 tons) to justify pickup by charter airfreight services. The industry thus faces a chicken-and-egg type of problem, as production will not be forthcoming until adquate markets and prices (and hence air freight facilities) are guaranteed. Further development of cold storage facilities at the airport, with private finance, should reduce this bottleneck.

4.130   Airfreight costs have increased substantially over the last few years. Effective rates are now around US$1.50/kg. The cost of air transport and packaging averages between 50 and 75 percent of product cost landed in Europe. High air transport costs make most fresh vegetables uncompetitive, but a wide range of floricultural products remain highly competitive. Within Africa it can be expected that much of the out-of-season vegetable production, where product differentiation is hard, will become concentrated in West and North Africa where current airfreight rates of under US$1.00/kg make them hard to compete with. Equivalent rates from Kenya are currently around US$1.20/kg, but are expected to rise substantially, which will affect Kenya's vegetable exports.

4.131 With limited airfreight capacity, Uganda should concentrate on developing floricultural products to take advantage of a competitive edge in transport costs. Worldwide, major flower exporters are working with airfreight rates of US$2.00/kg and above (table 20).

Table 20: Airfreight from Country to European Market		
Country	Flowers (US$ /kg)	Horticulture (US$ /kg)
Kenya	1.59 to 2.00	1.9 (rising)
Ghana		0.91 (air cargo) 0.65 (charter
Zambia	1.51	
South Africa	1.85	1.16 (financial rand) 1.46 (official rand)
Colombia	1.85 + 7 %	
Zimbabwe	2.00 (rising to 2.26)	1.27 (rising)
Barbados		0.83
Trinidad		0.71 (at a 2 ton break point)
Jamaica		0.86 0.70 (after negotiations)
Malaysia	3.47	
Thailand	2.35	1.35
Chile		2.60
Peru		1.69
Senegal		1.16
Ivory Coast		0.90
The Gambia		0.70 (air cargo) 0.90 (air charter)
Morocco	1.04	
Nigeria	0.90	0.75 (air cargo) + 5% 0.60 (air charter) + 5%
U.S.A. (Miami)	1.69 to 1.85	
Israel	1.48	

4.132 Policies and legislation strongly support the expansion and diversification of exports through the private sector. The Investment Code introduced at the beginning of 1991 created a favorable environment for foreign investors and there is evidence that a substantial number of individuals and companies are seriously considering investing in Uganda. The export certificate scheme is now well-established, together with streamlined export documentation and the new CD3 form. Export formalities are now easier for exporters, although some duplication still exists. Phytosanitary certification at the airport remains problematic because of poor discipline. The Investment Authority has sensibly set up a one-stop information point for foreign investors. Much more promotion needs to be targeted at specific companies, however.

4.133   The Export Policy Analysis and Development Unit (EPADU) was established in the Ministry of Planning and Economic Development to tackle policy issues and to kick-start export development by resolving key bottlenecks for exporters. EPADU has succeeded in its pioneering role, and now has to settle down to longer-term support of the sector. In this regard, closer coordination with the Export Promotion Council in MCIC -- a competing but though less well-developed institution -- will be necessary to avoid duplication.

4.134   The financial system remains a significant bottleneck to export development. Even basic financial transactions such as check cashing and clearing are inadequate. The export credit guarantee and export refinance schemes were only recently put into place. While the Export Finance and Guarantee Scheme launched by the Bank of Uganda played a crucial role in increasing non-traditional exports, many banks still seem to be reticent to participate in other schemes. Working capital is expensive and hard to obtain. Term finance is not available locally, and investors depend on own resources or donor finance for investment funding. Venture capital, especially equity capital, the most appropriate source of funding for the new, untested, high-risk, high-return types of investment necessary to develop this sector of the agricultural economy, is also not available.

4.135   **Market Prospects**. The European market offers supply opportunities for a whole range of specialist off-season horticultural commodities. While wholesale prices for fruit and produce look particularly attractive, most commodities are so perishable that airfreighted supply is the only possible means of transport. This places a considerable cost on the operation. Quality standards are rigorous and increasing, and there is little room for substandard material.

4.136   Certain fresh fruits (pineapples, bananas) and vegetables such as garlic are seafreighted to Europe. Development of this sector will depend on significant improvements in transport efficiency. The movement in the market (which supports the steady and increasing prices) is toward produce that has been handled in a cold chain from harvest to market. The lack of seafreight container traffic from Uganda reduces alternatives and competitiveness.

4.137   The Middle East markets are close, giving Uganda an advantage on transport costs. Purchasing power is strong, markets are large enough to warrant interest, and quality standards are not as rigorous as in Europe. Important niche markets exist--the largest and highest-priced cardamom market is in the Middle East, dominated by Saudi Arabia. These advantages have to be set against the frequent problems experienced in dealing with Middle East customers, and the different structure to their markets. Saudi Arabia and the Gulf States both offer excellent markets for fresh horticultural produce, but entry is difficult. In Saudi Arabia, for example, the major importers like to source a full range of produce from a supplier, creating a disadvantage for Uganda under present supply conditions.

4.138   As discussed previously, the regional market has potentially a large demand for food and other processed products from Uganda. In the medium term, a wider range of spices and essential oils could be developed. Both Kenya and Tanzania are looking at development of a range of spices, spice seeds, and essential oils to supply local needs and replace imports. Uganda has the potential to become a competitive supplier to neighboring and the other countries in the region.

4.139   **A Strategy for Growth**. The major constraints to growth include the human and technical resource base, key infrastructural components (roads, storage, airport facilities, container facilities), and the responsiveness of the financial system. It is advocated that Uganda follow a two-pronged approach to develop the sector. Uganda should continue its successfully initiated policy of enhancing the investment climate for foreign entrepreneurs, while resolving the general constraints that affect rapid market-based growth. In addition, however, the Government should continue with targeted efforts through EPADU and other agencies to assist the private sector in specific industries like vanilla and cardamom, to overcome development obstacles and identify and supply foreign markets.

4.140   Export market requirements are demanding in terms of product type, size, quality, packaging, delivery schedule, and frequency. In view of the lack of competitiveness in the fresh vegetable market mentioned previously, and the constraints on air transport in the short-term, the most appropriate products for export diversification are high-value and preferably low-volume items, especially the less-perishable products. The recommended crops are those nontraditional crops that are already being profitably exported but would benefit from product development and other forms of technical assistance. A more targeted approach would enhance export volumes and values: simsim; spices, especially vanilla, cardamom, dried ginger, and dried chillies; hides and skins, especially Wet-Blue hides; fish; some textiles; and beans and maize for the regional market.

4.141   Simsim was the largest single export item after coffee in 1990-1991 (US$10.7m), and simsim, maize and beans accounted for almost half of exports other than coffee, tea, cotton, and tobacco (para 1.18). Exports of pineapple and Asian vegetables to Europe continue--but at very low profit margins, because of air freight costs and relatively low prices. While small-scale entrepreneurs can exploit this market and make a valid contribution to exports, these crops are not considered sufficiently profitable and most of the foreign exchange earnings are swallowed by air freight charges. In contrast, the processing of pineapples into a frozen concentrate for export to world markets, especially the U.S.A., may be a more profitable route for pineapple exports.

4.142   There are other high-value crops with export potential, already grown in Uganda, which will require some more product and process development before they can be properly exploited. These include essential oils, especially lemongrass, citronella and palmarosa; processed cashew nut, which would require the privatization and rehabilitation of the plant at Soroti; Ndizi (marketed as "apple banana"); and fresh ginger (production of the Hawaiian variety and with exports only in November and early December).

4.143   As, and when, air freight connections and reliable regular schedules are established, more attention should be paid to the highest-value cut flowers--for example, roses--and other high-value fresh produce. Other essential oil crops which should be seriously considered for export development and which can have outstanding export value include patchouli, geranium, chamomile, tuberose, and pyrethrum. Vegetable oils are perhaps a good example for assessment in an import-substitution strategy.

4.144   Infrastructural development is needed if exports are to be diversified. The key areas here are improving airport passenger and cargo handling facilities and encouraging major airlines to begin scheduled passenger flights on wide-bodied aircraft with direct connections to European cities; maintaining the cold storage facilities at the airport and studying special refrigeration needs for export development, before further investment in such facilities; establishing a commercially run central communications and office facility for use by exporters and foreign investors, that provides efficient telephone, fax, telex, and secretarial services; accelerating feeder road rehabilitation; and changing the Uganda Railways rolling stock to accommodate greatly increased container traffic, and structuring the Port Bell facility as a container terminal.

4.145   The Government should give priority to negotiating transport agreements with Kenya and Tanzania to station neighboring country customs officers in Kampala--or Port Bell in the future. Such officers would preclear export freight, especially container cargo, and thus reduce border delays and handling costs; permit the transport of refrigerated containers on Ugandan registered trucks; and coordinate railway schedules and the creation of container express trains with rapid transhipment between container ports, Kampala and Mombasa.

4.146   Many of the proposed export crops require skills and technologies that are not generally available in Uganda. These can be obtained by technical assistance and on-the-job training financed by foreign investors or donors, and technical school and university courses. Some key areas for additional training are postharvest technology of perishable and durable crops, crop processing, engineering, and farm management. The Bureau of Standards, if strengthened, could play a role in providing guidance to the private sector on setting and monitoring appropriate product quality standards at each stage of the production and post harvest handling process.

4.147   Ventures into unfamiliar agricultural production and transformation processes require rapid and flexible adaptive research support. An applied research facility should be set up, ostensibly at Makerere, where faculty and students can engage in applied research for local industry, financed with a mixture of commercial, Government, and donor funding. Research could lead--and support--testing the production and processing of high-potential commodities for Uganda.

4.148   There is a need for long term funding, equity based if possible, to support these ventures. Government should try to encourage the entry of foreign venture capital firms by providing all the usual incentives for foreign investment. With the proposed Financial Sector Adjustment Operation in place, the Government, with donor support, should consider creating a line of medium-term credit, handled by the Bank of Uganda through the commercial banking system to support this type of venture. This line of credit will have to be fashioned carefully, given the high business risks in this field, but the payoffs in export growth could be high. USAID has experience with a similar line of credit in support of agro-industry development.

Food

4.149   Food production is the most widespread economic activity in Uganda. It accounts for 74 percent of agriculture of GDP, which is 60 percent of national output (fig. 3). The foods produced in Uganda are high in starch. Bananas account for 50 percent of total tonnage, and root crops another 35 percent. Cereals account for 10 percent of food production, and pulses the remaining 5 percent (fig. 36).

4.150   Growth in the agricultural economy in 1981-90 has been due to the very strong growth in food production, rebounding from the trough of 1980-81. Trend growth in the value of food production was 3.3 percent per year, pulling agricultural GDP growth up to 2.8 percent per year. The value of cash crop output increased only marginally at 0.9 percent per year.

4.151   In spite of its strong performance however, food production (in tonnage) only surpassed 1970 production levels in 1988 (fig. 37). Rapid growth in the 1980s has in fact been reversing the decline of 1976-80, and catching up with the levels of output achieved in the early 1970s. Population

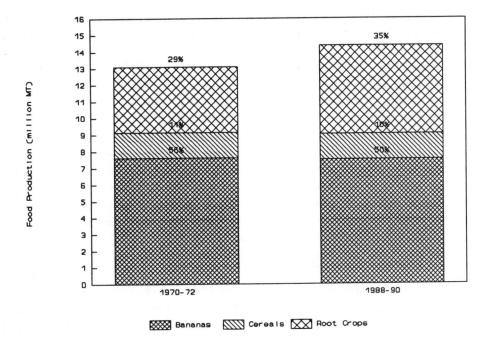

Figure 36   Food Production in Millions of Tons, and Shares of Select Food Crops, 1970-72 and 1988-90

Figure 37   Food Production Index Compared With the Real Kampala Food Price Index, 1970-90

growth did not slow during the troubled years, however, and food production per capita is now well below the levels recorded in the early 1970s (fig. 37).

4.152   Real food prices--deflated by the Low Income Consumer Price Index--increased sharply during the disruptions of war in 1979-80) and 1985-86. During 1981-90, however, food prices appear to have remained stable, and have even declined somewhat, except for 1989 when food prices rose sharply (fig. 37). This stability can be attributed to the rapid growth in output accommodating the rise in incomes and in population. Since 1981, real food prices have remained at levels well below those of the 1970s, in spite of the decline in food production per capita.   This apparent difference may be due to difficulties in collecting statistics in 1979-80. It can also be explained by the much lower per capita income levels that prevailed as of 1979 (fig.38), which kept demand--and thus prices--down. The income elasticity of demand for food in a poor country such as Uganda can be expected to be between 0.95 and 1.0. 73/ Per capita income dropped by 30 percent between 1970 and 1980. Food production dropped by 20 percent, which would imply that real prices can be expected to have declined.

4.153   It is reasonable to ask whether food production has responded to food prices. When the war years (1979-81 and 1985-86) are withdrawn from the computation, simple regression results indicate the food production per capita in a given year is closely correlated with the real price of food for the previous year (fig. 37)

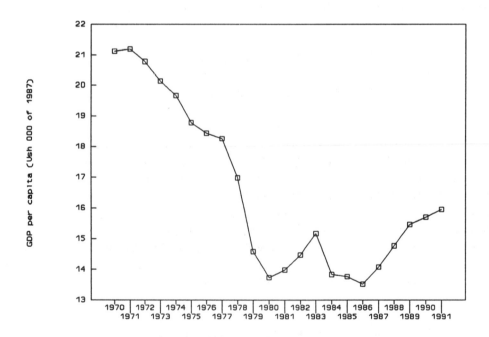

Figure 38   Real GDP per Capita in Ush of 1987, 1970-91

73/   Alderman, op. cit., p. 38.

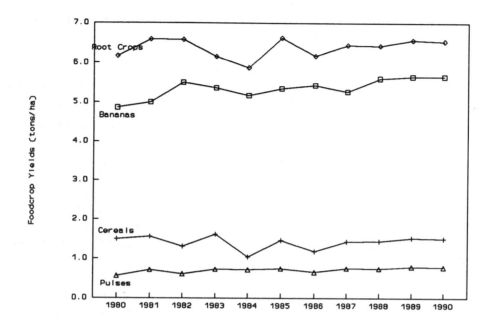

Figure 39   Average Yields for Selected Food Crops in Tons per Ha, 1980-90

4.154   The main food crop is bananas. It accounts for one-third of the 3.9 million ha under food. Seven other crops each have between 7 and 10 percent of area under food: beans, cassava, groundnuts, maize, millet, sorghum, and sweet potatoes.

4.155   Banana production in 1990 returned to the 7.5 million to 8 million tons yearly level reached in 1970-72. The increase in plantain output has been due to a rapid expansion in the area cultivated. Plantain yields appear to have been falling since the 1970s, from 8 tons to 8.5 tons/ha in the early 1970s, to 5.0 to 5.5 tons/ha during the mid-to late 1980s. These yield changes may be due to changes in yield estimation methods. There may however be a decline, due to the swings in production incentives, which affect the level of husbandry--no purchased inputs are used in banana production--and hence the yield. Since 1980, yield levels for bananas have gradually increased, albeit from a low base. The presence of a viral disease (called black sigatoka) has been detected in Uganda recently, and its effect is gradually spreading. While Ugandan bananas appear to be more resistant to virus than West African varieties, urgent research work is needed to identify or develop resistant plants and propagate them.

4.156   Yields for other food crops do not appear to have declined as precipitously as for bananas. Indeed, the 1980s, where the data are more reliable, the general trend was for yields to remain stable, or increase, as for cassava (fig. 39). It is true that yields for most crops are well below potential farm level output levels. The challenge to research and extension staff is to develop profitable and reliable methods of raising these yields using technology available to the small farmer.

4.157   **Market Prospects**. The market for food is domestic and regional. As mentioned previously, the domestic market for food can be expected to grow rapidly. A recent study in neighboring

Rwanda, where income levels and diet are comparable to Uganda's, shows an income elasticity of demand for food of 0.96. 74/ With population projected to grow at around 3.1 percent per year, and income per capita continuing to grow at 1.0 to 2.0 percent per year, demand for food--at constant relative prices--should continue to grow at 4 to 5 percent.

4.158 Food crop prices, while more volatile, have generally held up better than those for cash crops, providing the incentives for the shift into food crop cultivation as noted above. The ratio of farmgate coffee prices to banana prices has dropped from early 1970 levels, except for a dramatic increase between 1981 and 1984 when concerted efforts were made to improve the incentives for coffee production, and a second increase in relative coffee prices in 1991 (fig. 40).

4.159 Growth in food production will also be stimulated by the expansion of the monetized market. The possibility of selling food for cash will increase as roads are improved and extended, and as urban populations grow. In addition, if banana yields are affected severely by black sigatoka over the next five to ten years, and if mealybug infestation of cassava arrives in Uganda, as in neighboring countries, a fairly massive shift to consumption of other food crops can be expected.

4.160 **A Strategy for Growth.** The strategy for growth in food crop production should incorporate two approaches: acknowledgement and indirect support for bringing new land into crops, and support for an increase in land and labor productivity in areas now farmed. Food crop production in Uganda has always been based upon low purchased input systems. It has never been significantly affected by research or extension. Past increases in food crop production have always come from an increase in crop area, as new families are formed and move to open up their own farms. The expansion of cultivated areas under food crops is expected to continue, especially as security improves, with underutilized areas brought into production through inter-district and inter-regional migration and investment. However, increasing pressure on land in different districts is unavoidable, and will lead to increased labor-to-land ratios, more intensive practices, and increased yields--if returns to labor are to be maintained.

4.161 To increase the returns to labor in support of extensification increased attention must be given to mechanization. At current costs and crop prices there will be little scope for tractorization. The focus should be on ox-drawn cultivation. Attention should be given to: (a) overcoming the security and destocking constraints in the traditional heartland of ox cultivation in the Eastern Region; (b) providing support to the newly emerging ox cultivators in Tororo, Apac, and Karamoja; (c) promoting ox-power cultivation in other areas where livestock availability, soil type, terrain, vegetation, and social attitudes are favorable; (d) investigating the role of ox-drawn carts in releasing labor from current systems of transport; and adopting policies that foster private-sector grain milling to reduce the time taken by women on hand grinding.

4.162 The intensification of technology being advocated in a recent MAAIF-MFAD report on foodcrop development 75/ is not attractive financially at unsubsidized fertilizer prices. Much of the yield increase is expected to derive from the use of inorganic fertilizer. In Uganda a farmer has to sell 12 to 16 kg of grain to purchase 1 kg of nitrogen (depending on the fertilizer type). This compares with 2 or 3 kg of grain to one of nitrogen in developed countries. The response ratios of

---

74/   von Braun and others, op. cit., p. 66.

75/   Ministry of Agriculture and Manpower for Agricultural Development Project, Accelerated Foodcrop Production Strategy, Kampala, April 1990, p.20.

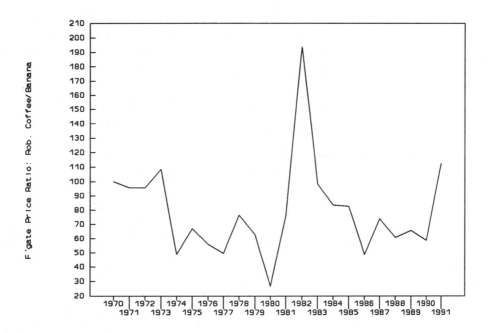

Figure 40   Ratio of Farmgate Prices of Robusta Coffee and Bananas, 1970-91

grain to nitrogen for millet, sorghum, and open pollinated maize range from five fifteen so that none of these crops can give attractive returns to fertilizer use at current price ratios. The lower-valued root crops give poorer returns. The use of fertilizer on food crops at present is practically nil. Hybrid maize with high levels of management can give more attractive returns and this should be the focus of attention for high-input cropping.

4.163   The other arm of the Government strategy for growth through the use of yield-increasing technology is the widespread use of improved seed. At present there are no varieties available of sorghum, millet, beans, or groundnuts that would attract widespread interest from farmers at commercial seed prices. An improved open pollinated maize has recently been developed but experience across the rest of Africa is that there is limited demand for such material at commercial seed prices. The focus of a seed industry would be restricted to hybrid maize.

4.164   The major constraint on field-level productivity in Uganda is from pests and diseases rather than soil fertility. The long-term solution to these lies with plant breeding and propagation rather than with purchased inputs. Resources therefore need to be concentrated on identifying and developing varieties with genetic resistance to the major pests and diseases. Once resistant varieties are obtained, the Government should arrange for multiplication and distribution. The strategy for food crop development advocated in this report is based on mounting an intensive research effort focussed on disease resistance, mentioned above, and an extension service focusing on the distribution of new vegetative planting material and the most labor-efficient methods of raising yields through changes in cultural practices. In the food crop subsector these research and extension efforts will have to be supported completely from Government sources. The Pilot Extension Project and the Agricultural Research Project, prepared for possible Bank financing, would address these questions.

4.165   Bananas, sweet potatoes and cassava, which contribute 85 percent of food production, all offer the opportunity for major yield increases through planting material with genetic tolerance or resistance to black sigatoka, fusarium wilt, nematodes, and weevils, affecting bananas; cassava mosaic, the green spider mite, cassava bacterial blight; and sweet potato viruses.

4.166   The success of this kind of approach depends on an effective agricultural research establishment in the development of the disease-resistant varieties, and an extension service to introduce and disseminate the improved varieties and provide instruction in improved husbandry. The crops mentioned above are all vegetatively propagated and the widespread dissemination of pest-and disease-tolerant material acceptable to farmers would depend on a network of multiplication centers, not on a centralized seed company. A seed company probably would not show interest in sale of vegetatively propagated planting material, given the ease with which it can be multiplied and dispersed within a farming community.

4.167   The organization and management of this activity will depend on human resources and not capital expenditure. Research on cassava varieties resistant to mosaic is well-advanced. A program for the multiplication and dissemination of mosaic-resistant cassava should be able to start soon. Research on sweet potatoes is just starting and research on disease resistant bananas is in its infancy, in spite of the enormous economic importance of this crop.

4.168   Uganda is fortunate in that there appears to be considerable scope for increasing the yields of its dominant food crops without resort to annual foreign exchange expenditures on chemical inputs. At a later stage, when it becomes clear that some constraints remain which cannot be overcome through plant selection and breeding, further advances may be possible through inputs that are financially more attractive than they are today.

4.169   Sorghum and millet respond relatively little to fertilizer and are unlikely to offer opportunities for profitable fertilizer use. They were researched intensively in the past with little effect, and it may be some time before further progress can be made increasing yields with a financially attractive package of seed or inputs.

4.170   Two strategies for maize production are likely to develop. The first approach, which would cover most maize farmers, depends on the use of a Government-funded extension service and would concentrate on making modest gains to yield through improved advice on cultural practices for what is a new crop for many growers. The second approach is restricted to the development of a group of "specialist" farmers with the financial and managerial capability of using hybrid seed and inorganic fertilizer. Such a production system would require:

- confidence in the capacity of the maize market to absorb large increases in output (the maize market collapsed in 1988 from overproduction). This confidence should be enhanced by the improvement in regional export prospects, a shift into grains as incomes increase, and the increased production of maize byproducts such as alcohol, starches, oils, and meals;

- reliable and secure private sector input procurement and distribution systems;

- farmers with above-average resources to finance the more input-intensive production system; and

- proof that maize production with a high-input, high-output technology would be profitable and competitive with other crops in a given ecological area.

4.171 Beans and groundnuts have not provided attractive returns to purchased inputs in the past and are less likely to do so under the current economic conditions. Intensified research is expected to produce more disease-and pest-resistant material but it will be some time before this is generally available. Groundnut multiplication rates are quite low and experience elsewhere has been that it takes a long time to switch a major part of the crop to a new variety. Breeding, localized seed multiplication, and advice on improved husbandry would be the basic strategies for these crops, but change would require an extended period, even with an effective program.

4.172 Because much of Ugandan food production is dominated by bananas, cassava, and sweet potatoes--all of which are eaten soon after harvest and are not stored in significant quantities--there is less risk of post harvest loss than with crops which have to be stored over many months. The major local grains, millet and sorghum, store particularly well. Some introduced sorghums do not store well and thus have not gained widespread popularity. Groundnuts and soya beans suffer little post-harvest loss where grown in a suitable environment. Maize and beans--9 percent of production--are the most susceptible to post-harvest loss. However cheap and practical methods already exist to control loss so they are not a long-term threat to production.

Sugar

4.173 Sugar processing was the largest industrial venture in Uganda before 1972. Climatic conditions for cane cultivation on the northern shores of Lake Victoria are good. Production peaked in 1970 at 154,100 tons of processed sugar. By 1985, production had fallen to 1,000 tons of sugar. Imports increased to 46,000 tons in 1986, but per capita consumption has declined dramatically. From levels of around 14 kg per capita in the early 1970s, which are comparable to consumption levels in surrounding countries, per capita sugar consumption dropped to below 5 kg per capita in the 1980s. The household expenditure survey of 1989-90 shows average household consumption to be on the order of 3.5 kg to 4.0 kg per capita per annum. The cost of sugar imports, about US$ 15 million in 1986, declined to US$ 2.4 million in 1989 and US$ 0.8 million in 1990.

4.174 There are three sugar factories: Kakira and Lugazi, near Jinja, and Kinyala near Masindi, in the West. Production in Kakira and Lugazi ran at around full capacity of 140,000 tons in 1968-70. Production declined to 69,000 tons in 1973, after the Asians were expelled from Uganda, and continued down to 2,400 tons in 1980.   The slow recovery to about 3,000 tons in 1984 and 1984 was frozen in 1986 and 1987. Since 1988, recovery has been dramatic, however--assisted by rehabilitation finance from IDA, the International Finance Corporation, the African Development Bank, and other donors. Output of processed sugar in 1990-91 was about 30,000 tons. Cane is drawn mainly from nucleus estates (around 8,000 ha in Kakira and 10,000 ha in Lugazi) and from outgrowers (2,600 ha in Kakira) (table 21). The Kinyala estate has never performed close to its 35,000 ton total capacity. Completed in the mid 1970s, production peaked at 3,500 tons in 1978 before operations were stopped a few years later.

4.175 Since 1986 the Government has supported the rehabilitation of the Lugazi and the Kakira sugar complexes. The rehabilitation of the Kinyala plant, now under way with funding from international donors, will permit the restoration of production capacity to about 170,000 tons of sugar by 1997. The rehabilitation of Lugazi and Kakira is well-advanced. The Overseas Development Association has funded a management firm to initiate operations at Kinyala. The foreign exchange savings at this level of output and consumption--net of replacement parts and other imported inputs, is in the order of US$75 million per year. It is estimated that domestic demand, which has been constrained by high prices, low incomes, and lack of supplies, will expand to meet these production levels.

Table 21: Status of Sugar Industry 1991							
	Kakira		Lugazi		Kinyala	Total	
	Target	Actual	Target	Actual	Target	Target	Actual
Cane Area (ha)	10,600	5,456	9,500	7,571	9,400	20,100	13,027
Cane Harvested (ha)		2,385		2,717			5,102
Factory Capacity (tc/d)	2,500	1,200	2,200	2,200	1,500	4,700	3,400
Cane Yield (t/ha)	105 t/ha	70 t/ha		83 t/ha			
Cane Crushed (t)	700,000	167,000	600,000	225,500	380,000	1,680,000	392,500
Sugar Produced (t)	74,200	14,400	60,000	15,600	37,000	171,200	30,000
Sugar Yield (%)		8.6%		6.9%			

4.176   In March 1991 following its broad policy of trade liberalization, the Government abandoned the system of administratively determining producer and consumer prices for sugar. Wholesale prices, to be set by competing sugar producers and importers, will reflect assessments of domestic supply and demand. In late 1991 the wholesale price of sugar charged by the two sugar producers was Ush540 per kilogram (US$0.50/kg at the market exchange rate), which is comparable to the prices charged by importers of sugar after tax and duty (and above import parity).

4.177   **Market Prospects.** Uganda's eventual demand for sugar over the next decade will eventually outstrip the production capacity of the existing factories. The income elasticity of demand for sugar is high, especially at the low levels of per capita consumption occurring in Uganda. An income elasticity for sugar of 3.17 for rural dwellers was estimated in a recent study in Rwanda. [76] Projections using consumption levels of the early 1970s imply total demand of about 250,000 tons in the mid 1990s, two-thirds greater than the maximum expected output. Given the high cost of importing sugar into Uganda, which includes transport from the coast, an import-substitution strategy makes economic sense. Even if international sugar prices were to drop 40 percent below Bank forecast levels at full development, the rehabilitation of the Kakira sugar complex would be viable in economic terms.

4.178   **Strategy for Growth.** The Government is meeting one key objective--reducing import costs-- with the successful rehabilitation of this industry. With most of the industry in private hands, and the determination of the domestic price subject to market forces, a key policy question for the Government relates to the level of protection from imports accorded to the sugar industry. The real price of sugar has gone up along with the increase in domestic output (fig. 41). The price of sugar to the consumer in Kampala in June 1991 was Ush 710 per kg at the consumer level, [77] equivalent

---

[76]   Joachim von, Braun, et al. op. cit., p. 66.

[77]   MPED, Key Economic Indicators, 6th Issue, July 1991, Table 19.

to US$0.76 per kg at the market exchange rate (US$760 per ton). Sugar was US$186 a ton FOB in the Caribbean in April-June 1991. 78/ While the domestic price appears to be well above import parity rates the Government has agreed that sufficient protection should be provided over the next few years, to enable the sugar factories to reinvest in plant, equipment, and estate development while maintaining profitability. The recent review of the Kakira sugar project indicates that operations are, and will continue to be, profitable at current prices. 79/ The agreement with IDA is that imports would be taxed to keep the wholesale price, CIF Kampala, at not less than US$400 per ton. It appears that, at current wholesale prices, demand for sugar is not as strong as expected and that inventories have been increasing. This, coupled with the high level of domestic prices, would indicate a need for the sugar producers--and traders--to reduce the price of sugar in real terms over the medium term. The Government should use the threat of increased--or lower-cost--importation to ensure that consumers pay a reasonable price for this commodity. While controlling the effects of international competition on the industry, the Government should allow the development of local competitors and not discourage the development of other small-scale refineries by the private sector. Their profitablility and longevity should be market determined.

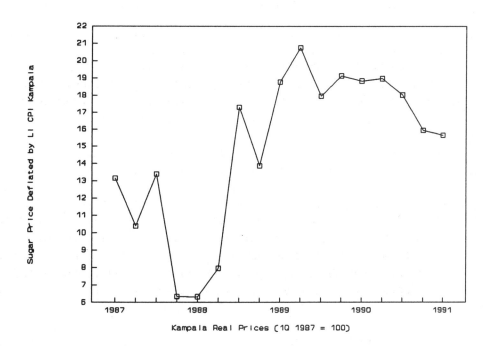

Figure 41   Quarterly Sugar Price in Kampala Deflated by the Low Income Consumer Price Index, 1987-91

78/   World Bank, "Commodity Price Data Sheet", International Trade Division, March 18, 1992.

79/   World Bank/AfDB-AfDF, "Mid Term Review - Aide Memoire," November 1991.

4.179   A second but related policy decision facing the sector refers to the pricing of cane purchases from the outgrowers. Cane producers are locked into a monopsony market. As with the price of greenleaf tea, some kind of governmental regulation on a fair minimum cane price is required to ensure that a portion of the rents from sugar production are passed down to the cane producers. Studies by the Bank of Uganda's Agricultural Secretariat on the Kakira estate coupled with conditionality under the IDA credit for that enterprise, will lay the foundation for policy.

Livestock and Dairy

4.180   Livestock products contributed 16 percent to agriculture GDP in 1990, down from 20 percent in 1980. Output from this sector has not grown significantly in real terms during the 1980s. Indeed, MAAIF statistics show that in 1987 the national cattle herd declined by 25 percent, and the sheep and goat herd by 36 percent, as a result of civil insecurity and cattle rustling in the North and Northeast. As of 1986, however, the strong resurgence of the dairy industry in the Southwest has caused livestock subsector GDP to grow at 4.9 percent per annum.

4.181   The 1990-91 livestock population was estimated by MAAIF to be about 4.3 million head of cattle, 3.04 million goats, 0.83 million sheep, and 0.62 million pigs. The national poultry flock is estimated at 10 million to 12 million birds. According to the 1989-90 Household Expenditure Survey, West and Southwest Uganda are currently the richest in livestock, with about two head of cattle per household, compared with one per household in the rest of the country.

4.182   Cattle are the most important type of livestock, in numbers and value. The national cattle herd which once numbered between 5 and 5.5 million animals was decimated during the fifteen years of civil war and disruption, and was only back up to 4.9 million by 1990. While outright slaughter accounts for some of the decline, the major reason for the reduction in herd size is the resurgence of a series of diseases that had previously been eradicated or controlled.

4.183   Mixed-farming smallholders and pastoralists own over 90 percent of the national cattle herd. Pastoralists are found mostly in the northeast (Karamoja) and in the Southwest--in Mbarara, Bushenyi and Masaka districts. Commercial dairy farming is based on some 140,000 animals of imported dairy breeds (mainly Frisian) and crosses with indigenous cattle. Commercial dairy farming developed primarily around the northern and western shores of Lake Victoria, and in the Southwest. This industry declined dramatically in the area because of the war of 1979-81. As of 1987, milk production has grown steadily in southwestern Uganda which now produces about 90 percent of marketed processed milk. A commercial beef ranching sector was built up in the 1960s and early 1970s and by 1984 produced about 20 percent of Uganda's beef. The IDA-supported Beef Ranching Development Project (Cr. 130-UG), implemented from 1969 to 1972, contributed to that growth. Ranches have suffered heavily from banditry and only about 50 ranches in the Southwest, out of a total of 400 nationwide, remain viably stocked. Commercial poultry and pig production, almost entirely in small household units, grew steadily from 1950 to 1970. The subsequent decline in those industries has been largely the result of a decline in grain milling and livestock feed.

4.184   Natural grass-dominated communal pastures provide almost all feed for indigenous livestock. Exotic and crossbred dairy animals susceptible to tickborne diseases are usually confined to fenced farms or kept in small enclosures. Some are hand fed on a cut-and-carry--zero grazing--basis. A survey by MAAIF of dairy farmers with exotic or crossbred animals shows that 46 percent of these farmers own only one or two cattle, most of the farmers now practice zero grazing and most are women.

4.185   The indigenous Zebu cattle total some 70 percent of the cattle population, followed by the indigenous Sanga (Ankole) with 15 percent, and the intermediates--crosses between the previous two breeds--with 13 percent. The remaining 2 percent are the exotic breeds, brought into Uganda since 1960 for the dairy and beef industry. The Zebu have low production coefficients and milk yields. Cows mature at about 4 years, calve every second year, and produce about 350 liters per lactation. Calf mortality is extremely high, at about 25 to 30 percent. Mortality for cattle is high, at about 7 percent. For imported breeds and crossbreds, the mortality rates are reversed: about 5 percent for calves and 10 percent for cattle, the calving rate is about 60 percent, and average milk production about 1,750 liters per lactation. While not providing as much meat and milk as exotics, local breeds are better adapted to local conditions and have higher resistance to trypanosomiasis and tick-borne diseases. Average cattle slaughter carcass weights in Uganda are estimated at about 150 kg.

4.186   Indigenous sheep and goat breeds predominate. The pig herd is a mix of European breeds and indiscriminate crosses. Indigenous poultry and crosses with imported breeds are found in the traditional sector while imported specialized layers, broilers and dual-purpose birds are used in the commercial sector. Production coefficients for sheep and goats are comparable to those in other parts of East Africa. Offtake is estimated at between 30 and 35 percent and mortality rates at between 20 and 30 percent. Slaughter carcass weights are 12-14 kg for sheep and goats. Production coefficients for pigs and poultry are very poor in the traditional sector.

4.187   The formal industry to supply milk to urban areas was only set up in the early 1960s with the Uganda Milk Processing Limited to supply Kampala and Jinja with milk imported from Kenya (45,000 liters per day). During the next fifteen years more than 3,000 dairy farmers established themselves using exotic breeds and crosses to supply the urban markets. Following the creation of the Government-owned Uganda Dairy Corporation in 1967, output expanded, and by the early 1970s Uganda had reached self-sufficiency with some 55,000 liters per day procured through a network of collection centers. The old Mbale dairy was taken over by the UDC in 1967. It had a nominal capacity of 30,000 liters per shift. By 1986, the collecting, processing, and marketing infrastructure was totally run-down due to lack of maintenance and looting. Other smaller dairies operated for short periods. The Toro Dairy Cooperative Society in Fort Portal which started in 1964 operated a small processing plant for about five years up to 1975, marketing up to 5,000 liters of pasteurized milk daily in nearby towns and trading centers. It subsequently closed due to management problems, was revived in 1989, and currently provides cooling for about 2,000 liters/day. Average milk consumption which was on the order of 40 liters per capita per year has now dropped to 20 liters.

4.188   By 1986 the formalized liquid milk supply system had collapsed. All the processed milk supplied to urban areas (mainly Kampala) by UDC was recombined from products imported by WFP. Since then, milk collected through the formal system has been increased from virtually nothing to more than nine million liters--or 50 percent of processed milk sales in 1990--the highest level since 1973. During the 1991 wet season all the milk sold by UDC in Kampala was indigenously produced. It is unlikely that imports of recombined milk will be required in the forseeable future, even to compensate for production fluctuations between the wet and dry seasons. Kampala and Jinja are supplied from a collection point in Mbarara, serving the Southwest. The number of farmers delivering milk to UDC has increased from less than 400 in 1986 to almost 6,000 in 1991. Whereas in 1989 about 12,000 liters per day were being shipped from Mbarara to Kampala, in mid 1991 some 70,000 liters per day were being sent up. The nominal capacity of the Kampala dairy is 65,000 liters per day. Operations are inefficient, however, and renovation of the plant has been initiated.

4.189   Milk collection, processing, and marketing for the urban markets is now monopolized by the Uganda Dairy Corporation. By procuring milk in the Southwest, the Uganda Dairy Corporation has supported a strong resurgence in milk production in the region. However, the areas around Kampala in Luwero and Mubende which provided much of the fresh milk previously have recently started to participate in the flourishing urban market through the "informal market". Up to 50 percent of the Kampala market for milk is supplied from the informal sector. The Luwero and Mubende regions will have a strong cost advantage over the Southwest in supplying Kampala, and can be expected to exercise a strong competitive pressure in the future. Prices for pasteurized milk are fixed by the Government, and only cover the Uganda Dairy Corporation's cash operating costs. In the past no allowances have been made for capital improvement. Farmgate milk prices in the South (about US$ 0.13 per liter), while low by international standards, have induced a strong supply response.

4.190   Problems with animal health are the main constraint on livestock production in Uganda. Livestock and poultry diseases can be conveniently summarized as follows: Major epidemic cattle diseases such as Rinderpest and Contagious Bovine Pleuropneumonia (CBPP); Diseases needing serious attention such as Trypanosomiasis, tickborne diseases, Foot and Mouth Disease, and Helminthiasis; Zoonoses such as Rabies, Brucellosis, Anthrax, and Tuberculosis; Relatively minor diseases such as Blackquarter, Hemorrhagic Septicaemia, Ephemeral Fever, Lumpy Skin disease, Contagious Caprine Pleuropneumonia, and African Swine Fever; and Poultry diseases such as Newcastle Disease, Fowl Pox, Fowltyphoid, Coccidiosis, Marck's disease, and Leukosis.

4.191   Uganda was free from Rinderpest from 1966 to 1979, when the breakdown of controls allowed the disease to spread into the Northern and Central Regions. The Emergency (1988) and the Pan African (1990) Rinderpest Campaigns have checked the spread of Rinderpest. Some 2.7 million cattle have been vaccinated. The emphasis is on surveillance and control.

4.192   CBPP was confined in Karamoja until 1979, when it spread to the rest of the country. It is a difficult disease to eradicate, and continuous vaccination at the rate of 4 million doses a year will be necessary. It is expected that the vaccine will be produced locally after January 1992.

4.193   Trypanosomiasis is endemic. Once-reclaimed areas are now reinfected. The disease is combated through vector controls, and by chemotherapy of infected animals. Projects focusing on tsetse eradication and trypanosomiasis treatment are underway with funding from EEC, OAU, and UK.

4.194   The most common tickborne diseases are East Coast Fever (the main killer of exotic cattle), anaplasmosis, heart water, and babesiosis. Ticks are controlled by dipping and spraying, but cost-effective levels of acaricide application have not been determined. The expense of the acaricides encourages use of a weak dosage, which then leads to the development of resistance in the ticks.

4.195   **Market Prospects.** The medium-term binding constraint on livestock production in Uganda will be demand and not supply. With continued problems of disease, Uganda's formal access to overseas export markets will be limited for many years. Demand for livestock will depend on the domestic and regional market. The weakness of domestic demand for livestock products is reflected in very low prices for meat (beef and pork) at present. The price for beef in Kampala in late 1991 was about Ush600/kg. At the same time, the price for cattle was about

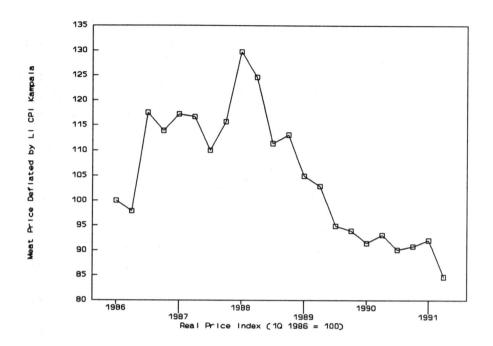

Figure 42   Quarterly Price of Beef Deflated by Kampala Low Income Consumer
Price Index, 1986-91

Ush300/kg liveweight (equivalent to about US$0.30/kg), only 15 to 20 percent of prices received
by producers in Europe or the USA. Real meat prices in Kampala, the main cash market,
increased in real terms from 1986 through to a peak in early 1988, as insecurity in the North and
Northeast affected the availability of livestock. Since then, beef prices have been in a secular
decline which has still to turn. Real beef prices were 35 percent below their 1988 peak, in mid
1991 (fig. 42). The situation for pork and fish is not much better.

4.196   The prospects for increased demand for meat products, if income per capita
continues to increase, are good. The income elasticity of demand for meat is high. It was
estimated at between 0.95 and 1 for low income families in Sudan and Sierra Leone, and 4.4 in
rural Rwanda. 80/ The Household Budget Survey shows a high income elasticity of demand
for livestock products, roughly 1.5. Incomes per capita have declined in Uganda since the early
1970s, to a final trough in 1986/87 (fig. 40). If income per capita continue to grow at a rate of
1.5 percent per annum--as it has since 1987 (fig. 40)--and the population grows at the projected
3.1 percent per annum, there should be a healthy 4 to 6 percent per annum growth in meat
demand (and hence output) at constant relative prices. Although the population has increased by
65 percent since 1970, however, income levels in real terms are still 30 percent below what they
were then. An income elasticity of demand of 2.0 or more for meat, coupled with the 30 percent

---

80/   Alderman, op cit p. 81, 82 and
             von Braun and others, op. cit., p. 66.

decline in income, would mean a drop of more than 60 percent in consumption--which would cancel out the effect of the population increase since 1979 (at constant relative prices).

4.197   The farm-gate milk price is also extremely low by international standards if peri-urban milk producers adjacent to Kampala are excluded. The price was Ush130/kg (about US$0.14) in September 1991 for milk delivered to collection centers in the Southwest, without an allowance for transport costs incurred by the farmer. It is less than half the farmgate price received by European and American farmers but about equal to the price received by New Zealand producers for milk destined for processing into dairy products. Although the price around Kampala was relatively high at about Ush 250-300/kg (about US$0.28 to 0.33/kg) this can only be taken advantage of by producers able to sell fresh milk direct to consumers.

4.198   At about Ush750/kg liveweight (about US$0.85/kg), poultry is much closer to international prices than are cattle or pigs. Allowing for the higher poultry liveweight-to-meat ratio (75 percent) over cattle (50 percent), poultry meat prices are about Ush1,000/kg (US$ 1.11), above beef at Ush600/kg (about US$0.60), indicating that poultry meat is a luxury product in Uganda.

4.199   There appears to be substantial demand for goat meat, and the industry should develop on the basis of local demand.   Export potential to the Middle East is limited.

4.200   **A Strategy for Growth.** There is good potential for medium-term growth in this industry. Consumption is likely to continue to increase, as incomes go up and families return to previous consumption levels. If increased reliance on imports is to be avoided, conditions should be created for a resurgence of local production. Climate and fodder availability are well suited for this type of development. A strategy for reducing the disease burden depends on improving the efficacy of the animal health service, (Chapter III).

4.201   The government has been preparing a Master plan for the dairy subsector, with assistance from DANIDA. The Master plan is expected to formulate a strategy for development of the dairy subsector to include the following components:

- For the domestic market, competition among milk processors should be fostered, and consumer substitution between natural and pasteurized milk should be permitted. Sale of untreated milk should continue to be permitted. Pasteurizing should be used mainly to increase the durability of milk transported long distances from producer to consumer. In this vein, the Government should ensure that prices for milk--raw or pasteurized--and milk products are determined by market forces; Consumers are encouraged to boil raw milk; other organizations are permitted to compete with the Uganda Dairy Corporation in milk pasteurization; farmers are encouraged to form local and regional cooperative organizations, to manage cooling and transporting milk to urban centers; and while private or cooperative sector competition is allowed to develop, the Dairy Corporation is maintained under Government sponsorship. This is to guarantee a supply of pasteurized milk to urban centers, and to foster supply response at the farm level. The Uganda Dairy Corporation should eventually be privatized, preferably to cooperatives or farmers associations involved in milk production and transport. The inactive Mbale plant should be sold off immediately.

- 119 -

- For <u>regional milk production</u> it should be recognized that producers in the environs of Kampala have a strong price advantage in supplying the city. The farmgate price adjacent to Kampala is at least double that in the South. It can be expected that eventually the main suppliers of Kampala and Jinja will be from the surrounding districts. The South will continue to provide milk to fill the deficit but it is unlikely that demand will grow much further. Regional surpluses will have to be channeled into milk-based products (butter, cheese). In this regard it should be noted that milk used for processed products like cheese will realize a substantially lower price than milk in the liquid consumer market; the pricing and collection strategy for the Southwest should adjust to the region's competitive advantage compared with other areas of the country; and facilities for processing milk into dairy products should be developed in the Southwest;

- An efficient <u>artificial insemination</u> service can improve the productivity and management of the dairy industry. The Government-run service will be privatized shortly. It is suggested that, in addition to the rather costly cold chain, the privately-run insemination service test the possibility of providing fresh semen on-farm as well. The sires used for this service should be certified by a National Dairy Control Board, to ensure that the quality of the dairy herd is improved. The most cost-effective approach would dominate and be continued.

- Uganda is self-sufficient in milk during the wet season but relies still on reconstituted milk for a substantial part of the Kampala supply in the dry season. The UDC expects to meet about 70 percent of the 1991 demand from domestic sources, compared with about 45 percent last year. <u>Substitution for imported milk</u> can be encouraged further--and eventually eliminated--by better phasing of the calving season; better feeding and herd management; and the development of a fresh-milk-processing capacity that can absorb the difference between total milk production and liquid milk demand in the wet season. When milk production drops in the dry season, it will go down to levels which bring it into balance with consumer demand for fresh milk. The development of a butter, cheese, and other byproduct market is of crucial importance to this strategy.

4.202   The delicacy of the incentive structure in the dairy industry--and the need for setting and maintaining standards on milk quality, improvement of dairy breeds, a pricing policy for the period of governmental participation, and management during the divestiture and development of private sector capacity--indicate the need for a dairy industry control board. This board should include representatives from the industry and Government, and have a small staff of high-level professionals.

4.203   Uganda is grossly understocked for <u>red meat production</u> at present. Meat production for the domestic market can be expected to increase rapidly, as domestic prices rise. The reestablishment of security in the North and Northeast--areas of traditional extensive livestock production--will also contribute to increase production. Improvements in the animal health situation are also a precondition for further investments in higher-quality breeds and increased pasture productivity. Once the animal health problems have been resolved, Uganda is well-placed to compete in the world market for beef.

4.204   The reinstating of security in traditional livestock zones, and the control of the main diseases can be expected to give an impetus to another livestock product: <u>draft power</u> for crop cultivation. This, in turn, should enhance labor productivity, incomes, and output.

4.205   <u>Small ruminants</u> are particularly import to small subsistence farmers. Special attention needs to be given to strengthening the animal health and extension services for small ruminants. Legume trees and shrubs, for example, have a special role to play in smallholder goat production. Goats will attract most interest and a special effort should be made to test and popularize dual-purpose breeds to provide milk--and meat--for home consumption.

4.206   <u>Pig production</u> on small farms faces the risk of African Swine Fever. However, there is good scope for improving the traditional production systems. At present the age at slaughter is twice as high as it need be. More attention should be given to animal health, feeding, and management. The animal research facility should be charged with improving the traditional production systems within small-farmer-resource constraints.

4.207   <u>Poultry</u> has an important role to play in meeting future needs for animal products. The traditional backyard system using indigenous or upgraded birds can be improved by changing breeds and giving attention to disease control (for example, vaccination), feeding, and management. Research establishments should look into improved backyard poultry production systems. Priority should be given to the development of commercial or semicommercial production--both dual-purpose birds, and specialized layers and broilers. The private sector can handle this, but backstopping will be needed on disease problems (vaccinations and poultry pathology). Research will be needed on animal nutrition--including feed analysis--and husbandry. Facilities will need to be provided to overcome the day-old-chick constraint. Investments for day-old-chick production should be in the hands of private licensed operators.

Fish

4.208   About 42,000 square km of Uganda is under water--18 percent of the country. 81/ Lake Victoria is the largest body of water and the most important source of fish. Lakes Kyoga, Albert, Edward and George--among the most productive of the country's 165 lakes and swamps--are a rich resource, providing fish and irrigation water, while reducing temperature extremes, and increasing rainfall.

4.209   The most common fish subject to commercial exploitation are the Nile Perch and the Nile Tilapia, from the ninety species in the country. Potential sustainable yield from Uganda's waters has not been accurately estimated. The quantification of this resource, and the establishment of sustainable exploitation policies is the most important next step in this subsector. At present the most generally accepted estimate is that the sustainable harvest is about 300,000 tons per annum, about 20 above the current catch.

81/   This section draws heavily on the MAAIF/Agricultural Secretariat, "Fisheries Subsector Assessment," September 1991.

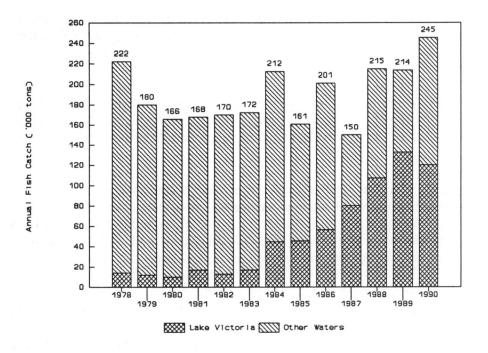

Figure 43 Annual Catch of Fish From Lake Victoria and Other Lakes in Thousands of Tons, 1978-90

4.210 The commercial harvest has averaged between 170,000 and 220,000 tons over the past 13 years (fig. 43). In 1990-91 the catch increased sharply, and an estimated 245,000 tons was harvested, worth about Ush34.3 billion ex-canoe (about US$34 million in September 1991). Lake Victoria, which used to account for under 10 percent of the national fish catch, has been increasing its share rapidly, and now provides 50 percent of the total. This is due to the rise in the importance of the Nile Perch, to be found principally in Lake Victoria and Lake Kyoga.

4.211 Fishing technology is artesanal. There are some 18,000 canoes in the industry, 2,400 of them motorized. These serve some 75,500 artesanal fishermen and their families, and the fishing appears to be profitable. Fresh fish prices, ex canoe, are about Ush200/kg. In addition two pair-trawlers (four boats) were recently introduced in Lake Victoria, operated by the Sino-Uganda Fisheries Joint Venture Co. Ltd. out of Entebbe.

4.212 The harvesting of fish is regulated by the so-called Fish and Crocodiles Act of 1951, revised in 1964. This law sets limitations on minimum fish size--18 inches for Nile Perch--and on aspects of fishing technology. Trawling is permitted in Uganda (but not in Kenya) and a minimum mesh size of 5 inches is required. Regulations are enforced by the Fisheries Department of the MAAIF, which has 500 staff stationed around the country. Regional staff also collect statistics on fish harvests and provide advice on catching, processing,and marketing. Research staff operate the Fish Technology Laboratory in Entebbe, and the Uganda Freshwater Fisheries Research Organization in Jinja. As in other parts of the MAAIF, the effectiveness of the Government's functions is hampered by shortages of trained staff, and inadequate salaries and operating budgets. Governmental research, extension, and surveillance have been assisted under donor projects funded by UNDP/FAO (stock assessment and research), IDRC-Canada (biology, ecology, and population dynamics of Nile Perch), EEC (artesanal fisheries rehabilitation); UNDP/FAO, Italian Aid (artesanal fishing Lake Victoria); IFAD/IDA (artesanal fishing in Lake Kyoga).

4.213   While governmental monitoring capacity is limited, overfishing is not yet considered a threat to the overall fish population. The harvest from Lake Victoria, however, is felt to be at its upper limit. The effect of the introduction of more intensive fishing techniques could cause the harvest levels to exceed sustainable limits.

4.214   **Market Prospects.** Fish are either sold fresh in the vicinity of the lakes, or dried and marketed through small traders and the local market infrastructure. Hygiene is poor, and specialized facilities are minimal. It is an attractive business opportunity, and recently a series of private sector, and joint venture firms have been established, processing fish for the premium local market, or export. Market prospects are good. In 1990 registered exports of fish totaled 1,664 tons worth US$1.4 million. Exports of 520 tons of frozen or chilled fish were handled by nine companies. Some 818 tons of smoked, dried, or salted fish were exported by twenty three firms. In 1991 this volume practically tripled to some 4,700 tons worth US$ 5.3 million. The key market for dried, smoked fish is Kenya. Fresh chilled or frozen fish are placed mainly in Gibraltar, Greece, the Netherlands, or the United Kingdom. There are an additional six 6 companies which have received Governmental approval, and are due to initiate operations shortly.

4.215   Actual export levels are higher than this however. Much of the catch from Lakes Albert, Edward, and George is taken into Rwanda, Sudan and Zaire and much of the trade in fish into Kenya and Tanzania is not monitored. There is does not appear to be any limit to the size of the export market.

4.216   Domestic consumption of fish increased starting in the early 1970s, and is now a significant portion of the national diet. It is estimated that fish consumption is between 8 and 13 kg per capita per annum 82/ and provides more than 50 percent of animal protein intake. Fresh fish prices at the dock in mid 1991 were about Ush200/kg (US$ 0.09/lb). The price of dried Nile Perch in Kampala in the same period was about Ush700/kg (US$ 0.32/lb). Unit export values were US$1.32/kg (US$ 0.60/lb) for fresh chilled fillets, and US$0.92/kg (US$0.42/lb) for smoked, dried, or salted fish.

4.217   **Strategy for Growth.** The export market for Uganda's fish appears to offer good prospects. As with other products, the problems are in the processing, transport, and delivery methods. At the harvesting level, it is feared that fisherment use predatory methods which may affect the maintenance of the fish population. It is not clear that harvests can be increased substantially, for lack of clear information and analysis. Areas for governmental action in the sector include:

> ●   Five research and monitoring questions involve the sustainability of the fishing industry. First, is Lake Victoria being overfished? The recent expansion of capital intensive extraction and processing operations could threaten the long term viability of the industry. A second question is

---

82/   MPED, Uganda National Household Budget Survey (1989-90), and MAAIF/Agricultural Secretariat, Fisheries Sectoral Background Paper, September 1991.

whether will the Nile Perch and the Tilapia will decimate the diversity of species in Lakes Kyoga and Victoria, beyond recovery? In the past ten years the variety of species in Lake Victoria and Kyoga has diminished, due to the predatory expansion of the Nile Perch, introduced in 1960. It is expected however--based on cursory information--that the Nile Perch population will stabilize soon. The dynamics of the populations of these species merits continuous monitoring and study. Third, is pollution from Kampala, Jinja, and other lakeside cities--or runoff from agricultural development--affecting the fish population? Fourth, is the current fishing, processing, and marketing technology appropriate--or can profitability be enhanced? Regulation of catch can be achieved through technology requirements. And fifth is the need to identify and put in place more effective methods to control the rapid spread of the water hyacinth, which is threatening fish populations in the lakes and rivers. To answer these and other questions, systematic long-term sampling and surveillance should be developed, so that regulation and other types of intervention can be adjusted to prevent any long-term damage to the resource, and the industry. Initial steps in this direction are being taken, but additional support is necessary. Monitoring capabilities are very limited.

- The Government's capacity and techniques for regulation should be strengthened to match the rapid development of the industry. Monitoring should focus on the long-term sustainable use of the fish resource, and implications for harvest methods and levels. The development of industry standards for export products could improve Uganda's standing in international markets.

- As with other agricultural enterprises, profitability is affected by transportation and communication costs. Governmental investment in infrastructure to improve the quality of roads, docks, and communication facilities will assist in maintaining the profitability of the industry, as returns decline with increased competition. The development of the road and rail links to the lakes in the West, would foster an increase in the fish harvest. If properly regulated, these additional sources of fish can be tapped in a sustainable basis for the export market.

V. AN AGRICULTURAL DEVELOPMENT STRATEGY

Previous Bank Strategy Proposals

The 1960 Bank Review and Recommendations

5.1   This is not the first time the World Bank has reviewed agriculture in Uganda. The Bank has done so twice before, in 1960 and 1983.

5.2   In 1960 a mission visited Uganda to review development prospects for the economy. The agriculture sector was analyzed in depth. The development objectives and priorities outlined in 1960 are similar to those expressed in this report. The measures proposed for achieving the objectives, however, were different.

5.3   As at present, the 1960 mission identified the agricultural sector meriting the Government's priority attention in attempts to stimulate growth:

> "It is our view that, in the present circumstances, investment in agriculture will bring greater returns--in terms of expanded output and incomes--than comparable investments in almost any other sector of the economy." 83/

Then, as now, the mission noted:

> "... the need to diversify Uganda's exports and particularly to place less reliance on increased coffee production, in view of the world market situation."

And,

> "... in view of the need to find a quick yielding source of growth ... the mission's program leans heavily on a substantial increase in cotton output in the short run. We do, however, propose a fuller development of livestock output through disease control and better marketing arrangements as a main means of diversification; for the rest, we also propose increasing the output of some minor crops and tea. Another important element in the program to achieve results in the short run should be to improve the quality of coffee through improved marketing techniques." 84/

5.4   Uganda's population of 6.5 million in 1960 had more than doubled to more than 16 million by 1990. Cash crop production in 1990, however, is at about the same levels as in 1960, or--in sugar and cotton--has dropped (table 22).

83/   World Bank, The Economic Development of Uganda, Johns Hopkins Press, 1962, p.96.

84/   World Bank, The Economic Development of Uganda, p. 96.

Table 22: Comparison of Production of Selected Cash Crops: 1960 vs 1990		
	1960	1990
Coffee Beans	117,000 tons	127,000 tons
Made Tea	7,000 tons	6,700 tons
Lint Cotton	360,000 bales	32,000 bales
Sugar	93,000 tons	29,000 tons
Livestock	US$ 900,000 85/	N/A

5.5   The Bank's prescription at that time for long-term measures included: (a) "improved general education and more vigorous dissemination of progressive techniques of production"; (b) "completing the change in the tenure system"--extending freehold rights--to induce investment and care of property; (c) development of the cooperative movement, seen as a key element in improving the responsiveness of rural services (marketing, credit, and supply of consumer goods and inputs), while containing exploitation by intermediaries; and (d) strengthened agricultural research. To foster short-term growth, recommendations were based on the transfer of capital to agriculture, aimed at increasing labor productivity. This was to be achieved by targeted subsidies for key implements and inputs, such as (ox-drawn) ploughs, cultivators, weeders, carts, seed drills, barbed wire, coffee trays, power hullers, pulpers, cattle kraals, and pump sprayers and insecticides for cotton--valued at US$6.6 million annually over four years. 86/ Building up the extension service, which then focused on assisting a reduced number of "progressive farmers," was advocated to complement the capital transfer.

The Agriculture Sector Memorandum of 1984

5.6   In 1983, the World Bank sponsored a further review of the agricultural sector. The country was recovering from the Amin years and the war with Tanzania. Again, complete reliance on the agricultural sector for growth was recommended, as were policies which focused on: "(a) rehabilitating the traditional export subsectors of coffee, cotton, tea and tobacco; (b) developing non-traditional exports; and (c) removing the technical, institutional and labor constraints to the sector's development". 87/ The objectives for the sector are familiar. Strategies to revitalize the agricultural economy included measures to: (a) improve price-setting methodology and timeliness for export crops; (b) "reduce the margins of the processing and marketing intermediaries" of the four major export crops; (c) balance revenue generation with production incentives, in designing taxation policy for export crops; and (d) focusing on the constraints peculiar to different agroecological zones through a series of regional agricultural development strategies. 88/

85/   US$ of 1960 expressed in US$ of 1990

86/   World Bank, op.cit. p.143.

87/   World Bank, Uganda - Agricultural Sector Memorandum. The Challenge Beyond Rehabilitation., 5044-UG, July 30, 1984, p. i.

88/   Ibid. p. vii.

5.7   The 1983 report recognized the problems posed by a nonresponsive export sector. As a result of the recommendations, a massive physical rehabilitation of the export industry was undertaken (Agriculture Rehabilitation Project, Cr 1328-UG). But, the 1983 recommendations to improve production incentives relied on administrative control to increase processing efficiency in the parastatal export monopolies, and to improve the responsiveness of Government-set prices and margins to market forces. These measures were inadequate. Although farmgate prices were increased significantly at the beginning of the decade, they were then allowed to decline in real terms, reducing production incentives. Processing margins were set too wide, reducing processing efficiency. With the rapid decline of real international prices for all of Uganda's exports in the late 1980s, poor yields and low processing efficiency have hampered Uganda's ability to compete in a much more agressive world market.

The Macroeconomic Framework

5.8   The economy was in severe disarray when the National Resistance Movement Government came into power in 1986. To restore macroeconomic balance and establish a framework for sustainable growth, the Government has put in place a series of reforms, with the assistance of the donor community.

5.9   Macroeconomic policy in Uganda 89/ is built on the framework set by the Economic Recovery Program (ERP) launched in May 1987 with support from the Bank, the IMF, and other donors. The main objectives of the ERP have been to restore internal financial stability and sharply reduce the rate of inflation (running at an annual rate of 360 percent in 1987), reduce imbalances in external accounts; improve producer incentives; improve the allocation and use of public resources; rehabilitate the infrastructure; and increase growth.

5.10   Despite strong initial measures in the first two years, which included a 77 percent devaluation, a one-time tax on liquid assets, increases of 100 to 400 percent in the Government controlled farmgate prices of export crops, and improvements in the allocation of foreign exchange, the Government failed to control fiscal and monetary aggregates. Inflation remained high and the trade deficit increased. Real GDP responded to the re-establishment of security and the rehabilitation of infrastructure however, and growth was 6.8 percent in FY 1988 and FY 1989.

5.11   The continued fall in the price of coffee caused the foreign exchange position to worsen considerably. In 1990 the Government addressed the adjustment program with renewed vigor. The currency was devalued by 40 percent, and a mechanism of periodic mini-devaluations established. The parallel market in foreign exchange was legalized, and beginning in 1992 the official exchange rate was determined by a circumscribed auction system. Fiscal and monetary policies were tightened as of 1990. Tax revenues outside the coffee tax were raised, and the expansion of credit for crop finance controlled. These measures were rewarded by a rapid fall in inflation, which fell from 243 percent in FY 88 to 29 percent in FY 90.

5.12   Recent developments are not as promising. The imbalance between Government revenue and expenditure has worsened in FY 92, causing fiscal controls to falter. The rapid expansion of

---

89/   This section drawn from World Bank Yellow Cover Report 10512-UG, "Uganda - Managing Public Expenditure", March 31, 1992, p. 1.

domestic credit to finance the fiscal deficit has caused the year-on-year inflation rate to jump to 39 percent in February 1992. The momentum of economic growth also appears to have slowed. Real GDP grew by 4.8 percent in FY 90 and an estimated 4.2 percent in FY 91, about two-thirds of the growth rates of the previous two years. The balance of payments position remains precarious. Coffee prices have continued to decline, reaching a historic low in February 1992, when Uganda was receiving US$0.70/kg of coffee. Coffee export earnings declined from US$282 million in FY 89 to US$ 126 million in FY 91. External debt now totals US$2.6 billion, and arrears exceed US$400 million.

Government Objectives for the Agricultural Sector

ASAC Letter of Development Policy

5.13   The Government's objectives for the agricultural sector are stated in the "Letter of Agricultural Policy" of November 1990 which set the stage for the Agriculture Sector Adjustment Program 90/:

> "Our economy is dominated by agriculture, and remains dependent on growth in the agricultural sector. Such growth has to meet the rising food requirements of a growing population. Through exports it also has to generate foreign exchange earnings to enable us to import agricultural inputs which we are not able to produce on our own, modernize our economy, and improve the living standards of our people."

These broad goals translate into the following two development objectives: to increase agricultural productivity, especially in food crop production, raising incomes and preventing expansion into marginal agricultural lands; and to diversify the production base and reduce the heavy dependence on coffee for exports and government revenue.

Way Forward II

5.14   More recently, the country's medium-term sectoral development strategy from 1991 to 1995 has been spelled out by the Government in the MPED's "Way Forward II." The objective is to develop a "self-sustaining" economy which:

> "largely uses its own raw materials in its manufacturing industries to produce capital goods and other inputs into the primary sectors of the economy... Such an economy has an internal dynamism that enables it to exist with a measure of independence and to cushion itself from the vagaries of world markets and external shocks." 91/

The statement emphasizes that:

90/   World Bank, "Report and Recommendation of the President of the International Development Association to the Executive Directors on a Proposed IDA Credit of SDR 69.5 Million to the Republic of Uganda in Support of an Agricultural Sector Adjustment Credit," P-5431-UG, November 27, 1990.

91/   MPED, "Way Forward II", August 1991, p. 7.

"the Government will follow a mixed economy strategy. Uganda has already begun a process of liberalization, moving towards policies which work through markets. This by no means implies that the role of the state is to be reduced, but rather that the role be altered to meet the requirements of a modern, mixed economy. Public institutions will continue to play a key role in establishing the infrastructure and policy environment conducive to private sector initiative and development." 92/

5.15   The "Way Forward II" acknowledges that the major engine of growth is expected to be agriculture and provides a statement of strategy with which this report agrees. The objectives for Government intervention in the sector over the next five years, as formulated by the Agriculture Policy Committee are:

"to raise yields by the adoption of appropriate technology through strengthened agricultural research and extension institutions;

to promote increased diversification in export crops, by creating competitive systems for processing and marketing of agricultural produce through reform of marketing institutions, enhanced export incentives, adequately remunerative producer prices, and more efficient public spending;

to facilitate financial stabilization by controlling credit expansion through improved institutional arrangements for financing crop procurement, and financial restructuring of marketing intermediaries;

to promote employment creation;

to promote self-sufficiency in food."

5.16   The intent of this report is to bring the different elements of the agricultural sector together in a coherent framework, and provide a sense of priorities for action over time and across the sector. There is only one area where we would suggest an adjustment to the agricultural growth strategy. It is stated in the "Way Forward II," that past increases in agricultural output have been due mainly to area expansion. The analysis provided in this report supports this statement, and leads, further, to the proposition that future growth in agricultural output will continue to rely to a large extent, on increases in cultivated area. Yet this aspect of agricultural growth has received little attention in the "Way Forward II" and other strategy statements. It has implications for labor flows, migratory patterns, ethnic tensions, land tenure disputes, infrastructural development, environmental regulation and protection, and social service expansion. We argue in this report that there are still large areas of high-to-medium potential-- underutilized land that are being brought into cultivation through a natural process of internal migration. Such slow migratory patterns should be acknowledged and indirect guidance provided. Extensification can be relied on to more readily increase output per labor day, which results in immediate increases in welfare.

92/   MPED, "Way Forward II", p.1

5.17   On a related topic, it is our opinion that the emphasis in the "Way Forward II" on yield increases as the only source of growth 93/ is misplaced. Both technological change and a continued expansion in area cultivated will continue to determine growth in agriculture over the next decade.   We also feel that the estimates of gains in food and export crop yields attainable through "improved technology which is already available" 94/ are overly optimistic. The yield increases obtainable from the release of higher-yielding, disease-resistant varieties of cassava, coffee, and other crops are not questioned. At issue is whether the technology based on the increased use of inorganic fertilizer and other chemical inputs is feasible and profitable for the Ugandan smallholder. The yield increases from the use of fertilizer shown in table 3 of the "Way Forward II" report--taken from the "Accelerated Food Crops Production Strategy"--are misleading, because the fertilizer applications and husbandry improvements (and hence additional labor) needed to achieve these yields are not necessarily profitable at market prices. Unsubsidized fertilizer prices (not extant in Uganda at present) are too high, and crop prices are too low for most food crops for fertilizer use to be profitable. The exception perhaps is the case of relatively high-resource farmers growing hybrid maize (see Chapter IV).

Lessons From This Review

5.18   As a prelude to proposing a strategy to support growth in agriculture, this section summarizes the main conclusions of this report, and lists the market and production constraints that determine Uganda's alternatives in its drive to promote growth and alleviate poverty.

5.19   Three main conclusions on the nature of past performance and the possibilities for future expansion emerge from this report: agricultural expansion has resulted from the rapid increase in the production of food for a resurgent domestic market, the increase in food production has resulted from expansion in area cultivated, and the international markets for Uganda's traditional export crops have become much more competitive than in the early 1970s.

Growth in Food Production

5.20   The engine of growth in the 1980s has been the reestablishment of peace and security, combined with release of the foreign exchange constraint, rehabilitation of key infrastructure, and the adoption of free-market policies including the decontrol of food prices and trade. This has resulted in an expansion in food production as production and marketing costs fell and the population tried to recapture consumption levels of the mid-1970s. Food production has led growth both in 1980-90 and since the advent of the current Government in 1986. Trend growth in food production was 3.3 percent per annum for the decade, and 5.9 percent per annum since 1986. Since 1986, growth in agricultural demand has been led by the urban demand for food. The rapid rise in urban incomes--and demand--resulted in part from the refurbishment of industries, services and Government, undertaken with high levels of donor support.

5.21   Food has become an attractive cash crop. For fifteen years--with the exception of the early 1980s and 1991 (Figure 40)--the relative returns on production of food versus cash crops

---

93/   MPED, "Way Forward II", p. 15 para 59.

94/   MPED, "Way Forward II", p. 20, para 87.

has been above the levels of the early 1970s. Because access to land is almost universal, wages needed to hire labor away from own production have risen as well. The rise of labor costs has squeezed profit margins on estates. With lower returns to export-crop production, farmers' time devoted to export crops has declined, affecting yields and quality. The main cash earners for rural families are now food crops or dairy products sold in urban areas, rather than the export crops of the 1970s.

5.22   One consequence of having food as the engine of agricultural growth is the dependence on the growth in domestic demand for continued impetus. Based on projected population and income increases, the domestic market is expected to increase at no more than 3 to 4 percent per year over the next decade (para 6.8). Much of the potential for growth through import substitution in the dairy, sugar, and tobacco subsectors has already been exploited. During 1991 and early 1992, the markets for "matoke" (bananas--the main foodcrop), milk, sugar, beef, and maize has been soft. And real food prices have been falling in the last half of the decade, except for a sharp increase in 1989. If current levels of growth in the domestic market are to continue, the focus will have to be on raising rural incomes through technological change and increases in labor productivity, diversifying of export markets, and raising urban incomes through increased import substitution and processing of local raw materials.

5.23   Growth in agricultural output slowed considerably in 1990. From increases of 6.2 and 6.4 percent in 1988 and 1989, growth dropped to 3.4 percent in 1990. The main cause of the slowdown was the slow growth in food crop production, down to 3.5 percent in 1990 from 7.5 percent the previous year. Export crop output actually declined by 11 percent in 1990, reflecting poor production incentives for coffee in previous years. The drop in growth in the food sector could have resulted from a several factors: completion of the reoccupation of the cultivated areas abandoned in the 1970s; the successful substitution for imported foods, such as sugar and milk; the saturation of the domestic market for food, given income levels; and the slow growth in incomes in nonfood sectors of the economy.

Expansion of Area Cultivated

5.24   Agricultural growth this decade has been due to an expansion in cultivated area, rather than an increase in yields. The area under cultivation--4.6 million ha--is still below the level of the late 1970s. Food crop cultivation, at 4.3 million ha, is at the levels of the early 1970s. Cash crop cultivation--at 0.3 million ha, due to the decline of cotton--is less than half the level of the 1960s. Agricultural land, while not limiting growth for the country as a whole, is a constraint in certain, high-potential, high-population regions in the Southwest and Northeast (table 1). There is a gradual inter-regional migration, from the most densely populated areas to less-populated regions of good potential. Reestablishing peace north of Lake Kyoga will make large underutilized areas available for cultivation. The area currently under cultivation, while utilizing the regions of highest potential, is still less than 30 percent of potentially cultivable areas.

Competition in International Markets

5.25   There has been a sea change in the international prices of Uganda's traditional export crops: coffee, tea, and cotton face much lower prices in real terms now than in the early 1970s. Prospects for trend improvements are limited. Profits and rents from these crops, most of which were captured by Government, have been severely reduced to keep the country competitive in international markets. Successful international competition now requires continued increases in the efficiency of export production and processing with little margin for taxation. Uganda, due to its excellent agricultural resources, is a low-cost producer in these three crops and with improved efficiency in the processing industries can expect to profitably sell all it can produce.

5.26   The regional market for food, especially maize and beans, can be expected to increase. Uganda's landlocked status and reliable rainfall provide it with the opportunity to supply food cheaply to several of neighbors--one of whom, in any given year, can be expected to be undergoing a drought. Growth in this market depends however, on the annual food import requirements of a client country in a given poor agricultural year, and may not go beyond 300,000 to 400,000 tons of food per year.

Structural Adjustment in Agriculture and Constraints to Growth

Agriculture Rehabilitation Project

5.27   Government's efforts to reform the production and marketing arrangements in agriculture since 1980 have received support from two IDA funded projects supporting sectoral adjustment: a) the Agriculture Rehabilitation Project (ARP) Cr 1328-UG of February 1983, and b) the Agriculture Sector Adjustment Credit, (ASAC), Cr 2190-UG of December 1990. Under the ARP the physical rehabilitation of export processing facilities in the cotton, coffee and tea sectors was successfully financed. No provision had been made for supporting operational reforms, however, and not all of the facilities have been used profitably. The ARP also financed a large share of agricultural imports between 1983 and 1991, when it closed. Perhaps the most important contribution was support for the newly established Interministerial Agricultural Policy Committee and its executive arm, the Agricultural Secretariat in the Bank of Uganda. Through this structure, Government kept in touch with production and incentives problems facing farms and processing industries and was able to implement ARP conditionality which required that farmgate prices for export crops be adjusted to maintain production incentives. While still administered by Government, prices and margins for export crop purchase and processing were adjusted upwards during the early 1980s to maintain production and export incentives within a monopolistic, state controlled system. There was some response in the coffee, tea, cotton, and tobacco sectors, subsequently dampened by security problems in the mid 1980s, the collapse of international markets (Figure 6), and a decline in real farmgate prices.

Agriculture Sector Adjustment Credit

5.28   ASAC was designed in 1990 to address the salient issues in adjustment of agriculture and their macroeconomic ramifications.   ASAC's main focus was to control credit expansion for crop finance, and improve export marketing efficiency and production incentives for coffee which provides over 90 percent of export revenue. In addition, funds were provided to improve policy making in the agricultural sector, and strengthen agricultural research and extension capacity. The project has been successful, and provides a model for how to proceed in the liberalization of other export crop marketing systems. Government has gone beyond the conditionality set forth in the operation in order to achieve the agreed objectives.   Control of credit expansion to finance the purchase of the coffee crop, the largest single source of demand for funds in the financial system (Figure 9), has been achieved by shifting the responsibility for providing this credit to the commercial banks, thus removing the Bank of Uganda from its position as financier of last resort and improving Government's capacity to monitor developments in the subsector. Inflation declined from around 240 percent per annum in FY 1988 to around 30 percent in FY 1990 (para

5.11). Coffee exports have been maintained in a time of declining world prices (Figure 29), by improving processing efficiency and farmgate production incentives. First, this was achieved through the promotion of competition. The monopoly control on exports held by CMB was dismantled. Participation by cooperative unions and private sector exporters was promoted. Government-imposed farmgate prices and marketing margins have been discontinued. The farmgate price of coffee has risen in real terms (Figure 10). CMB's regulatory functions were shifted to a separate Uganda Coffee Development Authority (paras 4.29-4.56). Second, Government has significantly reduced its tax on coffee exports, so that present coffee export earnings are converted at the market rate of exchange, and the tax rate is a flat 5 percent on export value. In addition to conditionality on coffee marketing and rural credit policy, ASAC is strengthening Government's policy formulation capacity for agriculture with technical assistance and training in the three main Ministries: MAAIF, MCIC and MPED. The Agricultural Secretariat, the locus for policy analysis in agriculture, continues to be assisted, although its role has shifted from administration of export prices and margins towards monitoring of product and inputs markets and prices, and providing analytical support for further adjustment and regulatory initiatives of Government. Agricultural research and extension are scheduled to receive long term support under two IDA funded projects, recently appraised, prepared with resources provided under ASAC. Also, ASAC provides support for the promulgation of a new Land Law which would extend freehold tenure. ASAC has addressed the first tier of constraints to agricultural growth. There is still an agenda for adjustment in agriculture, which is discussed below.

Constraints to Growth

5.29 Growth in agriculture in Uganda has been hampered during the 1980s by a series of structural constraints related to: (i) Government control of food and export crop marketing and pricing which inhibited incentives to improve the quality and quantity of output in the farm and factory; (ii) inadequate transportation infrastructure and shortage of vehicles; (iii) shortages of foreign exchange, and high and unpredictable inflation; and (iv) physical insecurity. In addition, agricultural growth has been held back by a series of institutional factors which include: (v) ineffective Government research and extension services; and (vi) segmented, inefficient and discriminatory markets for capital, labor, and agricultural inputs. The effects of the above mentioned constraints on the development of each subsector are described, by institution and by crop, in Sections III and IV of the Main Report.

5.30 Over the past six years, many of the structural constraints to growth in agriculture listed above have been removed. As the sectoral analysis undertaken in the Main Report indicates that since 1986 growth in the agricultural sector has been due, at different times, to: (i) the re-establishment of peace and security in the Center, South and West, which resulted mainly in increases in cultivated area under food; (ii) the decontrol of food marketing; (ii) improvements in transportation infrastructure between food producing areas and Kampala; (iv) rehabilitation of production and processing capacity for estate-based cash crops (tea, sugar); (v) decontrol of coffee processing and export marketing, which prevented serious declines in output, and (vi) the establishment of an open market in foreign exchange, which has provided an incentive for the development of non-traditional agricultural exports. The effects of the structural changes in the framework for agricultural growth undertaken over the past 6 years will continue to work themselves out during the 1990s. Increased competition in the coffee industry should result in improved processing and export marketing efficiency. Open markets in foreign exchange will result in investment export oriented industries. The rehabilitation of the tea sector will proceed slowly, helped by the resolution of Custodian Board cases.

5.31   There is still an agenda for structural change in agriculture. Rapid increases in output in the cotton sector could result from changes in ownership and the introduction of more efficient management, improved access to credit, and increased competition amongst ginneries and export marketing agents.   Adjustment in the cotton sector will be fairly complex and cumbersome however, given the dispersed location and ownership of ginneries, and the significant changes in ownership, management and finances involved. In tea, half of the gardens and many factories have yet to be rehabilitated. The process is contingent on progress in the divestiture of Government-owned enterprises, the resolution of ownership claims for tea estates held by the Custodian Board, and the restructuring of factory ownership and management in the smallholder tea sector.

5.32   The quickest gains from structural change have already been captured. The constraints to economic growth now facing the agricultural economy are not so easily dealt with. This point has already been made for food (para 5.23). Continued growth in agriculture will have to come from joint improvements in: (i) technology generation and dissemination; (ii) the responsiveness of the capital market and the availability of long-term finance; (iii) access and infrastructure for hitherto underutilized areas; (iv) the re-establishment of peace and security North of Lake Kyoga; (v) the fluidity of the labor market; and (vi) tenure security and the establishment of freehold tenure. The gradual release of constraints to growth in these areas will result from improvements in the effectiveness of Government in the provision of essential public goods and the establishment of indirect regulatory mechanisms. All these efforts require a long-term commitment to slow, steady change.

An Agricultural Sector Strategy

Development Objectives and Priorities

5.33   To design a development strategy for agriculture priorities in the use of scarce financial and managerial resources should be set. The Government's objectives in stimulating growth in the agricultural sector are to meet the country's food requirements, generate foreign exchange, and improve living standards (paras 5.13-5.14).   Rapid growth in the food sector since 1986 has returned the country to food self sufficiency and brought about a broad based increase in rural incomes.   The most fragile aspect of the recovery program in Uganda now is the lack of response in exports--which must grow in value in the next few years if economic growth is to be sustained. The capacity to finance imports has declined sharply due to the drop in coffee prices. Imports in 1990 were 3.5 times export revenue (para 1.21). The availability of concessional donor funding to continue to bridge this gap is unlikely to be sustained at current levels,95/ and additional private sector finance is practically unavailable.

5.34   The strategy to be followed must also acknowledge that <u>the nature of agricultural growth will have to change</u> over the next ten years.   The lead will have to shift, from food production for the domestic market, to production of raw materials for processing and/or direct export. Over the past 6 years improvements in physical security in rural areas, reductions in economic uncertainty and inflation, increased availability of foreign exchange, and reductions in transport costs have driven the increases in agricultural GDP.   The most responsive sector was food

---

95/   Mr. F.X. Colaço, Director, Eastern Africa Department, assessing the outcome of the Annual Meetings of September 1992 at Departmental Meeting of September 25, 1992.

production, for the market and for own consumption, where marketing and pricing controls had been removed early on. Food production, excluding livestock, grew at 5.9 percent per annum between 1986 and 1990. Growth in export crop production languished due to continued Governmental interference, depressed world markets, and financial and managerial weaknesses in the marketing and processing industries.

5.35 The scope for continued rapid growth in food production will be limited in future, due to its dependence on the size of the domestic market. Growth in domestic demand for food will be limited to growth due to the increase in population, and increases in per capita income induced by expansion in urban based industries and services, and revitalized agricultural exports, the new lead subsector. Even if these factors are all large and positive, they are unlikely to generate more than a 3-4 percent per annum increase in the demand for food (paras 4.13-4.16). This is below population growth, and will generate only a 1 percent increase in per-capita income.

5.36 In light of these imperatives, the report argues for a two pronged agricultural development strategy. In the short term, the agenda for adjustment and investment should continue to focus on increasing agricultural exports in traditional cash crops as rapidly as possible, while seeking diversification amongst the least investment-intensive non-traditional agricultural exports. This will provide for a new source of growth in the sector, not limited to expansion of the internal market, and will address one of the key macroeconomic disequilibria and constraints to sustainable growth. In the medium term, deeper measures should be taken to diversify agricultural exports, improve technology generation and dissemination in the sector, and reduce transactions costs, entry barriers and market failures in the land, labor and capital markets as described below.

5.37 The short term strategy advocates continued efforts to regain market share in traditional exports: cotton, coffee and tea. While production margins are very thin, and international prices low, our analysis shows that Uganda, due to its excellent natural conditions, is a low cost producer of these products and can compete in international markets even at depressed prices if processing and marketing efficiency is restored (paras 4.18-4.21). There is need for a rapid restructuring and liberalization of the cotton ginning and export marketing industry. In coffee, choice of export routes should be liberalized. In tea, Government should divest itself of parastatal factories and estates and conclude the Custodian Board review process, which is keeping a large number of the estates out of production. These changes would generate significant increases in foreign exchange, and have a broad based income generation effect in rural areas.

5.38 At the same time, short term measures should be taken to support the process of export diversification, which can grow very rapidly, as experience with sesame and fish exports in recent years indicates. Priority should be given to dry goods such as sesame, tobacco, hides and skins, spices and other products which do not rely too heavily on specialized packaging, critical transportation timing, expensive cooling infrastructure, and a commitment to constant, standardized quality deliveries. While the contribution to agriculture GDP from these crops is small (under 5 percent) their contribution to exports has been rising rapidly, and reached 20 percent in 1990 with the collapse in the price of coffee.

5.39 In the medium term, the report argues that a series of measures are needed to support further diversification in agricultural exports. While expansion in the traditional export markets based on more efficient processing and production will increase foreign exchange revenue, these crops will not provide large profits. Development of high value specialized crop exports will increase returns and taxable profits, and stabilize export revenue. Government's role in developing these new activities should be indirect. Its focus should be on reducing unnecessary regulation, improving transport infrastructure and telecommunications, and smoothing the responsiveness of the land, labor and financial markets to profitable production opportunities. In addition, to raise rural incomes and ease the growth in food production, Government should take indirect measures to improve migration into underutilized areas of good agricultural potential. This will reduce the hunger for land in the densely populated districts of the Southwest and the Northeast, and permit labor augmenting technology to be used, increasing output per person. Careful management of this process will be needed to minimize environmental costs. Growth in yields is another key element of the agricultural strategy. Many traditional food and cash crops face disease and husbandry problems. Experimentation with new high value crops will require a high class, responsive research and extension service. Continued support for agricultural research and extension services is argued for, as is the need to provide improved monitoring and regulation of the use of natural resources --grazing lands, forests and fish -- as population pressures are exacerbated.

5.40   The growth strategy advocated in this report should take place within bounds set by acceptable levels of environmental impact, self-determination and equity. The approach utilized in promoting growth should lead to sustainable use of natural resources, enable local communities to participate and direct the development process, and provide the largest number of employment opportunities possible to the rural poor. Uninhibited pursuit of a strategy to expand cultivated area could result in the mining of poor soils and the devastation of natural vegetation without providing a base for sustained increase in crop or livestock agriculture. Under the proposed strategy, policies which lead to increased internal migration should take into consideration the rights of the residents of the receiving areas, as well as the difficulties of adjustment faced by both incoming as well as resident families. Decisions on how production-processing-marketing relationships are structured, and the use of smallholder outgrower production schemes, can have broad beneficial effects. Prevention of concentration of land ownership through judicious management of titling and tenure of public lands will also benefit the rural poor. The effects of the proposed strategy on the alleviation of rural poverty, and the development of sustainable farming systems and participatory production relationships are noted below (para 5.65) following the description of the growth strategy.

Short Term Strategy: An Export Action Plan

5.41   **Coffee.** With coffee exports 80 to 100 percent of annual exports in the past fifteen years, it has been the clear initial target for improvements. As described in paras 4.29-4.56, and para 5.28, .64 above, over the past two years there have been a series of radical reforms in the structure of the domestic coffee processing and export business: opening the industry to competition, reducing governmental control, and taxation. The policy reforms have gone as far as was necessary to set the stage for a competitive, aggressive attempt to win back some of the country's share of the world coffee market. No further basic changes in export policy in the coffee sector should be made for at least three years. While continuing evaluation of the effectiveness of current policies should continue, the industry should be allowed to adjust to the market-oriented framework established to date. With a flat 5 percent tax, and exports converted at the bureau exchange rate, there are strong incentives for exporters to raise quality and volume as much as possible. However, it will take time for the incentives to filter back through the processing industry to the producers. There is, however, one area where action in the short term will significantly improve export incentives and reduce uncertainty:

- Coffee exporters should be allowed to select the most competitive export channel and route (road or rail), and export inspections and customs procedures should be streamlined to reduce wasted time and resulting cost increases.

5.42 **Cotton.** The third largest export earner (after sesame seed) in 1990-91, <u>cotton should be the focus of the Government's efforts to raise export earnings</u>. The reasons are compelling.

- At market-based prices and reasonable levels of ginning efficiency--well above current levels--even low-input, low-output cotton production as practiced in Uganda is profitable;

- An important constraint to increased efficiency and growth in the sector is the lack of competition in ginning and export marketing. This can be solved with changes in policy, adjustments in laws and regulations, and assistance in rationalizing ginnery ownership. Ginneries are now held entirely by cooperative unions and many of these are insolvent;

- The production response from farmers is expected to be rapid. In spite of the unsatisfactory system of cotton purchases and payment now in place--with routinely long delays--some 70,000 ha were planted in 1991. When payment is adequate and prompt, the incentives for increased production should be strong;

- The regions north of Lake Kyoga, where cotton has traditionally been grown, are not as severely affected by security problems as they were one or two years ago, and the situation is improving;

- Capital has already been invested in a partial refurbishing of nominal ginning capacity, which far exceeds current output;

- The key ingredients to improving operations in the cotton sector--working capital finance, and managerial and technical skills--can be provided by private entrepreneurs without additional Governmental involvement once it is clear that a stable policy based on freely convertible export earnings and a competitive ginning and export marketing environment are put in place.

5.43 The steps necessary to revitalize the cotton sector include:

- The re-establishment of peace and security in production regions North of Lake Kyoga;

- The revocation of the Lint Marketing Board's monopoly on cotton exports, and other restrictive provisions of the LMB Act,

- The revocation of area monopsony power provided to cooperatives in the purchase of seed cotton, and other restrictive provisions of the Cotton Act,

- Provision of assistance to cooperative unions to enable them to solve financial and managerial constraints, and increase use of their ginning facilities. Sale, lease and/or management contracts with viable private sector entities are envisaged;

- The establishment of a cotton development authority, funded by a small cess (less than 1 percent) on cotton exports, to assure quality standards, promote the industry at home and abroad, and fund research and extension once industry profitability has been established.

5.44   Tea. Whereas the estate sector has by and large been privatized, there remains the question of the tea estates and factories of the Government owned Agriculture Enterprises Ltd (AEL). These estates are inefficiently run well under capacity. Privatization of their operations would permit these resources to be brought back into operation, with gains in employment and foreign exchange to the country.

- The Government should divest itself of AEL holdings in the tea sector as soon as private sector buyers with capacity to make full and profitable use of the assets have been identified.

5.45   Nontraditional Agricultural Exports. The other area for immediate attention, where the production response can be rapid is in nontraditional agricultural exports. Growth can be quick as the progression from 1989-90 to 1990-91 indicates when NTAEs jumped from US$2.1 million to US$23.8 million. The most important products include sesame seed, beans, maize, other cereals, hides and skins, fish, and fruit and vegetables. This rapid growth must be supported. But markets for these products are small and volatile. The measures to foster this type of growth are indirect, and focus on the need to improve the reliability and efficiency of export channels, and facilitate access to term finance. Measures would include:

- Review of the functions of the Export Policy Analysis and Development Unit, the Export Promotion Council, and the Investment Authority, in order to harmonize their policy making, promotional and regulatory activities and simplify the array of review and approval procedures faced by potential investors and entrepreneurs. These agencies should jointly develop a plan to address potential constraints to new investors in Uganda which would improve export facilities, including regular air freight availability to Europe, reduce license and approval procedures, provide specialized communication services, and provide specialized export processing and storage infrastructure for key industries.

- A mechanism to improve the availability of local and foreign funding to qualified investors. During the time that the financial sector is under adjustment, the need for exports in the short term may justify the creation of a dedicated line of credit, or the establishment of an organization capable of providing venture capital finance and reducing the business risk to investors with likely new projects.

Medium-Term Agricultural Development Strategy

5.46   The medium-term strategy outlines Government's role in inducing structural change and investment in agriculture until the turn of the century. The framework for the strategy cites the need for Government intervention in three main areas: (a) improving incentives for agricultural production and processing, (b) improving the efficiency of the land, labor, and capital markets, and (c) inducing technological change through improvements in agricultural research and extension, and strengthening management of natural resources.

5.47   Incentive Framework. Government administration of prices and processing and marketing margins in the agricultural sector has been almost completely discontinued. Only cotton, tobacco, cocoa and tea continue to have farmgate prices set by fiat.   Government intervention in the sector will be justified to: (a) take direct or indirect measures to increase efficiency in processing, mainly through the promotion of competition, and (b) enter the market on the side of the producer in cases where processing industries exercise monopsony control on crop purchase prices. The cotton, tea and sugar subsectors are cases in point. The implementation of these measures is very dependant on accurately designed policies and programs which achieve desired objectives without diminishing production and investment incentives.

5.48   The key entity in the <u>formulation of Government policy</u> in the sector is the Agriculture Policy Committee, which brings together the top civil servants in the Agriculture, Finance and Economic Planning, Commerce and related ministries, the Bank of Uganda and the Uganda Commercial Bank. Much effort has been made in recent years (under ARP, ASAC and various donor funded Technical Assistance projects) to develop Government's policy analysis and formulation capacity. The agriculture planning departments in the MAAIF, MCIC and MFEP have all received support, as has the Agricultural Secretariat of the Bank of Uganda, the executive arm of the Agriculture Policy Committee. The system has worked well to date. Many of the major reforms liberalizing marketing, processing and exports have been successfully carried out under this structure. The system now has to be redesigned to play a role in the more indirect management appropriate in a market based economy. A Task Force constituted under the APC has addressed the question of planning and policy formulation for the agricultural sector. 96/ Points made in this report include the need to:

- Establish comprehensive and reliable sources of regular data on product and factor prices across the country. The series generated by the Agricultural Secretariat surveys is a good start. The long awaited Agricultural Census should be completed by MAAIF and published as soon as possible. Government survey procedures for crop production estimates should be reviewed for accuracy, and a system for prediction should be evolved to provide early warning of possible shortages in food crops.

- Strengthen policy analysis and strategic thinking in the Ministry of Agriculture, Animal Industry and Fisheries, to enable it to lead in the formulation of sectoral development policy;

- Consolidate the interministerial planning framework for annual budgeting and public investment program review in the agricultural sector, under the leadership of MFEP;

- Encourage producers and agro-industries to organize their own associations to represent their points of view before the policy makers. Such associations should be encouraged to "self regulate" their industry in their own interest;

- Maintain, for the present, the use of an Agricultural Policy Committee for the formulation of agricultural development policy, with the Agricultural Secretariat as

---

96/   Government of Uganda, APC, "Programme for Strengthening Agricultural Sector Planning (PASP)", Report of the Task Force on Agriculture Sector Planning, Kampala, January 1922.

an executive arm. This system is flexible and efficient, and has proven well able to bring about consensus, and produce results to date.

5.49   In the coffee industry, competition is developing in export processing and marketing following the recent structural adjustment process (para 5.28). The recent Cabinet decisions freeing producer prices and processing and marketing margins to market forces and allowing exporters to convert coffee export proceeds at the bureau exchange rate, should fundamentally improve the incentive environment in the industry, assure fair competition between cooperatives and private-sector operators, and improve the responsiveness of the coffee industry to international conditions. In addition to the recommendations made for the short-term plan, the report notes that:

- Coffee sector incentive policies, on pricing, taxation and licensing should be stabilized for at least three years, to allow the industry to adjust to the new rules. Monitoring of industry parameters should be constant to permit a Government response to unpredictable destabilising events;

- Measures should be designed and enforced by UCDA to prevent collusion and maintain competition among coffee processors and exporters;

- Privatization of the Coffee Marketing Board Limited should be completed, with ownership shares gradually sold off to the private sector;

- Alternative export sale procedures should be assessed--including an auction--to maximize medium-term export revenue, establish a fair basis for tax assessment, provide an open, fair pricing process, and encourage buyer commitment to the Ugandan product.

5.50   Measures to revitalize the processing side of the cotton industry have been spelled out in the short term plan. In the medium term, attention should be given to the production side. Cotton yields and acreage will respond to the efforts made to strengthen the inputs supply market, the rural financial market and to improve the responsiveness and relevance of Government's agricultural research and extension services. A resurgence of oxen based ploughing and cultivation will occur when the security situation in the Teso, Lango and Acholi areas improves sufficiently for farmers to hold animals without fear of rustlers. In addition, particular attention should be given to:

- Assistance in restocking with animals for draft powered land preparation and cultivation;

- Refinement and improvement of the cotton seed varieties by agroecological area. Previously adapted varieties have been mixed up.

5.51   In the tea industry, to improve processing efficiency and increase output in estate and UTGC factories, the following measures are recommended, in addition to those noted under the short-term plan:

- For the UTGC and its factories, reform should follow the plan outlined by the proposed EEC project, whereby factory management is separated from the extension and overhead-support functions of UTGC and put in the hands of a professional management concern, and factories are eventually sold off to the farmers who use them;

- Retention accounts for foreign exchange earned from tea exports should be brought under strict supervision of the Bank of Uganda and gradually phased out in favor of the open market in foreign exchange;

- UTGC's monopoly over procurement of green leaf should be removed. Factories should be encouraged to enter directly into contracts with outgrowers, which include leaf collection, input supply, and credit recovery. UTGC should play the role of "buyer of last resort" in order to maintain an equitable farmgate greenleaf price;

- Deliberations by the Custodian Board on ownership of private sector tea estates should be concluded, under the framework provided by the IDA-funded Structural Adjustment Credit, and incentives provided for the rapid rehabilitation of privately owned factories and gardens,

5.52   In the sugar industry, incentives for domestic production--with freely determined domestic market prices and competing privately owned producers--will be determined by trade policy. While the sugar industry is being rehabilitated--which may last another five years--competition from imports should be regulated through tariffs to permit the sugar producers to realize prices of more than US$400 per ton needed to permit profitable factory operation and self-financing of the rehabilitation works.

5.53   **Product- and Factor-Market Efficiency and Infrastructure.** Government influence on the functioning of markets supporting agricultural growth will, for the most part, be indirect. The key indirect instruments will be reforms in the financial market, a retreat from the inputs market, and investments in transportation and communication infrastructure, as discussed below. Direct intervention and change will need to be fostered amongst farmer cooperatives and in land markets.

5.54   The major player in rural factor and product markets in Uganda over the past twenty years has been the farmer cooperative network. The existence of this network, its infrastructure, and the loyalty of its customers means that rural cooperatives and their unions can continue to be play an important role. Increased liberalization in rural trade and processing means, however, that these organizations will have to compete with other private sector entrants. Steps should be taken to assist cooperatives to emerge from their protected environment and take advantage of trade and processing opportunities. In this regard:

- Market protection for cooperatives should be reduced, to force competition with private enterprises. At the same time, special social taxes and obligations imposed on cooperatives should be reviewed to avoid raising operating costs and placing cooperatives at a competitive disadvantage;

- Legislation governing the democratic operation of cooperatives should be used by Registrar to make the management cadres of primary societies and their unions more responsive to the majorities in the membership. At the same time, the Registrar's powers of direct intervention in the cooperative system should be diminished;

● Technical assistance in finance and management will be needed in the cooperative system, to assist in the rationalization and divestiture of businesses, the negotiation of joint ventures with private entrepreneurs (especially in cotton), and the improvement of operating efficiency and profitability. Subsidies on this technical assistance may be needed in its initial phases, to achieve the necessary restructuring of these entities;

5.55   The market for agricultural inputs is distorted by Government participation, and by the difficulties of operating an import-based business in a rapidly changing macroeconomic environment. Steps should be taken to reduce market distortions and improve industry responsiveness by having:

● MAAIF withdraw from the physical distribution and sale of agricultural inputs. Donated fertilizer should be made available at commercial prices ex Kampala to the private trade for sale to farmers,

● Inputs--including donations of fertilizer--made available through donor-funded agricultural projects should be sold by the Government through auctions, or in other ways that will develop the private trade.

● MAAIF should foster a dialogue with major consumers and suppliers of fertilizers pesticides and animal husbandry chemicals to identify and promote the importing of products which, consistent with agronomic requirements of various soils and crops, can provide the required nutrients or active ingredients at minimum cost to the country and the farmer.

5.56   The development of rural financial markets will have to follow on the measures being taken under the recently appraised Financial Sector Adjustment Credit (FSAC), proposed for IDA support. In addition to reestablishing confidence in the financial system and improving prudential capabilities of the Bank of Uganda, the following measures advocated under FSAC should improve the responsiveness of rural financial markets:

● Restructuring and recapitalizing the Cooperative Bank and the Uganda Commercial Bank both of which have wide rural branch networks that can mobilize rural savings and supply finance to rural enterprises. Effective use of the branch network will depend on the development of a "branch orientation" in the commercial financial system which emphasizes the development of a lending relationship, and a deposit-taking relationship with customers. Branch managers should be encouraged (within the bounds of prudence) to identify and encourage local business development;

● Restructuring the development finance institutions. The supply of medium-term finance is crucial in the modernization of agroprocessing infrastructure;

● Maintenance of positive savings and lending rates, leading toward a freely floating system;

- Continued testing of innovative approaches to market-based rural lending and saving. These pilot approaches should combine group-based savings and lending schemes with crop marketing and production finance, while directing programs to needy areas, the rural poor, and rural women in an attempt to use informal-finance methods to create sustainable village-level financial contracts and organizations. Such community-based pilot schemes should interact effectively with the "informal" financial network, make it more liquid, and link it more closely to commercial finance.

5.57   The operation of land markets is a delicate area, confused by the existence of a reform decree passed in 1975 whose provisions have been only partly implemented. The approach proposed in this report is to:

- Focus tenure-related efforts on the mechanisms for the resolution of tenure-related disputes in the short term. The land market appears to work well in most areas under traditional tenure systems,

- Regulate access to hitherto unoccupied--or underdeveloped--areas and public lands in ways which foster smallholder occupancy, and ownership by persons committed to making the land produce. Speculative concentration of land holding in public lands and unoccupied areas should be avoided. Supportive treatment for smallholder immigrants, and extension of squatters rights where appropriate, should be provided;

- Pass new land legislation, after sufficient national discussion to obtain broad agreement, which would re-establish freehold tenure. Mailo tenancies would be separated from the mailo estate and vested in the Land Commission. The Commission may then grant this land in freehold to the mailo tenant. The rights of customary tenants on public lands would be restored, and tenants permitted to obtain freehold tenure. Freehold tenure will reduce the land-related barriers to migration by labor and small farmers which are inherent in many customary tenure systems;

- Once agreement on the new land legislation and regulation has been reached, the Land Offices through which the legislation will be implemented should be strengthened.

5.58   Whether there are obstacles to the functioning of the rural labor market is not clear. Cursory observation indicates that it functions fairly well and that labor responds predictably to employment opportunities around the country--migrating when the expected returns outweigh remuneration from local jobs and the costs of moving. The absence of migrant workers of Rwandan origin since the early 1980s has affected production relationships and wages for export crop production in estates and on smallholder farms. Migration of poorer farmers from the land-poor Southwest to the western and central areas continues. Migrants work farms of established owners and establish their own holdings, especially in the West. When the returns to food production improved in the latter half of the 1980s, the flow of migrant labor diminished. The flow of labor into urban areas has only gradually started again. Urban incomes are, on average, 69 percent higher than in rural Uganda, and rural areas have grown at 5.9 percent per annum, above the national average growth rate of 2.5 percent. Further work is needed to identify labor flows, the nature of the work contract, the influence of customary tenure arrangements in different regions, and ways Government can influence the efficiency of this market. The location of improvements in schools, hospitals, and rural feeder and access roads, combined with improved access to land and tenure security under a freehold system, can facilitate the flow of families from overpopulated areas into areas of labor shortage where land is still available for smallholder use.

5.59   The role of Government in developing strategically placed rural infrastructure cannot be overemphasized. The efficiency of all the markets discussed above depends on the availability of reliable, low-cost transport and effective power and communications networks. Rural feeder and access roads play a vital role in determining whether and how a region is developed. The location and design of rural infrastructure can determine whether development of an area is environmentally benign. The availability of health and schooling facilities seriously affects population movements and the human costs of migration and development. For this reason, this report recommends:

- The planning of rural infrastructure--roads, schools, and health care facilities-- should be closely coordinated with agricultural development expectations, and environmental degradation considerations in regional, and district-level development plans. Such plans, which could be developed with full community participation as part of the "decentralization to the districts" initiative, would smooth the flow of labor to areas of opportunity. The negotiation of these "zoning plans" would sharpen the tradeoffs between environmental preservation and economic growth;

- Rural infrastructure development should be planned--and executed--with the full knowledge and cooperation of the communities affected. Such communities should be encouraged to participate in operation, maintenance, and rehabilitation of this infrastructure.

- Attention should be paid to providing guidelines for public and private investment in irrigation projects. Certain high value crops produced for export (flowers, vegetables) require irrigation due to the highly controlled husbandry process and marketing schedule to be followed. In other cases, the unreliability of rainfall will justify water catchment or river based irrigation to supplement moisture availability for both crops and livestock. Also, certain areas adjacent to lakes can be utilized for paddy rice production, such as the scheme supported by the Chinese in Kibimba between Jinja and Tororo. General studies of the feasibility of irrigation schemes in the most likely areas of the country should be undertaken, gathering basic data on moisture availability, soil quality and topography, crop profitability, farmer and community interest, and other factors. The use of different levels of technology should be included in the assessment. Such studies can guide public and private decision makers on the social and financial profitability of such investments. The studies should differentiate between public sector investments (justified by the lumpiness of the initial investment), and those schemes which can be funded privately.

5.60   **Research and Extension Services and Natural Resource Management.** Research is vital to the development strategy identified for the agricultural sector. Although expansion of cultivated areas is expected to continue in the medium-term, technological change will play an increasingly important role in agricultural growth. For resource-poor smallholder farmers, faced with limited cropping alternatives, technological change embodied in higher-yielding or disease-resistant-seed or planting stock, a chemical, or a husbandry technique can provide one of the few affordable means of raising incomes. Government is moving, with IDA assistance, toward the establishment of a centralizing National Agricultural Research Organization, which will improve the efficacy of this service, set the research agenda and stabilize funding. Existing research institutes will belong to this organization. Funding--and the agenda--for research will come from: (a) Government, for work on the broad array of food and livestock problems, where cost recovery is difficult; (b) export crop-related "cesses"--in coffee, tea, sugar, and cotton--to support crop-specific research programs; and (c) privately funded requests to resolve specific production problems. Measures would be taken under the IDA financed project to improve the incentives for collaboration with farmers and extension staff, in the production of research results which are relevant and profitable to adopt.

5.61   Increased agricultural output and rural incomes are important Government objectives. The country cannot wait for the gradual dissemination of technological improvements through word of mouth and curiosity. To speed technological change, the Government should continue to operate an extension service dedicated to the dissemination of appropriate profitability-enhancing, environmentally-appropriate technology. Linking the widely dispersed, broadly diversified users of this service to its costs is difficult. For this, and equity reasons, the Government, with IDA assistance, will continue to fund a redesigned, streamlined, national extension service. The focus will be to provide intensive, high quality technical assistance through a "unified" service on all aspects of agricultural production. Management will be compatible with the "T & V" system. Extension staff will initially cover select portions of priority districts, extending coverage where economically justified, and as budgetary funding permits. Private operations--especially one such as tobacco production--with tightly linked input finance, production, and marketing, can be expected to finance their own, crop-specific extension agents.

5.62   On natural resource management Governmental departments charged with controlling the use of forest and fish resources, and with management of wildlife, are notoriously weak and underfunded. These organizations should be restructured and performance incentives provided so that the regulatory legislation and framework can begin to function. Natural resources and wildlife are under severe pressure due to population growth and fuelwood needs (forests), and due to incentives to export (fish).

5.63   For the above-mentioned Government services to be effective in rural areas, personnel should have strong performance incentives, as well as the vehicles and equipment and supplies necessary for operation in difficult and taxing environments. For this reason:

- Funding for Government agricultural research, extension and natural resource management services should be given high priority within the National Budget. Annual budgetary allocations of locally generated resources in support of agriculture-related services, with emphasis on research and extension, be increased to at least 0.75 percent of GDP (about US$ 17 million in 1990).

- The NARO, the extension service and the natural resource management services should have terms of service remunerative enough strongly motivate innovative and responsive performance.

- A portion of the funding by the NARO of its institutes be provided on a "results" basis, with continued funding contingent on the production of usable conclusions.

Environmental Impact of Agricultural Growth

5.64   There has been a clear environmental cost to the years of civil disorder from which the country is emerging. Uganda's wildlife, forests, fish, grazing lands and other natural resources are in danger of being overused, polluted and driven to extinction. Soil erosion is a problem in high-population density, high rainfall areas. Natural resource management programs and policies have broken down during the period of civil unrest, and have yet to be re-established.   The strengthening of the Government services related to regulating natural resource use, wildlife management and conservation, as mentioned above, will have to be accomplished quickly if the irretrievable loss of high forests and wildlife is to be avoided. Measures taken in this regard should incorporate the needs, interests and participation of the local residents. The encouragement of natural migration patterns into under-utilized areas will have to be undertaken following careful assessment of soil quality and sustainable agricultural potential to prevent settlement in regions unsuitable for stable development. These measures have been described above, and are contingent on the development of a strong management and regulatory capacity for natural resources within Government, as well as on the use of environmental, agricultural and social criteria in the planning of new roads, schools and hospitals. Within crop agriculture, environmental criteria will have to be used by the research and extension services to develop solutions to pest and disease problems that are as benign as possible. The rapid development of cotton advocated in the report is based on the continued use of the traditional low-input, low-output methods.   As productivity and input use rise, care should be taken by the extension service and Government to limit pesticides to those with minimal environmental consequences.

The Alleviation of Rural Poverty

5.65   The strategy developed above is intended to cause agricultural GDP to grow as rapidly as possible in the next five to ten years, within the bounds imposed by climate, soils, markets, and the capacities of Uganda's institutions. Food production is widely dispersed, with all smallholder farmers producing food both for own consumption and the cash market. The structure of export crop production is also based on the use of large numbers of farmers, each of whom produces small quantities of the crop for a central processing center. The implication is that, once the processing industries have become competitive, growth in exports will carry with it strong backward linkages to the rural population. For this reason there is, in broad terms, **a close correlation between measures that produce agricultural growth, and those that will contribute to a reduction in rural poverty.** But, some aspects of the growth strategy are likely to have a greater effect on rural poverty--and gender differences--than others. For example:

- The rehabilitation of the **cotton industry** is likely to have a broad rural-poverty mitigation effect.

    o   Cotton was grown by thousands of smallholder farmers in the North and Northeast. These areas have been under severe security-related restrictions until recently, which significantly diminished economic activity. Although grown using low-input low-output--environmentally neutral--techniques, cotton provides cash and an excellent seed bed for the follow-on crop of millet;

o   Cotton ginning is labor intensive, and can generate substantial wage employment;

o   Cotton can be produced easily in certain areas in the West, contributing to the opening of new areas there;

- The enforcement of carefully designed minimum cane and greenleaf prices, guaranteeing farmers a share of the export parity price can prevent factory owners from exploiting their strong monopsony positions in these industries. There may be a case for such a system in the cotton industry. This would depend on an assessment of the ability of farmers to sell to competing ginneries. There appears to be sufficient competition in the coffee industry not to warrant such interference.

- The use of **outgrower production** strategies for rainfed industrial crops such as tea and sugar, can include more families (as families) in the export industry and in the cash generation possible from such an industry. A detailed assessment would be warranted in each case, however. While riskier for factories than for nucleus estates--in that supplies are not as secure or well regulated--such an approach could save an estate the costs of recruitment, supervision, and investments in living facilities.

- The inclusion of **inheritance rights for women** in the newly designed land legislation can permit women to continue to raise families and pursue their own lives upon the death of a spouse.

- The formalization of **squatter rights** within well-defined circumstances taking into consideration ethnic differences and customary land rights--and the facilitating of smallholder occupancy of environmentally suitable public lands and unoccupied areas--can give smallholders from the poorer, crowded areas easier legal access to the underutilized regions in the West and North.

- The use of **rural women's groups** in the design of pilot rural savings and credit schemes can help incorporate women into the financial system, and provide finance for trade and food production, activities that rural women specialize in.

- The maintenance of an open, **unregulated market in liquid fresh milk** permits small one-and two-cow operations on the periphery of Kampala and near other urban areas to participate in a lucrative market.

- Support for **small rural processing and service enterprises**--sewing, brickmaking, metalwork, carpentry, and bicycle repair--provides additional rural employment in the production of articles and services that would otherwise be imported from the metropolis.

VI. IMPLICATIONS FOR PUBLIC EXPENDITURE AND GROWTH PROSPECTS

Public Expenditure

6.1   The management of public expenditure in Uganda has been the topic of a recent Bank report.97/ This section draws on that report, and on the directions outlined in the preceding section.

6.2   Public services in the early 1980s had been devastated by the neglect, lack of funding, and loss of qualified staff during the Amin regime of 1971-79. While staff were still on the payroll, few of the original services were provided. Since then, the Government has been gradually rebuilding its capacity to direct the economy and provide social and economic support services.

6.3   In addition to its role defining sectoral development policies, the Government budget supports agricultural development in four basic ways: (a) through the generation and dissemination of technological change via research and extension services and the production of seeds and planting materials; (b) through the training of future farm managers, and staff, policymakers, and Government personnel in the management of agricultural enterprises, at diplomate colleges and Makerere University; and (c) in the provision of rural roads, rural electrification, telecommunications, marketing structures and market information; and (d) through direct investment in productive enterprises, in the sugar, tea, and livestock sectors, for example.

6.4   The absolute amount of locally generated governmental resources allocated to agriculture-related services (at 0.5 percent of GDP), and its share of the Government budget (at 4 percent of total locally funded expenditure) are very low by international standards. However, with Government revenue of only 8.1 percent of GDP supporting expenditure of 16.4 percent of GDP in FY 1991 98/ it is clear that more resources are not forthcoming. A shift in expenditure out of defense could provide more resources for agriculture, but the likelihood of dramatic change is low.

6.5   Government support for agriculture will probably continue at current levels. The challenge is to make more effective use of existing resources. The problems of public sector services for agriculture have been detailed in the recent public expenditure reviews 99/ and include:

- Raising funding allocations per staff position. Staff are inadequately paid, vehicles and facilities are poor, and travel and training allowances are too low. With a ceiling on real resources, staffing levels have to be radically reduced to permit those who remain to be more effective. A retrenchment program is being designed by the Ministry of Public Service, with support and under conditionality from the IDA-funded Structural Adjustment Project.

97/   World Bank, "Public Choices for Private Initiatives," 9203-UG, February 12, 1991.

98/   World Bank, "Uganda - Managing Public Expenditure," 10512-UG, Yellow Cover, March 31, 1992, p.4.

99/   World Bank, "Public Choices for Private Initiatives," 9203-UG, Volume II, February 12, 1991, pp 11-18.

- Shedding those functions that can be better performed by the private sector. In this category are the Namulalere Agricultural Mechanization Center, about seventeen government-owned and run state farms, 20 beef ranches and dairy farms, the veterinary drug supply service, and clinical veterinary services.

- Rationalizing the parallel field services offered by the formerly separate Ministry of Agriculture and Ministry of Animal Industries and Fisheries will result in more effective use of a fewer staff.

- Concentrating ministry resources in the essential programs of research and extension, which will be relied on to produce and disseminate basic technology. In 1988-89 the allocation for research and extension was less than 40 percent of the total recurrent budget.

6.6   Recommendations for the for Government and donor development expenditure include :

- Increasing the allocations for rehabilitation of feeder roads and the creation of district rural road maintenance capabilities. The planned allocation for feeder roads in 1992-93 in the Rehabilitation and Development Plan is US$ 15.5 million, 39 percent of the planned expenditure on roads, and 3.5 percent of annual planned development expenditure of US$483 million. An allocation of 10 percent of the annual development budget would not be inappropriate.

- Only 13 percent of the four-year development budget has been allocated to agriculture and related services--and only a small proportion of this will go into agricultural research. The returns to labor and land from agricultural production are still at very low levels. Further resources are needed to boost productivity in this sector, so that it can support the industrialization of the economy. The recommendation is to eventually raise the resources devoted to agricultural research to at least 1 percent of GDP, or US$24 million per year, 5 percent of the development budget. A portion of this could be funded from crop-specific export taxes, administered through crop-specific regulatory agencies.

- Smoothing the disbursement of Government counterpart funding--where delays holds up the disbursement of much larger amounts of donor funds--using procedures formulated under the recent Bank report, "Managing Public Expenditure."

- Focusing development expenditure on the creation of Government's regulatory and monitoring capacity, especially as the liberalization of marketing and processing gets under way in the traditional export sector. The creation of the UCDA in the coffee sector, should provide a pilot exercise for similar efforts in tea and cotton.

Prospects for Growth in Agriculture

6.7   Growth in the sector--particularly in agricultural exports--should raise incomes and consumer demand in the country. This section provides a brief treatment of growth prospects in the food sector, broadly defined to include livestock products, and the export sector. The nature of agricultural growth will have to change over the next ten years. Due to the limitations imposed by the expansion of the domestic market, in order to maintain a high growth rate in the sector the lead will have to shift from food production for the domestic market, to production of raw materials for processing and/or direct export.

Food

6.8   The most responsive sector since 1986 has been food production for the market and for own consumption, where marketing and pricing controls had been removed early on. Improvements in physical security in rural areas, reductions in economic uncertainty and inflation, increased availability of foreign exchange, and reductions in transport costs have all contributed to the rapid growth in this sector.   Food production, excluding livestock, grew at 5.9 percent per annum between 1986 and 1990.   Growth in export crop production languished due to continued Governmental interference, depressed world markets, and financial and managerial weaknesses in the marketing and processing industries.

6.9   The scope for continued rapid growth in food production will be limited in future, due to its dependence on the size of the domestic market.   In developing a point estimate for growth in the demand for food, we have used 0.95 as the income elasticity of demand for all food, a projected population growth rate of about 3.1 percent, 100/ a per capita income growth rate of some 1.5 percent per year (this is the average for the decade) and assumed constant relative prices.   On this basis the demand for food is estimated to grow at around 4.5 percent per annum. This is also the rate at which supply would have to grow to keep relative prices constant.   This estimate of growth in the food sector is very sensitive to percapita income growth, and could vary between 3 and 5 percent per annum, depending on what happens to GDP per capita.   With no growth in per capita income, food production would still have to grow at 3.1 percent per year, to keep up with the projected population increase.

6.10   The structure of the demand for food is likely to change.   As incomes rise, there could be a significant shift out of root crops into livestock products.   The Rwanda study and the Uganda Household Budget Survey both support the hypothesis that the income elasticity of demand for livestock products is much higher than for food as a whole, well above 1 and perhaps as high as 3.   Conversely, the demand for starchy foods is likely to decline.   The income elasticity of demand for bananas, cassava, and other root crops--the basis of the Ugandan diet--is estimated to be well below one.

6.11   Yields in the food sector have remained relatively stable or increased slightly during the 1980's.   The exception is bananas, the largest single crop, accounting for 50 percent of the tonnage of food produced, where the trend decline in yields since 1970 is statistically significant. In forecasting trend growth into the next century, it is assumed that efforts to revitalize research and extension, and respond to production problems with improved inputs and husbandry will result at least in a stabilization of overall yields, and may indeed improve them.   It is envisaged that agricultural growth resulting from technological change and productivity improvements would not surpass 1.9 percent per annum (para 6.13).

100/   World Bank, "Uganda - Social Sector Strategy", Report No. 10765-UG, page 2. The projected population growth rate is based on recent surveys of fertility and mortality rates Demographic and Health Survey of 1988/89. The intercensal population growth rate of 2.6 percent per annum (1980-1991) is understood to be lower than the projected rate of increase, due to circumstances affecting morbidity which are not expected to reoccur.

6.12   Returns to improved security, and better transportation and communications infrastructure will continue to influence agricultural output, especially in the North and Northeast, but the influence of these factors is expected to be slight when compared with their impact since 1986. In light of the limitations of the above-mentioned opportunities for growth in food production, it is forecast that average annual growth over the next seven years will not exceed 5 percent per annum, and is likely to be in the range of 3.5 to 4.5 percent. To put this in perspective, the annual increase in the value of food crop production between 1981 and 1990 has averaged 3.3 percent. From 1986 through 1990, the recovery years, growth in food crop production has been 5.9 percent per year.

6.13   A series of long term projections for all sectors of the economy was undertaken in the context of the World Bank Country Economic Memorandum 101/, and are noted in table 25 below. The projected growth rates for food production of 3.2 percent per annum would be realized both from a growth in cultivated area of about 1.3 percent per annum, and also from an increase in factor productivity of 1.9 percent per annum.   The changes in factor productivity are quite high, given the slow growth in yields and labour productivity over the past decade, but could be achieved if the research system succeeds in addressing disease problems in matoke, cassava and other key crops, and technology dissemination through the extension service and the private sector inputs supply markets is effective.

6.14   The consequences on the structure of production of the type of expansion depicted above should also be noted. There is a clear shift towards maize production/consumption, as incomes rise.   The relative shares of domestic food production which are implicit in the above projections are noted in table 23 below:

Table 23: Changes in the Shares of Total Foodcrop Production (in percentages)			
Crop	Actual 1991	Projected 2005	Percentage Change in Share
Matoke	30.2	24.4	-19.2
Millet	11.1	11.1	0
Maize	8.5	17.2	+101.8
Sorghum	6.1	5.5	-10.6
Sweet Potatos	11.8	9.4	-19.7
Rice	3.1	3.0	-1.3
Cassava	8.4	8.2	-1.6
Beans	10.7	9.2	-13.7
Others	10.2	11.9	+16.7
Total Foodcrops	100.0	100.0	

101/   World Bank, Country Economic Memorandum, "Growing Out of Poverty", Report No. 10715-UG, Green Cover version, December 9, 1992, Chapter 5.

Export Crops

6.15   The markets for Uganda's traditional export crops: robusta coffee, tea and cotton are depressed. In spite of this, there are compelling reasons for continuing to push for reform and productivity improvements in these subsectors: (i) there is large underutilized capacity which can be brought into operation again at reasonable marginal cost; (ii) there are stands of the perennial crops which could be brought back into production again quickly at well below establishment costs; (iii) production and processing techniques are well known in the smallholder population, the main source of output; (iv) markets are very elastic. Uganda's market share in a given commodity is small, and it will be able to sell all it can profitably produce without influencing the price.

6.16   The **cotton** sector should grow rapidly, if the liberalization measures proposed in the report (paras 4.87 - 4.90) are successfully put in place, and substantial amounts of private sector capital and managerial expertise--local and foreign--enter the industry. A major precondition for growth in this subsector is the continued reduction in security problems north of Lake Kyoga, in the traditional cotton growing areas. The projection is that, if the program is successful, cotton exports could go from 20,000 to 250,000 bales in five years. While this is well within ginning capacity and historical limits, it would be a huge undertaking. The implied growth rate is about 40 percent per year over seven years. Were this successful, exports would increase by some US$60 million per year at current prices.

6.17   Production in the **coffee** sector--with the liberalization of processing and export marketing that has taken place, and improvements in the production and continued dissemination of the new planting stock--should rise by perhaps 4 to 5 percent per annum. A return to export levels of the early 1970s--3.2 million bags--would add another US$ 50 million at current prices.

6.18   In **tea**, the sale of AEL to competent private owners, and the revitalization of the UTGC and the smallholder sector should bring back the 10,000 ha of planted tea, currently awaiting rehabilitation and unproductive. This would imply a doubling of production and exports of some 10,000 tons of made tea by 1997.

6.19   On the other hand, **non-traditional agricultural exports** such as maize, sesame seed, fish, beans, hides and skins have grown very rapidly in recent years. From US$ 4 million in 1989, export value reached US$ 23.8 million in 1990 and US$ 42.6 million in 1991, 24 percent of total exports. A careful review of growth possibilities, given current production, shipping, and marketing constraints, indicates that total annual exports from this subsector could reach some US$100 million in seven years, about US$80 million over 1990 levels. Most of the growth would come initially from sesame seed, maize, hides and skins, and spices and essential oils. Floriculture, fruits, and vegetables would pick up later in the period.

6.20   An optimistic scenario for the largest export sectors is set forth in the table 24 below, and *shows how the value of exports could be more than doubled* over the next five to seven years. This projection assumes that the action programs proposed in this report are implemented and succeed in bringing traditional exports back to historical levels, while promoting the rapid growth of non-traditional, high value agricultural exports. Base prices and exports are for 1990, and the projections are for seven years.

Table 24: Projection of Potential Export Performance Under Export Action Plan, through 1997			
	1990	1997	Annual Growth Rate
Volumes ('000 MT)			
Coffee Beans	142.40	195.00	4.6 %
Cotton Lint	3.80	45.00	42.3 %
Made Tea	4.80	16.00	18.8 %
Value (million US$)			Incremental Value (US$ M)
Coffee Beans	141.60	193.90	52.30
Cotton Lint	5.80	68.70	62.90
Made Tea	3.60	15.50	11.90
Non Traditional Agricultural Exports	20.00	100.00	80.00
TOTAL	171.00	378.10	207.10

6.21   As mentioned above, longer term projections (through the year 2005) have been developed in the context of the World Bank Country Economic Memorandum.   These projections of economic results focus on what could be achieved, if all goes well.   These projections thus represent a feasible target.   A summary of the results of these projections is provided in Table 25 below:

Table 25: Projected Average Annual Compound Growth Rates for Agriculture GDP for the Period 1992-2005 (in percentages)			
Subsector	Actual Growth Rates		Projected Growth Rates
	1981-1991	1986-1991	1992-2005
Foodcrops (Domestic)	3.2	4.8	3.2
Livestock Products (Domestic)	1.3	4.6	4.6
Horticulture, Spices, High Value Non-traditional Crops for Export			11.2
Traditional Export Crops	2.3	3.6	3.1
Food (Domestic Crops plus Livestock)			3.5
Exports (Traditional plus Non-Traditional)			9.5
Agriculture GDP (Monetary and Non-Monetary)	2.9	4.9	5.0

6.22   If these targets are met, it will mean that a series of profound and positive changes will have taken place in export agriculture in Uganda, enabling it to play its role of generating the foreign exchange needed to support continued development in agriculture and other sectors with higher returns to labor.

STATISTICAL ANNEX

CONTENTS

UGANDA GDP AT FACTOR COST, 1981 – 1991, AT CONSTANT (1987) PRICES (Million Shillings)

INDUSTRY GROUP	1981	1982	1983	1984	1985	1986	1987	1988	1989	1990	1991
Agriculture	49,313	52,945	56,200	52,216	53,257	52,773	52,683	59,264	63,267	65,495	67,880
Cash crops	3,820	6,047	5,672	5,343	5,559	5,342	5,558	5,316	5,706	5,469	6,837
Food crops	25,854	27,051	30,438	26,230	27,966	28,289	30,088	32,539	35,706	36,808	36,918
Livestock	14,635	14,735	14,862	14,558	13,998	13,403	13,960	15,068	15,565	16,151	16,759
Forestry	1,266	1,325	1,390	1,356	1,283	1,264	1,419	1,567	1,534	1,605	1,686
Fishing	3,738	3,787	3,838	4,729	4,451	4,475	1,658	4,774	4,756	5,462	5,680
Mining & Quarrying	391	495	537	473	371	365	302	286	330	622	755
Manufacturing	6,367	7,395	8,005	7,747	6,993	6,576	7,683	9,424	11,223	12,062	13,762
Coffee, Cotton, Sugar	558	667	622	600	510	483	520	707	1,023	1,240	1,794
Manufactured food	414	635	665	619	638	548	737	942	960	1,063	1,216
Miscellaneous	5,395	6,093	6,718	6,528	5,845	5,545	6,426	7,775	9,240	9,759	10,752
Electricity/Water	637	675	702	746	772	833	885	911	972	1,049	1,134
Construction	5,179	5,492	5,245	4,764	4,633	5,055	7,022	7,709	8,158	8,490	8,886
Retail/Wholesale	24,897	26,669	28,265	27,885	26,768	26,199	28,620	32,078	35,348	37,262	39,318
Transport/Communication	5,562	5,910	6,408	6,869	7,137	7,698	8,165	8,704	9,136	9,474	9,869
Road	3,900	4,047	4,385	4,873	5,184	5,512	5,821	6,327	6,753	6,955	7,303
Rail	451	554	596	610	468	543	576	592	648	738	710
Air	202	192	261	168	192	212	286	271	286	296	315
Communication	1,009	1,117	1,166	1,218	1,293	1,431	1,482	1,514	1,449	1,485	1,541
Community services	18,183	19,144	19,718	19,884	20,167	20,947	21,618	22,882	24,280	25,807	27,445
General government	5,993	6,053	6,113	6,174	6,236	6,299	6,383	6,489	6,618	6,765	6,932
Education	4,238	4,579	4,741	5,026	4,937	5,090	4,935	5,180	5,501	5,964	6,583
Health	1,319	1,355	1,386	1,411	1,437	1,476	1,515	1,556	1,598	1,641	1,686
Rents	3,333	3,642	3,817	3,510	3,688	4,044	4,482	5,071	5,677	6,231	6,696
Miscellaneous	3,300	3,515	3,661	3,763	3,869	4,038	4,303	4,586	4,886	5,206	5,548
TOTAL MONETARY	110,529	118,725	125,080	120,584	120,098	120,446	126,978	141,258	152,714	160,261	169,049
Agriculture	65,758	68,402	76,242	67,139	71,319	72,124	75,734	80,285	85,270	87,382	88,886
Food crops	56,734	59,248	66,946	57,956	62,245	63,087	66,310	70,292	74,916	76,535	77,599
Livestock	6,808	6,886	6,967	6,694	6,569	6,467	6,765	7,250	7,539	7,870	8,217
Forestry	1,749	1,795	1,850	1,899	1,949	2,011	2,077	2,147	2,221	2,295	2,361
Fishing	467	473	479	590	556	559	582	596	594	682	709
Construction	552	586	609	620	632	656	696	754	816	879	947
Owner Occupied Dwellings	4,332	4,449	4,553	4,635	4,719	4,846	4,977	5,111	5,250	5,391	5,536
TOTAL NON-MONETARY	70,642	73,437	81,404	72,394	76,670	77,626	81,407	86,150	91,336	93,652	95,369
TOTAL GDP	181,171	192,162	206,484	192,978	196,768	198,072	208,385	227,408	244,050	253,913	264,418
GDP PER CAPITA	13,787	14,238	14,951	13,726	13,750	13,475	14,003	14,668	15,327	15,528	15,746
POPULATION EST. ('000)	13,141	13,496	13,811	14,059	14,310	14,699	14,881	15,504	15,923	16,352	16,793

Source: MFEP, Background to the Budget — 1992/93, June 1992

Table 2

UGANDA
AGRICULTURE IN GDP, AND ANNUAL GROWTH, 1981 – 1991 (constant 1987 Ush millions)

	1981	1982	1983	1984	1985	1986	1987	1988	1989	1990	1991
GDP	181,171	192,162	206,484	192,978	196,808	198,072	208,385	227,408	244,050	253,913	264,418
Agriculture GDP	115,071	121,347	132,442	119,355	124,616	124,897	128,417	139,549	148,537	152,877	156,766
Monetary	49,313	52,945	56,200	52,216	53,297	52,773	52,683	59,264	63,267	65,495	67,880
Non Monetary	65,758	68,402	76,242	67,139	71,319	72,124	75,734	80,285	85,270	87,382	88,886
Population ('000)	13,141	13,496	13,811	14,059	14,313	14,699	14,881	15,504	15,923	16,352	16,793
Rural Population ('000)	11,875	12,131	12,392	12,658	12,930	13,209	13,493	13,783	14,080	14,383	14,692
Agriculture GDP per Rural Inhabitant	9.7	10.0	10.7	9.4	9.6	9.5	9.5	10.1	10.5	10.6	10.7
Annual Increase in Agriculture GDP		5.45%	9.14%	-9.88%	4.41%	0.23%	2.82%	8.67%	6.44%	2.92%	2.54%
ANNUAL GROWTH IN GDP		6.07%	7.45%	-6.54%	1.98%	0.64%	5.21%	9.13%	7.32%	4.04%	4.14%
ANNUAL GROWTH IN AGRICULTURE		5.45%	9.14%	-9.88%	4.41%	0.23%	2.82%	8.67%	6.44%	2.92%	2.54%
Cash crops		58.30%	-6.20%	-5.80%	4.79%	-4.59%	4.04%	-4.35%	7.34%	-4.15%	25.01%
Food crops		4.49%	12.84%	-13.55%	7.16%	1.29%	5.50%	6.67%	7.56%	2.46%	1.04%
Forestry		0.83%	0.96%	-2.64%	-3.22%	-3.39%	4.30%	7.69%	3.52%	3.97%	3.98%
Livestock		3.48%	3.85%	0.46%	-0.71%	1.33%	6.75%	6.24%	1.10%	3.86%	3.77%
Fishing		1.31%	1.34%	23.21%	-5.87%	0.54%	-55.50%	139.73%	-0.37%	14.84%	3.99%

Rural Population: 1980 — 11625
Rural Population: 1991 — 14692
Rural Population Growth: 2.15%

Table 3

UGANDA

SHARES OF GDP IN AGRICULTURE

(based on GDP in current prices)

	1981	1982	1983	1984	1985	1986	1987	1988	1989	1990	1991
GDP	2,805	3,950	5,991	9,490	24,743	59,126	211,384	593,128	1,112,414	1,495,258	2,103,892
Agriculture GDP	1,545	2,188	3,539	5,176	15,028	36,615	131,417	353,304	677,044	812,459	1,082,044
Monetary	680	1,037	1,550	2,370	6,439	15,448	55,683	154,627	287,330	358,797	500,616
Non Monetary	865	1,151	1,989	2,806	8,589	21,167	75,734	198,677	389,714	453,662	581,428
Non-Mon/GDP	30.8%	29.1%	33.2%	29.6%	34.7%	35.8%	35.8%	33.5%	35.0%	30.3%	27.6%
Non-Mon/Agric.	56.0%	52.6%	56.2%	54.2%	57.2%	57.8%	57.6%	56.2%	57.6%	55.8%	53.7%
Agriculture Share											
of GDP:	55.1%	55.4%	59.1%	54.5%	60.7%	61.9%	62.2%	59.6%	60.9%	54.3%	51.4%

SUBSECTORAL SHARES

Monetized

	1981	1982	1983	1984	1985	1986	1987	1988	1989	1990	1991
Agriculture	100%	100%	100%	100%	100%	100%	100%	100%	100%	100%	100%
Cash crops	6%	14%	13%	14%	11%	12%	10%	8%	7%	9%	16%
Food crops	46%	42%	52%	49%	52%	53%	54%	51%	57%	53%	46%
Livestock	38%	32%	25%	26%	31%	28%	25%	30%	25%	26%	26%
Forestry	3%	3%	3%	2%	2%	2%	3%	3%	3%	3%	3%
Fishing	7%	9%	8%	8%	4%	5%	8%	8%	8%	9%	9%

Non Monetized

	1981	1982	1983	1984	1985	1986	1987	1988	1989	1990	1991
Agriculture	100%	100%	100%	100%	100%	100%	100%	100%	100%	100%	100%
Food crops	81%	81%	87%	86%	86%	87%	88%	85%	87%	85%	85%
Livestock	10%	10%	10%	10%	10%	10%	10%	10%	10%	10%	10%
Forestry	3%	3%	3%	3%	3%	3%	3%	3%	3%	3%	3%
Fishing	1%	1%	1%	1%	1%	1%	1%	1%	1%	1%	1%

	1981	1982	1983	1984	1985	1986	1987	1988	1989	1990	1991
AGRICULTURE GD	1,545	2,188	3,539	5,176	15,028	36,615	131,417	353,304	677,044	812,459	1,082,044
Cash crops	44	144	195	343	680	1,896	5,558	12,463	20,798	31,082	80,064
Food crops	1,013	1,374	2,526	3,556	10,715	26,447	96,398	247,346	505,111	578,546	725,470
Livestock	375	484	576	899	2,906	6,410	20,725	67,767	107,162	140,272	191,693
Forestry	62	78	107	155	402	1,012	3,496	11,076	19,651	27,259	35,936
Fishing	51	108	135	223	325	850	5,240	14,652	24,322	35,300	48,881
TOTAL AGRICULT	100.0%	100.0%	100.0%	100.0%	100.0%	100.0%	100.0%	100.0%	100.0%	100.0%	100.0%
Cash crops	2.8%	6.6%	5.5%	6.6%	4.5%	5.2%	4.2%	3.5%	3.1%	3.8%	7.4%
Food crops	65.6%	62.8%	71.4%	68.7%	71.3%	72.2%	73.4%	70.0%	74.6%	71.2%	67.0%
Livestock	24.3%	22.1%	16.3%	17.4%	19.3%	17.5%	15.8%	19.2%	15.8%	17.3%	17.7%
Forestry	4.0%	3.6%	3.0%	3.0%	2.7%	2.8%	2.7%	3.1%	2.9%	3.4%	3.3%
Fishing	3.3%	4.9%	3.8%	4.3%	2.2%	2.3%	4.0%	4.1%	3.6%	4.3%	4.5%
GDP	181,171	192,162	206,484	192,978	196,808	198,072	208,385	227,408	244,050	253,913	264,418
AGRICULTURE SHA	55.1%	55.4%	59.1%	54.5%	60.7%	61.9%	62.2%	59.6%	60.9%	54.3%	51.4%
Cash crops	1.6%	3.6%	3.3%	3.6%	2.7%	3.2%	2.6%	2.1%	1.9%	2.1%	3.8%
Food crops	36.1%	34.8%	42.2%	37.5%	43.3%	44.7%	45.6%	41.7%	45.4%	38.7%	34.5%
Livestock	13.4%	12.3%	9.6%	9.5%	11.7%	10.8%	9.8%	11.4%	9.6%	9.4%	9.1%
Forestry	2.2%	2.0%	1.8%	1.6%	1.6%	1.7%	1.7%	1.9%	1.8%	1.8%	1.7%
Fishing	1.8%	2.7%	2.3%	2.3%	1.3%	1.4%	2.5%	2.5%	2.2%	2.4%	2.3%

Source: MFEP, Background to the Budget — 1992/93, June 1992

Table 4

UGANDA
RECURRENT REVENUE PERFORMANCE
(million new Uganda Shs.)

Source of Revenue	1980/81	1981/82	1982/83	1983/84	1984/85	1985/86	1986/87	1987/88	1988/89	1989/90	Prelim 1990/91
Income Tax	4.7	22.7	24.8	62.5	97.6	156.3	569.9	1517.6	4770.0	8756.5	12177.1
PAYE	1.2	2.6	2.8	3.2	8.9	13.1	34.1	92.7	495.0	688.7	941.3
Other 1/	3.5	20.2	22.1	59.3	88.8	143.2	535.8	1424.9	4275.0	8067.8	11235.7
Export Taxes	1.1	67.6	160.6	412.1	941.8	1914.8	1996.5	5274.5	5425.0	11925.0	12195.7
Coffee	1.1	67.6	160.6	412.1	941.8	1891.3	1996.5	5259.0	5370.0	11921.4	12195.7
Other	-	-	0.0	0.0	0.0	23.6	0.0	15.5	55.0	34.6	-
Customs Duty	5.7	51.7	64.0	93.2	142.9	176.4	594.9	1865.9	7792.0	22830.5	45711.5
Excise Duty	1.0	18.4	28.4	34.8	55.5	97.3	340.8	1710.5	4905.0	6460.0	12377.7
Sales Tax 2/	10.7	74.8	105.5	176.8	318.7	422.3	1265.5	6651.8	17549.0	28106.6	34490.8
Commercial Transaction Levy	0.5	2.0	4.7	11.1	17.4	22.7	67.7	375.0	931.0	1945.5	3123.2
Foreign Exchange Profits	-	-	115.0	79.1	-	-	-	-	-	-	-
Freight Charges	..	..	13.1	13.5	24.9	50.6	52.0	616.7	-	-	-
Other Tax Revenue 3/	1.2	6.7	6.3	46.0	2.9	3.4	119.3	308.7	1378.0	4140.1	4751.5
Non Tax Revenue					19.1		-1.7		6969.0	2294.5	3101.5
TOTAL RECURRENT REVENUE	24.9	243.8	522.4	929.1	1620.8	2843.8	5004.9	18320.7	49719.0	86458.7	127929.0

Source: Ministry of Planning and Economic Development, Background to the Budget 1989–1990; July 1989.
Ministry of Planning and Economic Development, Background to the Budget 1985–86; June 1985.

1/ Includes selective income levy, company and individual profits.
2/ Sales tax on local manufactured goods and imports.
3/ Includes motor vehicles and other license fees and appropriations-in-aid. For 1980/81 and 1981/82 includes Public Sector
Investment Contribution.
NOTE: ".." means not available.

Doc: NACCTS03

Table 5

UGANDA
RECURRENT EXPENDITURE BY MINISTRY
(million new UShs.)

	1980/81	1981/82	1982/83	1983/84	1984/85	1985/86	1986/87	1987/88	1988/89	1989/90	Prelim 1990/91
President's Office	71.2	11.2	20.0	26.6	100.7	172.4	339.1	951.2	1435.8	3095.0	2804.9
Judiciary	0.6	1.3	1.5	2.2	6.2	10.1	58.3	115.6	208.8	503.8	557.2
National Assembly	0.5	1.4	2.4	2.9	5.4	7.2	48.5	112.6	356.9	738.0	1508.8
Audit	0.1	0.2	0.2	0.5	1.4	1.2	12.4	24.3	44.2	63.7	148.7
Public Service	1.1	3.1	5.3	5.4	15.2	32.1	101.9	278.8	898.3	1769.6	1281.5
Foreign Affairs	2.6	9.9	33.3	30.8	50.0	106.4	385.9	655.3	1822.8	3905.2	2678.1
Justice	0.4	0.6	0.9	1.1	1.9	3.0	19.2	63.6	149.5	156.2	414.4
Finance	11.6	67.3	122.3	64.2	561.9	1430.4	1786.0	8543.2	12838.8	14888.5	3044.1
Commerce	0.2	0.6	0.7	1.6	2.9	3.4	22.1	39.9	106.2	253.0	284.1
Agriculture	3.0	7.4	8.6	13.6	29.9	39.6	168.5	443.0	963.0	1151.5	1426.7
Animal Industry	1.8	3.1	4.5	7.1	23.3	36.0	131.9	258.9	718.5	860.9	1264.5
Lands and Surveys	1.8	5.1	5.1	8.7	16.8	23.5	33.9	80.4	210.2	1002.1	1012.5
Education	14.0	43.4	67.9	126.3	279.1	527.5	887.8	4716.9	7985.1	12437.3	18564.3
Health	4.9	11.7	21.3	27.0	65.9	88.3	180.4	622.0	1833.5	3305.9	5213.1
Youth, Culture & Sport	0.9	1.7	2.4	3.3	12.9	18.1	47.7	85.6	134.2	754.3	545.3
Works	2.6	5.7	6.8	13.5	52.0	135.5	273.9	482.7	976.4	2172.9	1889.9
Transport	0.9	3.1	2.6	3.9	7.0	8.7	43.1	61.5	111.9	320	309.1
Information	0.9	1.9	3.2	6.8	11.9	20.6	62.0	75.0	232.1	399.5	435.9
Industry & Technology	0.1	0.4	0.7	0.8	2.2	3.0	10.9	25.2	71.6	115.8	135.9
Labor	0.9	2.0	2.9	4.3	8.9	111.4	25.1	47.1	218.7	205.6	418.9
Defense	39.2	56.8	67.9	166.5	356.3	1026.9	2212.4	6383.1	16781.4	34696.6	40221.7
Internal Affairs	0.7	1.8	1.5	2.2	3.2	5.5	30.7	93.1	104.9	533.4	279.2
Police	5.2	9.4	18.1	23.1	46.1	87.0	287.8	733.7	1536.5	2610.4	4324.4
Prison	3.8	10.0	12.2	12.8	26.4	45.2	160.5	397.8	843.9	2183	1231.5
Local Government	4.4	10.5	13.5	21.6	37.6	46.9	170.1	381.5	1409.4	1648.6	3763.2
Planning	0.3	0.7	1.3	2.8	3.9	3.7	22.0	26.7	134.9	120.7	215.1
Co-operatives	0.5	1.1	1.4	2.4	6.2	8.5	22.2	79.9	208.7	295.4	593.2
Tourism & Wildlife	0.3	0.9	1.1	1.7	3.3	5.1	30.8	58.4	174.4	247.2	332.1
Regional Cooperation	0.6	1.4	1.5	4.3	10.5	9.0	36.0	128.7	214.8	25	-
Prime Minister's Office	-	-	0.4	0.9	1.2	5.8	16.0	37.1	93.7	304.6	364.3
Environment	..	..	4.8	7.8	12.3	95.6	7.7	94.1	336.3	306.4	347.3
Rehabilitation	1.0	3.9	0.2	0.5	1.0	3.7	242.7	566.5	1046.5	1351.5	671.6
Energy	0.0	0.1	0.1	0.1	0.2	0.2	11.1	21.1	76.8	126.1	83.9
Mulago Hospital	..	..	0.0	0.0	0.0	0.0	41.1	216.8	584.8	1196.3	1849.2
Housing	..	2.3	2.3	5.7	7.1	11.9	45.3	85.5	215.6	242.1	361.1
Water Minerals Devt.	..	..	-	-	-	-	51.8	206.1	284.4	365	805.6
Inspectorate of Govt.	..	..	-	-	-	-	-	12.1	53.5	119.1	129.3
Makerere University	..	..	-	-	-	-	-	-	1224.6	2197.6	2780.9
Central Purchasing	..	0.1	-	-	-	-	-	-	432.5	1044.5	798.9
Namalere Workshop	..	..	-	-	-	-	-	-	191.4	255.8	306.1
State House	..	..	-	-	-	-	-	-	778.6	2118.1	2352.1
Constitutional Affairs	..	..	-	-	-	-	-	-	17.6	482.6	841.6
Reconstruction & Devt.	..	..	-	-	-	-	-	-	13.0	69.8	182.6
Women in Development	..	..	-	-	-	-	-	-	12.6	89.4	95.2
Karamoja Development	..	..	-	-	-	-	-	-	8.3	73.3	83.3
Mass Mobilization	..	..	-	-	-	-	-	-	255.1	1165.1	1364.1
Public Service Commission	-	-	-	-	-	-	-	-	-	64.5	102.3
Unallocated	-	-	-	-	-	-	-	-	-	3491.6	-
TOTAL	111.9	280.1	438.9	602.9	1771.0	4133.2	8026.5	27205.0	58350.7	105522.5	108417.7

Source: Ministry of Planning and Economic Development, Background to the Budget 1989-1990; July 1989.
 Ministry of Planning and Economic Development, Background to the Budget 1985-86; June 1985.

1/ Table includes expenditure on statutory items.
NOTE: ".." means not available.

Doc: NACCTS04

Table 6

UGANDA
DEVELOPMENT BUDGET BY MINISTRY 1/
(million new Uganda Shs.)

	1980/81	1981/82	1982/83	1983/84	1984/85	1985/86	1986/87	1987/88	1988/89	1989/90	Prelim 1990/91
President's Office	1.0	5.6	7.7	8.7	19.8	53.3	63.7	300.2	396.0	95.8	515.9
Judiciary	0.1	0.3	0.0	0.2	0.5	0.4	1.0	10.0	28.6	69.7	68.3
National Assembly	0.2	0.4	0.5	0.4	1.0	5.9	24.8	29.3	87.5	117.5	1624.8
Audit	0.0	0.1	0.2	0.3	0.5	1.1	1.1	2.4	13.3	82.6	66.3
Public Service	0.1	0.2	0.3	1.3	5.4	10.6	4.4	6.9	67.2	515.1	103.5
Foreign Affairs	0.0	0.1	0.9	0.1	1.6	8.1	10.1	18.3	10.3	21.4	12.1
Justice	0.0	0.1	0.1	0.1	0.3	0	11.2	4.2	53.5	34.5	13.6
Finance 1/	3.1	22.0	9.5	45.9	136.2	216.8	417.6	1457.0	1526.0	3446.5	5136.5
Commerce	0.0	-	0.1	0.1	0.2	0.4	5.4	10.3	12.7	352.0	24.1
Agriculture	7.3	7.1	9.8	3.9	9.1	69.1	166.7	151.0	402.3	692.5	1339.5
Animal Industry	1.4	7.6	3.9	6.2	22.0	39	90.3	332.6	604.0	123.8	367.9
Lands and Surveys	0.7	2.6	4.7	14.4	34.0	52.7	4.4	25.4	211.4	224.8	28.1
Education	1.8	7.5	4.7	6.1	14.4	36.2	205.9	194.9	323.4	533.6	1956.0
Health	0.8	3.1	4.9	2.9	14.1	5.8	32.3	17.6	293.0	302.9	850.0
Youth, Culture & Sport	0.3	0.3	0.2	0.3	13.5	10.6	53.6	23.6	46.1	37.6	53.2
Works	1.4	3.6	3.7	13.3	18.2	71.3	264.7	1147.8	1242.5	4405	8640.3
Transport	0.3	1.3	0.3	3.7	0.8	0.6	1.8	4.1	72.6	628.8	353.5
Information	0.0	0.5	0.6	3.0	17.2	8.5	23.3	106.0	117.2	202.2	152.5
Industry & Technology	-	0.0	0.0	0.3	0.5	0.6	0.9	3.6	4.8	26.7	22.7
Labor	0.0	0.3	0.2	0.5	0.2	2.4	6.1	-	13.3	11.8	61.3
Defense	9.7	16.7	23.3	25.8	28.5	33.2	400.1	2229.0	3800.0	4242.2	20735.5
Internal Affairs	0.9	3.7	5.4	5.1	5.8	15.6	118.4	341.6	407.8	997.3	1057.7
Police	-	-	-	-	-	-	-	-	-	730.9	-
Prison	-	-	-	-	-	-	-	-	-	53.8	-
Local Government	0.6	0.5	0.3	7.2	2.8	21.5	40.8	224.8	383.0	1006.3	5136.0
Planning	0.0	0.2	1.6	0.8	1.4	4.2	6.6	106.9	68.8	96.4	2221.9
Co-operatives	0.0	0.1		2.4	5.3	6.7	62.6	52.6	141.4	243.0	245.5
Tourism & Wildlife	0.1	0.2	0.1	1.2	1.5	1.2	9.0	4.9	24.1	23.9	67.9
Regional Cooperation	0.1	0.9	0.9	1.5	1.0	0.3	1.8	89.4	8.9	5.7	-
Prime Minister's Office	-	-	0.1	0.1	1.6	5.9	12.3	10.0	71.3	23.8	142.0
Environment							9.5	11.9	74.2	55.4	359.1
Rehabilitation	0.1	0.1	0.3	0.3	0.9	1.2	9.0	0.8	16.9	7.3	20.8
Power, Posts & Telecomms	-	0.0	0.0	0.4	0.3	3.1	-	-	-	-	-
Energy	..	..	-	-	-	-	3.4	67.0	60.9	7.7	16.1
Mulago Hospital	..	..	-	-	-	-	26.4	29.2	153.4	419.7	273.1
Housing	..	4.9	4.0	8.4	19.5	23.2	96.6	2221.3	296.1	667.9	476.5
Water Minerals Devt.	..	..	-	-	-	-	51.5	116.9	169.8	1138.9	440.7
Inspectorate of Govt.	..	..	-	-	-	-	-	7.2	2.3	27.9	40.0
Makerere University	..	..	-	-	-	-	-	-	121.8	228.1	353.7
Central Purchasing	-	0.0	-	-	-	-	-	-	-	119.1	4.0
Namalere Workshop	..	..	-	-	-	-	-	-	420.3	37.8	1.3
State House	..	..	-	-	-	-	-	-	200.0	476.3	1378.1
Constitutional Affairs	..	..	-	-	-	-	-	-	9.2	397.1	25.2
Reconstruction & Devt.	..	..	-	-	-	-	-	-	19.6	45.7	72.3
Women in Development	..	..	-	-	-	-	-	-	12.0	18.8	1.3
Karamoja Development	..	..	-	-	-	-	-	-	53.6	263.0	148.8
Mass Mobilization	..	..	-	-	-	-	-	-	31.8	106.0	93.5
Public Service Commission	-	-	-	-	-	-	-	-	-	538.0	-
Unallocated	-	-	-	-	-	-	-	-	-	-2433.8	-
TOTAL	**30.0**	**89.9**	**88.3**	**165.0**	**377.9**	**709.5**	**2237.1**	**9358.7**	**12072.9**	**21469.0**	**54700.9**

Source: Ministry of Planning and Economic Development, Background to the Budget 1989-1990; July 1989.
    Ministry of Planning and Economic Development, Background to the Budget 1985-86; June 1985.

1/ Includes contributions to international organizations.
NOTE: ".." means not available.

Doc: NACCTS05

UGANDA
SUMMARY OF GOVERNMENT BUDGETARY AND FINANCIAL OPERATIONS
(million new Uganda Shs.)

BUDGET/FINANCIA	1980/81	1981/82	1982/83	1983/84	1984/85	1985/86	1986/87	1987/88	1988/89
RECURRENT BUDGET									
Revenue	27.3	243.9	522.4	902.9	1620.9	2843.8	5005.0	22262.3	45290.2
Expenditure	111.9	280.1	438.7	789.8	1781.0	4133.2	8026.5	27205.0	58350.7
Deficit/Surplus	-84.6	-36.2	83.7	113.1	-160.1	-1289.4	-3021.5	-4942.7	-13060.5
DEVELOPMENT BUDGET									
Revenue	5.8	34.9	5.8	45.0	78.0	384.4	853.0	5640.0	11408.4
Expenditure	30.1	89.9	88.2	160.3	356.3	709.5	2237.1	16048.7	29888.9
Deficit/Surplus	-24.3	-55.0	-82.4	-115.3	-278.3	-325.1	-1384.1	-10408.7	-18480.5
Unallocated Items 1/	-11.3	63.0	-166.8	-219.2	-192.4	-23.7	-4405.6	9852.4	17105.0
TOTAL DEFICIT	-97.7	-154.2	-165.4	-221.5	-630.8	-1638.3	-8811.2	-5499.1	-14436.0
FINANCING									
External (Net)	7.7	10.0	36.3	30.1	134.7	474.3	1362.0	556.1	12912.0
Domestic	90.0	144.2	129.0	191.4	496.1	1164.0	4195.0	4943.0	1524.0
Bank	88.0	133.2	113.7	-69.3	538.9	775.2	2182.0	4481.0	978.0
Nonbank	2.0	11.0	15.4	260.7	-42.8	388.8	2013.0	462.0	546.0
TOTAL FINANCING	97.7	154.2	165.4	221.5	630.8	1638.3	5557.0	5499.1	14436.0

Source: Ministry of Planning and Economic Development, Background to the Budget 1989-1990; July 1989.
Ministry of Planning and Economic Development, Background to the Budget 1985-86; June 1985.

1/ Balancing item.

Doc: NACCTS06

UGANDA

MARKETED PRODUCTION OF EXPORT CROPS (thousand tons)

	1978	1979	1980	1981	1982	1983	1984	1985	1986	1987	1988	1989	1990°
Coffee 1/	121.2	103.0	135.2	97.5	166.6	157.4	138.7	155.0	143.3	160.3	156.4	188.2	189.9
of which:													
Robusta	118.9	98.3	130.0	93.0	152.3	142.8	128.6	144.4	134.7	151.2	144.5	178.0	179.6
Arabica	23.3	4.7	4.8	4.5	14.3	14.6	10.1	10.6	8.6	9.1	11.9	10.2	10.3
Cotton 1/	20.4	7.6	6.1	4.1	5.1	10.0	12.2	10.0	8.9	5.8	5.0	4.8	5.9
Tobacco 2/	1.4	0.8	0.4	0.1	0.6	1.6	2.0	1.6	0.9	1.3	2.6	3.8	-
Tea 3/	10.9	1.8	1.5	1.7	2.6	3.1	5.2	5.8	3.3	3.6	3.5	4.6	6.7
Sugar (Raw)	8.0	5.2	4.3	3.8	3.3	3.1	2.4	0.8	-	-	6.2	-	-
Cocoa	0.2	0.2	0.1	0.1	0.1	0.2	0.3	0.2	0.1	0.1	0.2	0.5	1.0

AREA PLANTED OF EXPORT CROPS (thousand hectares)

	1978	1979	1980	1981	1982	1983	1984	1985	1986	1987	1988	1989	1990
Coffee 1/	223.0	224.0	224.0	224.0	224.0	224.0	224.0	224.5	224.7	224.7	224.7	237.6	240.0
of which:													
Robusta	190.0	191.0	191.0	191.0	191.0	191.0	191.0	191.5	191.7	191.7	191.7	208.1	210.0
Arabica	33.0	33.0	33.0	33.0	33.0	33.0	33.0	33.0	33.0	33.0	33.0	29.5	30.0
Cotton 1/	677.5	417.0	312.4	121.3	150.3	169.6	199.4	160.0	180.0	140.0	98.9	106.0	69.0
Tobacco 2/	4.1	3.7	3.3	0.6	1.1	3.8	3.2	2.9	1.4	2.1	2.7	3.8	-
Tea 3/	20.9	20.9	20.9	20.9	20.9	20.9	20.9	20.9	20.9	20.9	20.9	20.9	
Sugar (Raw)	31.3	37.5	31.0	31.0	31.0	31.0	31.0	31.0	31.0	31.0	31.0	31.0	
Cocoa	14.4	14.5	14.5	14.5	14.5	14.5	10.5	14.5	14.5	14.5	14.5	10.0	10.0

YIELD PLANTED OF EXPORT CROPS (tons per hectare)

	1978	1979	1980	1981	1982	1983	1984	1985	1986	1987	1988	1989	1990
Coffee (Clean)	0.54	0.46	0.60	0.44	0.74	0.70	0.62	0.69	0.64	0.71	0.70	0.79	0.79
of which:													
Robusta (kg kiboko)	1159	953	1260	902	1477	1385	1247	1396	1301	1461	1396	1584	1584
Arabica (kg parchm)	883	178	182	170	542	553	383	402	326	345	451	432	429
Cotton (kg seed)	93	56	60	104	104	181	188	192	152	127	156	139	263
Tobacco (flue/fired)	0.34	0.22	0.12	0.17	0.55	0.42	0.63	0.55	0.64	0.62	0.96	1.00	-
Tea (Green Leaf)	2.61	0.43	0.36	0.41	0.62	0.74	1.24	1.39	0.79	0.86	0.84	1.10	
Sugar (Raw)	256	139	139	123	106	100	77	26	0	0	200	0	
Cocoa	14	14	7	7	7	14	29	14	7	7	14	50	100
Area of Export Crops	971	718	606	412	442	464	489	454	473	433	393	409	319

Source: Ministry of Planning and Economic Development, the following "Background to the Budget": 1989-90 of July 1989, 1985-86 of July 1985, 1991-92 of July 1991
1/ Annual figures refer to CROP YEAR of coffee and cotton ending in September and October respectively, in the year indicated. It should be noted that planting, weeding, spraying, etc. in the case of cotton are carried out in the calendar year in which the CROP YEAR starts.

Table 9

UGANDA
COMPOSITION OF EXPORTS, VOLUME AND VALUE

	1970	1971	1972	1973	1974	1975	1976	1977	1978	1979	1980	1981	1982	1983	1984	1985	1986	1987	1988	1989	1990	1991
VOLUME: '000 TONS																						
Coffee 1/	191.2	174.6	214.2	192.4	187.2	176.6	153.1	113.4	113.7	143.1	110.1	128.3	174.7	144.3	133.2	151.5	140.8	148.2	144.2	176.50	141.50	127.40
Cotton	78.1	68.7	66.1	64.7	36.2	25.6	19.2	9.9	11.7	3.6	2.3	1.2	1.8	7.0	6.7	9.6	4.9	3.4	2.1	2.30	3.80	7.80
Tea	15.0	15.3	20.7	19.2	16.7	17.1	11.7	8.8	8.7	1.4	0.5	0.5	1.2	1.3	2.5	1.2	2.8	2.1	3.1	3.20	4.80	7.10
Tobacco	2.0	2.2	2.5	1.5	1.1	1.3	1.1	1.8	1.2	0.4	0.3	-	-	0.7	0.7	0.3	-	-	0.0	0.50	2.30	2.50
Maize													1.6	29.7	29.7	9.8	2.2	-	-	13.3	26.7	33.10
Beans																				1.08		
Copper	16.5	16.8	14.1	9.7	9.0	7.8	5.4	2.5	6.2	4.4											-	
UNIT VALUE: US$/KG																						
Coffee	0.74	0.80	0.75	0.93	1.20	0.82	2.03	5.00	2.75	2.98	3.1	1.9	2.0	2.4	2.7	2.3	2.8	2.1	1.8	1.5	1.0	0.90
Cotton	0.63	0.73	0.80	0.74	1.07	0.86	1.18	1.60	1.69	1.78	1.8	1.9	1.8	1.6	1.8	1.5	1.0	1.2	1.4	1.7	1.5	1.50
Tea	0.89	0.89	0.87	0.82	0.94	0.73	0.95	1.46	0.95	1.00	0.6	0.6	0.7	0.9	1.3	0.8	1.1	0.9	1.0	1.0	0.7	1.00
Tobacco	1.30	1.38	1.08	1.32	1.22	1.31	1.81	2.01	1.50	2.25	1.0	-	-	1.3	2.1	1.3	-	-	-	1.2	1.2	1.90
Maize													0.4	0.4	0.3	0.3	-	-		0.05	0.16	0.13
Beans																						
Copper	1.41					0.92			0.31	0.11												
VALUE: US$ MILLION																						
Coffee	142.0	140.3	161.2	178.2	224.0	144.6	310.9	567.0	312.7	425.9	341.3	243.8	349.4	346.3	359.6	348.5	394.2	307.5	265.3	262.8	140.40	120.80
Cotton	49.1	50.3	53.0	48.0	38.9	22.1	22.8	15.8	19.8	6.4	4.1	2.3	3.2	11.2	12.1	14.0	5.1	4.1	3.0	4.0	5.80	11.70
Tea	13.3	13.6	17.9	15.7	15.7	12.5	11.2	12.9	8.3	1.4	0.3	0.3	0.8	1.2	3.3	1.0	3.1	1.9	3.1	3.2	3.60	6.80
Tobacco	2.6	3.0	2.7	2.0	1.3	1.7	2.0	3.6	1.8	0.9	0.3	0.0	0.0	0.9	1.5	0.4	0.0	0.0	0.0	0.6	2.80	4.50
Maize											0.0	0.0	0.6	12.1	8.9	2.9	0.0	0.0	0.3	1.5	3.30	4.20
Beans																				0.60	4.20	4.30
Copper	23.2					7.2			1.9	0.5												
Simsim																					5.20	10.50
Re-exports	1.9					0.6																
Other Exports	47.1					8.7			8.7	4.6	2.2	2.5	0.7	2.1	6.6	4.3	3.1	3.1	2.9	2.8	10.00	22.00
Total Unadjusted	279.2					197.4			353.2	439.7	348.2	248.9	354.7	373.8	392.0	371.1	405.5	316.6	274.6	275.5	175.3	184.90
Adjusted	-17.6					-20.0			-32.1	-43.4	-29.1	-3.4	-7.6	-6.1	15.9	7.9	1.3	17.0	-8.3	2.2	2.5	
TOTAL EXPORTS	261.6					177.4			321.1	396.3	319.1	245.5	347.1	367.7	407.9	379.0	406.8	333.6	266.3	277.7	177.80	184.90

Source : Ministry of Planning and Economic Development, Background to the Budget 1990 – 1991, July 1990.

Note: Data for 1970, 1978, 1979 are drawn from World Bank Report No. 5595-UG, June 5, 1985.

UGANDA
AREA PLANTED OF SELECTED FOOD CROPS
THOUSAND/HECTARES

	1970	1971	1972	1973	1974	1975	1976	1977	1978	1979	1980	1981	1982	1983	1984	1985	1986	1987	1988	1989	1990
Plantain																					
Bananas (Matoke)	909	905	916	974	1063	1097	1180	1240	1287	1173	1173	1180	1199	1209	1209	1210	1210	1336	1302	1322	1379
Cereals																					
Finger Millet	582	714	497	636	510	484	498	527	510	313	279	300	330	341	332	300	342	324	371	381	376
Maize	300	280	415	314	388	475	527	429	450	272	258	260	285	295	347	289	322	307	345	430	389
Sorghum	311	307	318	287	367	311	326	280	286	187	167	170	200	207	206	190	208	203	233	231	240
Rice									24	12	11	12	15	17	17	14	19	16	17	20	44
Wheat									7	3	8	4	5	5	4	5	5	5	6	5	4
TOTAL	1193	1301	1230	1237	1265	1270	1351	1236	1277	787	723	746	835	865	906	798	896	855	972	1067	1053
Root Crops																					
Sweet Potatoes	444	495	508	400	506	550	564	467	476	256	231	350	372	457	387	359	407	398	417	405	414
Irish Potatoes									37	21	24	25	28	30	17	25	19	26	27	36	34
Cassava	539	508	371	483	485	618	512	540	529	322	302	310	331	372	401	300	362	345	361	392	371
TOTAL	983	1003	879	883	991	1168	1076	1007	1042	599	557	685	731	859	805	684	788	769	805	833	819
Pulses																					
Beans 1/	300	459	309	359	408	408	436	338	388	227	224	299	364	398	385	334	397	373	445	480	495
Field Peas 1/									34	19	17	18	20	32	16	17	18	22	23	24	22
Cow Peas 1/									80	43	38	41	45	46	49	44	50	42	46	47	72
Pigeon Peas 1/									105	58	50	55	60	62	72	60	67	60	64	68	79
TOTAL	414	634	427	496	564	564	602	467	607	347	329	413	489	538	522	455	532	497	578	615	668
Oilseeds																					
Groundnuts 1/	251	291	291	222	267	243	213	234	234	122	95	110	120	124	172	124	177	126	179	189	191
Soya Beans 1/	5	4	7	5	6	6	8	6	6	4	4	5	6	6	11	10	12	10	17	18	37
Sim-sim 1/	50	91	82	89	92	112	106	119	137	60	65	70	80	95	86	76	80	74	81	92	124
TOTAL	306	386	380	316	365	361	327	359	377	186	164	185	206	225	269	210	269	210	277	299	352
Total Annuals	2896	3324	2915	2931	3184	3363	3356	3068	3303	1919	1773	2029	2261	2487	2502	2147	2485	2331	2632	2814	2892
TOTAL FOOD AREA	3805	4229	3831	3905	4247	4460	4536	4308	4590	3092	2946	3209	3460	3696	3711	3357	3695	3667	3934	4136	4271
Food Area Per Rural Capita (ha/cap)	0.42	0.46	0.40	0.40	0.43	0.44	0.43	0.40	0.42	0.27	0.25	0.27	0.29	0.30	0.29	0.26	0.28	0.27	0.29	0.29	0.30

Source: Ministry of Planning and Economic Development, Background to the Budget 1990-91, July 1990.
   Ministry of Planning and Economic Development, Background to the Budget 1985-86; June 1985.
1/ Pulse area inferred for 1970-78, based on 1978-1990 ratio.

Table 10

UGANDA
PRODUCTION OF SELECTED FOOD CROPS
THOUSAND/TONS

	1970	1971	1972	1973	1974	1975	1976	1977	1978	1979	1980	1981	1982	1983	1984	1985	1986	1987	1988	1989	1990
Plantain																					
Banana (Matoke)	7657	7557	7634	8126	8879	9106	8137	8531	8855	6090	5699	5900	6596	6487	6250	6468	6565	7039	7293	7469	7791
Cereals																					
Finger Millet	783	650	594	643	591	682	567	578	561	481	459	480	401	545	332	480	427	518	578	610	564
Maize	389	421	500	419	430	570	674	566	594	453	286	342	393	413	338	354	322	357	440	624	584
Sorghum	462	348	419	380	345	467	390	344	351	316	299	320	270	407	247	310	280	315	344	347	360
Rice									26	15	17	15	19	22	20	19	21	20	23	27	62
Wheat									14	5	17	8	10	12	7	8	8	10	13	11	8
TOTAL	1634	1419	1513	1442	1366	1719	1631	1488	1546	1270	1078	1165	1093	1399	944	1171	1058	1220	1398	1619	1578
Root Crops																					
Sweet Potatoes	1570	1425	1224	1252	1786	1953	2002	1659	1689	1272	1200	1300	1487	1843	1630	1664	1865	1674	1716	1658	1780
Irish Potatoes									293	131	166	175	196	209	132	168	98	185	190	248	238
Cassava	2578	2417	2650	2132	2350	2992	2838	2993	2028	2100	2072	3034	3127	3239	2969	2700	2900	3101	3271	3568	3339
TOTAL	4148	3842	3874	3364	4136	4945	4840	4652	4010	3503	3438	4509	4810	5291	4731	4532	4863	4960	5177	5474	5357
Pulses																					
Beans	388	222	237	170	196	326	337	253	291	182	133	240	237	314	295	267	267	299	338	389	396
Field Peas 1/									14	6	7	8	10	12	13	8	10	11	12	12	11
Cow Peas 1/									31	22	16	18	20	37	39	35	39	37	38	38	58
Pigeon Peas 1/									42	19	26	25	28	29	25	28	30	27	42	46	55
TOTAL 1/	388	222	237	170	196	326	337	253	378	229	182	291	295	392	372	338	346	374	430	485	520
Oilseeds																					
Groundnuts	244	251	234	212	200	194	177	193	187	80	70	90	90	99	102	93	118	122	134	145	172
Soya Beans	5	4	7	5	4	4	8	6	6	3	3	5	6	7	8	8	10	8	14	16	37
Sim-sim									40	16	20	25	35	42	39	33	35	33	36	45	62
TOTAL	249	255	241	217	204	198	185	199	233	99	93	120	131	148	149	134	163	163	184	206	271
Total Output	14076	13295	13499	13319	14781	16294	15130	15123	15022	11191	10490	11985	12925	13717	12446	12643	12995	13756	14482	15253	15517
Food Production	1439	1325	1311	1261	1364	1466	1326	1292	1251	909	830	925	974	1008	892	884	887	916	941	966	959
Per Capita (kg/cap)	100	92	91	88	95	102	92	90	87	63	58	64	68	70	62	61	62	64	65	67	67

Source: Ministry of Planning and Economic Development, Background to the Budget 1989-90; July 1989.
Ministry of Planning and Economic Development, Background to the Budget 1985-86; June 1985.

	1970	1971	1972	1973	1974	1975	1976	1977	1978	1979	1980	1981	1982	1983	1984	1985	1986	1987	1988	1989	1990
Food Production Per Capita (kg/cap)	100	92	91	88	95	102	92	90	87	63	58	64	68	70	62	61	62	64	65	67	67

Table 11

Table 12

UGANDA
YIELDS OF SELECTED FOOD CROPS
TONS/HECTARE

	1970	1971	1972	1973	1974	1975	1976	1977	1978	1979	1980	1981	1982	1983	1984	1985	1986	1987	1988	1989	1990
Plantain																					
Bananas	8.42	8.35	8.33	8.34	8.35	8.30	6.90	6.88	6.88	5.19	4.86	5.00	5.50	5.57	5.17	5.35	5.43	5.27	5.60	5.65	5.65
Cereals																					
Finger Millet	1.35	0.91	1.20	1.01	1.16	1.41	1.14	1.10	1.10	1.54	1.65	1.60	1.22	1.60	1.00	1.60	1.25	1.60	1.56	1.60	1.50
Maize	1.30	1.50	1.20	1.33	1.11	1.20	1.28	1.32	1.32	1.67	1.11	1.32	1.38	1.40	0.97	1.22	1.00	1.16	1.28	1.45	1.50
Sorghum	1.49	1.13	1.32	1.32	0.94	1.50	1.20	1.23	1.23	1.49	1.79	1.88	1.35	1.97	1.20	1.63	1.35	1.55	1.48	1.50	1.50
Rice									1.08	1.25	1.55	1.25	1.27	1.29	1.18	1.36	1.11	1.25	1.35	1.35	1.41
Wheat									2.00	1.67	2.13	2.00	2.00	2.40	1.75	1.60	1.60	2.00	2.17	2.20	2.00
TOTAL	1.37	1.09	1.23	1.17	1.08	1.35	1.21	1.20	1.21	1.61	1.49	1.56	1.31	1.62	1.04	1.47	1.18	1.43	1.44	1.52	1.50
Root Crops																					
Sweet Potatoes	3.54	2.88	2.41	3.08	3.53	3.55	3.55	3.55	3.55	4.97	5.19	3.71	4.00	4.03	4.21	4.64	4.58	4.21	4.12	4.09	4.30
Irish Potatoes									7.92	6.24	6.92	7.00	7.00	6.97	7.76	6.72	5.16	7.12	7.04	6.89	7.00
Cassava	4.78	4.76	7.14	4.41	4.83	4.84	5.54	5.54	3.83	6.52	6.86	9.79	9.45	8.71	7.40	9.00	8.01	8.99	9.06	9.10	9.00
TOTAL									3.85	5.85	6.17	6.58	6.58	6.16	5.88	6.63	6.17	6.45	6.43	6.57	6.54
Pulses																					
Beans	1.29	0.48	0.77	0.47	0.48	0.80	0.77	0.75	0.75	0.80	0.59	0.80	0.65	0.79	0.77	0.80	0.67	0.80	0.76	0.81	0.80
Field Peas 1/									0.41	0.32	0.41	0.44	0.50	0.38	0.81	0.47	0.56	0.50	0.52	0.50	0.50
Cow Peas 1/									0.39	0.51	0.42	0.44	0.44	0.80	0.80	0.80	0.78	0.88	0.83	0.81	0.81
Pigeon Peas 1/									0.40	0.33	0.52	0.45	0.47	0.47	0.35	0.47	0.45	0.45	0.66	0.68	0.70
TOTAL 1/									0.62	0.66	0.55	0.70	0.60	0.73	0.71	0.74	0.65	0.75	0.74	0.79	0.78
Oilseeds																					
Groundnuts	0.97	0.96	0.80	0.95	0.75	0.80	0.83	0.82	0.80	0.66	0.74	0.82	0.75	0.80	0.59	0.75	0.67	0.97	0.75	0.77	0.80
Soya Beans	1.00	1.00	1.00	1.00	0.72	0.58	0.96	1.00	1.00	0.75	0.75	1.00	1.00	1.17	0.73	0.80	0.83	0.80	0.82	0.89	1.00
Sim-sim									0.29	0.27	0.31	0.36	0.44	0.44	0.45	0.43	0.44	0.45	0.45	0.49	0.50
TOTAL									0.62	0.53	0.57	0.65	0.64	0.66	0.55	0.64	0.61	0.78	0.66	0.69	0.77

Source: Ministry of Planning and Economic Development, Background to the Budget 1989-90; July 1989.
Ministry of Planning and Economic Development, Background to the Budget 1985-86; June 1985.

Table 13

UGANDA
LIVESTOCK PRODUCTION

	1970	1971	1972	1973	1974	1975	1976	1977	1978	1979	1980	1981	1982	1983	1984	1985	1986	1987	1988	1989
Cattle 1/	4280.5	4223.9	4472.6	4628.7	4773.3	4867.9	4989.5	4911.1	5245.6	5242.2	4770.6	4745.4	4821.1	4871.3	4993.1	5000.0	5200.0	3905.2	4259.8	4183.7
Sheep	827.5	915.0	887.9	921.3	996.5	1051.0	1097.0	1138.9	1195.8	1255.6	1318.4	1384.3	1453.5	1035.5	1602.0	1674.0	1680.0	682.8	690.1	644.1
Goats	1801.4	2211.8	1953.0	2100.8	1872.8	2168.7	2299.7	2384.8	2609.1	2624.3	2543.6	2670.8	2804.3	1978.9	3091.0	3246.0	3300.0	2502.8	2110.0	2279.7
Pigs	63.5	87.5	88.2	74.6	71.5	93.1	122.0	161.2	169.2	177.7	186.6	195.9	205.7	232.8	227.0	238.0	250.0	470.4	452.3	552.9
Poultry 2/	..	..	..	..	..	..	..	..	407.4	154.0	377.0	176.2	324.4	1000.0	1200.0	3000.0	5000.0	8330.0	..	..

Source: Ministry of Planning and Economic Development, Background to the Budget 1990 – 1991, July 1990.
Ministry of Planning and Economic Development, Background to the Budget 1985-86; June 1985.
WB Report No. 7439-UG: Uganda Towards Stabilization and Economic Recovery; September 26, 1988
Upto 1977: Source: "Livestock Development and Marketing Study in Uganda", Winrock International, Morrilton Arkansas, May 1984, Page 19.

1/ Dairy and beef cattle.

2/ Total number of birds on commercial farms including chickens, geese, turkeys and ducks.

NOTE: ".." means not available

Doc: APRYLD08

UGANDA
FRESH MILK COLLECTION AND RECONSTITUTED MILK SALES
('000 liters)

	Fresh Milk Collection	Reconstituted Milk Sales
1972	19,526	
1973	16,389	
1974	6,174	
1975	5,087	
1976	4,263	
1977	2,479	
1978	764	
1979	451	
1980	123	8,625
1981	233	6,368
1982	494	16,432
1983	672	15,199
1984	2,455	19,142
1985 (Jan – Jun)	3,043	14,214
1986	198	12,949
1987	2,116	15,514
1988	2,836	6,005
1989 (estimated)	5,400	..

Source: Agricultural Policy Committee, "The Economics of Livestock
        Production in Uganda – Milk, Meat, Hides and Skins", May 1988.
        Government of Uganda, Livestock Services
        Project Preparation Report, July 1989.

NOTE: ".." means not available

Table 15

UGANDA

PRODUCTION OF ROUND-WOOD TIMBER, PROCESSED WOOD PRODUCTS, CHARCOAL AND OTHER FOREST PRODUCTS

('000)

		1977/78	1978/79	1979/80	1980/81	1981/82	1982/83	1983/84	1984/85	1985/86	1986/87	1987/88	1988/89
Round Wood Timber													
Logs	Cubic Meter	51.0	60.0	51.0	65.0	66.0	75.0	77.0	83.0	33.0	50.0	83.00	80.00
Poles and Fence Posts	Cubic Meter	10.0	11.0	15.0	20.0	17.0	22.0	22.0	30.0	40.0	43.0	70.0	71.000
Fuel Wood	Cubic Meter	70.0	77.0	104.0	150.0	130.0	170.0	190.0	250.0	300.0	340.0	410.0	530.00
Processed Wood Products													
Sawn Timber	Cubic Meter	21.0	21.0	19.0	23.0	23.0	25.0	26.0	28.0	10.0	25.0	30.0	29.00
Particle/Chip Board	Cubic Meter	..	0.0	0.0	0.1	-	-	-	-	-	-	-	-
Plywood and Block Board													
Board	Square Meter	140.0	150.0	130.0	145.0	80.0	398.0	400.0	500.0	180.0	450.0	600.0	680.00
Paper Boxes	Square Meter	720.0	750.0	700.0	800.0	180.0	190.0	-	-	-	250.0	350.0	410.00
Matches (small size)	Cartons 1/	9.0	9.0	9.0	10.0	12.0	2.5	-	-	-	-	-	-
Matches (large size)	Cartons 2/	-	-	-	-	1.6	1.7	-	6.0	7.0	8.0	15.0	15.00
Paper & Paper Products	Tons	1.0	0.9	1.0	1.2	0.2	1.5	1.6	2.0	2.0	3.0	7.0	7.00
Charcoal & Other Forest Products	Tons	27.0	27.0	28.0	30.0	35.0	37.0	38.0	40.0	45.0	57.0	70.0	73.00

Source: Ministry of Planning and Economic Development; Background to the Budget 1989–90; July 1989.
Ministry of Planning and Economic Development; Background to the Budget 1985–86; June 1985

1/ Cartons of 10 gross small–size match boxes each
2/ Cartons of 200 large–size match boxes each

Doc: APRYLD11

Table 16

UGANDA
FISH PRODUCTION AND VALUE BY LAKE REGION

	1978	1979	1980	1981	1982	1983	1984	1985	1986	1987	1988	1989	1990
PRODUCTION (THOUSAND TONS)													
Lake Victoria	14.2	12.0	10.0	17.0	13.0	17.0	44.8	45.6	56.5	80.0	107.1	132.4	119.9
Lake Albert	20.6	17.0	13.0	6.0	10.0	4.0	4.0	6.0	9.0	8.9	12.5	13.9	19.5
Albert Nile	5.7	4.5	3.2	3.0	1.0	4.0	1.9	1.6	0.3	2.5	1.0	1.9	1.4
Lake Kyoga	167.0	133.0	131.0	130.0	138.0	140.0	150.0	100.0	128.0	48.0	86.7	54.7	94.9
Lakes Edward, George & Kazinga Channel	11.8	9.6	7.0	5.0	6.9	6.0	10.4	6.6	6.3	6.5	5.9	5.6	5.5
Lake Wamala	1.8	2.0	1.0	3.8	0.5	0.7	0.5	0.3	0.4	0.5	0.4	1.0	-
Other Waters	1.1	1.8	0.7	3.0	0.6	0.6	0.7	0.7	0.4	3.3	1.0	4.0	4.0
TOTAL	222.2	179.9	165.9	167.8	170.0	172.3	212.3	160.8	200.9	149.7	214.6	213.5	245.2
VALUE (MILLION NEW UGANDA SHILLINGS)													
Lake Victoria	0.65	3.00	3.00	8.02	13.00	10.54	83.72	160.14	470.65	2400.00	6923.00	14297.00	21410.00
Lake Albert	2.31	4.25	3.90	1.93	4.22	1.92	2.67	20.10	45.00	144.00	786.00	1899.00	2110.00
Albert Nile	0.04	1.13	0.96	0.97	0.42	1.98	3.24	5.36	1.50	4.00	52.00	199.00	270.00
Lake Kyoga	7.50	33.25	39.30	34.30	83.21	112.00	117.00	81.27	294.40	1000.00	6017.00	6237.00	9490.00
Lakes Edward, George & Kazinga Channel	0.89	2.40	2.10	1.37	3.83	3.99	8.31	15.99	12.98	169.00	368.00	699.00	600.00
Lake Wamala	0.09	0.50	0.30	2.15	0.41	0.60	0.59	0.51	0.60	1.50	18.00	61.00	-
Other Waters	0.03	0.45	0.27	0.76	0.25	0.36	0.51	0.58	0.60	132.00	65.00	227.00	400.00
TOTAL	11.51	44.98	49.83	49.50	105.34	131.39	216.04	283.95	825.73	3850.50	14229.00	23619.00	34280.00

Source: Ministry of Planning and Economic Development ; Background to the Budget 1990 – 1991, July 1990.
Ministry of Planning and Economic Development; Background to the Budget 1985–86; June 1985.

Doc: APRYLD13

Table 17

UGANDA
SUMMARY OF AGRICULTURAL SECTOR SURVEY : 1986/87
('000)

District	No. of Households	AGRICULTURAL SYSTEM				NO. OF LIVESTOCK			
		Livestock	Crops	Mixed	Fishing	Cattle	Pigs	Sheep	Goats
CENTRAL:									
Kampala 1/	43.51	5.99	28.29	8.08	1.15	13.63	25.72	7.00	10.29
Luwero	74.26	2.31	59.57	10.24	2.14	88.75	19.51	4.79	15.38
Masaka	112.02	5.24	63.13	41.34	2.31	256.89	50.89	16.89	84.02
Mpigi	66.09	4.25	42.70	16.86	2.28	117.94	39.45	10.39	29.34
Mubende	124.61	3.82	90.12	30.45	0.22	267.50	66.57	24.28	52.91
Mukono	120.78	6.46	68.68	39.02	6.62	108.57	29.30	16.63	60.97
Rakai	71.05	3.43	57.26	9.04	1.32	163.65	26.17	16.97	70.59
TOTAL	612.32	31.50	409.75	155.03	16.04	1016.93	257.61	96.95	323.50
WESTERN									
Bundibugyo	11.27	0.86	8.19	1.06	1.16	52.54	0.96	6.10	16.52
Bushenyi	69.59	0.51	63.23	5.00	0.85	145.33	3.98	42.94	132.61
Hoima	61.09	0.12	58.41	1.31	1.25	32.02	13.01	16.60	79.72
Kabale	68.38	0.04	65.78	2.27	0.29	51.68	5.17	43.41	80.50
Kabarole	97.82	2.03	80.53	14.83	0.43	143.91	13.49	46.32	134.79
Kasese	38.79	1.38	32.91	2.52	1.98	43.21	34.65	22.03	116.05
Masindi	5.72	0.22	4.98	0.23	0.29	39.90	5.76	2.82	25.85
Rukungiri	33.56	0.51	28.60	4.03	0.42	55.41	3.43	30.55	79.75
TOTAL	386.22	5.67	342.63	31.25	6.67	564.00	80.45	210.77	665.79
NORTHERN									
Arua	25.02	0.04	11.97	12.02	0.99	94.96	17.68	35.06	171.25
Moyo	9.73	0.02	7.11	2.54	0.06	15.99	0.18	7.57	16.99
Nebbi	26.45	0.31	23.29	1.83	1.02	57.23	6.42	21.96	88.84
TOTAL	61.2	0.37	42.37	16.39	2.07	168.18	24.28	64.59	277.08
EASTERN									
Iganga	58.3	1.04	44.02	12.06	1.18	128.84	7.50	13.44	130.73
Jinja	15.94	0.44	10.95	4.50	0.05	14.59	4.69	1.99	24.91
Kamuli	42.34	2.59	24.94	13.57	1.24	122.87	12.69	6.85	70.22
Kapchorwa	10.39	0.11	4.42	5.86	0.00	30.20	1.76	9.48	22.61
Kumi	23.97	0.32	7.67	15.81	0.17	134.88	16.43	22.03	64.79
Mbale	52.23	2.69	26.13	23.36	0.05	68.99	19.69	22.74	97.68
Tororo	139.89	2.07	73.62	63.29	0.91	248.67	24.00	59.97	142.18
TOTAL	343.06	9.26	191.75	138.45	3.60	749.04	86.76	136.50	553.12
ESTIMATE OF GRAND TOTAL (including missing 7 districts)	1402.8	46.80	986.50	341.12	28.38	3905.20	470.40	682.80	2502.80

Source: **Ministry of Planning and Economic Development; Background to the Budget 1989-90; July 1989.**

1/ Includes Entebbe town.

Doc: APRYLD14

Table 18

UGANDA
SUMMARY OF AGRICULTURAL SECTOR SURVEY : 1986/87
('000)

District	No. of Households	AGRICULTURAL SYSTEM				NO. OF LIVESTOCK PER FARM			
		Livestock	Crops	Mixed	Fishing	Cattle	Pigs	Sheep	Goats
CENTRAL:									
Kampala 1/	43.51	14%	65%	19%	3%	0.3	0.6	0.2	0.2
Luwero	74.26	3%	80%	14%	3%	1.2	0.3	0.1	0.2
Masaka	112.02	5%	56%	37%	2%	2.3	0.5	0.2	0.8
Mpigi	66.09	6%	65%	26%	3%	1.8	0.6	0.2	0.4
Mubende	124.61	3%	72%	24%	0%	2.1	0.5	0.2	0.4
Mukono	120.78	5%	57%	32%	5%	0.9	0.2	0.1	0.5
Rakai	71.05	5%	81%	13%	2%	2.3	0.4	0.2	1.0
TOTAL	612.32	5%	67%	25%	3%	1.7	0.4	0.2	0.5
WESTERN									
Bundibugyo	11.27	8%	73%	9%	10%	4.7	0.1	0.5	1.5
Bushenyi	69.59	1%	91%	7%	1%	2.1	0.1	0.6	1.9
Hoima	61.09	0%	96%	2%	2%	0.5	0.2	0.3	1.3
Kabale	68.38	0%	96%	3%	0%	0.8	0.1	0.6	1.2
Kabarole	97.82	2%	82%	15%	0%	1.5	0.1	0.5	1.4
Kasese	38.79	4%	85%	6%	5%	1.1	0.9	0.6	3.0
Masindi	5.72	4%	87%	4%	5%	7.0	1.0	0.5	4.5
Rukungiri	33.56	2%	85%	12%	1%	1.7	0.1	0.9	2.4
TOTAL	386.22	1%	89%	8%	2%	1.5	0.2	0.5	1.7
NORTHERN									
Arua	25.02	0%	48%	48%	4%	3.8	0.7	1.4	6.8
Moyo	9.73	0%	73%	26%	1%	1.6	0.0	0.8	1.7
Nebbi	26.45	1%	88%	7%	4%	2.2	0.2	0.8	3.4
TOTAL	61.2	1%	69%	27%	3%	2.7	0.4	1.1	4.5
EASTERN									
Iganga	58.3	2%	76%	21%	2%	2.2	0.1	0.2	2.2
Jinja	15.94	3%	69%	28%	0%	0.9	0.3	0.1	1.6
Kamuli	42.34	6%	59%	32%	3%	2.9	0.3	0.2	1.7
Kapchorwa	10.39	1%	43%	56%	0%	2.9	0.2	0.9	2.2
Kumi	23.97	1%	32%	66%	1%	5.6	0.7	0.9	2.7
Mbale	52.23	5%	50%	45%	0%	1.3	0.4	0.4	1.9
Tororo	139.89	1%	53%	45%	1%	1.8	0.2	0.4	1.0
TOTAL	343.06	3%	56%	40%	1%	2.2	0.3	0.4	1.6
ESTIMATE OF GRAND TOTAL (including missing 7 districts)	1402.8	3%	70%	24%	2%	2.8	0.3	0.5	1.8

Source: Ministry of Planning and Economic Development; Background to the Budget 1989-90; July 1989.

1/ Includes Entebbe town.

Doc: APRYLD15

UGANDA
PROFITABILITY AND COMPETITIVENESS OF EXPORT CROPS – MAY 1991

Units: Shs/Kg

Table 19

Item	Cotton			Coffee (Arabica)			Coffee (Robusta)			Tea			Cocoa			Cashew Nut		
	Financial	Foreign	Local	Financial	Foreign	Local	Financial	Foreign	Local	Financial	Foreign	Local	Financial	Foreign	Local	Financial	Foreign	Local
OUTPUT																		
Av. Exp pce. US $/Kg	1.55	1.55	-	1.81	1.81	-	1.00	1.00	-	1.21	1.21	-	1.10	1.10	-	10.00	10.00	-
Value of Output Shs/Kg	1395.00	1395.00	-	1629.00	1629.00	-	900.00	900.00	-	1089.00	1089.00	-	990.00	990.00	-	9000.00	9000.00	-
OFF-FARM COSTS																		
Processing Costs	259.00	147.63	111.37	182.08	27.31	154.77	138.40	41.52	96.88	-	-	-	118.10	35.43	82.67	1009.70	403.88	605.82
Marketing Costs	277.57	166.54	111.03	168.76	101.26	67.50	175.76	105.46	70.30	462.39	309.80	152.59	88.32	57.41	30.91	828.00	703.80	124.20
Collection Costs	61.78	3.09	58.69	28.48	1.42	27.06	33.54	1.68	31.86	87.80	35.12	52.68	-	-	-	858.59	85.86	772.73
Sub-Total	598.35	317.26	281.09	379.32	129.99	249.33	347.70	148.65	199.05	550.19	344.92	205.27	206.42	92.84	113.58	2696.29	1193.54	1502.75
NET VALUE	796.65	1077.74		1249.68	1499.01		552.30	751.35		538.81	744.08		783.58	897.16		6303.71	7806.46	
ON-FARM COSTS																		
Seeds	-	-	-	-	-	-	-	-	-	-	-	-	-	-	-	-	-	-
Fertil/Chemicals	42.00	29.40	12.60	80.67	56.47	24.20	60.32	-	60.32	58.85	41.20	17.66	38.50	26.95	11.55	-	-	-
Hired Labour	202.50	-	202.50	88.28	-	88.53	71.66	-	71.66	113.85	-	113.85	111.38	-	111.38	-	-	-
Transport/Others	22.50	-	22.50	7.15	-	7.15	12.06	-	12.06	13.75	-	13.75	12.38	-	12.38	22.00	-	22.00
Family Labour	594.72	-	594.72	303.05	-	303.05	297.64	-	297.64	66.90	-	66.90	350.90	-	350.90	546.85	-	546.85
Fixed Costs (Eg.Depr,Annuity etc.)	64.72	32.36	32.36	74.28	37.14	37.14	62.43	31.22	31.22	49.31	24.66	24.66	74.84	37.42	37.42	143.67	71.84	71.84
Sub-Total	926.44	61.76	864.68	553.43	93.61	460.07	504.11	31.22	472.90	302.66	65.85	236.81	588.00	64.37	523.63	712.52	71.84	640.69
TOTAL COSTS	1524.79	379.02	1145.77	932.75	223.60	709.40	851.81	179.87	671.94	852.85	410.77	442.08	794.42	157.21	637.21	3408.81	1265.37	2143.44
NET OUTPUT VALUE	-129.79	1015.98		696.25	1405.40		48.19	720.13		236.15	678.23		195.58	832.79		5591.19	7734.63	
DRC Ratio		1.13			0.50			0.93			0.65			0.77			0.28	
DRC		1014.97			338.19			625.16			586.63			688.64			249.41	
IVA		1015.98			898.10			490.13			678.23			823.79			7734.63	

1. The market foreign exchange rate of Ug.Shs 900/= for one Us.Dollar has been used in working out the output value and DRC values, except in case of coffee.

2. The market exchange rate of Ug. 900/= to the dollar has been used for both Arabica and Robusta coffee. It is expected that the market rate of exchange will be applied to coffee exports as of January 1992.

3. Local costs have not been adjusted for distortions in the economy.

Doc: APRYLD16

Table 20

UGANDA
AVERAGE UNIT PRICE : CMB EXPORTS
(US$ per Kg)

	1982/83	1983/84	1984/85	1985/86	1986/87	1987/88	1988/89	1989/90
October	179.64	236.18	279.55	220.30	269.50	196.71		
November	196.40	246.36	271.83	225.20	277.98	194.87		
December	201.01	244.71	261.78	239.77	283.91	228.52		
QI	194.51	241.13	273.89	226.40	276.21	205.17		
January	220.30	239.31	261.54	267.90	265.19			
February	235.10	245.50	255.67	292.43	240.18			
March	238.38	266.01	240.61	330.27	237.36			
QII	231.58	254.10	251.25	297.52	247.26			
April	235.54	262.99	245.48	317.52	216.76			
May	236.33	266.76	247.60	319.16	195.21			
June	231.15	262.68	244.27	275.47	193.07			
QIII	234.11	264.22	245.62	301.23	202.15			
July	229.43	276.48	236.95	270.70	192.18			
August	238.63	257.96	221.16	250.23	191.73			
September	231.13	272.52	224.47	257.14	190.95			
QIV	233.77	269.06	228.59	261.69	191.55			
TOTAL	224.24	256.59	245.20	273.88	220.98			

Memorandum items:

	1983	1984	1985	1986	1987	1988	1989	1990
1st HY	232.70	259.96	247.99	300.06	222.27			
2nd HY	237.74	271.15	227.88	266.68	193.02			
TOTAL-	235.47	264.78	237.21	283.36	206.01			

	1982/83	1983/84	1984/85	1985/86	1986/87	1987/88	1988/89	1989/90
TOTAL-FY		248.61	258.40	261.01	244.99			

Source: Coffee Marketing Board, Uganda

Doc: COFFEE04

UGANDA
AVERAGE REAL PRODUCER PRICE OF COFFEE
(Average 1983/84 = 100; Deflated by mid-Income CPI)

Month	1983 Nominal Price	1983 Real Index	1984 Nominal Price	1984 Real Index	1985 Nominal Price	1985 Real Index	1986 Nominal Price	1986 Real Index	1987 Nominal Price	1987 Real Index	1988 Nominal Price	1988 Real Index	1989 Nominal Price	1989 Real Index
			Actual						Actual					
January	50.0	60.7	100.0	105.9	210.0	93.0	470.0	90.6	850.0	48.7	2400.0	49.6	6000.0	44.3
February	50.0	61.6	100.0	109.3	210.0	92.4	470.0	98.2	850.0	46.9	2900.0	57.6	6000.0	41.8
March	50.0	60.5	100.0	103.6	210.0	89.8	470.0	90.1	850.0	45.8	2900.0	57.4	6000.0	39.4
April	50.0	59.0	100.0	96.5	210.0	82.7	470.0	85.4	850.0	38.6	2900.0	45.2	6000.0	37.9
May	50.0	56.6	100.0	92.7	210.0	80.9	850.0	145.2	1625.0	59.6	2900.0	41.1	6000.0	36.4
June	80.0	89.4	130.0	125.4	270.0	101.1	850.0	125.7	2400.0	105.2	2900.0	37.3	6000.0	35.0
July	80.0	88.7	130.0	117.0	270.0	99.0	850.0	137.8	2400.0	97.5	6000.0	68.9	6000.0	33.9
August	80.0	89.7	130.0	113.0	270.0	88.9	850.0	118.0	2400.0	94.2	6000.0	63.8	6000.0	32.7
September	80.0	87.2	130.0	102.0	270.0	87.7	850.0	101.5	2400.0	75.8	6000.0	59.1	6000.0	31.6
October	80.0	85.8	130.0	83.0	270.0	82.8	850.0	87.8	2400.0	74.5	6000.0	54.7	6000.0	30.6
November	100.0	109.2	210.0	125.5	270.0	77.9	850.0	63.2	2400.0	64.5	6000.0	50.7	6000.0	29.6
December	100.0	106.1	210.0	110.8	470.0	120.6	850.0	50.9	2400.0	54.7	6000.0	46.9	6000.0	28.6
Average Calendar Year			130.8	107.1	261.7	91.4	723.3	99.5	1818.8	67.2	4408.3	52.7	6000.0	35.1

	1983/84	1984/85	1985/86	1986/87	1987/88	1988/89
Average Fiscal Year	100.0	99.3	99.3	75.3	62.4	48.2
Average Coffee Year	105.5	94.6	106.1	67.8	56.1	40.4
Average Real Price (CofYr)	100.0	89.6	100.6	64.3	53.2	38.3
Total Deliveries (CofYr)	100.0	111.7	103.3	115.6		
Total Exports (CofYr)	100.0	99.2	95.0	90.6		
Memorandum: 1/						
Coffee Deliveries to CMB	2312.4	2583.4	2388.1	2672.6		
Coffee Exports	2519.0	2500.0	2392.2	2283.3		

Source: Coffee Marketing Board, Uganda

1/ Data for coffee year and in bags per thousand.

Table 22

UGANDA
PRODUCERS' SHARE IN EXPORT PRICE
(New Uganda Shillings)

Month	1983 Ush/US$	1983 Sales Ush/Kg	1983 Producer Share(%)	1984 Ush/US$	1984 Sales Ush/Kg	1984 Producer Share(%)	1985 Ush/US$	1985 Sales Ush/Kg	1985 Producer Share(%)	1986 Ush/US$	1986 Sales Ush/Kg	1986 Producer Share(%)	1987 Ush/US$	1987 Sales Ush/kg	1987 Share(%)
January	1.07	2.36	21.2	2.41	5.78	17.3	5.39	12.55	16.7	14.61	39.13	12.0	14.00	37.13	22.9
February	1.12	2.63	19.0	2.53	6.22	16.1	5.28	13.51	15.5	14.70	42.99	10.9	14.00	33.63	25.3
March	1.17	2.78	18.0	2.74	7.29	13.7	5.79	13.93	15.1	14.70	48.55	9.7	14.00	33.23	25.6
April	1.20	2.82	17.7	2.92	7.68	13.0	5.93	14.56	14.4	14.70	46.68	10.1	14.00	30.35	28.0
May	1.28	3.03	16.5	2.92	7.80	12.8	6.00	14.87	14.1	14.60	46.60	18.2	37.00	72.23	22.5
June	1.39	3.21	24.9	3.08	8.08	16.1	6.00	14.66	18.4	14.00	38.57	22.0	60.00	115.84	20.7
July	1.55	3.56	22.5	3.38	9.35	13.9	6.00	14.22	19.0	14.00	37.90	22.4	60.00	115.31	20.8
August	1.66	3.97	20.1	3.74	9.65	13.5	6.00	13.27	20.3	14.00	35.03	24.3	60.00	115.04	20.9
September	1.76	4.07	19.6	4.00	10.90	11.9	6.00	13.47	20.0	14.00	36.00	23.6	60.00	114.57	20.9
October	1.86	4.38	18.3	4.46	12.46	10.4	6.80	14.98	18.0	14.00	37.73	22.5	60.00	118.03	20.3
November	2.07	5.09	19.6	5.46	14.85	14.1	8.70	19.59	13.8	14.00	38.92	21.8	60.00	116.92	20.5
December	2.34	5.72	17.5	5.52	14.44	14.5	12.75	30.57	15.4	14.00	39.75	21.4	60.00	137.11	17.5
Average Calendar Year			19.6			14.0			16.7			18.3			22.2
Average Fiscal Year						17.2			14.4			15.8			23.4

Source: Coffee Marketing Board, Uganda

Table 23

UGANDA
TRENDS IN PRODUCERS' SHARE IN EXPORT RECEIPTS, IN REAL PRODUCER PRICES AND IN WORLD MARKET PRICES
(Indices: 1983/84 = 100)

Month	1983			1984			1985			1986			1987			1988			1989		
	Domestic Producer Share	Real Price	World Price (US$)	Producer Share	Real Price	World Price (US$)	Producer Share	Real Price	World Price (US$)	Producer Share	Real Price	World Price (US$)	Producer Share	Real Price	World Price (US$)	Producer Share	Real Price	World Price (US$)	Producer Share	Real Price	World Price (US$)
January	123	61	89	101	106	97	97	93	106	70	91	108	133	49	107		50				44
February	110	62	95	93	109	99	90	92	103	63	98	118	147	47	97		58				42
March	104	61	96	80	104	107	88	90	97	56	90	133	149	46	96		57				39
April	103	59	95	76	97	106	84	83	99	58	85	128	163	39	88		45				38
May	96	57	95	74	93	108	82	81	100	106	145	129	131	60	79		41				36
June	145	89	93	93	125	106	107	101	99	128	126	111	120	105	78		37				35
July	131	89	93	81	117	112	110	99	96	130	138	109	121	97	78		69				34
August	117	90	96	78	113	104	118	89	89	141	118	101	121	94	77		64				33
September	114	87	93	69	102	110	116	88	91	137	101	104	122	76	77		59				32
October	106	86	95	61	83	113	105	83	89	131	88	109	118	75	79		55				31
November	114	109	100	82	125	110	80	78	91	127	63	112	119	65	79		51				30
December	101	106	99	84	111	106	89	121	97	124	51	115	102	55	92		47				29
Average Calendar Year	114	80	95	81	107	107	97	91	96	106	100	115	129	67	86		53				35
Average Fiscal Year					100	100		99	105		92	107	136	75	100		62				

Source: Coffee Marketing Board, Uganda

Notes:

1. Producer's real price: Based on minimum price set by CMB for unprocessed cherries (Kiboko), thus excluding primary societies' and union's (or private processor's) margins, and excluding domestic transport costs. Deflated by the mid-income Kampala CPI.

2. Producer's share: Based on average export price (FOB Mombasa) at the official exchange rate and on the minimum producer's price.

3. Export price: Average monthly price in US$ for actual exports of CMB, derived from revenue and quantity data in export bills.

Table 24

UGANDA

PRODUCERS' SHARE IN EXPORT PRICE (ADJUSTED FOR CONVERSION TO CLEAN COFFEE)

(New Uganda Shillings)

Month	1983			1984			1985			1986			1987		
	Ush/US$	Sales Ush/Kg	Producer Share(%)	Ush/US$	Sales Ush/Kg	Producer Share(%)	Ush/US$	Sales Ush/Kg	Producer Share(%)	Ush/US$	Sales Ush/Kg	Producer Share(%)	Ush/US$	Sales Ush/Kg	Producer Share(%)
January	1.07	2.36	39.3	2.41	5.78	32.0	5.39	12.55	30.9	14.61	39.13	22.2	14.00	37.13	42.4
February	1.12	2.63	35.2	2.53	6.22	29.8	5.28	13.51	28.7	14.70	42.99	20.2	14.00	33.63	46.9
March	1.17	2.78	33.3	2.74	7.29	25.4	5.79	13.93	28.0	14.70	48.55	18.0	14.00	33.23	47.4
April	1.20	2.82	32.8	2.92	7.68	24.1	5.93	14.56	26.7	14.70	46.68	18.7	14.00	30.35	51.9
May	1.28	3.03	30.6	2.92	7.80	23.7	6.00	14.87	26.1	14.60	46.60	33.7	37.00	72.23	41.7
June	1.39	3.21	46.1	3.08	8.08	29.8	6.00	14.66	34.1	14.00	38.57	40.7	60.00	115.84	38.3
July	1.55	3.56	41.7	3.38	9.35	25.7	6.00	14.22	35.2	14.00	37.90	41.5	60.00	115.31	38.5
August	1.66	3.97	37.2	3.74	9.65	25.0	6.00	13.27	37.6	14.00	35.03	45.0	60.00	115.04	38.7
September	1.76	4.07	36.3	4.00	10.90	22.0	6.00	13.47	37.0	14.00	36.00	43.7	60.00	114.57	38.7
October	1.86	4.38	33.9	4.46	12.46	19.3	6.80	14.98	33.3	14.00	37.73	41.7	60.00	118.03	37.6
November	2.07	5.09	36.3	5.46	14.85	26.1	8.70	19.59	25.6	14.00	38.92	40.4	60.00	116.92	38.0
December	2.34	5.72	32.4	5.52	14.44	26.9	12.75	30.57	28.5	14.00	39.75	39.6	60.00	137.11	32.4
Average Calendar Year			36.3			25.9			30.9			33.9			41.1
Average Fiscal Year						31.9			26.7			29.3			43.3

Source: Coffee Marketing Board, Uganda

Out-turns: 1 Kg. of coffee (robusta kiboko) = 0.54 Kg. of clean robusta coffee.

UGANDA

PRODUCTION AND EXPORTS OF COFFEE FROM 1964-65

	Robusta Deliveries MT	Arabica Deliveries MT	Total Deliveries MT	Robusta Prod'n MT	Arabica Prod'n MT	Total Prod'n MT	Robusta Exports MT	Arabica Exports MT	Total Exports MT	Robusta Exports '000 Bags	Arabica Exports '000 Bags	Total Exports '000 Bags
1964 / 1965	135978	4588	140566									
1965 / 1966	122774	5642	128416				122760	5640	128400	2046	94	2140
1966 / 1967	124888	8945	133833				124860	8940	133800	2081	149	2230
1967 / 1968	92888	13155	106043	121000	15000	136000	92880	13140	106020	1548	219	1767
1968 / 1969	183429	14884	198313	225000	25000	250000	183420	14880	198300	3057	248	3305
1969 / 1970	179826	14132	193958	182000	15000	197000	179820	14100	193920	2997	235	3232
1970 / 1971	159260	16222	175482	147000	13000	160000	159240	16200	175440	2654	270	2924
1971 / 1972	162886	20825	183711	150000	23000	173000	162900	20820	183720	2715	347	3062
1972 / 1973	195532	18142	213674	236000	24000	260000	195540	18120	213660	3259	302	3561
1973 / 1974	180504	18069	198573	182000	14000	196000	180480	18060	198540	3008	301	3309
1974 / 1975	182000	17000	199000	185000	15000	200000	181980	16980	198960	3033	283	3316
1975 / 1976	123108	13956	137064	131000	9000	140000	123120	13980	137100	2052	233	2285
1976 / 1977	151620	4310	155930	148000	12000	160000	151620	4320	155940	2527	72	2599
1977 / 1978	117591	3644	121235	108000	9000	117000	118080	3660	121740	1968	61	2029
1978 / 1979	100005	3040	103045	103000	9000	112000	100020	3060	103080	1667	51	1718
1979 / 1980	130391	4804	135195	112000	10000	122000	130380	4800	135180	2173	80	2253
1980 / 1981	93027	4519	97546	112000	10000	122000	93000	4500	97500	1550	75	1625
1981 / 1982	152210	14269	166479	175000	12000	187000	152220	14280	166500	2537	238	2775
1982 / 1983	142705	14716	157421	175000	13000	188000	142680	14700	157380	2378	245	2623
1983 / 1984	126210	12530	138740	178000	14000	192000	126180	12540	138720	2103	209	2312
1984 / 1985	142210	10800	153010	189000	15000	204000	142140	10800	152940	2369	180	2549
1985 / 1986	133343	9945	143288	184000	14000	198000	133320	9960	143280	2222	166	2388
1986 / 1987	149037	11963	161000	196000	15000	211000	148920	11940	160860	2482	199	2681
1987 / 1988	145806	10314	156120			0	143460	10140	153600	2391	169	2560
1988 / 1989	162512	11496	174008	238118	23628	261746	176460	10380	186840	2941	173	3114
1989 / 1990	120867	8550	129417				132431	9469	142397	2207	158	2365
1990 / 1991	126466	13799	140265				114240	9660	123900	1904	161	2065
1991 / 1992												

Table 26

UGANDA
EVOLUTION OF THE PRICE OF ROBUSTA, AT FARM LEVEL, AND EXPORTS

Year	Kiboko Min 1/ Price Ush/Kg	Clean Min 2/ Price Ush/Kg	Exchange Rate Official Ush/US$	Exchange Rate Market Ush/US$	Average Export Price US$/Kg	Robusta Adjusted Export 4/ Price US$/Kg	Robusta Farmgate Price US$/kg (Official)	Share in Official Export Price	Robusta Farmgate Price US$/kg (Market)	Share in Market Export Price	Export Price
1981	0.19	0.36	0.50	0.50	1.90	1.61	0.72	45%	0.72	45%	100%
1982	0.43	0.79	0.94	2.58	2.00	1.69	0.84	49%	0.30	18%	100%
1983	0.68	1.27	1.54	4.07	2.40	2.03	0.82	40%	0.31	15%	100%
1984	1.28	2.38	3.60	6.05	2.70	2.29	0.66	29%	0.39	17%	100%
1985	2.57	4.75	6.74	18.37	2.30	1.95	0.70	36%	0.26	13%	100%
1986	6.92	12.81	14.27	65.33	2.80	2.37	0.90	38%	0.20	8%	100%
1987	17.54	32.48	40.83	174.00	2.07	1.76	0.80	45%	0.19	11%	100%
1988	44.50	82.41	106.25	423.00	1.84	1.56	0.78	50%	0.19	12%	100%
1989	60.00	111.11	234.17	570.54	1.49	1.26	0.47	38%	0.19	15%	100%
1990	75.00	138.89	431.92	718.08	0.99	0.84	0.32	38%	0.19	23%	100%
1991	165.00	305.56	620.00	810.13	1.04	0.88	0.49	56%	0.38	43%	100%

1/ per Kg Kiboko
2/ per Kg Clean Coffee
3/ Outturn Kiboko to Clean Coffee   0.54
4/ 9 percent of exports is Arabica. Arabica receives 180% of Robusta price.
      Factor   1.18   port price to robusta price

UGANDA
KAMPALA COST OF LIVING INDEX, LOW INCOME GROUP
(August 1981 = 100)

	Food	Drink & Tobacco	Fuel & Lighting	Household Goods	Clothing	Weighted Avg. Index	Annual % Change
Weights	70.0	11.0	8.0	2.0	9.0	100.0	
1981 August	100.0	100.0	100.0	100.0	100.0	100.0	
September	102.4	80.0	95.7	99.0	122.8	101.2	
October	97.3	88.8	86.0	99.0	134.4	98.8	
November	92.6	89.2	77.8	86.5	102.2	91.6	
December	88.5	89.7	77.1	86.5	96.4	88.1	
1982 January	87.8	90.4	63.3	115.4	123.6	90.4	
March	100.6	90.4	106.1	114.0	120.0	102.1	
May	108.7	72.4	94.3	118.9	140.0	106.6	
July	113.9	73.3	110.6	124.9	122.5	109.9	
September	134.5	73.7	102.2	129.5	113.9	122.4	21.0
November	156.3	78.7	84.5	132.3	117.5	138.3	51.0
December	152.6	75.8	113.0	126.6	127.6	136.8	55.3
1983 January	143.6	77.3	116.5	119.7	124.5	130.7	44.6
February	136.1	93.4	113.2	115.0	126.5	127.4	24.8
March	138.6	94.9	120.5	115.0	126.5	129.8	27.1
April	158.0	97.9	119.4	116.3	128.4	143.3	34.5
May	163.2	100.9	124.4	122.0	136.0	148.4	39.2
June	160.0	92.3	129.0	122.0	136.0	145.6	32.5
July	165.6	96.9	126.2	124.7	161.4	152.2	38.5
August	173.0	98.0	118.6	128.7	161.4	156.7	28.0
September	187.7	99.5	123.6	130.4	161.3	167.1	36.5
October	203.7	100.6	117.7	128.0	161.3	177.4	28.3
November	196.0	98.6	118.5	130.1	155.8	171.7	24.2
December	189.9	100.9	132.6	140.1	164.7	170.2	24.4
1984 January	197.0	100.9	139.3	141.2	161.7	175.3	34.1
February	178.6	105.3	148.3	144.2	169.8	165.0	29.5
March	189.5	106.8	150.0	152.1	176.0	173.6	33.7
April	206.9	115.9	154.7	149.2	176.0	186.6	30.2
May	203.9	117.1	164.7	149.3	178.5	185.8	25.2
June	197.9	118.3	160.6	151.3	177.5	181.5	24.7
July	206.5	128.6	190.6	172.0	229.1	196.6	29.2
August	221.5	122.5	186.5	178.7	207.7	203.8	30.1
September	250.8	118.7	187.6	179.1	230.8	225.1	34.7
October	298.6	142.3	210.2	203.6	240.6	250.2	41.0
November	313.9	174.7	183.6	202.8	234.8	274.8	60.0
December	393.1	211.8	239.0	266.0	242.5	339.7	99.6
1985 January	431.7	248.1	365.0	315.9	375.4	394.6	125.1
February	432.7	224.3	415.7	339.4	381.8	397.8	141.1
March	462.3	250.9	367.1	354.4	396.2	418.8	141.2
April	571.5	268.6	394.7	402.4	405.5	498.6	167.2
May	568.9	275.5	350.6	436.8	481.6	502.3	170.3
June	579.2	270.1	352.8	478.8	490.4	511.0	181.5
July	566.0	289.1	390.4	482.3	485.2	507.3	158.0
August	636.0	349.6	546.2	482.3	485.2	574.4	181.8
September	669.1	379.0	489.1	570.0	507.0	600.3	166.7
October	885.6	369.9	503.4	581.3	524.5	746.7	198.4
November	937.8	403.8	491.1	579.5	541.7	786.1	186.1
December	1113.8	465.9	594.7	729.9	622.3	932.5	174.5

- 182 -

UGANDA
KAMPALA COST OF LIVING INDEX, LOW INCOME GROUP
(August 1981 = 100)

Table 27
Page 2 of 2

	Food	Drink & Tobacco	Fuel & Lighting	Household Goods	Clothing	Weighted Avg. Index	Annual % Change
Weights	70.0	11.0	8.0	2.0	9.0	100.0	
1986 January	-	-	-	-	-	-	-
February	1014.8	489.1	639.8	930.4	1136.6	936.2	132.9
March	1024.8	670.6	736.3	925.5	1241.4	980.3	131.6
April	1238.2	617.9	733.3	1216.3	1263.0	1131.4	123.7
May	1362.4	653.5	891.6	1365.7	1338.4	1244.7	144.7
June	1500.9	705.7	875.0	1324.9	1384.2	1349.3	160.9
July	1307.7	758.1	962.8	1537.5	1508.9	1242.4	142.4
August	1361.4	940.8	1058.0	1699.0	1872.6	1343.6	131.4
September	1590.1	1113.5	1165.6	1899.6	2092.9	1555.2	156.5
October	1779.7	1217.8	1155.9	2216.9	2624.9	1752.8	130.7
November	2249.3	1474.8	1159.9	2353.2	2557.9	2106.8	163.2
December	2446.2	1670.9	1357.7	2525.0	2903.7	2316.6	144.1
1987 January	3065.8	1868.5	2257.8	2932.1	3195.9	2878.5	-
February	3580.2	1894.8	2590.2	3274.0	4701.2	3410.4	264.3
March	3680.0	2074.0	2681.5	3377.6	4886.7	3526.0	259.7
April	4328.5	2168.2	3621.8	3459.9	4979.1	4075.5	260.2
May	4822.4	2344.4	4111.8	3459.9	4979.1	4479.8	259.9
June	4042.1	1959.6	3674.6	4138.6	5640.8	3929.4	191.2
July	3917.8	2594.2	2468.1	4480.5	5569.8	3816.2	207.2
August	4014.0	2384.4	2434.3	6059.5	5782.3	3908.4	190.9
September	4485.8	3407.8	2159.8	6955.1	7948.9	4542.2	192.1
October	5278.3	3377.1	2367.5	7187.4	7723.3	5096.5	190.8
November	5970.1	4706.6	3517.9	6681.1	8038.3	5835.3	177.0
December	6608.5	4056.0	4705.6	7535.0	9118.7	6419.9	177.1
1988 January	7058.7	7106.3	4978.9	9169.0	12527.7	7432.0	158.2
February	8147.2	5968.2	9658.7	9717.7	11572.4	8368.1	145.4
March	8651.8	6653.5	11839.4	11512.9	13149.3	9149.0	159.5
April	9939.2	5968.2	11674.6	12237.1	13939.8	9230.0	126.5
May	10858.3	5970.7	12562.8	12742.4	15534.8	10915.6	143.7
June	11373.7	6083.7	13451.1	11944.0	15843.5	11371.7	189.4
July	14883.9	7729.5	14924.8	14223.3	20472.9	14590.0	282.3
August	17139.9	9247.3	17280.7	15183.8	22366.9	16714.3	327.6
September	16976.6	8295.6	14200.2	14175.8	16289.4	15681.7	245.2
October	16688.6	8054.4	14200.2	13794.4	15892.3	15410.2	202.4
November	18387.5	8225.7	13556.7	14494.8	15629.6	16557.2	183.7
December	18196.0	8256.1	13672.2	15123.4	19308.7	16779.4	161.4
1989 January	19001.5	9813.2	11328.0	14165.7	19382.1	17314.5	133.0
February	19653.0	9806.7	13620.5	15234.8	20927.0	18113.6	116.5
March	20484.4	10808.6	15461.9	16232.2	22036.0	19072.9	108.5
April	24076.5	11266.4	12747.2	13737.8	26346.2	21758.5	135.7
May	25158.0	10291.6	12980.8	17006.9	25885.8	22520.3	106.3
June	25724.3	11097.7	20244.0	18635.6	25733.2	23536.0	107.0
July	28090.1	12749.5	18762.5	17522.5	27613.5	25033.6	72.4
August	27826.8	13860.1	18690.5	18219.9	27707.0	25019.6	50.6
September	30632.8	13869.0	16010.2	18548.7	29296.4	26824.9	72.7
October	35612.2	14931.1	16060.8	18493.9	30281.6	30366.0	99.0
November	35169.0	17740.8	19022.2	18698.7	30281.6	30666.4	87.5
December	36287.7	17607.2	19677.8	19063.3	27985.0	31250.2	88.2
1990 January	34878.2	17535.0	22121.9	21901.8	38139.0	31553.8	84.4
February	33003.5	19339.6	24375.0	21406.2	38139.0	30694.2	71.3
March	33277.2	21696.1	21018.3	21023.8	37952.1	30847.6	63.3
April	33115.4	19079.4	19728.7	20566.0	37952.1	30299.1	40.8
May	31685.5	19079.4	19855.9	20894.2	37952.1	29368.4	32.3
June	29718.3	19079.4	23803.4	20877.4	37706.7	28366.0	22.2
July	27499.1	20304.8	22876.8	21590.9	38924.2	27095.5	8.2
August	29793.2	19950.4	22275.2	21030.8	35459.4	28140.3	12.5
September	32487.3	19844.0	24573.9	20909.9	36873.2	30292.3	12.9

Source: Ministry of Planning and Economic Development, Background to the Budget 1990 – 1991, July 1990.

Table 28
Page 1 of 2

UGANDA
KAMPALA COST OF LIVING INDEX, MIDDLE-INCOME GROUP
(April 1981 = 100)

	Food	Drink & and Tobacco	Fuel and Lighting	Trans-port	Clothing	Other Consumer Goods	Other Manuf. Goods	Weighted Average Index	Annual % Change
Weights	41.0	17.0	6.0	10.0	14.0	10.0	2.0	100.0	
1981 April	100.0	100.0	100.0	100.0	100.0	100.0	100.0	100.0	
May	..	..	..	..	..	..	..	..	
June	136.8	131.8	152.4	103.2	343.6	136.7	235.8	164.4	
July	127.4	113.2	124.7	244.5	334.7	130.4	235.3	168.0	
August	126.5	114.0	124.7	244.5	328.8	118.0	205.2	165.1	
September	125.1	109.8	124.7	244.5	324.7	115.6	210.2	163.1	
October	121.8	106.1	123.6	245.2	328.6	125.3	203.5	162.5	
November	123.7	110.9	121.5	245.2	330.2	122.0	201.5	163.8	
December	124.2	104.9	120.1	245.2	330.5	124.8	200.3	163.2	
1982 January	118.2	112.7	139.6	341.2	341.3	124.6	207.3	174.5	
February	127.5	115.9	139.6	341.2	349	129.7	242	181.1	
March	146.9	113.9	145.3	341.2	348.6	136.6	245.1	189.8	
April	167.7	120.9	144.6		351.3	141.8	235.3	200.2	100.2
May	158.7	118.7	146.0	341.2	342.3	145.3	194.2	194.5	
June	169.0	112.1	162.2	354.6	343.7	143.9	205.3	200.2	21.8
July	171.2	119.1	190.8	306.6	349.5	147.7	178.7	199.8	18.9
August	181.4	120	189.4	306.6	350.7	160.1	190.4	205.7	24.6
September	186.1	119.6	194.6	306.6	347.2	147.0	230.3	206.9	26.9
October	195.9	125	236.8	306.6	347.7	146.1	231.4	214.4	31.9
November	205.8	117.8	267.7	315.6	349.1	152.4	233.3	220.8	34.8
December	199.3	123.3	267.7	320.1	354.7	150.2	232.9	220.1	34.9
1983 January	207.8	125.3	267.7	433.4	331.8	151.0	214.8	231.7	32.8
February	199.2	126.6	269.1	433.4	326.8	149.3	252.4	228.4	26.1
March	209.5	125.8	268.4	433.4	325.9	146.1	266.8	232.3	22.4
April	226.3	122.5	271.3	433.4	329.8	145.7	233.6	238.6	19.2
May	246.2	128.5	285.9	433.4	333.0	146.6	247.2	249.5	28.3
June	246.5	137.0	308.5	436.6	334.4	149.0	244.0	253.1	26.4
July	241.9	145.5	304.9	442.3	335.6	146.8	262.4	253.4	26.8
August	239.1	136.3	307.8	449.0	334.6	143.2	268.2	251.1	22.1
September	264.4	127.0	307.1	449.0	332.7	143.5	241.7	259.1	25.2
October	275.7	123.3	307.1	449.0	331.4	138.3	236.2	262.3	22.3
November	261.6	124.9	358.3	449.0	334.4	142.9	240.3	260.8	18.1
December	259.4	124.5	385.0	506.0	331.1	143.5	240.0	266.7	21.2
1984 January	253.6	125.5	385.7	506.0	334.9	151.2	235.4	265.8	14.7
February	228.3	131.3	387.8	506.0	343.8	149.2	226.6	257.4	12.7
March	260.5	131.2	444.5	506.0	345.5	154.1	233.2	274.8	18.3
April	296.2	144.6	452.4	506.0	341.5	156.1	235.6	291.9	22.3
May	281.5	171.7	452.4	619.3	346.5	168.4	221.6	303.5	21.6
June	259.7	154.7	491.6	619.3	349.5	163.2	232.0	294.1	16.2
July	293.6	163.7	494.5	632.9	360.4	166.6	218.5	312.7	23.4
August	315.2	162.0	495.9	632.9	372.0	173.8	216.9	323.6	28.9
September	351.0	162.7	1508.6	632.9	513.6	177.5	217.6	419.4	61.9
October	373.2	195.9	1504.3	672.9	515.0	195.9	241.7	440.4	67.9
November	421.6	226.9	1583.0	672.9	524.0	236.0	244.8	475.6	82.4
December	522.6	270.3	1669.7	688.7	546.3	275.5	253.4	538.4	101.9
1985 January	611.3	349.2	1682.5	992.5	600.7	341.7	366.3	635.8	139.2
February	629.8	399.8	1674.7	992.5	607.7	366.0	418.1	656.0	154.9
March	653.3	310.2	1681.8	992.5	636.9	392.1	443.1	658.0	139.4
April	773.2	358.4	1669.7	992.5	628.4	396.9	433.8	713.7	144.5
May	795.4	375.7	1774.7	992.5	645.5	409.6	475.6	736.5	142.7
June	814.4	417.8	1779.4	1019.5	634.5	398.8	456.7	751.5	155.5
July	813.4	461.4	1793.7	1019.5	663.0	413.6	526.2	766.2	145.0
August	978.2	521.4	1781.6	1019.5	674.4	492.7	520.0	852.6	163.5
September	1005.9	516.7	1790.8	1019.5	665.6	510.8	617.0	866.3	106.6
October	1100.4	380.5	1084.5	1019.5	668.0	563.8	1232.8	857.4	94.7
November	1104.2	483.6	1084.5	1019.5	1084.5	564.4	1110.5	932.4	96.0
December	1254.4	500.6	1135.5	1154.7	1135.5	636.6	1110.5	1027.8	90.9

UGANDA
KAMPALA COST OF LIVING INDEX, MIDDLE-INCOME GROUP
(April 1981 = 100)

	Food	Drink & and Tobacco	Fuel and Lighting	Trans- port	Clothing	Other Consumer Goods	Other Manuf. Goods	Weighted Average Index	Annual % Change
Weights	41.0	17.0	6.0	10.0	14.0	10.0	2.0	100.0	
1986 January	1586.3	958.4	2229.4	1834.7	1343.4	1047.6	1829.2	1460.0	129.6
February	1426.0	720.5	2229.4	1834.7	1343.4	974.2	1829.2	1346.5	105.3
March	1494.4	929.3	2242.9	1834.7	1608.4	1112.2	2127.0	1467.7	123.1
April	1655.8	850.4	2236.5	1834.7	1618.5	1284.9	2606.7	1548.3	116.9
May	1826.9	813.6	2260.1	1834.7	1777.2	1394.9	2597.7	1646.7	123.6
June	2198.8	1263.3	2256.5	1834.7	1905.3	1457.6	2727.8	1902.2	153.1
July	1804.8	1101.3	2275.1	1834.7	1918.5	1640.8	2738.1	1734.6	126.4
August	1845.4	1596.7	2706.3	2957.0	1997.1	2008.1	2969.5	2025.9	137.6
September	2231.2	1648.1	4525.5	2957.0	2181.5	2037.5	4225.0	2355.9	171.9
October	2671.4	1734.5	4522.7	2957.0	3235.8	2069.3	5258.3	2722.3	217.5
November	2841.5	1693.6	4559.8	2957.0	9945.6	1965.3	5095.8	3713.0	298.2
December	4655.1	2285.3	4735.5	3917.0	10031.6	2193.9	4704.5	4690.8	356.4
1987 January	4511.9	2508.1	4615.5	3917.0	10665.6	3451.2	5693.4	4897.1	235.4
February	4841.3	2273.8	4745.2	4020.3	10867.3	3602.8	7837.5	5096.7	278.5
March	4890.1	2780.8	4846.1	4020.3	10604.6	4330.3	6450.0	5217.1	255.5
April	5937.0	3005.8	4777.7	4020.3	13804.3	4645.6	7800.0	6187.0	299.6
May	6793.7	4404.2	6703.4	4728.3	18112.4	5810.9	6583.4	7657.7	365.0
June	5111.5	2891.7	6594.9	4728.3	17742.0	3666.1	5166.7	6409.6	237.0
July	6035.2	3650.0	6580.6	4728.3	17623.5	3844.5	5166.7	6917.6	298.8
August	6123.9	3575.0	6313.9	4700.0	17623.5	4335.5	4700.0	6962.2	243.7
September	7492.9	4358.3	23456.8	4821.6	18985.7	4554.5	4666.7	8909.4	278.2
October	7700.0	4600.0	23465.3	4821.6	18729.9	4787.9	6500.0	9060.1	232.8
November	10286.6	4600.0	23741.8	4821.6	19355.9	7185.6	6500.0	10464.6	181.8
December	12117.7	7100.0	23772.5	4821.6	23467.0	8039.4	7000.0	12313.1	162.5
1988 January	11948.2	8350.0	24453.7	6821.6	28251.6	9614.2	11000.0	13604.3	177.8
February	13451.1	6100.0	25695.1	6821.6	28981.0	10692.9	11666.7	14135.8	177.4
March	14000.4	6733.3	24782.2	6821.6	26783.7	12347.4	9000.0	14218.4	172.5
April	14654.3	5775.0	24782.2	6821.6	35661.2	12063.3	9500.0	15548.0	151.3
May	17863.7	5925.0	26457.9	6821.6	43750.4	12063.3	9500.0	18122.4	136.7
June	21637.6	8191.7	26457.9	6821.6	54516.3	13097.4	13666.7	21749.0	239.3
July	23811.3	10775.0	29065.3	21821.6	65760.2	15012.4	19000.0	26608.1	284.6
August	23728.9	10333.3	29065.3	21821.6	63777.8	12660.2	19000.0	25986.5	273.3
September	24127.6	9820.8	29065.3	21821.6	62848.8	12882.3	17833.3	25931.7	191.1
October	24581.0	9579.2	29065.3	21821.6	60988.9	13010.8	14500.0	25762.3	184.4
November	25666.1	9291.7	29065.3	21821.6	62327.9	12582.3	14500.0	26302.9	151.4
December	25735.9	9366.7	33914.3	21821.6	64892.6	12582.3	15000.0	27004.2	119.3
1989 January	25754.5	10480.0	33914.3	21821.6	68397.4	13261.0	15000.0	27759.7	104.1
February	27891.7	10363.3	34677.2	21821.6	75481.9	13889.6	15500.0	29726.6	110.0
March	28494.4	13370.8	118206.1	15821.6	78680.6	15096.4	15500.0	35465.2	149.4
April	32383.2	13383.3	119477.5	15821.6	80927.1	14889.4	18500.0	37431.8	140.8
May	34007.9	14744.2	121419.2	15821.6	82576.2	14731.2	19000.0	38730.0	110.7
June	34413.8	14196.7	132953.0	15821.6	89298.7	14911.7	21583.3	40511.6	86.2
July	39340.3	15950.0	136535.3	15821.6	87613.3	16017.0	23000.0	42942.3	61.4
August	41138.1	15472.5	139329.1	15821.6	85588.9	14816.2	21000.0	43328.8	66.7
September	46623.5	15575.0	141543.3	15821.6	83561.8	15128.1	22500.0	47401.7	75.5
October	50091.6	17223.4	149598.9	15821.6	79169.2	15618.1	22500.0	48349.7	82.9
November	49050.7	19191.7	144201.3	19821.6	86236.1	16163.9	25000.0	49461.7	83.3
December	51392.6	19058.3	146020.1	19821.6	83436.6	1618.6	25000.0	50154.2	81.1
1990 January	49654.8	19825.0	145384.2	19821.6	85401.4	18160.7	25000.0	48706.2	75.5
February	47803.8	20225.0	161431.8	19821.6	87085.4	19049.8	19000.0	49182.8	65.5
March	45328.3	20550.0	176206.6	19821.6	94807.6	20459.4	16333.3	50278.3	41.8
April	45753.1	19350.0	193414.7	19821.6	93465.0	20698.6	16333.3	51117.0	36.6
May	43690.5	18820.0	210875.4	19821.6	91381.8	19975.8	15666.7	50851.6	31.3
June	40467.5	18695.0	248873.8	19821.6	94839.0	19998.5	17333.3	52308.5	29.1
July	40750.5	20166.7	256081.4	23821.6	99046.4	19953.9	17333.3	54091.6	26.0
August	44887.3	19966.7	267665.5	23821.6	99696.2	20419.5	18333.3	56606.3	30.7
September	47589.6	20466.7	308487.6	39200.0	102573.1	20572.4	18266.7	62203.1	36.7

Source: Ministry of Planning and Economic Devlopment, Background to the Budget 1990 - 1991, July 1990.

Table 29

UGANDA

AVERAGE MARKET PRICES: AVERAGE MARKET PRICES FOR SELECTED CONSUMER GOODS IN KAMPALA

(New Uganda Shillings)

Items	Unit	1986 QI	1986 QII	1986 QIII	1986 QIV	1987 QI	1987 QII	1987 QIII	1987 QIV	1988 QI	1988 QII	1988 QIII	1988 QIV	1989 QI	1989 QII	1989 QIII	1989 QIV	1990 QI	1990 QII	1990 QIII	1990 QIV	1991 QI
Banana (Matoke)	1 Kg	2.31	3.53	3.18	5.90	7.24	9.13	6.35	13.68	16.61	20.87	29.73	34.21	37.95	44.43	48.33	85.20	65.63	56.80	47.95	81.70	87.22
Maize Meal	1 Kg	5.71	6.51	3.69	5.33	8.33	11.92	26.64	34.03	44.72	48.33	93.05	111.67	135.77	202.33	284.86	300.00	294.00	250.67	220.00	264.00	289.33
Groundnuts	1 Kg	13.84	18.67	10.91	20.45	21.59	29.43	61.40	111.17	132.63	179.78	233.98	274.17	255.43	454.99	387.6	377.86	340.66	336.31	366.59	533.96	460.78
Sugar	1 Kg	19.30	24.88	6.67	8.00	44.81	44.92	56.67	38.00	55.33	90.00	282.00	233.50	360.04	484.63	463.37	548.27	590.00	589.33	584.09	580.00	608.67
Dry Fish	1 Kg	38.99	51.22	37.25	44.22	59.73	85.68	208.16	232.11	340.17	601.75	827.55	1025.64	988.33	988.69	1190.76	1531.16	1592.20	1106.66	1516.00	1355.00	1388.00
Sweet Potatoes	1 Kg	2.45	3.02	1.98	3.21	4.26	3.83	8.14	16.45	23.69	27.81	39.47	55.15	36.09	49.64	79.36	91.83	70.00	47.17	53.48	88.98	112.58
Dry Beans	1 Kg	5.18	6.07	2.79	4.46	7.02	13.42	40.30	65.69	61.33	82.77	105.60	108.55	113.87	199.77	182.5	186.17	178.56	175.24	198.68	263.89	210.70
Dry Cassava	1 Kg	2.75	3.33	1.82	2.90	3.58	5.17	17.92	22.78	31.67	36.42	54.45	57.33	60.00	77.91	93.43	116.00	130.00	119.39	111.67	111.67	110.21
Green Vegetables	1 Kg	8.68	9.88	7.37	8.35	14.26	19.98	47.89	39.73	88.64	110.22	192.45	112.50	166.40	210.14	216.6	182.64	230.00	277.51	316.65	203.82	239.70
Bread	1 Kg	20.91	30.32	17.23	23.61	33.70	23.53	106.67	139.65	218.40	286.99	409.51	390.00	423.63	580.00	691.00	708.26	735.91	700.00	706.48	730.00	762.67
Tea	1 Kg	44.33	53.89	34.17	43.06	48.53	84.72	303.33	288.89	625.00	637.77	833.33	994.45	1059.72	1063.33	1199.98	1602.44	2000.00	2000.00	2000.00	2000.00	2000.00
Salt	1 Kg	7.08	13.67	9.00	8.43	4.61	13.96	32.72	46.36	101.33	91.95	127.96	95.91	101.30	125.69	139.67	143.33	159.63	151.08	152.30	172.40	202.31
Cooking Oil	1 Pepsi Bottle	15.00	19.78	28.17	28.22	48.89	57.22	45.42	47.39	56.33	158.50	219.11	198.11	213.86	225.89	242.23	259.66	247.00	236.67	234.17	237.50	245.00
Milk	1/2 Liter	2.67	3.08	2.36	5.67	10.44	17.08	20.83	24.72	30.69	38.89	65.83	71.67	75.08	74.79	101.38	117.09	120.89	118.42	116.34	118.33	122.00
Rice	1 Kg	17.88	24.21	20.67	26.76	47.14	59.68	43.62	65.58	85.04	227.89	216.67	201.67	251.82	325.69	320.99	358.66	465.33	441.33	352.00	404.00	464.67
Tomatoes	1 Kg	9.76	5.57	3.76	5.17	5.13	11.97	57.73	66.97	117.44	109.95	103.93	117.33	133.21	172.93	214.00	131.20	257.21	184.09	190.57	172.85	166.68
Onions	1 Kg	17.34	17.10	8.47	14.25	17.62	40.97	66.15	162.23	178.46	217.75	195.17	223.64	199.01	390.23	438.90	514.03	440.80	578.97	709.30	546.00	355.27
Meat	1 Kg	24.20	30.83	20.56	29.71	48.24	61.00	112.67	167.67	274.56	340.55	438.89	460.55	486.55	581.35	592.30	653.33	693.33	700.00	706.67	800.00	866.67
Native Beer	1 Beer Bottle	2.38	2.56	3.33	5.00	6.83	7.33	7.50	11.67	22.08	23.33	36.11	40.00	41.67	48.33	54.33	69.66	74.66	80.00	80.00	85.00	100.83
Bottled Beer	1 Beer Bottle	22.00	20.75	32.50	42.78	56.67	76.67	95.00	150.00	216.67	150.00	256.11	251.11	280.43	364.52	455.33	493.33	522.00	450.00	540.00	606.67	746.67
Cigarettes	1 Stick Kali	0.23	0.31	0.43	0.75	1.00	1.00	1.45	1.94	3.21	3.18	3.86	3.44	5.00	4.80	5.98	7.92	9.44	10.00	10.00	10.00	10.00
Charcoal	1 Kg	1.85	2.27	1.47	1.86	3.79	4.91	7.82	10.93	35.45	74.29	49.99	41.66	57.11	59.94	74.37	71.63	83.39	81.04	13.83	90.57	111.87
Paraffin	1/2 Liter	3.83	4.61	5.17	5.67	10.83	28.33	10.00	18.33	66.67	100.00	100.00	100.00	63.26	84.37	94.17	109.45	128.33	130.00	156.67	236.94	345.83
Soap	1 Kg	41.01	49.25	34.87	37.06	81.36	76.21	133.54	183.85	328.97	399.52	506.46	411.17	325.49	370.14	339.90	326.50	396.20	393.50	421.99	446.29	465.87
Sheet (American)	1 Meter	22.00	26.27	32.44	45.83	66.67	90.83	87.50	116.67	158.33	203.33	310.00	321.66	312.78	333.33	366.67	350.00	365.00	500.00	547.22	562.50	600.00
Cotton Blanket	One	177.70	267.33	338.33	476.44	632.50	770.83	1262.22	1540.83	2235.33	2450.00	2588.89	2613.67	2802.78	3427.78	3458.33	3475.00	3733.00	3555.50	3433.33	3522.22	3511.11
Nylci Material	1 Meter	25.25	33.67	45.89	79.50	122.22	171.67	158.33	171.11	237.56	331.83	450.00	390.56	422.44	505.55	515.00	517.00	800.00	800.00	883.33	900.00	983.33

Source: Ministry of Planning and Economic Development, Background to the Budget 1990 - 1991, July 1990.
World Bank Report No. 7439-UG; Uganda Towards Stabilization and Economic Recovery.

Table 30
Page 1 of 2

UGANDA
AVERAGE KAMPALA MARKET PRICES FOR SELECTED CONSUMER GOODS
INCLUDED IN THE MIDDLE-INCOME GROUP INDEX

Item	Wheat	Soft Drinks	Sportsman	Rex	Colgate	Matches	Cycle Tyre	Cycle Tube	Nytil Plain	Nytil Khaki
Unit	1 Kg.	1 Bottle	1 Packet	1 Packet	Medium	1 Box	One	One	1 Meter	1 Meter
1981 January	-	-	-	-	-	-	-	-	-	-
February	-	-	-	-	-	-	-	-	-	-
March	-	-	-	-	-	-	-	-	-	-
April	2.00	0.80	2.00	3.00	1.00	0.10	15.00	5.00	1.70	3.00
May	-	-	-	-	-	-	-	-	-	-
June	3.93	1.00	3.00	3.33	1.50	0.18	27.25	14.50	3.25	3.79
July	5.29	1.00	2.71	3.15	1.50	0.17	28.81	13.93	2.80	3.50
August	5.17	1.00	2.00	2.64	1.50	0.16	30.96	10.20	2.45	2.95
September	4.40	0.99	2.20	2.81	1.50	0.17	33.06	10.00	2.29	2.81
October	4.41	1.00	2.16	2.62	11.70	0.18	33.65	9.13	2.38	3.14
November	4.36	1.00	2.09	2.54	1.70	0.17	31.90	9.52	2.43	3.13
December	4.04	1.04	2.03	2.33	1.70	0.18	29.75	10.11	2.50	3.10
1982 January	4.09	1.41	1.98	2.58	1.70	0.17	30.05	10.71	3.37	3.52
February	3.94	1.53	2.07	2.60	1.80	0.18	33.84	12.92	3.37	3.47
March	3.95	1.55	2.07	2.45	2.00	0.18	34.54	13.00	3.46	3.80
April	3.56	1.58	2.01	3.00	2.00	0.21	35.58	11.67	3.50	3.88
May	3.61	1.52	1.98	3.00	2.00	0.21	29.68	9.53	2.86	3.58
June	3.57	1.32	2.00	2.32	2.00	0.20	31.41	10.06	3.12	3.78
July	3.62	1.43	1.99	2.02	2.00	0.20	27.08	8.84	3.26	4.29
August	3.19	1.50	1.89	2.00	1.97	0.22	28.20	9.64	3.64	4.33
September	3.53	1.51	2.00	2.77	2.10	0.20	31.09	12.67	3.40	4.00
October	3.63	1.53	2.00	2.69	1.95	0.22	29.79	13.21	3.44	4.13
November	3.52	1.46	1.98	2.46	2.05	0.23	32.50	12.50	3.35	4.33
December	3.71	1.50	2.01	2.35	2.09	0.21	31.50	12.79	3.66	4.48
1983 January	3.88	1.50	2.01	2.27	2.33	0.21	30.41	11.34	3.69	4.54
February	3.68	1.50	2.31	2.76	2.63	0.20	29.81	15.30	3.44	4.27
March	3.54	1.50	2.19	2.84	2.46	0.19	30.83	16.40	3.41	4.22
April	3.28	1.46	2.01	2.52	2.45	0.19	29.33	13.58	3.26	4.12
May	3.20	1.50	2.46	2.84	2.44	0.19	29.79	14.79	3.43	4.28
June	3.33	1.50	2.96	3.63	2.66	0.18	31.99	13.74	3.54	4.35
July	3.50	1.50	2.29	6.50	2.61	0.18	35.00	14.57	3.52	4.27
August	3.35	1.50	2.39	4.50	2.61	0.18	34.58	15.29	3.50	4.16
September	3.45	1.50	2.22	2.73	2.71	0.17	32.01	13.50	3.48	4.17
October	3.48	1.50	2.08	2.57	2.73	0.15	31.14	13.24	3.33	4.02
November	3.51	1.50	2.20	2.68	2.77	0.17	32.09	13.35	3.59	4.10
December	3.65	1.50	2.10	2.57	2.67	0.16	32.40	13.20	3.41	3.95
1984 January	3.46	1.50	2.06	2.58	2.69	0.19	31.46	13.05	3.85	3.88
February	3.52	1.50	2.06	2.64	2.80	0.17	30.98	12.33	4.48	3.38
March	3.43	1.52	1.98	2.54	2.86	0.19	30.45	13.17	4.40	4.10
April	3.49	1.60	2.43	3.07	3.01	0.18	31.42	13.08	4.18	4.17
May	3.56	1.59	2.64	7.58	3.14	0.19	30.17	12.10	4.50	4.38
June	3.96	1.69	2.47	3.35	3.10	0.18	31.53	12.69	4.42	4.13
July	3.59	1.73	2.43	3.08	3.14	0.18	30.29	11.75	5.15	5.00
August	4.45	1.78	2.56	3.06	3.23	0.21	28.08	12.33	5.70	6.00
September	4.60	2.08	2.66	3.15	3.29	0.21	29.50	11.92	6.06	5.95
October	5.46	2.20	2.70	3.43	3.45	0.27	32.50	13.33	6.25	5.81
November	6.21	2.46	3.16	4.18	3.27	0.48	33.83	13.20	6.50	6.05
December	8.55	2.60	5.01	6.04	4.12	0.54	33.50	14.17	7.40	7.58
1985 January	12.29	3.77	7.64	9.43	5.55	0.58	52.38	19.17	10.31	10.62
February	11.77	4.07	4.92	5.69	7.18	0.54	62.72	20.90	10.93	11.75
March	10.55	3.93	4.92	6.40	7.28	0.53	65.33	22.53	12.08	12.94
April	10.03	3.96	5.28	5.88	7.55	0.50	66.75	21.13	11.45	13.58
May	10.19	4.07	5.38	6.39	7.56	0.54	71.67	23.67	11.92	15.00
June	9.74	5.55	4.95	5.97	7.47	0.52	65.00	24.00	11.77	13.50
July	9.79	6.23	4.98	5.83	8.43	0.51	75.36	27.50	13.20	16.50
August	12.70	6.20	8.50	9.20	11.00	0.53	67.50	29.50	13.50	18.00
September	12.67	6.20	8.59	9.02	10.37	0.51	80.08	35.00	12.88	20.00
October	19.92	5.58	7.72	8.50	10.19	0.50	160.83	69.97	13.06	20.33
	13.74	5.38	7.53	8.53	10.11	0.51	146.50	62.21	13.00	21.28
December	14.79	5.40	8.29	9.36	11.86	0.65	146.50	62.21	16.00	23.50

Table 30
Page 2 of 2

UGANDA
AVERAGE KAMPALA MARKET PRICES FOR SELECTED CONSUMER GOODS
INCLUDED IN THE MIDDLE-INCOME GROUP INDEX

Item	Wheat	Soft Drinks	Sportsman	Rex	Colgate	Matches	Cycle Tyre	Cycle Tube	Nytil Plain	Nytil Khaki
Unit	1 Kg.	1 Bottle	1 Packet	1 Packet	Medium	1 Box	One	One	1 Meter	1 Meter
1986 January	25.00	15.00	20.00	20.00	20.00	1.50	238.75	103.33	25.13	40.60
February	22.50	10.56	13.44	15.56	20.22	1.17	238.25	103.33	25.13	40.60
March	23.07	14.44	10.67	13.67	21.56	1.36	241.67	132.14	28.11	39.83
April	26.88	14.14	10.00	13.17	22.25	1.64	350.00	144.00	29.29	38.67
May	28.11	11.14	10.00	12.89	26.00	1.72	370.00	136.43	37.50	47.25
June	28.19	15.43	18.56	21.00	26.44	1.79	383.33	145.00	38.00	62.50
July	33.75	15.28	20.00	20.00	30.22	2.06	391.43	143.33	39.13	64.60
August	40.00	18.40	27.67	48.33	37.22	2.21	403.33	162.50	46.71	67.00
September	53.33	19.20	23.56	34.38	38.88	2.19	662.50	201.67	53.88	73.33
October	51.94	25.00	23.78	26.22	39.00	2.00	850.00	242.50	58.89	90.71
November	50.83	25.00	27.44	30.89	35.33	2.17	850.00	226.25	59.29	93.75
December	58.89	31.67	39.78	41.11	43.89	2.19	433.33	226.00	69.29	95.83
1987 January	71.07	39.17	40.00	42.43	65.00	3.31	10000.00	236.00	105.00	110.00
February	73.33	33.00	36.50	45.00	76.25	3.00	1500.00	283.75	100.00	150.00
March	73.33	45.00	37.50	47.13	75.83	6.25	1050.00	295.00	96.67	125.00
April	80.00	38.33	43.13	50.38	79.17	7.11	1500.00	280.00	108.00	150.00
May	132.50	50.00	75.00	85.00	115.00	6.50	775.00	400.00	135.00	261.00
June	75.00	40.00	50.00	70.00	70.00	5.00	650.00	300.00	90.00	220.00
July	75.00	50.00	60.00	90.00	80.00	5.00	650.00	300.00	90.00	230.00
August	90.00	50.00	50.00	90.00	100.00	5.00	600.00	270.00	90.00	230.00
September	115.00	70.00	50.00	80.00	100.00	5.00	650.00	250.00	110.00	200.00
October	115.00	70.00	60.00	80.00	100.00	5.00	900.00	350.00	100.00	200.00
November	135.00	50.00	60.00	80.00	100.00	15.00	900.00	350.00	130.00	230.00
December										
1988 January	125.00	80.00	100.00	120.00	200.00	15.00	1800.00	500.00	180.00	230.00
February	150.00	70.00	100.00	120.00	200.00	20.00	2000.00	500.00	180.00	250.00
March	150.00	80.00	100.00	130.00	200.00	20.00	1800.00	350.00	180.00	250.00
April	175.00	75.00	100.00	130.00	200.00	20.00	1800.00	350.00	180.00	250.00
May	250.00	75.00	100.00	130.00	200.00	20.00	1800.00	350.00	180.00	250.00
June	275.00	80.00	150.00	180.00	250.00	20.00	2000.00	700.00	250.00	400.00
July	250.00	130.00	170.00	250.00	300.00	20.00		900.00	350.00	500.00
August	250.00	130.00	200.00	250.00	200.00	20.00		900.00	350.00	470.00
September	250.00	130.00	165.00	200.00	270.00	20.00		850.00	350.00	470.00
October	275.00	130.00	155.00	200.00	250.00	20.00		550.00	350.00	430.00
November	250.00	120.00	150.00	200.00	250.00	20.00		500.00	350.00	430.00
December	275.00	120.00	160.00	200.00	250.00	20.00		500.00	350.00	430.00
1989 January	264.00	120.00	236.00	282.00	270.00	20.00	3000.00	500.00	367.00	500.00
February	285.00	112.00	240.00	286.00	290.00	20.00	3000.00	550.00	394.00	550.00
March	375.00	150.00	280.00	337.00	350.00	19.00	3000.00	550.00	366.67	533.33
April	440.00	150.00	280.00	340.00	286.00	20.00	3000.00	850.00	387.50	500.00
May	450.00	150.00	281.00	294.00	310.00	20.00	2700.00	1000.00	432.50	500.00
June	450.00	150.00	288.00	324.00	310.00	20.00	3000.00	1075.00	466.67	566.67
July	600.00	150.00	340.00	430.00	320.00	22.00	2700.00	1300.00	450.00	575.00
August	612.00	147.00	290.00	422.00	310.00	19.00		1200.00	425.00	600.00
September	585.00	150.00	306.00	406.00	296.00	20.00	2700.00	1350.00	470.00	550.00
October	650.00	156.00	412.00	510.00	310.00	20.00			474.00	550.00
November	612.00	200.00	406.00	496.00	330.00	20.00	3000.00	1500.00	511.00	580.00
December	645.00	210.00	406.00	486.00	340.00	24.00	3000.00	1500.00	530.00	583.33
1990 January	640.00	210.00	406.00	506.00	350.00	27.50	3000.00	900.00	570.00	610.00
February	650.00	200.00	470.00	540.00	370.00	29.00	3000.00		600.00	637.00
March	650.00	200.00	540.00	700.00	350.00	29.00			590.00	1120.00
April	640.00	178.00	520.00	700.00	350.00	30.00			570.00	1040.00
May	650.00	166.00	496.60	690.00	350.00	28.00	2300.00	800.00	610.00	1033.00
June	637.50	156.00	506.00	700.00	350.00	28.00	2500.00	900.00	620.00	1075.00
July	606.25	196.00	400.00	620.00	350.00	27.50	2500.00	900.00	675.00	1120.00
August	687.50	192.00	400.00	600.00	360.00	27.00	2800.00	900.00	680.00	1075.00
September	650.00	200.00	440.00	600.00	360.00	28.00	2720.00	920.00	640.00	1140.00
October	660.00	200.00	392.00	592.00	350.00	26.00	2730.00	900.00	640.00	1160.00
November	675.00	200.00	400.00	600.00	370.00	28.75	3260.00	900.00	687.50	1060.00
December	650.00	230.00	400.00	600.00	380.00	28.75	2980.00	900.00	660.00	1050.00
1991 January	633.30	200.00	420.00	596.00	380.00	28.33	3000.00	912.50	700.00	1162.00
February	681.00	200.00	400.00	600.00	380.00	26.25	3220.00	937.50	720.00	1220.00
March	680.00	250.00	400.00	600.00	410.00	30.00	3340.00	1000.00	760.00	1230.00
April	700.00	250.00	420.00	620.00	420.00	28.00	3380.00	1000.00	780.00	1100.00
May	680.00	237.50	400.00	600.00	410.00	29.00	3500.00	916.60	780.00	1160.00

Table 31

UGANDA
MINIMUM PRODUCER PRICES FOR SELECTED EXPORT CROPS
(New Uganda Shillings)

Effective Date	Year	Annual Average Robusta Price	LI Cons Price Index	New Cons Price Index	Months Validity	COFFEE Robusta (Kiboko)	COFFEE Arabica (Bugisu Grade P)	TOBACCO Flue-cured (Grade TOI)	TOBACCO Fire-cured (Grade I)	SEED COTTON (AR)	SEED COTTON (BR)	TEA (Green Leaf)	COCOA
Apr 1981					4	0.07	0.14	0.14	0.09	0.06	0.01	0.03	
9 May 1981	81	0.19	96.0		5	0.20	0.37	0.79	0.54	0.15	0.03	0.04	
9 Oct 1981					3	0.35	0.65	0.79	0.54	0.30	0.06	0.06	
Dec 31 1981													
1 Jan 1982	82	0.43	114.7		6	0.35				0.30		0.10	
7 Jun 1982					6	0.50	0.93	1.00	0.67	0.40	0.08	0.15	0.30
Dec 31 1982													
1 Jan 1983					4	0.50	1.02	1.15	0.75	0.50		0.15	
9 May 1983	83	0.68	153.4		2	0.60	1.40	1.50	1.00	0.60		0.25	0.40
1 Jul 1983					5	0.80	1.76	2.00	1.39	0.90	0.50	0.40	0.80
21 Dec 1983					1	1.00				0.90		0.45	1.30
Dec 31 1983													
1 Jan 1984					6	1.00						0.45	
1 Apr 1984	84	1.28	216.8		4	1.30	2.30	2.20	1.50	1.20	0.62	0.70	1.30
Jul 1984					2	2.10	3.50	3.30	2.20	1.80	0.90	0.80	1.90
Nov 1984													2.20
Dec 31 1984													
1 Jan 1985					6	2.10	4.60	5.90	3.90	1.80	1.00	0.80	4.20
20 Jun 1985	85	2.57	572.5		5	2.70	8.30	8.00	5.60	2.20	1.50	1.20	5.50
22 Dec 1985					1	4.70				3.20		1.40	
1 Jan 1986					5	4.70				3.20		1.40	
27 May 1986	86	6.92	1405.0		1	8.50	16.92	10.00	7.00	4.00	2.00	5.00	22.00
Dec 31 1986						8.50				4.00		5.00	
1 Jan 1987					6	8.50				4.00		5.00	
May 1987	87	17.54	4285.6		7	24.00	43.66	38.00	25.00	19.00	10.00	10.00	30.00
Dec 31 1987													
1 Jan 1988	88	44.50	12692.7		6	29.00	50.00	90.00	55.00	32.00	18.00	10.00	
Jul 1988				78.1	6	60.00	110.00	220.00	117.00	80.00	42.00	20.00	75.00
Dec 31 1988													
1 Jan 1989					12	60.00	110.00	250.00	140.00	80.00	42.00	20.00	
Mar 1989	89	60.00	22668.7		6	60.00	110.00	410.00	210.00	130.00	65.00	30.00	
Jun 1989				139.4	4	60.00	110.00	410.00	210.00	130.00	65.00	35.00	
Dec 31 1989													
1 Jan 1990					2	60.00	180.00	480.00	480.00	160.00	65.00	35.00	
May 1990								480.00	480.00			35.00	
Jul 1990	90	75.00	30669.4		6	75.00	350.00	480.00	480.00	160.00		35.00	
Nov 1990				188.6		120.00	350.00			220.00	110.00	35.00	
Dec 31 1990													
1 Jan 1991						120.00						35.00	
Mar 1991	91	165.00	39938.6		6	120.00	350.00			220.00	110.00	35.00	
Jul 1991				245.6	6	120.00	471.00			300.00		45.00	
Dec 31 1991						210.00						60.00	

Source: Background to the Budget 1991 - 1992, July 1991.

UGANDA
EVOLUTION OF KAMPALA SUGAR PRICE

		Nominal Sugar Ush/Kg 1/	Nominal Sugar Ush/Kg 2/	LI CPI	LI CPI (Jan–Mar 1986=100)	Deflated Sugar Price 1/ (Jan–Mar 1987=100)	Index	Deflated Sugar Price 2/ (Jan–Mar 1986=100)	Index	Domestic Sugar Prod'n	Nominal Meat Price 2/	Meat Price Defl. by LI CPI 1Q 1986 =100	Meat Price Index 1Q 1986 =100
1986	1		19.30	33	100			19.30	100		24.2	24.2	100
	2		24.90	43	130			19.15	99		30.8	23.7	98
	3		13.30	48	145			9.20	48		41.1	28.4	118
	4		16.00	72	216			7.42	38		59.4	27.6	114
1987	1	44.81	89.60	114	340	13.17	100	26.33	136		96.5	28.4	117
	2	44.92	89.80	144	432	10.40	79	20.79	108		122.0	28.2	117
	3	56.67	56.70	141	423	13.39	102	13.40	69		112.7	26.6	110
	4	38.00	38.00	200	599	6.34	48	6.34	33		167.7	28.0	116
1988	1	55.33	55.30	292	874	6.33	48	6.32	33	0	274.6	31.4	130
	2	90.00	90.00	377	1129	7.97	61	7.97	41		340.6	30.2	125
	3	282.00	282.00	544	1629	17.32	131	17.32	90		438.9	27.0	111
	4	233.50	233.50	562	1683	13.87	105	13.87	72	7534	460.6	27.4	113
1989	1	360.04	360.03	640	1917	18.79	143	18.79	97		486.6	25.4	105
	2	484.63	484.60	780	2334	20.76	158	20.76	108		581.4	24.9	103
	3	463.37	463.37	861	2578	17.97	136	17.97	93	15859	592.3	23.0	95
	4	548.27	551.60	956	2864	19.14	145	19.26	100		651.1	22.7	94
1990	1	590.00	590.00	1046	3131	18.84	143	18.84	98		693.3	22.1	91
	2	589.33	589.33	1037	3106	18.97	144	18.97	98		700.0	22.5	93
	3	584.09	584.10	1082	3239	18.03	137	18.03	93		706.7	21.8	90
	4	580.00	580.00	1215	3640	15.94	121	15.94	83	28913	800.0	22.0	91
1991	1	608.67	608.67	1299	3890	15.65	119	15.65	81		866.7	22.3	92
	2	722.67	722.67	1396	4182			17.28	90		856.7	20.5	85

1/ Background to the Budget (1990/91 and 1991/92)
2/ Key Economic Indicators, 6th Issue: July 1991

Table 33

UGANDA
GROSS MARGIN AND RETURNS TO FAMILY LABOUR FOR EXPORT AND COMPETING CROPS – MAY 1991
(Using Handhoe)

CROP	Yield Kg/Ha	Producer Price Shs/KG	Value of Output Shs/KG	Variable Cost Shs/Ha	Gross Margin Shs/Ha	Gross Margin US$/Ha	Family Labour Pd/Ha	Return per Personday Shs/Pd	Return per Personday US$/Pd	Rank
A.Perennial Crops										
Coffee (R)	1,100	120	132,000	92,916	39,084	44	290	135	0.15	18
Coffee (A)	750	350	262,500	117,734	144,766	163	285	508	0.57	13
Tea (GL)	5,000	45	225,000	187,980	37,020	42	105	353	0.40	15
Cocoa (WB)	1,200	180	216,000	76,640	139,360	157	220	633	0.71	7
Matooke	9,000	45	405,000	220,000	185,000	208	310	597	0.67	8
B.Seasonal Crops										
Cotton	550	220	121,000	55,287	65,713	74	177	371	0.42	14
Maize	2,000	60	120,000	79,313	40,687	46	122	334	0.38	16
Beans	750	150	112,500	54,604	57,896	65	104	557	0.63	11
Groundnuts	800	300	240,000	105,872	134,128	151	207	648	0.73	6
Soyabeans	1,000	160	160,000	53,422	106,578	120	114	935	1.05	2
Simsim	400	300	120,000	43,959	76,041	86	138	551	0.62	12
Cassava	7,500	20	150,000	95,183	54,817	62	182	301	0.34	17
S.Potatoes	4,000	30	120,000	54,628	65,372	74	110	594	0.67	9
F.Millets	1,500	100	150,000	51,218	98,782	111	167	592	0.67	10
Sorghum	1,600	100	160,000	51,787	108.213	122	160	676	0.76	5
Paddy Rice 1/	1,750	210	367,500	62,762	304,738	343	307	993	1.12	1
Tobacco (Flue) *	950	700	665,000	358,910	306,090	345	380	806	0.91	3
Tobacco (Fire) *	800	490	392,000	168,500	223,500	252	280	798	0.90	4

1/ Price in Paddy equivalent (conversion to milled white rice is 60%).

NOTE: * Costs for Tobacco are still to be updated.

2/ Converted to US $ at an exchange rate of Ush   888

Table 34

UGANDA
INDEX OF INDUSTRIAL PRODUCTION : MONTHLY SUMMARY FOR INDEX GROUPS
(Base 1987 = 100)

Period	Food Process-ing	Drinks and Tobacco	Textiles and Clothing	Leather and Footwear	Timber Paper etc.	Chemical Paint & Soap	Bricks and Cement	Steel & Steel Products	Miscel-laneous	ALL ITEMS
NO. OF ESTABS	49	12	13	7	19	16	11	17	17	161 ++
WEIGHT	20.7	26.1	16.3	2.3	9.0	12.3	4.3	5.3	3.7	100.0
ANNUAL										
1982	106.7	48.6	196.7	77.9	68.2	64.6	163.7	81.6	87.6	97.4
1983	103.7	59.8	177.6	152.8	79.6	68.8	177.4	118.5	124.3	103.7
1984	99.8	79.4	136.9	175.5	88.7	61.2	156.5	110.7	139.5	101.1
1985	93.9	84.8	98.9	86.9	76.8	58.6	122.7	133.1	139.1	91.1
1986	85.3	82.2	92.9	90.0	72.0	58.8	120.6	105.9	141.0	86.1
1987	100.0	100.0	100.0	100.0	100.0	100.0	100.0	100.0	100.0	100.0
1988	128.0	139.6	121.8	62.0	135.1	111.2	94.5	87.2	134.0	123.7
1989	153.7	143.7	132.7	62.9	169.4	162.9	109.0	98.9	204.2	145.2
1990	170.1	155.2	116.3	74.9	181.1	183.9	154.2	106.1	181.0	154.3

Note: In the tables, the symbol '+' is used to indicate that, in addition to the individual establishments covered in the index, production data for coffee and tea processing, as advised by the respective marketing boards, is included.

SOURCE: Statistics Department, MPED

Table 35

UGANDA

AGRICULTURAL WAGE RATE AND HIRE CHARGES IN RURAL AREAS - MAY 1991

(Rates and Charges in Shillings)

DISTRICT	AGRICULTURAL WAGE RATE				TRACTOR RATES		OX-PLOUGH RATES		SPRAYER	TRANSPORT (PER KM)					
	Casual Labour (Per day)	Permanent Labour (@ month)	Contract Labour Ploughing @ Ha	Weeding @ Ha	First Ploughing @ Ha	Second Ploughing @ Ha	First Ploughing @ Ha	Second Ploughing @ Ha	@ HA	HEAD LO (30-50KG)	BICYCLE (50-100KG)	WHEELBAR (50-100KG)	TRACTOR TRAILER (100KG)	PICK-UP (100KG)	TRUCK (100KG)
MBALE	450	7,500	25,000	-	25,000	25,000	20,000	17,500	1,000	150	200	200	200	200	150
KAPCHORWA	450	4,500	20,000	-	25,000	25,000	20,000	16,000	750	200	250	250	200	200	150
TORORO	500	4,500	20,000	-	25,000	25,000	17,500	15,000	1,250	200	200	250	200	200	200
IGANGA	450	6,000	20,000	-	25,000	25,000	20,000	20,000	1,250	250	250	300	200	200	200
JINJA	500	6,000	25,000	-	25,000	25,000	-	-	1,500	250	250	250	200	200	200
MASAKA	450	8,000	15,000	-	25,000	15,000	-	-	1,500	300	250	300	250	250	200
MPIGI	500	10,000	15,000	-	25,000	20,000	-	-	-	200	250	300	250	400	250
LUWERO	450	15,000	32,000	-	32,000	22,500	-	-	2,000	300	300	300	200	250	250
MUBENDE	350	6,000	20,000	-	25,000	20,000	-	-	-	250	200	300	250	200	200
HOIMA	500	8,000	25,000	-	25,000	20,000	-	-	-	200	300	500	250	250	200
MASINDI	450	5,000	25,000	-	32,000	-	-	-	-	250	200	350	250	250	200
KASESE	400	6,000	30,000	-	30,000	20,000	-	-	-	300	400	200	250	200	-
KABAROLE	400	-	-	-	25,000	20,000	-	-	-	250	300	300	250	200	200
RUKUNGIRI	400	6,000	18,750	-	32,000	-	-	-	-	200	300	300	350	200	200
BUSHENYI	400	5,000	20,000	-	25,000	12,500	-	-	-	250	300	200	250	250	-
MBARARA	450	6,000	17,500	-	25,000	20,000	-	-	1,500	250	250	200	300	300	-
UGANDA -AVE.	444	6,469	20,516	-	26,625	18,438	19,375	17,125	1,344	238	263	281	241	208	163
-MODE.	450	6,000	20,000		25,000	20,000	20,000	17,500	1,500	250	250	300	250	200	200

Note: In Kapchorwa, donkeys and Bullock Carts are used to transport agricultural produce.
Charges for 100kg weight are Shs. 350 for a donkey, and Shs 300 for a cart per km.

Table 36

UGANDA
STRUCTURE OF INTEREST RATES
(Percent per Annum)

	1981 June	1981 Oct	1982 July	1982 Dec	1983 Jan	1983 July	1983 Dec	1984 Jan	1984 July	1984 Dec	1985 Jan	1985 July	1985 Dec	1986 Jan	1986 May f/	1986 Dec	1987 July	1988 July	1988 Dec	1989 March	1989 Dec	1990 March
BANK OF UGANDA																						
Ways and Means	2.5	5.0	2.0	2.0	2.0	2.0	2.0	2.0	2.0	2.0	2.0	2.0	2.0	2.0	5.0	5.0	5.0	15.0	15.0	15.0	15.0	15.0
Re-discount Rate	7.0	9.0	10.0	10.0	12.5	14.5	14.5	14.5	23.0	23.0	23.0	23.0	23.0	23.0	35.0	35.0	32.0	38.0	38.0	48.0	48.0	48.0
Bank Rate to Commercial Banks	8.0	10.0	11.0	11.0	13.5	15.5	15.5	15.5	24.0	24.0	24.0	24.0	24.0	24.0	36.0	36.0	31.0	45.0	45.0	55.0	55.0	55.0
TREASURY BILLS																						
35 Days	4.7	8.0	9.0	11.0	10.0	12.0	12.0	12.0	20.0	20.0	20.0	20.0	20.0	20.0	30.0	30.0	23.0	33.0	33.0	38.0	38.0	38.0
63 Days	4.9	8.5	9.5	11.0	11.0	11.0	13.0	13.0	21.0	21.0	21.0	21.0	21.0	21.0	32.0	32.0	25.0	35.0	35.0	40.0	40.0	40.0
91 Days	5.1	9.0	10.0	12.0	12.0	1.0	14.0	14.0	22.0	22.0	22.0	22.0	22.0	22.0	35.0	35.0	28.0	38.0	38.0	43.0	43.0	43.0
GOVERNMENT STOCKS																						
5 Years	8.5	11.0	12.0	12.0	12.0	12.0	12.0	12.0	25.0	25.0	25.0	25.0	25.0	25.0	40.0	40.0	30.0	38.0	40.0	45.0	45.0	45.0
10 Years	9.5	11.5	12.5	12.5	12.5	12.5	12.5	12.5	26.0	26.0	26.0	26.0	26.0	26.0	45.0	45.0	32.0	40.0	42.0	47.0	47.0	47.0
15 Years	10.5	12.0	13.0	13.0	13.0	13.0	13.0	13.0	27.0	27.0	27.0	27.0	27.0	27.0	-	-	35.0	45.0	45.0	50.0	50.0	50.0
COMMERCIAL BANKS																						
Deposit Rates:																						
Demand Deposits	0.0	0.0	0.0	0.0	opt.	opt.	opt.	opt.	5.0	5.0	5.0	5.0	5.0	5.0	10.0	10.0	7.0	15.0	15.0	20.0	20.0	20.0
Savings Deposits	5.0	8.0	9.0	9.0	11.0	11.0	13.0	13.0	18.0	18.0	18.0	18.0	18.0	18.0	28.0	28.0	18.0	28.0	28.0	33.0	33.0	33.0
Time Deposit:																						
3-6 Months	0.0	0.0	0.0	0.0	-	-	-	-	20.0 a/	20.0	-	20.0	20.0	20.0	25.0	25.0	15.0	28.0	28.0	33.0	33.0	33.0
4-12 Months	0.0	0.0	0.0	0.0	-	-	-	-	20.0 a/	20.0	-	20.0	20.0	20.0	30.0	30.0	20.0	30.0	30.0	35.0	35.0	35.0
Minimum One Year	5.0	12.0	13.0	13.0	15.0	15.0	15.0	17.0	22.0	22.0	22.0	22.0	22.0	22.0	35.0	35.0	22.0	32.0	32.0	37.0	37.0	37.0
More than One Year	6.0	neg.	neg.	neg.	neg.	neg.	neg.	neg.	neg.	neg.	neg.	neg.	neg.	neg.	neg.	neg.	neg.	neg.	neg.	neg.	neg.	neg.
Lending Rates: d/																						
Agriculture	8.0	13.0	14.0	14.0	16.0	16.0	18.0	18.0	24.0	24.0	24.0	24.0	24.0	24.0	38.0	38.0	22-25 a/	32-35 a/	32-35 a/	min 25.0 w/	s/25-40	s/25-40
Export & Manufac.	12.0	14.0	15.0	15.0	17.0	18.0	19.0	19.0	24.0	24.0	24.0	24.0	24.0	24.0	38.0	38.0						
Commerce cf	12.0	15.0	16.0	22.0	16-22	19.0	22.0	22.0	25.0	25.0	25.0	25.0	25.0	25.0	40.0	40.0	30.0 b/	40.0 b/	40.0 b/	max 50.0	b/50	b/50
Unsecured cf	12.0	17.0	17.0	20.0	22.0	22.0	22.0	22.0	26.0	26.0	26.0	26.0	26.0	26.0	42.0	42.0						

Source: Ministry of Planning and Economic Development, Background to the Budget 1990 - 1991, July 1990.
World Bank Report No. 7439-UG; Uganda Towards Stabilization and Economic Recovery.

a/ Short term commercial nature
b/ Exceeding one year
cf Maximum rate
d/ Effective rates
f/ Effective June 16, 1984
neg.: Negotiable
opt.: Optional

Table 37

UGANDA
OFFICIAL EXCHANGE RATE
(New Uganda Shillings per US$)

Month	1981	1982		1983		1984 a/		1985	1986 Fixed		1987	1988	1989	1990			1991	
	Window 1	Window 1	Window 2	Window 1	Window 2	Window 1	Window 2	Auction	Priority	Market	Official	Official	Ordinary	S.I.P b/	Official	Market	Official	Market
January	0.076	0.860		1.070	2.350	2.410	2.990	5.390	14.790		14.000	60.000	165.000		375.000		570.00	778.50
February	0.078	0.860		1.120	2.300	2.530	3.030	5.570	14.800		14.000	60.000	165.000		379.000		600.00	800.00
March	0.079	0.858		1.166	2.360	2.740	3.200	5.790	14.800		14.000	60.000	200.000		379.000		620.00	814.50
April	0.080	0.859		1.197	2.680	2.920	3.180	5.930	14.800		14.000	60.000	200.000		379.000		640.00	847.50
May	0.081	0.874		1.283	2.755	2.920	3.260	6.000	14.000	50.000	14.000	60.000	200.000		384.000		670.00	
June	0.768	0.942		1.388	2.900	3.070	3.070	6.000	14.000	50.000	14.000	60.000	200.000		397.000			
July	0.794	0.987		1.551	2.937	3.380	3.380	6.000	14.000	50.000	60.000	150.000	200.000	400.000	440.000	637.00		
August	0.817	0.992	3.000	1.665	2.936	3.740	3.740	6.000	14.000		60.000	150.000	200.000		440.000	697.00		
September	0.805	0.991	3.000		2.710	4.000	4.000	6.000	14.000		60.000	150.000	200.000		480.000	730.50		
October	0.791	0.997	2.000	1.856	2.955	4.460	4.460	6.800	14.000		60.000	150.000	340.000		480.000	725.00		
November	0.783	1.017	2.520	2.067	3.260	5.460	5.460	8.700	14.000		60.000	150.000	370.000		510.000	750.50		
December	0.856	1.048	2.400	2.338	3.025	5.520	5.520	12.750	14.000		60.000	165.000	370.000		540.000	768.50		
Average	0.50	0.94	2.58	1.39	2.76	3.60	3.77	6.74	14.27	50.00	40.83	106.25	234.17	400.00	431.92	718.08	620.00	810.13

Source: Ministry of Planning and Economic Development, Background to the Budget 1990 – 1991, July 1990.
World Bank Report No. 7439–UG; Uganda Towards Stabilization and Economic Recovery.

a/ Windows unified in June 1984
b/ Special import program
c/ October 1 to October 24.
d/ October 25 to October 31.
e/ November 1 to November 28.
f/ November 29 to November 30.

Table 38

UGANDA
POPULATION – THE 1969 & 1980 CENSUS RESULTS & PROVISIONAL MID-YEAR PROJECTIONS

Region & Districts	1969 Census '000	1980 Census '000	1991 Census '000	Average Annual Growth (1969-80)	Average Annual Growth (1980-91)	Area (Sq. Km.) Total	Area (Sq. Km.) Land	Land Density (/Sq Km 1980)	Land Density (/Sq Km 1991)	Percent Urban 1980 4/	Percent Urban 1991 4/	Sex Ratio Males/'000 Females 1980
CENTRAL												
1 Kampala 1/	330.7	458.5	773.5	3.0	4.9	238	198	2,316	3,907	100.0	100.0	1026
2 Kalangala	6.8	8.6	16.4	2.2	6.0	5,716	445	19	37	0.1	8.5	
3 Kiboga		138.7	140.8		0.1	4,336	4,583	30	31	-	3.6	
4 Luwero	315.2	412.5	449.2	2.5	0.8	9,198	8,539	48	53	4.9	9.2	1033
5 Masaka	451.2	622.6	831.3	3.0	2.7	10,611	5,518	113	151	6.1	10.1	1016
6 Mpigi	513.5	661.2	915.4	2.3	3.0	6,222	4,486	147	204	5.3	13.0	1033
7 Mubende	331.0	371.6	497.5	4.2	2.7	5,974	5,237	·71	95	3.2	7.0	1101
8 Mukono	541.0	634.3	816.2	1.5	2.3	14,242	4,594	138	178	8.1	12.2	1047
9 Rakai	182.6	274.6	382.0	3.8	3.0	4,973	3,889	71	98	1.5	4.1	985
Total	2672.0	3582.6	4822.3	2.7	2.7	61,510	37,489	96	129	18.0	24.4	1037
WESTERN												
10 Bundibugyo	79.4	112.2	116.0	3.2	0.3	2,338	2,097	54	55	3.8		1017
11 Bushenyi	410.7	524.7	734.8	2.3	3.1	5,396	4,906	107	150	0.8		913
12 Hoima	184.0	142.2	176.0	4.5	2.0	5,577	3,058	47	58	2.4		1020
13 Kabale	403.4	328.7	412.8	1.2	2.1	1,869	1,653	199	250	5.6		873
14 Kabarole	328.0	519.8	741.4	4.3	3.3	8,361	8,109	64	91	5.4		994
15 Kasese	164.1	277.7	343.0	4.9	1.9	3,205	2,724	102	126	10.2		1049
16 Kibale		152.1	219.3		3.4	4,625	4,719	32	46			
17 Kisoro		126.7	184.9		3.5	662	620	204	298			
18 Masindi	167.8	223.2	275.3	2.6	1.9	9,334	8,452	26	33	2.7		1064
19 Mbarara	450.5	688.1	929.6	3.9	2.8	10,839	10,587	65	88	3.5		963
20 Rukungiri	244.6	296.6	388.0	1.8	2.5	2,753	2,584	115	150	2.1		931
Total	2432.5	3392.0	4521.1	3.1	2.6	54,959	49,509	69	91	3.9		964
NORTHERN												
21 Apac	225.4	313.3	460.7	3.0	3.6	6,488	5,887	53	78	0.5	1.4	975
22 Arua	369.6	472.3	624.6	2.3	2.6	7,830	7,595	62	82	1.8	4.2	924
23 Gulu	223.7	270.1	338.7	1.7	2.1	11,735	11,560	23	29	5.9	12.7	947
24 Kitgum	240.1	308.7	350.3	2.3	1.2	16,136	16,136	19	22	5.0	2.9	949
25 Kotido	105.6	161.4	190.7	3.9	1.5	13,208	13,208	12	14	2.0	5.1	928
26 Lira	278.9	370.2	498.3	2.6	2.7	7,251	6,151	60	81	3.0	5.4	978
27 Moroto	164.7	188.6	171.5	1.2	-0.9	14,113	14,113	13	12	5.7	7.7	896
28 Moyo	90.0	106.5	178.5	1.5	4.8	5,006	4,668	23	38	3.0	5.7	974
29 Nebbi	204.1	233.0	315.9	1.2	2.8	2,891	2,781	84	114	1.5	7.6	919
Total	1902.1	2424.1	3129.2	2.2	2.3	84,658	82,099	30	38	3.0	5.4	944
EASTERN												
30 Iganga	470.2	643.9	944.0	2.9	3.5	13,113	4,823	134	196	4.7	4.8	964
31 Jinja	196.3	228.5	284.9	1.4	2.0	734	677	338	421	19.7	26.9	1068
32 Kamuli	278.3	349.6	480.7	2.1	2.9	4,348	3,332	105	144	1.6	1.6	982
33 Kapchorwa	64.5	74.0	116.3	1.3	4.2	1,738	1,738	43	67	2.8	3.9	1048
34 Kumi	190.7	239.5	237.0	2.1	-0.1	2,861	2,457	97	96	0.7	5.0	913
35 Mbale	421.4	556.9	706.6	2.6	2.2	2,546	2,504	222	282	5.6	8.7	996
36 Pallisa		261.2	356.0		2.9	1,564	1,919				1.0	
37 Soroti	379.9	476.6	430.5	2.1	-0.9	10,060	8,526	56	50	3.8	10.7	943
38 Tororo	527.1	407.2	554.0	2.3	2.8	2,989	1,981	206	280	4.2	11.5	949
Total	2528.4	3237.4	4110.0	2.3	2.2	39,953	27,957	116	147	5.0	7.8	970
UGANDA TOTAL 2/	9535.0	12636.1	16582.6	2.59	2.50	241,080	197,054	64	84	8.0	11.4	982

Source: Ministry of Planning and Economic Development, Background to the Budget 1989-1990: July 1989.

1/ Kampala District includes Kampala city and Entebbe municipality.
2/ District totals may not tally with the overall total because of rounding.
3/ The annual growth rate were not used to generate district projections.
4/ Percent urban is based on towns and trading centers of 400 people or more.
5/ Hoima, Kabale, Tororo, Mubende have growth rate based on old configuration.

Table 39

UGANDA
POPULATION
('000)

Region & Districts	Census 1969	Census 1980	PROJECTIONS 1981	1982	1983	1984	1985	1986	1987	1988	1989	1990
CENTRAL												
Kampala 1/	351.8	479.8	498.4	512.9	528.5	544.4	560.8	577.8	592.2	613.2	631.7	650.8
Luwero	315.2	412.5	429.3	441.1	453.0	465.2	477.8	490.7	503.9	517.5	531.5	545.8
Masaka	458.0	631.6	656.9	676.3	697.5	719.1	741.6	764.7	788.5	813.0	838.3	849.4
Mpigi	492.4	639.9	664.8	682.8	700.8	719.2	738.0	757.4	777.3	797.7	818.6	840.1
Mubende	331.0	510.3	531.1	549.0	570.7	593.2	616.5	640.6	665.6	691.5	718.3	746.1
Mukono	541.0	634.3	657.4	672.4	684.3	696.3	708.5	720.8	733.2	745.8	758.5	771.3
Rakai	182.6	274.6	285.8	295.2	306.4	317.9	329.8	342.2	355.0	368.2	382.0	396.2
Total	2,672.0	3,582.6	3,723.7	3,829.7	3,941.2	4,055.3	4,173.0	4,294.2	4,415.7	4,546.9	4,678.9	4,814.7
WESTERN												
Bundibugyo	79.4	112.2	116.7	120.5	125.0	129.7	134.5	139.5	144.7	150.0	155.6	161.3
Bushenyi	410.7	524.7	543.8	558.1	571.9	585.9	600.3	615.1	630.2	645.6	661.5	677.7
Hoima	184.0	294.3	306.2	316.9	330.3	344.1	358.4	373.2	388.6	403.0	421.2	438.4
Kabale	403.4	455.4	474.0	483.9	490.6	497.1	508.7	510.3	516.8	523.3	529.8	536.2
Kabarole	328.0	519.8	540.5	560.0	582.6	606.1	630.5	655.8	682.0	709.2	737.3	766.5
Kasese	164.1	277.7	289.0	299.7	313.4	327.6	342.4	357.8	373.7	390.3	407.4	425.3
Masindi	167.8	223.2	232.3	238.9	245.7	252.6	259.8	267.1	274.7	282.5	290.5	298.7
Mbarara	450.5	688.1	715.8	739.8	768.6	798.3	829.1	861.0	894.1	928.3	963.8	999.6
Rukungiri	244.6	296.6	309.8	317.3	323.9	330.6	337.4	344.3	351.4	358.6	365.9	373.3
Total	2,432.5	3,392.0	3,528.1	3,635.1	3,752.0	3,872.0	4,001.1	4,124.1	4,256.2	4,390.8	4,533.0	4,677.0
NORTHERN												
Apac	225.4	313.3	326.1	335.9	346.6	357.6	369.0	380.7	392.8	405.3	418.2	431.5
Arua	369.6	472.3	491.5	504.6	518.7	530.1	543.3	556.9	570.8	585.0	599.6	614.5
Gulu	223.7	270.1	281.2	288.0	293.7	299.6	305.5	311.6	317.7	324.0	330.4	336.8
Kitgum	240.1	308.7	320.1	328.6	336.9	345.4	354.1	363.0	372.1	381.0	391.1	400.9
Kotido	105.6	161.4	168.0	173.7	180.4	187.4	194.7	202.2	210.0	218.0	226.4	235.0
Lira	278.9	370.2	385.3	396.2	407.4	418.8	430.6	442.8	455.2	468.1	481.2	498.8
Moroto	164.7	188.6	197.2	201.5	204.6	207.7	210.9	214.0	217.2	220.4	223.6	225.8
Moyo	90.0	106.5	110.8	113.4	115.5	117.5	119.6	121.8	123.9	126.1	128.3	130.6
Nebbi	204.1	233.0	242.5	247.7	251.3	255.0	258.6	262.3	265.9	269.6	276.9	293.3
Total	1,902.1	2,424.1	2,522.7	2,589.6	2,655.1	2,719.1	2,786.3	2,855.3	2,925.6	2,997.5	3,075.7	3,167.2
EASTERN												
Iganga	470.2	643.9	670.0	687.7	710.9	732.7	755.1	778.5	802.1	826.7	852.0	878.1
Jinja	196.3	228.5	237.8	242.9	246.4	249.9	253.4	256.9	260.4	263.9	267.4	270.8
Kamuli	278.3	349.6	363.8	373.2	382.0	390.9	400.1	409.5	419.0	428.8	438.9	449.1
Kapchorwa	64.5	74.0	77.6	79.3	80.5	81.1	83.1	84.4	85.7	87.0	88.3	89.6
Kumi	190.7	239.5	248.5	254.9	260.8	266.9	273.1	279.4	285.9	292.5	299.2	306.1
Mbale	421.4	556.9	579.9	596.1	612.8	629.8	647.4	655.4	683.9	705.0	722.6	742.7
Soroti	379.9	476.6	496.1	508.8	520.7	532.9	545.3	558.1	571.1	584.4	598.4	611.9
Tororo	527.1	668.4	695.6	713.1	731.2	748.9	767.1	785.7	804.8	824.3	844.3	864.7
Total	2,528.4	3,237.4	3,369.3	3,456.0	3,545.3	3,633.1	3,724.6	3,807.9	3,912.9	4,012.6	4,111.1	4,213.0
UGANDA TOTAL 2/	9,535.1	12,636.2	13,143.8	13,510.4	13,893.6	14,279.5	14,685.0	15,081.5	15,510.4	15,947.0	16,398.7	16,871.9

Source: Minist Source: Ministry of Planning and Economic Development.Background to the Budget 1990 - 1991, July 1990

1/ Kampala District includes Kampala city and Entebbe municipality.
2/ District totals may not tally with the overall total because of rounding.
3/ The annual growth rate were not used to generate district projections.
4/ Percent urban is based on towns and trading centers of 400 people or more.

Table 40

UGANDA
MIGRATION 1980-1981

Region & Districts	District Growth as Ratio of Average Growth	Total Population Migrating ('000)	Percent Changes in Land Density	Changes in Land Density above Average Change
CENTRAL:				
1 Kampala	195%	171.8	69%	220%
2 Kalangala	242%	5.1	91%	290%
3 Kiboga	5%	-41.2	2%	5%
4 Luwero	31%	-92.1	9%	28%
5 Masaka	106%	14.2	34%	107%
6 Mpigi	120%	47.7	38%	123%
7 Mubende	107%	9.8	34%	108%
8 Mukono	93%	-16.2	29%	92%
9 Rakai	122%	21.6	39%	125%
Total	109%	120.8	35%	111%
WESTERN:				
10 Bundibugyo	12%	-31.2	3%	11%
11 Bushenyi	124%	46.2	40%	128%
12 Hoima	78%	-10.6	24%	76%
13 Kabale	84%	-18.6	26%	82%
14 Kabarole	131%	59.3	43%	137%
15 Kasese	77%	-21.4	24%	75%
16 Kibale	135%	19.7	44%	141%
17 Kisoro	140%	18.6	46%	147%
18 Masindi	77%	-17.6	23%	75%
19 Mbarara	111%	26.6	35%	112%
20 Rukungiri	99%	-1.2	31%	99%
Total	106%	69.7	33%	107%
NORTHERN:				
21 Apac	143%	49.6	47%	151%
22 Arua	103%	4.8	32%	103%
23 Gulu	83%	-15.8	25%	81%
24 Kitgum	46%	-54.8	13%	43%
25 Kotido	61%	-21.1	18%	58%
26 Lira	109%	12.5	35%	111%
27 Moroto	-34%	-76.0	-9%	-29%
28 Moyo	192%	38.7	68%	216%
29 Nebbi	112%	10.1	36%	114%
Total	94%	-52.0	29%	93%
EASTERN:				
30 Iganga	141%	99.0	47%	149%
31 Jinja	81%	-15.0	25%	79%
32 Kamuli	117%	21.9	38%	120%
33 Kapchorwa	168%	19.2	57%	183%
34 Kumi	-4%	-77.3	-1%	-3%
35 Mbale	87%	-24.2	27%	86%
36 Pallisa	114%	13.2		0%
37 Soroti	-37%	-195.0	-10%	-31%
38 Tororo	113%	19.6	36%	115%
Total	88%	-138.5	27%	86%
UGANDA TOTAL	100%	-0.0	31%	100%

1/ Growth above (immigration) or below (emigration) the national growth rate.

Table 41

UGANDA
POPULATION AND LAND AVAILABILITY BY DISTRICT

Region and District	Rural Population 1/ ('000)				Cultivable Land Area 2/ (Km2)	Density (Persons per Km2)				Average Area of land cultivated per person 3/ (ha)	Area Required for 1991 Population (Km2)	Percent Cultivable land used in 1991	Broad Soil Class	% Annum Growth in Rural Pop'n 1980-91
	1991	1980	1969	1959		1991	1980	1969	1959					
Central														
1 Mpigi	796	627	478	387	4406	181	142	108	88	0.38	3,025	69%	I	2.2%
2 Mukono	717	606	520	365	4061	177	149	128	90	0.38	2,725	67%	II	1.5%
3 Luwero	408	400	311	240	7986	51	50	39	30	0.38	1,550	19%	II	0.2%
4 Masaka	747	618	440	314	5542	135	112	79	57	0.34	2,540	46%	II	1.7%
5 Rakai	366	275	172	123	3500	105	78	49	35	0.34	1,244	36%	III	2.6%
6 Mubende	463	360	320	213	8963	52	40	36	24	0.32	1,482	17%	II	2.3%
Eastern														
7 Iganga	899	627	457	329	4489	200	140	102	73	0.328	2,949	66%	III	3.3%
8 Jinja	208	183	93	95	619	336	296	151	153	0.328	682	110%	II	1.1%
9 Kamuli	473	346	271	216	3694	128	94	73	58	0.328	1,551	42%	III	2.9%
10 Kapchorwa	112	75	64	49	1064	105	70	60	46	0.386	432	41%	II	3.8%
11 Kumi	225	239	189	161	2454	92	97	77	66	0.787	1,771	72%	III	-0.5%
12 Mbale	645	529	397	304	2022	319	262	196	150	0.384	2,477	122%	II	1.8%
13 Soroti	384	459	366	284	8407	46	55	44	34	0.787	3,022	36%	II/III	-1.6%
14 Tororo 5/	842	643	507	393	3887	217	165	131	101	0.387	3,259	84%	III	2.5%
Northern														
15 Apac	454	313	174	120	4962	91	63	35	24	0.542	2,461	50%	III	3.4%
16 Arua	598	463	359	257	6578	91	70	55	39	0.255	1,525	23%	III	2.4%
17 Gulu	296	255	232	151	11321	26	23	20	13	0.533	1,578	14%	IV	1.4%
18 Kitgum	340	301	206	127	13536	25	22	15	9	0.533	1,812	13%	IV	1.1%
19 Kotido	181	158	102	66	10352	17	15	10	6	N/A			III	1.2%
20 Lira	471	361	304	231	6950	68	52	44	33	0.542	2,553	37%	II	2.4%
21 Moroto	158	181	147	92	7540	21	24	19	12	N/A			IV	-1.2%
22 Moyo	168	103	87	29	4313	39	24	20	7	0.255	428	10%	IV	4.6%
23 Nebbi	292	229	201	119	2689	109	85	75	44	0.255	745	28%	II	2.2%
Western														
24 Bundibugyo	116	110	65	53	394	294	279	165	135	0.2	232	59%	III	0.5%
25 Bushenyi	735	521	408	294	3559	207	146	115	82	0.25	1,838	52%	II	3.2%
26 Hoima 5/	395	287	180	120	6633	60	43	27	18	0.316	1,248	19%	II/III	2.9%
27 Kabale 5/	598	430	429	354	2353	254	183	182	151	0.286	1,710	73%	II/III	3.0%
28 Kabarole	741	493	361	209	7607	97	65	48	27	0.25	1,853	24%	II/III	3.8%
29 Kasese	343	250	161	134	1478	232	169	109	90	0.2	686	46%	II	2.9%
30 Masindi	275	218	162	67	5369	51	41	30	13	0.316	869	16%	II	2.1%
31 Mbarara	930	665	434	233	9477	98	70	46	25	0.174	1,618	17%	III	3.1%
32 Rukungiri	388	295	209	129	1391	279	212	150	93	0.286	1,110	80%	II/III	2.5%

1/ National Census Figures.
2/ "Soil Productivity and Land Availability Studies": B.W. Langlands: Makerere 1974.
3/ Report on Uganda Census of Agriculture and Langlands, op cit.
4/ Langlands op cit. - I = Very good; II = Good; III = Moderate; IV = Poor.
5/ 1991 Census: Tororo + Pallisa, Hoima + Kibale, Kabale + Kisoro

Table 42

UGANDA
ESTIMATED AVERAGE LAND AND LIVESTOCK
PER HOUSEHOLD BY REGION IN UGANDA

ITEM	UNIT	REGIONS				
		Central	Eastern	Western	Northern	UGANDA
Farmland per household	Sq. Metres	13593	9762	17186	10984	13523
Other land per household	Sq. Metres	8367	11771	9589	15871	10263
Cattle per household	Number	0.97	1.36	2.11	0.67	1.37
Pigs per household	Number	0.35	0.18	0.46	0.4	0.35
Goats and sheep per household	Number	0.92	1.51	2.03	2.43	1.54
Poultry per household	Number	3.58	6.75	3.5	5.73	4.5

NOTE : The table is based on results of the Uganda National Household Budget Survey (1989–1990)

DISTRIBUTION OF LIVESTOCK BY REGION

	Central	Eastern	Western	Northern	UGANDA
AGGREGATE NUMBERS					
Total Households ('000)	1,065	672	867	284	2,887
Rural Households ('000)	802	573	783	278	2,436
Total Cattle ('000)	1,033	914	1,828	190	3,956
Total Pigs ('000)	373	121	399	113	1,011
Total Goats and sheep ('000)	980	1,015	1,759	689	4,447
Poultry ('000)	3,814	4,536	3,033	1,625	12,993
REGIONAL SHARES					
Total Households	37%	23%	30%	10%	100%
Rural Households	33%	24%	32%	11%	100%
Cattle 2/	26%	23%	46%	5%	100%
Pigs	37%	12%	39%	11%	100%
Goats and Sheep	22%	23%	40%	16%	100%
Poultry	29%	35%	23%	13%	100%

Based on Household Budget Survey, 1989–90
2/ Multiply coefficient per HH times Total Households

Table 43

**FREQUENCY AND PERCENTAGE DISTRIBUTION OF HOUSEHOLDS BY
MONTHLY HOUSEHOLD EXPENDITURE IN UGANDA**

Monthly Household Expenditure Class (Shs.'000)	URBAN Number of Households	Percent	RURAL Number of Households	Percent	TOTAL Number of Households	Percent
00 – 25	98,716	26.1	1,363,311	54.3	1,461,928	50.6
25 – 50	130,302	34.5	745,433	29.7	875,735	30.3
50 – 75	79,076	21.0	232,745	9.3	311,821	10.8
75 – 100	29,133	7.7	87,239	3.5	116,372	4.0
100 – 125	16,172	4.3	37,075	1.5	53,247	1.8
125 – 150	8,848	2.3	23,440	0.9	32,288	1.1
150 – 200	8,091	2.2	12,480	0.5	20,571	0.7
200 – 250	3,114	0.8	2,269	0.1	5,383	0.2
250 – 300	2,156	0.6	2,750	0.1	4,906	0.2
300 & Above	2,020	0.5	3,145	0.1	5,165	0.2
TOTAL	377,529	100.0	2,509,887	100.0	2,887,416	100.0

Notes : The table is based on the results of the Uganda National Household Budget
Survey (1989–1990)

The survey covered all districts of Uganda except Kumi and Soroti in the Eastern Region;
Gulu, Kitigum, Kotido, Lira and Moroto in the Northern region.

Source : Statistics Department, MPED

Table 44

LANDUSE
('000 hectares)

	1970	1971	1972	1973	1974	1975	1976	1977	1978	1979	1980	1981	1982	1983	1984	1985	1986	1987
Total Area	23,588	23,588	23,588	23,588	23,588	23,588	23,588	23,588	23,588	23,588	23,588	23,588	23,588	23,588	23,588	23,588	23,588	23,588
Total Land	19,955	19,955	19,955	19,955	19,955	19,955	19,955	19,955	19,955	19,955	19,955	19,955	19,955	19,955	19,955	19,955	19,955	19,955
Forest Land	6,315	6,310	6,310	6,308	6,305	6,300	6,250	6,210	6,160	6,110	6,060	6,010	5,960	5,910	5,860	5,810	5,760	5,710
Other Lands	3,660	3,615	3,545	3,467	3,386	3,248	3,167	3,207	3,185	3,235	3,215	3,185	3,155	2,745	2,595	2,545	2,490	2,540
Subtotal Forest/Other	9,975	9,925	9,855	9,775	9,691	9,548	9,417	9,417	9,345	9,345	9,275	9,195	9,115	8,655	8,455	8,355	8,250	8,250
Agricultural Area	9,980	10,030	10,100	10,180	10,264	10,407	10,538	10,538	10,610	10,610	10,680	10,760	10,840	11,300	11,500	11,600	11,705	11,705
Permanent Crops	1,200	1,230	1,250	1,280	1,314	1,382	1,466	1,515	1,530	1,530	1,600	1,640	1,660	1,700	1,700	1,700	1,705	1,705
Avail. Annual Crops	3,780	3,800	3,850	3,900	3,950	4,025	4,072	4,023	4,080	4,080	4,080	4,120	4,180	4,600	4,800	4,900	5,000	5,000
Cropped Land	4,980	5,030	5,100	5,180	5,264	5,407	5,538	5,538	5,610	5,610	5,680	5,760	5,840	6,300	6,500	6,600	6,705	6,705
Pasture/Cultivable	5,000	5,000	5,000	5,000	5,000	5,000	5,000	5,000	5,000	5,000	5,000	5,000	5,000	5,000	5,000	5,000	5,000	5,000
Irrigated Ag. Land	4	4	4	4	4	4	4	4	6	6	6	6	8	8	8	9	9	9
Other Irrigated Land	4	4	4	4	4	4	4	4	6	6	6	6	8	8	8	9	9	9

Source: FAO Fertilizer Yearbook (from BESD)

LANDUSE
('000 hectares)

	1970	1971	1972	1973	1974	1975	1976	1977	1978	1979	1980	1981	1982	1983	1984	1985	1986	1987
Total Area	100%	100%	100%	100%	100%	100%	100%	100%	100%	100%	100%	100%	100%	100%	100%	100%	100%	100%
Total Land	85%	85%	85%	85%	85%	85%	85%	85%	85%	85%	85%	85%	85%	85%	85%	85%	85%	85%
Landuse Ratio	5,022	5,022	5,057	5,097	5,139	5,211	5,277	5,277	5,313	5,313	5,348	5,388	5,428	5,658	5,758	5,808	NA	NA
Agricultural Area	10,030	10,030	10,100	10,180	10,264	10,407	10,538	10,538	10,610	10,610	10,760	10,760	10,840	11,300	11,500	11,600	11,705	11,705
Arable Permanent	5,030	5,030	5,100	5,180	5,264	5,407	5,538	5,538	5,610	5,610	5,680	5,760	5,840	6,300	6,500	6,600	6,705	6,705
Arable Land	3,800	3,800	3,850	3,900	3,950	4,025	4,072	4,023	4,080	4,080	4,080	4,120	4,180	4,600	4,800	4,900	5,000	5,000
Permanent Crops	5%	1,230	1,250	1,280	1,314	1,382	1,466	1,515	1,530	1,530	1,600	1,640	1,660	1,700	1,700	1,700	1,705	1,705
Pasture Land	21%	5,000	5,000	5,000	5,000	5,000	5,000	5,000	5,000	5,000	5,000	5,000	5,000	5,000	5,000	5,000	5,000	5,000
Forest Land	27%	6,310	6,310	6,308	6,305	6,300	6,250	6,210	6,160	6,110	6,060	6,010	5,960	5,910	5,860	5,810	5,760	5,710
Other Lands	16%	3,615	3,545	3,467	3,386	3,248	3,167	3,207	3,185	3,235	3,215	3,185	3,155	2,745	2,595	2,545	2,490	2,540
Irrigated Ag. Land	0%	4	4	4	4	4	4	4	6	6	6	6	8	8	8	9	9	9
Other Irrigated Land	0%	4	4	4	4	4	4	4	6	6	6	6	8	8	8	9	9	9

Source: FAO Fertilizer Yearbook (from BESD)

Table 45

UGANDA
DISTRIBUTION OF HOUSEHOLDS BY AREA OF FARMLAND POSSESSED BY REGION

AREA OF FARMLAND POSSESSED	CENTRAL		EASTERN		WESTERN		NORTHERN		UGANDA	
	Number of HH	Percent Landed	Number of HH	Percent Landed	Number of HH	Percent Landed	Number of HH	Percent Landed	Number of HH	Percent Landed
Urban	245,574		56,178		50,317		25,460		377,529	
Nil (urban)	263,062		99,209		83,900		5,725		451,896	
0-10	492,873	61.4	383,599	67.0	436,401	55.8	200,809	72.2	1,513,682	62.2
10-20	173,971	21.7	128,610	22.5	195,091	24.9	59,296	21.3	556,968	22.9
20-40	99,171	12.4	45,952	8.0	94,743	12.1	13,314	4.8	253,180	10.4
40-60	15,901	2.0	6,583	1.1	31,234	4.0	2,364	0.9	56,082	2.3
60-80	6,921	0.9	2,638	0.5	7,478	1.0	94	0.0	17,131	0.7
80-100	2,237	0.3	3,521	0.6	1,849	0.2	323	0.1	7,930	0.3
100 and above	11,121	1.4	1,875	0.3	15,812	2.0	1,739	0.6	30,547	1.3
TOTAL	1,065,257		671,987		866,508		283,664		2,887,416	
TOTAL with Land	802,195	100.00	572,778	100.00	782,608	100.00	277,939	100.00	2,435,520	100.00

Notes : The table is based on the results of the Uganda National Household Budget Survey (1989 - 1990)

The survey covered all districts of Uganda except Kumi and Soroti in the Eastern Region:
   Gulu, Kitigum, Kotido, Lira and Moroto in the northern reion.

Table 46

UGANDA
COMPOSITION OF EXPORTS, VOLUME AND VALUE

	1970	1971	1972	1973	1974	1975	1976	1977	1978	1979	1980	1981	1982	1983	1984	1985	1986	1987	1988	1989	1990
VOLUME: '000 TONS																					
Coffee 1/	191.2	174.6	214.2	192.4	187.2	176.6	153.1	113.4	113.7	143.1	110.1	128.3	174.7	144.3	133.2	151.5	140.8	148.2	144.2	176.50	142.40
Cotton	78.1	68.7	66.1	64.7	36.2	25.6	19.2	9.9	11.7	3.6	2.3	1.2	1.8	7.0	6.7	9.6	4.9	3.4	2.1	2.30	3.80
Tea	15.0	15.3	20.7	19.2	16.7	17.1	11.7	8.8	8.7	1.4	0.5	0.5	1.2	1.3	2.5	1.2	2.8	2.1	3.1	3.20	4.80
Tobacco	2.0	2.2	2.5	1.5	1.1	1.3	1.1	1.8	1.2	0.4	0.3	-	-	0.7	0.7	0.3	-	-	0.0	0.50	1.90
Maize													1.6	29.7	29.7	9.8	2.2	-	-	13.3	13.5
Beans																				1.08	-
Copper	16.5	16.8	14.1	9.7	9.0	7.8	5.4	2.5	6.2	4.4											
UNIT VALUE: US$/KG																					
Coffee	0.74	0.80	0.75	0.93	1.20	0.82	2.03	5.00	2.75	2.98	3.1	1.9	2.0	2.4	2.7	2.3	2.8	2.1	1.8	1.5	1.0
Cotton	0.63	0.73	0.80	0.74	1.07	0.86	1.18	1.60	1.69	1.78	1.8	1.9	1.8	1.6	1.8	1.5	1.0	1.2	1.4	1.7	1.5
Tea	0.89	0.89	0.87	0.82	0.94	0.73	0.95	1.46	0.95	1.00	0.6	0.6	0.7	0.9	1.3	0.8	1.1	0.9	1.0	1.0	0.8
Tobacco	1.30	1.08	1.32	1.32	1.22	1.31	1.81	2.01	1.50	2.25	1.0	-	-	1.3	2.1	1.3	-	-	-	1.2	1.2
Maize											-	-	0.4	0.4	0.3	0.3				0.05	0.20
Beans																					
Copper	1.41					0.92			0.31	0.11											
VALUE: US$ MILLION																					
Coffee	142.0	140.3	161.2	178.2	224.0	144.6	310.9	567.0	312.7	425.9	341.3	243.8	349.4	346.3	359.6	348.5	394.2	307.5	265.3	262.8	141.60
Cotton	49.1	50.3	53.0	48.0	38.9	22.1	22.8	15.8	19.8	6.4	4.1	2.3	3.2	11.2	12.1	14.0	5.1	4.1	3.0	4.0	5.80
Tea	13.3	13.6	17.9	15.7	15.7	12.5	11.2	12.9	8.3	1.4	0.3	0.3	0.8	1.2	3.3	1.0	3.1	1.9	3.1	3.2	3.60
Tobacco	2.6	3.0	2.7	2.0	1.3	1.7	2.0	3.6	1.8	0.9	0.3	0.0	0.0	0.9	1.5	0.4	0.0	0.0	0.0	0.6	2.20
Maize											0.0	0.0	0.6	12.1	8.9	2.9	0.0	0.0	0.3	1.5	1.60
Beans																				0.60	2.70
Copper	23.2					7.2			1.9	0.5											
Simsim																					
Re-exports	1.9					0.6														10.00	10.00
Other Exports	47.1					8.7			8.7	4.6	2.2	2.5	0.7	2.1	6.6	4.3	3.1	3.1	2.9	2.8	10.00
Total Unadjusted	279.2				197.4				353.2	439.7	348.2	248.9	354.7	373.8	392.0	371.1	405.5	316.6	274.6	275.5	177.5
Adjusted	-17.6				-20.0				-32.1	-43.4	-29.1	-3.4	-7.6	-6.1	15.9	7.9	1.3	17.0	-8.3	2.2	0.3
TOTAL EXPORTS	261.6					177.4			321.1	396.3	319.1	245.5	347.1	367.7	407.9	379.0	406.8	333.6	266.3	277.7	177.80

Source : Ministry of Planning and Economic Development, Background to the Budget 1990 – 1991, July 1990.

Note: Data for 1970, 1978, 1979 are drawn from World Bank Report No. 5595-UG, June 5, 1985.

1/ Coffee based on shipment.

Table 47

UGANDA
COMPOSITION OF IMPORTS 1/

Categories of Imports	1987 QI	QII	QIII	QIV	Total	1988 QI	QII	QIII	QIV	Total
Foods & Beverages	615	33	23	162	832	23	305	..	44	372
Salt	..	..	..	..	..	1000	..	..	..	1000
Sugar	3696	1195	2400	500	7791	200	..	..	..	200
Cigarettes	..	..	..	..	..	..	..	..	..	..
Alcoholic Beverages	123	..	..	210	123	2	11	..	59	73
Soap Cleaning & Polishing Preparations	52	..	..	..	262	..	53	..	..	53
Drugs, Medical & Pharmaceutical Products	441	211	70	610	1333	96	163	..	88	348
Textile Fabrics & Ready-Made Clothing	226	36	..	185	448	..	..	..	..	..
Motorcycles & Bicycles	915	..	..	740	1655	..	..	..	1	1
Road Motor Vehicles	719	96	1103	998	2916	257	261	69	203	790
Matches, Candles & Electric Installations	688	17	21	56	782	187	96	..	36	319
Household Equipment	494	..	284	2806	3584	25	..	..	..	25
SUBTOTAL: CONSUMER GOODS	7969	1589	3900	6267	19725	1791	890	69	431	3181
Rubber Tyres & Tubes	641	..	281	312	1233	125	..	..	328	453
Industrial & Agricultural Machinery	1099	1764	297	1658	4818	622	374	50	19	1065
Spare Parts	3709	581	1658	1645	7974	888	366	306	546	2106
Lime, Cement & Fabricated Constr. Materials	3763	3920	1645	8353	20294	5551	3719	5230	1654	16153
Precision Instruments	183	1	8353	139	328	..	305	3	..	308
Office Machines, Stationery Supplies & Books	1607	101	139	1769	4350	626	252	286	128	1292
Shoes Materials for Making Shoes	121	..	1769	29	171	..	..	16	62	78
Packing Materials	331	1500	29	1691	4001	1072	1186	465	190	2912
SUBTOTAL: PRODUCTIVE IMPORTS	11435	7868	8251	15596	43168	8884	6201	6356	2927	24368
OTHER GOODS 2/	17431	29094	14838	22591	83953	24297	22897	20508	18583	86285
GRAND TOTAL	36853	38550	26989	44454	146846	34792	29989	26933	21940	113834

Source: Ministry of Planning and Economic Development, Background to the Budget 1990 - 1991, July 1990.

1/ These are imports on a cash basis which do not include imports financed through external loans and grants or private foreign exchange, thus the difference
with the Balance of Payments estimates.

2/ Other Goods comprises: 1. Fuel & Petroleum; 2. Chemicals and 3. Miscellaneous Imports.

NOTE: " .. " means not available

Table 48

UGANDA
DIRECTION OF TRADE
(million US$)

Country/Region	1981	1982	1983	1984	1985	1986	1987	1988
EXPORTS:								
United States	98.64	151.64	100.45	88.56	108.09	126.73	77.73	56.46
United Kingdom	33.74	36.58	40.75	56.52	57.39	67.81	55.23	49.35
Belgium–Luxembour	0.33	2.06	1.78	1.79	5.46	5.68	5.45	5.75
France	22.68	30.04	34.63	37.24	26.79	38.92	34.98	38.19
Netherlands	17.90	8.88	10.54	16.45	15.53	26.09	27.99	39.14
F.R. of Germany	15.44	24.43	29.39	35.79	30.68	31.61	17.56	23.50
Italy	7.59	16.06	19.66	26.96	25.15	15.82	11.35	16.61
Spain	14.44	20.51	32.81	39.88	37.60	47.57	30.14	30.42
Other Europe	4.36	7.91	6.87	11.95	9.75	19.09	16.61	18.30
Japan	13.77	22.02	16.29	26.71	10.12	16.87	15.98	9.14
India	0.02	0.01	0.01	0.02	0.02	0.02	0.02	0.02
Other Asia	4.42	10.21	11.56	7.75	29.82	16.55	0.42	21.84
Kenya	1.61	2.25	1.17	1.19	1.24	1.31	1.57	1.88
Other Africa	12.14	12.67	11.58	18.69	11.20	8.99	3.26	4.14
Other Countries	9.67	11.63	9.14	15.45	11.10	6.62	12.21	13.50
TOTAL	256.75	356.90	326.63	384.95	379.94	429.68	309.08	328.20
IMPORTS:								
United States	7.48	9.35	4.51	3.52	5.17	4.62	20.46	17.38
United Kingdom	55.59	60.74	35.09	42.73	56.13	41.76	69.35	69.14
Belgium–Luxembour	7.81	8.58	14.28	12.90	9.90	5.06	4.83	8.78
France	21.11	10.41	10.17	13.99	4.68	5.75	8.28	5.30
Netherlands	3.54	7.83	5.74	5.55	8.66	14.51	7.96	11.39
F.R. of Germany	37.48	38.36	36.93	21.75	18.57	38.18	48.50	34.43
Italy	7.36	8.83	12.41	11.95	18.03	19.23	64.90	35.11
Spain	0.07	0.58	0.37	0.71	1.59	0.58	0.42	5.64
Other Europe	9.50	18.08	11.32	9.75	9.74	15.56	52.48	27.38
Japan	5.70	8.43	16.14	18.92	21.65	17.15	36.00	27.97
India	16.72	15.89	15.89	17.47	18.36	19.26	21.19	17.02
Other Asia	12.83	4.23	9.75	19.55	12.51	27.72	63.59	84.40
Kenya	127.95	110.50	113.20	103.77	108.96	114.40	137.29	164.74
Other Africa	11.44	1.53	3.05	4.52	3.87	7.90	4.32	5.04
Other Countries	4.59	18.26	14.25	14.41	8.68	8.92	5.08	7.76
TOTAL	329.17	321.60	303.10	301.49	292.93	329.62	537.43	521.48

Source: Ministry of Planning and Economic Development, Background to the Budget 1990-91; July 1990.

Table 49

UGANDA
BALANCE OF PAYMENTS
(million US$)

Country/Region	1982	1983	1984	1985	1986	1987	1988
CURRENT ACCOUNT	-69.9	-72.3	107.1	77.0	6.9	-169.8	-194.0
Trade Balance	-74.9	-60.4	65.7	114.9	-68.5	-300.8	-353.2
Exports F.O.B.	347.1	367.7	407.9	379.0	407.5	333.7	272.9
Imports C.I.F.	-422.0	-428.1	-342.2	-264.1	-476.1	-634.5	-626.1
Services (net)	-102.3	-115.4	-44.0	-98.9	-133.2	-113.6	-126.9
(Interest Charges) 1/	-26.3	-51.0	-36.8	-21.0	-41.3	-18.3	-24.1
Unrequited transfers	107.3	103.5	85.4	61.0	208.7	244.6	286.1
CAPITAL ACCOUNT	14.6	27.7	-88.3	-27.4	75.8	142.3	59.5
Medium and Long Term (net)	26.2	23.9	32.1	14.6	64.5	135.3	36.7
Inflows	96.8	163.7	120.8	85.6	104.4	239.7	239.1
Disbursements	70.0	112.8	109.7	85.6	104.4	180.0	207.6
Rescheduled Maturities 2/	16.8	11.1	-	-	-	9.7	9.7
Reschuled Arrears	10.0	39.8	11.1	-	-	23.9	-
Other	-	-	-	-	-	26.1	21.8
Outflows	-70.6	-139.8	-88.7	-71.0	-39.8	-104.4	-202.4
Amortization 3/	-43.8	-88.9	-77.6	-71.0	-39.8	-42.1	-39.8
Rescheduled Maturities 2/	-16.8	-11.1	-	-	-	-9.7	-9.7
Reschuled Arrears	-10.0	-39.8	-11.1	-	-	-23.9	-
Other	-	-	-	-	-	-28.7	-152.9
Short Term (net)	-11.6	3.8	-120.4	-42.0	11.3	7.0	22.8
Commercial Banks (net)	-8.3	-1.0	-23.2	-20.0	-	-	-
Trade Credit (net)	-3.3	4.8	-97.2	-22.0	11.3	7.0	22.8
NET CHANGE IN ARREARS 3/	22.4	8.3	-77.3	17.3	44.3	19.1	142.1
OVERALL BALANCE 3/	-32.9	-36.3	-58.5	66.9	127.1	-8.5	7.6
FINANCING	32.9	36.3	58.5	-66.9	-127.1	8.5	-7.6
Monetary Authorities 4/							
Change in Gross Reserves 5/	-34.3	-28.2	56.2	29.6	0.8	-19.0	-1.6
I.M.F. (net) 6/	82.3	85.4	-10.2	-89.5	-108.4	-6.8	5.5
Other (net) 7/	-15.1	-20.9	12.5	-7.0	-19.5	34.3	-11.5

Source: Ministry of Planning and Economic Development, Background to the Budget 1989-1990;
   July 1989.

1/ Some interest payments may be recorded under repayment of principal.

2/ Matching items for rescheduled maturities and arrears appear as capital inflows and capital outflows.

3/ Arrears included in overall balance; (+):increase in net arrears; (-) decrease in net arrears.

4/ End of period data; (+) increase in net liabilities; (-) decrease in net liabilities.

5/ (+) decrease in gross reserves; (-) increase in gross reserves.

6/ The movement in the net position has been based on end of the period data while the data for purchases and repurchases are shown at the value of the data at which they have taken place; the reconciliation of the latter with the former is accounted for by the fluctuations in the exchange rate for the U.S. dollar which on average appreciated in 1981-1982: the financing flow shown by end of the period data is therefore smaller than the flow which actually took place.

7/ Includes errors and omissions.

UGANDA
DELIVERIES OF MAIN EXPORT CASH CROPS : 1982-90
(tons)

Table 50

PERIOD	COFFEE**			TEA	TOBACCO
	Robusta	Arabica	Total		
Year					
1982	146,455	15,411	161,866	2,580	647
1983	134,089	14,135	148,224	3,054	1,650
1984	136,674	9,298	145,971	5,214	1,969
1985	133,848	10,147	143,995	5,758	1,613
1986	151,247	8,634	159,881	3,335	949
1987	158,002	9,065	167,067	3,511	1,214
1988	141,718	9,439	151,157	3,512	2,639
1989	161,154	7,888	169,042	4,658	3,456
1990	117,330	9,220	126,550	6,704	3,322
Month					
1989 Jan	16,863	1,037	17,900	378	0
Feb	16,682	1,051	17,733	248	0
Mar	13,849	754	14,603	273	5
Apr	14,985	1,045	16,030	384	55
May	14,154	525	14,687	409	78
Jun	6,797	497	7,294	424	32
Jul	15,863	560	16,423	319	71
Aug	16,853	227	17,080	280	276
Sep	12,688	445	13,133	381	673
Oct	10,290	347	10,637	458	977
Nov	11,214	786	12,000	470	943
Dec	10,917	614	11,531	634	346
1990 Jan	12,391	1,146	13,537	556	373
Feb	11,102	831	11,933	526	0
Mar	10,148	1,040	11,188	595	0
Apr	7,387	865	8,252	602	45
May	4,930	703	5,633	689	91
Jun	3,777	611	4,388	638	35
Jul	11,335	458	11,793	402	96
Aug	14,669	639	15,308	296	147
Sep	11,743	537	12,280	373	398
Oct	9,085	534	9,619	623	652
Nov	8,818	692	9,510	649	885
Dec	11,914	1,164	13,109	755	600
1991 Jan	14,582	1322	15,904	410	854
Feb	9,774	1500	11,274	556	n.a.
Mar	5,199	1,017	6,216	n.a.	n.a.

Note : ** From November, 1990 figures include those of the four Unions under the
"Union Export Services" authorized to export coffee.

Sources : Coffee Marketing Board, Uganda Tea Authority, B.A.T. (Uganda) Ltd.
and Union Export Services

Distributors of World Bank Publications

ARGENTINA
Carlos Hirsch, SRL
Galeria Guemes
Florida 165, 4th Floor-Ofc. 453/465
1333 Buenos Aires

**AUSTRALIA, PAPUA NEW GUINEA,
FIJI, SOLOMON ISLANDS,
VANUATU, AND WESTERN SAMOA**
D.A. Books & Journals
648 Whitehorse Road
Mitcham 3132
Victoria

AUSTRIA
Gerold and Co.
Graben 31
A-1011 Wien

BANGLADESH
Micro Industries Development
   Assistance Society (MIDAS)
House 5, Road 16
Dhanmondi R/Area
Dhaka 1209

   Branch offices:
   Pine View, 1st Floor
   100 Agrabad Commercial Area
   Chittagong 4100

   76, K.D.A. Avenue
   Kulna 9100

BELGIUM
Jean De Lannoy
Av. du Roi 202
1060 Brussels

CANADA
Le Diffuseur
C.P. 85, 1501B rue Ampère
Boucherville, Québec
J4B 5E6

CHILE
Invertec IGT S.A.
Americo Vespucio Norte 1165
Santiago

CHINA
China Financial & Economic
   Publishing House
8, Da Fo Si Dong Jie
Beijing

COLOMBIA
Infoenlace Ltda.
Apartado Aereo 34270
Bogota D.E.

COTE D'IVOIRE
Centre d'Edition et de Diffusion
   Africaines (CEDA)
04 B.P. 541
Abidjan 04 Plateau

CYPRUS
Center of Applied Research
Cyprus College
6, Diogenes Street, Engomi
P.O. Box 2006
Nicosia

DENMARK
SamfundsLitteratur
Rosenoerns Allé 11
DK-1970 Frederiksberg C

DOMINICAN REPUBLIC
Editora Taller, C. por A.
Restauración e Isabel la Católica 309
Apartado de Correos 2190 Z-1
Santo Domingo

EGYPT, ARAB REPUBLIC OF
Al Ahram
Al Galaa Street
Cairo

The Middle East Observer
41, Sherif Street
Cairo

FINLAND
Akateeminen Kirjakauppa
P.O. Box 128
SF-00101 Helsinki 10

FRANCE
World Bank Publications
66, avenue d'Iéna
75116 Paris

GERMANY
UNO-Verlag
Poppelsdorfer Allee 55
D-5300 Bonn 1

HONG KONG, MACAO
Asia 2000 Ltd.
46-48 Wyndham Street
Winning Centre
2nd Floor
Central Hong Kong

INDIA
Allied Publishers Private Ltd.
751 Mount Road
Madras - 600 002

   Branch offices:
   15 J.N. Heredia Marg
   Ballard Estate
   Bombay - 400 038

   13/14 Asaf Ali Road
   New Delhi - 110 002

   17 Chittaranjan Avenue
   Calcutta - 700 072

   Jayadeva Hostel Building
   5th Main Road, Gandhinagar
   Bangalore - 560 009

   3-5-1129 Kachiguda
      Cross Road
   Hyderabad - 500 027

   Prarthana Flats, 2nd Floor
   Near Thakore Baug, Navrangpura
   Ahmedabad - 380 009

   Patiala House
   16-A Ashok Marg
   Lucknow - 226 001

   Central Bazaar Road
   60 Bajaj Nagar
   Nagpur 440 010

INDONESIA
Pt. Indira Limited
Jalan Borobudur 20
P.O. Box 181
Jakarta 10320

IRELAND
Government Supplies Agency
4-5 Harcourt Road
Dublin 2

ISRAEL
Yozmot Literature Ltd.
P.O. Box 56055
Tel Aviv 61560

ITALY
Licosa Commissionaria Sansoni SPA
Via Duca Di Calabria, 1/1
Casella Postale 552
50125 Firenze

JAPAN
Eastern Book Service
Hongo 3-Chome, Bunkyo-ku 113
Tokyo

KENYA
Africa Book Service (E.A.) Ltd.
Quaran House, Mfangano Street
P.O. Box 45245
Nairobi

KOREA, REPUBLIC OF
Pan Korea Book Corporation
P.O. Box 101, Kwangwhamun
Seoul

MALAYSIA
University of Malaya Cooperative
   Bookshop, Limited
P.O. Box 1127, Jalan Pantai Baru
59700 Kuala Lumpur

MEXICO
INFOTEC
Apartado Postal 22-860
14060 Tlalpan, Mexico D.F.

NETHERLANDS
De Lindeboom/InOr-Publikaties
P.O. Box 202
7480 AE Haaksbergen

NEW ZEALAND
EBSCO NZ Ltd.
Private Mail Bag 99914
New Market
Auckland

NIGERIA
University Press Limited
Three Crowns Building Jericho
Private Mail Bag 5095
Ibadan

NORWAY
Narvesen Information Center
Book Department
P.O. Box 6125 Etterstad
N-0602 Oslo 6

PAKISTAN
Mirza Book Agency
65, Shahrah-e-Quaid-e-Azam
P.O. Box No. 729
Lahore 54000

PERU
Editorial Desarrollo SA
Apartado 3824
Lima 1

PHILIPPINES
International Book Center
Suite 1703, Cityland 10
Condominium Tower 1
Ayala Avenue, H.V. dela
   Costa Extension
Makati, Metro Manila

POLAND
International Publishing Service
Ul. Piekna 31/37
00-677 Warzawa

For subscription orders:
IPS Journals
Ul. Okrezna 3
02-916 Warszawa

PORTUGAL
Livraria Portugal
Rua Do Carmo 70-74
1200 Lisbon

SAUDI ARABIA, QATAR
Jarir Book Store
P.O. Box 3196
Riyadh 11471

**SINGAPORE, TAIWAN,
MYANMAR,BRUNEI**
Information Publications
   Private, Ltd.
Golden Wheel Building
41, Kallang Pudding, #04-03
Singapore 1334

SOUTH AFRICA, BOTSWANA
For single titles:
Oxford University Press
   Southern Africa
P.O. Box 1141
Cape Town 8000

For subscription orders:
International Subscription Service
P.O. Box 41095
Craighall
Johannesburg 2024

SPAIN
Mundi-Prensa Libros, S.A.
Castello 37
28001 Madrid

Librería Internacional AEDOS
Consell de Cent, 391
08009 Barcelona

SRI LANKA AND THE MALDIVES
Lake House Bookshop
P.O. Box 244
100, Sir Chittampalam A.
   Gardiner Mawatha
Colombo 2

SWEDEN
For single titles:
Fritzes Fackboksforetaget
Regeringsgatan 12, Box 16356
S-103 27 Stockholm

For subscription orders:
Wennergren-Williams AB
P. O. Box 1305
S-171 25 Solna

SWITZERLAND
For single titles:
Librairie Payot
Case postale 3212
CH 1002 Lausanne

For subscription orders:
Librairie Payot
Service des Abonnements
Case postale 3312
CH 1002 Lausanne

TANZANIA
Oxford University Press
P.O. Box 5299
Maktaba Road
Dar es Salaam

THAILAND
Central Department Store
306 Silom Road
Bangkok

**TRINIDAD & TOBAGO, ANTIGUA
BARBUDA, BARBADOS,
DOMINICA, GRENADA, GUYANA,
JAMAICA, MONTSERRAT, ST.
KITTS & NEVIS, ST. LUCIA,
ST. VINCENT & GRENADINES**
Systematics Studies Unit
#9 Watts Street
Curepe
Trinidad, West Indies

TURKEY
Infotel
Narlabahçe Sok. No. 15
Cagalogiu
Istanbul

UNITED KINGDOM
Microinfo Ltd.
P.O. Box 3
Alton, Hampshire GU34 2PG
England

VENEZUELA
Libreria del Este
Aptdo. 60.337
Caracas 1060-A